# Caressing
# OLD MEMORIES

OLEN G BARBER

Copyright © 2025 by Olen G Barber

HardCover: 978-1-964035-69-7
Paperback: 978-1-7374272-0-9
eBook: 978-1-7374272-1-6
Library of Congress Control Number: 2025904214

All rights reserved. No part of this publication may be reproduced, distributed, or transmitted in any form or by any electronic or mechanical means, without the prior written permission of the publisher, except in the case of brief quotations embodied in critical reviews and certain other noncommercial uses permitted by copyright law.

This is a work of nonfiction.

# ABOUT THE AUTHOR BIO FOR OLEN GETZEN BARBER

Olen Barber is a seventeen-year student of the school of hard knocks, a twenty-year veteran of the US Navy, a twenty-one-year Law Enforcement officer with the Arapahoe County Colorado, Sherif's Department, and a survivor of eighty-seven years of life.

During his school of hard knocks, he learned the need for a quality education and an honest and reliable reputation. The military gave him the opportunity to build a strong character and start his pursuit of an education. His Law enforcement career provided him with the opportunity to learn from experts in many fields.

Being blessed by God with a guardian angel, a very good memory and all the people who helped him and urged him to share his life story compelled him to write this book.

# ACKNOWLEDGEMENTS

I would like to pay special acknowledgements to all those people who reached out to me with a helping hand when I needed it. First and foremost, I need to thank my wife Audrey for her encouragement and examples with her excellent book, James Madison Ellis. I would like to give special thanks to Sandy Bain, a close friend for fifty plus years who volunteered to edit the book. Without their help this book would not have been possible.

# TABLE OF CONTENTS

About the author BIO for Olen Getzen Barber ................................................. iii
Acknowledgements .................................................................................... v
Chapter 1   Caressing Old Memories .......................................................... 1
Chapter 2   Neals ..................................................................................... 5
Chapter 3   Starting School ....................................................................... 12
Chapter 4   Leaving Neals ......................................................................... 16
Chapter 5   Uncle Chief's Farm .................................................................. 19
Chapter 6   Pup ........................................................................................ 23
Chapter 7   Tobacco ................................................................................. 31
Chapter 8   The Farm ................................................................................ 38
Chapter 9   Leaving Home ........................................................................ 64
Chapter 10  My First Job ........................................................................... 67
Chapter 11  Orange and Blue Diner ........................................................... 73
Chapter 12  Hank's Song ........................................................................... 78
Chapter 13  Considering the Military ......................................................... 83
Chapter 14  Western Union ....................................................................... 85
Chapter 15  String Fellows ........................................................................ 88
Chapter 16  Allis Chalmer ......................................................................... 91
Chapter 17  Choosing the Navy over the Army .......................................... 109
Chapter 18  The Long Train Ride to Boot Camp ......................................... 114
Chapter 19  Our Introduction to Boot Camp .............................................. 122
Chapter 20  Boot Camp Company 007 ...................................................... 128
Chapter 21  Heading to Norman Oklahoma ............................................... 134
Chapter 22  Home Again ........................................................................... 141
Chapter 23  Norman Oklahoma ................................................................. 144
Chapter 24  Aviation Electrician Class A School ......................................... 152

| Chapter 25 | VF-43 | 177 |
| Chapter 26 | GITMO | 187 |
| Chapter 27 | Life at McGuire | 206 |
| Chapter 28 | Wheeling, West Virginia | 224 |
| Chapter 29 | Leaving McGuire | 231 |
| Chapter 30 | Motorcycle | 234 |
| Chapter 31 | AE-B School | 242 |
| Chapter 32 | Transition to Hawaii | 248 |
| Chapter 33 | Tachikawa Japan | 259 |
| Chapter 34 | When Olen met Keiko | 279 |
| Chapter 35 | Singer Tommy Duncan | 285 |
| Chapter 36 | Keiko's introduction to America | 292 |
| Chapter 37 | NAS North Island | 306 |
| Chapter 38 | Imperial Beach | 321 |
| Chapter 39 | USS Hancock | 327 |
| Chapter 40 | U.S.S. Hancock Second Cruise | 347 |
| Chapter 41 | U.s.s. Hancock Last Cruise | 358 |
| Chapter 42 | Nas Imperial Beach | 366 |
| Chapter 43 | Leaving The Military | 389 |
| Chapter 44 | Investigation Division | 415 |
| Chapter 45 | Back To The Patrol Division | 433 |
| Chapter 46 | Detention Division | 440 |
| Chapter 47 | Remodeling The Jail | 446 |
| Chapter 48 | Jail Overcrowding | 450 |
| Chapter 49 | Overload Burnout | 459 |
| Chapter 50 | Special Assignment | 464 |
| Chapter 51 | The New Jail | 469 |
| Chapter 52 | Video Court System | 476 |
| Chapter 53 | Pope John Paul II | 479 |
| Chapter 54 | My Second Retirement | 481 |

# Chapter 1

# CARESSING OLD MEMORIES

I was born around nine P.M. on January 22, 1936, in a farmhouse located two miles from Baxley, Georgia. It was just 15 minutes before the doctor's arrival, a fact my dad often joked about, claiming it was the only instance in my life when I was in a hurry. Unfortunately, the doctor fell ill and passed away a few days after my birth, leading to an incorrect recording of my birth details.

During those challenging times, we faced difficulties. In the fall of that year, we moved to North Florida in search of work. My Dad found employment as a farm hand in the area of a small community called Haile, Florida, working on a farm owned by the Suggs Family.

I have some vague memories from when I was barely two years old. At that time, we were living in a simple frame house known as the sharecropper's house on the Suggs farm, where my dad worked as a farmhand. A particularly severe storm struck during that period.

The house itself was old, lacking ceiling or wall paneling. Its features included rough-cut wooden doors and shutters, matched with a floor of similar quality. Gazing upwards revealed the underside of the tin roof while looking down, exposed cracks in the floor. The shutters for the windows hung on metal hinges, resembling the door that used a piece of 2 x 4 with a 16-penny nail functioning as a latch to hold it closed.

The storm hit during the early afternoon with such force that it blew the door open and sent the latch flying across the room, hitting the back wall. In response, my mother urgently instructed my seven-year-old brother to "Hold Your Brother." At the time, I was sitting in the middle of the room inside a cardboard box. I can still vividly recall my brother gripping the box's end with both hands, looking directly at me with a mixture of determination and fear. His image remains ingrained in my memory, a snapshot of that moment from eighty-five years ago.

Another memory centers around my parents' efforts to secure the door against the storm. My Mom struggled to hold it shut while my dad hauled her big old Singer sewing machine to barricade the entrance. In my memory, they appeared young, vibrant, and strong. This cherished memory of their determination and teamwork continues to bring me joy, a testament to their resilience.

I also have fond recollections of the environment surrounding that old place. The yard was devoid of grass, just bare dirt. A dirt road ran alongside it, occasionally seeing wagons but rarely any motor vehicles due to their scarcity back then.

One day, while playing with our chickens on the road, a sudden noise frightened me profoundly. Lost in my play, I didn't notice an old Model T Ford approaching from behind until its horn blared. Startled, I sprinted back to the yard so swiftly that I was indoors before my mom could reach me. When she inquired if I had been on the road, I fibbed, pointing to the chickens. It might have been my first lie, but she didn't press the matter, allowing me to escape that time.

Lastly, one of my fondest memories from that place was when my brother returned home from school, playing with a yo-yo. I eagerly awaited him outside, overwhelmed with excitement as I had never seen a yo-yo before.

I considered it the most beautiful thing in the world. My brother had acquired it by trading an old pocketknife at school, a deal he thought was good, although Dad disagreed. As my brother and I grew older, we shared other wonderful memories, but those times were truly special and remain at the top of my cherished memories.

With the positive recollections, there were also unpleasant events. One day, a loud crashing noise drew our attention down the road. With my mom and my brother Derlwood, I hurried to the spot where a small local railroad, known as Peggy Railroad, intersected the road. An unfortunate incident had occurred: a train engine collided broadside with a car, pushing it down the tracks before coming to a halt. The driver's name was Willie Cleage.

The aftermath was chaotic, scattering car parts and debris along the tracks. Arriving at the scene, we were joined by other adults trying to manage the situation. Mom shielded Derlwood and me from the distressing scene, assigning us the task of clearing car parts while the adults tended to the more difficult aspects. Soon, a few other adults arrived to assist. The situation was grim and required a substantial amount of time to bring under control.

As the harvest season arrived, changes unfolded at the Suggs farm. The year's crops were disappointing, and employment opportunities in the area were dwindling. Consequently, Dad's brother Herman, who was married to Edith, the owner's daughter, along with their two sons David and Bobby, had to return to the Suggs farm. To accommodate them, Dad had to relocate to secure work. We moved roughly 10 miles away to a community called Neals.

Following our move for my father's work, some negative incidents occurred at the old sharecropper's house. While they affected other people, they weren't as personally impactful. Most of those memories have faded, except for one particularly somber episode that transpired there.

My uncle, Herman Barber, had wed Edith Suggs and moved into the old house with their two sons David and Bobby. Tragedy struck one day when Edith was cooking, causing the stove to explode, and set the house ablaze. David was with Mr. Suggs at the time, but unfortunately, Edith lost her life in the explosion and fire. Rushing to the scene, Mr. Suggs was only able to rescue Bobby from the front room. The house was completely consumed by flames. This memory remains haunting and unsuccessful in my recollections.

## Chapter 2

# NEALS

I remember that we had to move so Dad could find work. We moved about ten miles farther back into the woods to a place called Neals. It was a 900-acre farm settled in the late 1800s by someone with the last name of Miller. The farm was too isolated from the other communities for the hired help to commute, so some houses were built on the farm for the help to live in. One was a large three-bedroom house for a family, and there were some small units for general help.

Mr. Miller's widow still lived there with another couple named Garrison, who ran the place. Mrs. Miller and the Garrisons were from New York. I remember how we used to laugh at the way they talked. Understanding what they said was a big challenge.

Mr. Garrison was a short, stocky man with a bossy attitude. He would get all excited about the least minor problem, and I was too young to understand how serious the situation could be; I used to laugh at him. I guess you could say I thought he was very entertaining, and I would slip around to watch him.

Things at the new job did not go well at first. Dad had taken a job cutting pulpwood and was to be paid by the cord. It was extremely hard and dirty work. He would come home at night completely exhausted, covered in dirt, sweat, and pine tar. I don't know how we made it through the first two weeks until payday, but we did. With the job, we also got the use of a large house and a yard big enough for a garden and chicken coops for our chickens. The house was a big frame structure, like the one that the storm hit on the Suggs farm.

Then real trouble came when Dad went to get his pay. The amount he was offered for his work was less than it should have been. Dad did not have any formal education, but he had learned to count and to keep track of his earnings. He was a proud man who would not cheat you out of anything, but you best not try to cheat him. He refused to accept the amount offered and stepped aside until the rest of the crew went through the pay line. Then Dad and Mr. Garrison had some strong words. Dad explained to Mr. Garrison in a few simple words what he intended to do if he did not get the amount agreed upon. Dad was paid the correct amount, and then he quit the job.

I remember when he came home. He was terribly upset, and when he told Momma what happened, she started crying. Dad told Mom to start packing because we would have to move as soon as he could find a place to go. They were trying to figure out how they were going to survive with two kids and no job or place to live. I do not think I really understood the situation, but I sure felt some of the pain. I also remember that Dad had borrowed a shotgun to shoot some game with, and it was in the house. Dad looked down the path coming up to the house and saw Mr. Garrison walking toward the house, and I recall Dad telling Mom to get the shotgun and Mom pleading with Dad not to shoot him.

As it turned out, Mr. Garrison had come to apologize for the misunderstanding about the pay. After the misunderstanding was settled, he told Dad that he needed someone to take care of the farming and wanted Dad to do it. Farming was Dad's line of work, and Dad would now be paid by the hour, so he accepted the offer. It also turned out that Mr. Garrison had lent the shotgun to Dad, and Dad was going to return it, but Mr. Garrison insisted that Dad keep it for as long as he needed it. Mr. Garrison never wanted that old shotgun back, and it is still in our family somewhere.

I remember all the joy we felt that night after everything was straightened out. After a short period of time on his new job assignment, Dad came home from work one night and told Mom he had gotten a pay raise to $10.00 per week, rain, or shine. Mom was so happy. That was the first time in her life she knew how much money she could plan on for the next week. After a few weeks, Dad was able to buy our first car. It was old and worn out, but we loved it, and I got to ride inside for a change.

Between the time we moved to Neals, and I started school, I had a lot of time on my hands. My brother was big enough to help Mom with some of her work, and he went to school. Dad worked in the fields all day, and Mom had to take care of everything else, including me. There were a lot of ways for me to get into trouble, and I found most of them.

Dad had a big game rooster that did not like me. Every time I got in his area, he used me as his punching bag. He stood about as tall as I did, and he would fly into me and knock me down. Mom had to keep rescuing me from the rooster. Dad loved that old rooster, and he was proud of him.

One day when my brother was there, the rooster attacked me, and my brother hit him with a big stick and knocked him unconscious. Mom was afraid the rooster was dead, and she knew that Dad would be mad. She was able to revive the rooster by bathing his head in cool water. Well, she got him back on his feet ok, but for a while, he walked kind of funny. I do not remember him bothering me again after that.

I also remember the time I got bored one afternoon and went for a walk in the woods. I must have been the only one in Neals that did not think I was lost. Everyone in the area came looking for me. One of the searchers found me and made sure I got home. Mom and Dad were terribly upset but so happy that I was ok that I did not get punished. I really did enjoy the adventure of the walk.

I also remember learning just how easy it is to get seriously hurt or killed. I was too small to do most things to help Mom or Dad, but Mom would let me go to the field where Dad was working to tell him it was time to come home. Mom was trying to teach me how to tell time on the clock, and I would tell Dad that Mickey's big hand was pointing straight up and his little hand was pointing straight down, and that would indicate that it was 6 PM. and I would walk back to the house with him. Most of the time, he would be plowing with a mule, and he would help me up on the mule, and I would ride on him back to the stock pen. I was so small that when I sat on the mule, my feet would just touch the part of the trace chain that ran from the harness to the back band.

We used a thick leather collar, which held a set of wooden and metal Hames around the mule's neck.

We used chains to pull the plow, and they connected the plow to the Hames. They went from the Hames to a second item that went across the mule's back called a backband, and from there, the chains went to the plow.

When the mule was unhooked from the plow, you took the long part of the chain and hooked it to the top of the Hames, making a large loop in the chain. With my short legs, this worked like a ladder for me to climb up or down when I was getting on or off the mule.

One day, I found myself riding on the back of a mule, with Dad leading the way. However, as we approached the stock pen, things took an unexpected turn. Someone had come to see Dad and he was waiting by the fence. At the sight of this person, the mule became spooked. In response to the mule's behavior, two hogs from the pen managed to escape by darting under the mule.

The mule was seized by panic, attempting to bolt away while I clung on, only intensifying its fear. Dad was in a dilemma, trying to regain control of the mule while simultaneously freeing me from my position. Unfortunately, my right leg had slipped down behind the chain, wedged between the harness and the back band. Holding onto the harness with a vice-like grip, I remained trapped, and Dad couldn't release me with just one hand.

Observing the situation, the man by the fence rushed over to help. Dad let go of the mule and quickly extracted me from my precarious position. In the commotion, the mule bolted away in a panicked run.

All I got was bruises on my hands and the leg that was behind the chain, but if Dad had not gotten me loose from the mule, I would most likely have been killed.

After we had been there a year or so, my Granddad Barber started working on the place and moved into one of the small houses. He was by himself when he moved in, but later, he shared the house with a black man who had started working on the place. While Granddad lived there, sometimes we would all go fishing with him.

One day, we had planned to go night fishing at one of the nearby fishing ponds for what we called 'strike fishing.' In this technique, a long piece of straight metal, such as a spring leaf from a piece of equipment, was used to strike the fish. Our preparations included building a campfire and crafting torches to provide light. Just after dark, we would wade along the lake's edge with our torches, scanning the water for fish, primarily catfish, which tended to be bedded down in the shallows. The sudden light from the torches would momentarily blind them, allowing us to strike them accurately using the long piece of metal. Mastering the art of slow and quiet movement was crucial, and occasionally, we could even sneak up on larger fish.

Well, our trip almost ended in tragedy that day. It was just before dark, and Dad, Derlwood, and I went to join Grandpa and the guy sharing the house with him to go striking. Grandpa was getting ready to go, and Derlwood was sitting on the bottom step to the front Porch, and I was playing in the front yard. Dad and Grandpa were on the porch, and Grandpa asked the other guy living there to get the rifle.

Granddad had an old single-shot .22 caliber rifle that had seen its better days. It had the type of loading system that required you to cock the hammer back and push down the firing pin unit to load or unload the rifle. The hammer had the thumb grip partly broken off, and the only way you could check to see if it was loaded was to pinch the hammer between your thumb and finger and pull it back to the cocked position, then push the firing pin unit down.

As he was walking out onto the porch with the rifle to check it, he was trying to pinch the hammer between his thumb and finger and pull it into the cocked position when the hammer slipped out of his grip. The rifle was loaded, and it went off. The bullet just creased the top of

Derwood's head. His hair flew. It stunned him for a minute or so and gave him a permanent part through his hair. It cut a shallow crease in his scalp that required it to be cleaned and bandaged only. That was a good thing because the only professional medical assistance was hours away.

Dad's response to the situation was more dangerous than the gunshot. He grabbed the rifle from the guy who was checking it and was attempting to beat the guy with it when Grandpa got control of him. Derlwood was ok, but we did not get to go fishing.

There were a lot of good memories, but also some bad ones, like the start of World War II, and when I got sick with something called Bright's Disease. I was not expected to survive it, but an old country doctor named Whitlock would not give up, and he got me cured.

My best memory of being sick was when I got away with everything, but when I got well, that all ended. The doctor told Mom I could not eat anything fried in grease, and in those days, everything was fried. I loved fried potatoes, so Mom fried me some in butter, which did not make the doctor happy, but I loved them.

## Chapter 3
# STARTING SCHOOL

The first school I got to attend was Bell school, and that was the year that Pearl Harbor was bombed. I loved going to school because it was the only place I could go and be with my brother. I remember my teacher that year was Mrs. Proctor. We had to take a nap right after lunch each day, and she would walk around and play softly on the violin. That was the prettiest sound that I had ever heard.

Then one day, just before our nap, someone came into the room and whispered something to Mrs. Proctor. Her voice changed as she told us to stay in our seats, and she left the room. This had never happened before, and I just knew it was something bad, and I remember feeling scared. In a few minutes, my brother came to the door and motioned for me to come with him. He said that we had to go home early, and when I asked him what was wrong, he said someone had bombed us, and we were at war.

I remember that I was really scared because I did not truly understand what war was, but I kept remembering a picture of a battle scene with a lot of men fighting with swords.

The war changed everything. Things that we needed, like sugar and gas, became rationed, and we had to do without some of the things that we needed. The school bus situation changed, and my brother and I had to change schools.

We changed to a community school called Franklin. It was a big farmhouse that belonged to the owners of the Franklin farm. The school was supported by only one school bus with a lady driver, and that young lady was not only our school bus driver but the school principal and the only teacher. She was also the entire school administration.

The owners of the old farmhouse had remodeled it, leaving only the kitchen and one large room. They were a real, nice old couple, and now they volunteered to work there as the cook and janitor to help the school system out.

All the students that attended Franklin School rode to and from school on that bus. The large room was the only school room, and it had four rows of desks to accommodate the students. The school covered grades one through eight, and the older students had to help teach us younger ones. There was no electricity or running water in the building. There was a hand-operated pump in the yard, and we all had to bring our own glasses for drinking water. There were two small buildings outside that were used for restrooms, one for the girls and one for the boys.

A big wood-burning heater was to provide the heat for school in the winter, and a large wood-burning stove was for cooking. I liked the school because everyone was nice, and my brother and I were always together.

Our school bus pickup point was a mile through the woods from our house, and the only way to get there was to walk through the woods. In the wintertime, the only way to make the bus on time was to start before daylight. Some mornings we would build a fire at the bus pickup point to keep warm while waiting for the bus.

I can still remember that the cook was always waiting for us each morning with a bunch of homemade hot biscuits, peanut butter, and Sugar Cane syrup. She also made our lunches, so we got two hot meals each day. The older kids helped us younger kids, and everyone got along well. I remember that I really liked it there, but that only lasted about two years before we were sent back to Bell School.

One other good thing that happened was that dad bought a battery-operated radio. The only way that we got the news about the war or pending severe weather was over the radio. We could only listen to one short news report a day and the Grand Ole Opry on Saturday nights because we had to save the battery. We had the only radio in our community, and everyone came to our house on Saturday nights to hear the Grand Ole Opry. That was when I got hooked on country music. Boy, I loved that old radio.

At best, Dad only went to town once a month to buy supplies, and sometimes my brother and I would get to go. The only road to town was a dirt road through the woods, and it was difficult to drive. During rainy weather, Dad would have to drive the old farm log truck, but if the weather and roads were good, then Dad would drive the car. When my brother and I got to go, we would watch for Tortoises like the one in the picture.

We called them gophers, and when we saw one, we would yell out to stop, and we would get to catch them. We would normally catch about four or five on the way to town. There is a considerable amount of meat in them, and we would drive through black neighborhoods and sell them. We would get a quarter for each of the smaller ones, but we would get fifty cents apiece for the larger ones.

Dad let us keep the money we got, and we would feel like kings. We could buy candy and soda pop. Sometimes we would even get to see a movie. All the tough times just seemed like normal living to me, but those good times were so special that they all made successful Memories.

Just before the end of the war, Mr. Garrison took sick with cancer and died. It was a sad loss for my brother and me. He did not have any kids, and he really liked us. He always managed to give us a few toys for Christmas. Mrs. Miller sold the place to Nash Davis, who went by the name of Shorty.

Shorty was the proprietor of Silver Springs, an entertainment park renowned for its glass-bottom boat rides. He had managed to transform the park into an immensely prosperous enterprise. The Tarzan movie series, starring actor Johnny Weissmuller, was being filmed there. Additionally, Ross Allen's Rattlesnake Milking show drew crowds, contributing to the remarkable success. The income was substantial, to the extent that the government was claiming 90 percent of it in taxes. In search of a tax shelter, Shorty opted for the Neals property.

Shorty did not have any children of his own, but he had a niece that he loved very much and wanted her to have a horse and a place to ride it, and Neals also filled that need.

Prior to buying Silver Springs, Shorty was in the High Springs area and was known in the area. He asked Dad to stay on at Neals, but Dad had already entered a deal with his Uncle Chief Bullard, but Dad did agree to stay on until he got someone to take his place.

## Chapter 4

# LEAVING NEALS

We moved to Uncle Chief's farm in the fall, and the people were finishing up their harvest and still living in the sharecropper's house. We moved into a vacant house on an adjoining farm that was directly across the road from the main entrance to his farm.

The house belonged to Bryant Clark and was a nice little house that served All of our needs at that time. As soon as we arrived at the farm, Dad went to work helping with the harvest and the farm upkeep that Uncle Chief needed to be done.

I had a great time at the new location. At first, we were adjusting to the change in everything and the new chores we had to do. Mom,

Derlwood, and I had to get the Clark house set up for us to live in. I remember there were some problems getting our old wood stove into the house and working. It was like the one shown in the picture, but not as fancy.

They got the stove working, and Derlwood and I had to start cutting and hauling in a supply of wood. We also had an open-faced fireplace, and they burned a lot of wood.

As soon as the corn harvest started, Dad started getting part of the corn, and to store it, we had to get the corncrib at Clark's place cleaned up and ready. Part of the corn would be used for grinding into grits and cornmeal. To get the corn ready to be ground, we would have to sort out the best ears of corn and shuck them by hand. The best corn would have to be shelled and bagged. To help with this, Dad got an old hand-operated corn sheller like the one in the picture. Derlwood and I now had the job shelling and drying corn to be taken to the Gristmill in town to be ground into grits and corn meal. The remaining part of the corn would become feed for the mules.

The Gristmill would grind the corn for half the output. That was a good deal for the people in the area because some of the local stores in town would sell it as a non-label for a cheaper price.

We had to finish moving into the Clark house so we could register for our new school. We were now in a different school district and had to register in the High Springs school to start the next school year, which was starting in a few weeks. I was not looking forward to going back to school. I had just got started at Bell School when the war broke out, and I had to change to Franklin School.

That was a small group of students and only one teacher to get used to, but it was a lot harder to get to school and back home. Then I had to adjust to the Bell School all over again. Now I had everything to do all over again, and I liked the freedom of home and was not excited about a new school adventure.

There was a significant amount of work to be done at the Clark House and the corncrib area. Consequently, we were kept quite busy cleaning up and repairing the fences and horse stalls. The corn harvested had filled the corn crib with stock feed, and since Dad required mules to work with, he had managed to acquire a fine pair. By the time the mules arrived at the Clark House, we had their stalls prepared and ready.

The time flew by, and before I knew it, I was back in school. The teachers at the school were nice but very strict. We had to ride a bus like before, and it had a long route to run. They would run the route in one direction in the morning and then reverse it in the evening. That was to try to balance out how long the bus ride was for each student. I was in the middle of the route, so my time was the same both ways.

When I got home after school, I had chores to do before homework. The only light we had in the house was a couple of kerosene lamps. We had no electricity or running water. We still had the old battery-operated radio we had at Neals, but no battery. The war was over now, so we really did not listen to the news anymore, but I did miss the Grand Old Opry. Everybody was up before daybreak each day, and by dark, you were ready for bed.

# Chapter 5
# UNCLE CHIEF'S FARM

Looking back at that first year on Uncle Chief's Place, I don't know how we survived. I do not remember any time when we had any part of a day off. Everybody worked all day, every day. I remember that Mom looked more tired than she did at Neals, but she seemed happier. I think it was because she could now get the things she needed. I know the food was better at mealtimes. I think we felt better about everything now because Dad was now a sharecropper instead of just an hourly farm worker. He also got an old hand-operated corn sheller.

By the time we moved from Neals, the war was winding down, and most of the heavy fighting was over. The local men, who were serving in the military, were returning home. I was too young and isolated to remember much about the ones who were lost in the war, but I do remember that some of the ones who came back were crippled, but most of them that made it home were ok.

While I still have vivid memories of the beginning of the war, I don't have any clear memories of how I learned that the war was over, only that everyone was happier, and things were better. Some of the men who came home worked on the farms with us during harvest time. The men worked in the fields, and for the most part, the women worked at the barns and houses. The conversations that took place between the men were very exciting to this young lad. Sometime during the end of the war, some of the German Prisoners of war worked in the fields with us harvesting peanuts. The government had a labor program that allowed farm owners to get War prisoners and a guard by paying part of the expense.

The one's that I saw were very nice, and those who spoke English would talk to the men during their work breaks. One of the prisoners that came to the farm and worked with us had been educated somewhere in America, and he spoke excellent English. He enjoyed talking and telling funny stories that would get everyone laughing. I remember one of the things he said was, "Hitler said that we would be walking through America someday, but he did not say anything about this pitchfork."

I was so excited being a part of all that, and man, I would hang onto each word of their stories. Later in life, I learned more about what happened during the war, and that changed some of my feelings about war, but not my memories of the good times and experiences I had. While most of the Germans worked on the farms, the tobacco warehouses in Valdosta, Georgia worked for the Japanese POWs.

Uncle Chief's real name was E M Bullard. His sister was my Dad's Mother and my grandmother. Uncle Chief was a large man, and when he was sixteen years old, he stood just over six feet tall and weighed one hundred and eighty pounds. He had grown up during the time that the Railroad was expanding and worked in the woods with his family cutting timber for the Railroad. At the age of sixteen, he could stand up two freshly cut crossties and pick them up onto his shoulders and carry them to the pickup truck. He could also drink with the best of them when he could buy the whisky. The problem was he was too young to buy it. To buy whisky, you had to be eighteen years old.

He was big enough but not old enough, so he lied about his age and got an identification card that said he was eighteen years old. That also made him old enough for the Army, so he got drafted during World War

I. He was too scared to tell the military that he had lied about his age, and he served a tour of duty in the Army. He had some pretty, wild stories about that experience.

After he got out of the service, he got a farm in the High Springs area and settled down, except that he still liked to drink. High Springs is located just inside the Alachua County line, close to Columbia County. Well, at that time, Alachua County was a dry County and could not sell any kind of alcoholic beverage. Columbia County was wet and had juke joints just across the county line, which was the Santa Fe River.

About once a month, Uncle Chief would come to town to buy supplies, and he would visit those juke joints just across the river. By the time he headed home, he would be kind of drunk and had to drive through High Springs to get home. High Springs had a young police officer who insisted on arresting Uncle Chief and taking him to jail. This cost Uncle Chief his driver's license and money, and he did not think it was right. At first, Uncle Chief only complained about it and thought the officer would stop bothering him, but the young officer kept on arresting Uncle Chief.

On one of his trips to town, Uncle Chief had a bad case of the Flu, and while picking up his supplies, he noticed that the police officer was watching him. Uncle Chief got mad and decided it was time to get even with the officer. After loading up all his supplies, he made his normal trip across the river to the juke joints. This time he did not drink anything and just spent some time visiting with his friends.

After, he felt that enough time had passed that he could have gotten drunk. He started home. Like always before, the officer pulled him over. Uncle Chief played it up a little and let the officer take him to jail. The officer said something to the effect, "I got you again, and I'm going to keep you in jail till you are sober". Well, Uncle Chief was a good bit larger than the police officer, and he grabbed the officer and overpowered him. He grabbed the officer and took his gun, keys, and hat, and locked him in the jail. Later Uncle Chief went to the city Mayor's house and told the mayor, "I have got your officer locked up in your jail, and here is his stuff. When you think he is sober, you can let him out."

Well, Uncle Chief never said much about what that cost him, but that is how he got Chief for a nickname. I guess he liked that name because that was the only name he used, and even though there was no Indian blood in him or his wife, he always called her Bo or Squaw.

By the time we moved onto his farm, Uncle Chief had built up a large farm for that area. He had hired Dad to take over the farm on a fifty-fifty split basis. We also got to raise our own livestock, like cows and hogs, on an even split basis. The agreement also included the use of the large frame-type house with a fenced-in yard to live in and as much ground for a garden as we needed. There were three tobacco barns with wood-fired flue systems in them and a feed barn, and stock pens. All the farmland was cleared for cultivation and completely fenced.

## Chapter 6

# PUP

We still had the same old car that Dad had bought during our time at Neals, and by then, we had also acquired a dog we affectionately called Pup. In the photograph, you can see the old car, Derlwood, Pup, and me. Pup, a pit bull, proved to be an exceptional farm dog. She responded to commands when working with the livestock. If you instructed her to catch something, regardless of its size, she would chase it down and capture it.

Whether it was a hog or a cow, she had distinct techniques: she'd bite the ear of a hog and catch a cow by the nose. While mules and horses were beyond her control to hold, she would drive them into a corner of the fence and keep them contained there. Despite sustaining injuries multiple times, she never gave up. If you told her to watch over something, she would diligently guard it, preventing anyone else from getting close.

On one occasion, Uncle Chief had brought us some seed to plant, and Pup's task was to watch over the seed bag, ensuring birds and chickens wouldn't eat the valuable contents. Uncle Chief came by and wanted to check the seed. Well, that did not work out well. He was not going to let any dog keep him from looking at something he had bought and paid for keep him from looking at them, so he challenged her. She went into full defense mode and chased him away from the bag. That really made him mad at first, but after he settled down, he had a lot more respect for Pup.

She loved Derlwood the most, but she would always protect the smallest one in the group. Most of the time that would be me, and I liked that. With her help, some of the time I could handle my big brother. Without her help, I lost every fight we had.

Shortly after we started working Uncle Chief's farm, Dad got an old model A Ford that someone had converted to a flatbed truck. They cut off the rear of the car and built a flatbed just large enough to carry four fifty-five-gallon barrels.

I remember that it did not run when Daddy got it, but Derlwood and Dad got it running ok. They built sideboards all the way around the truck bed. That made it a good water truck.

We were keeping some cows in a pasture that was about two miles from the farmhouse, and we had to haul water to them. That little truck was just what we needed for that job. Since it was all on private property, Dad let Derlwood drive the truck.

We would pump the water and fill the barrels just to get to drive the truck. The pup would ride in the back with the water barrels trying to protect the truck from all those tree limbs that were hitting the truck.

She would try to bite every limb that hit the truck, and of course, the limb would slap her in the face, and she would just get madder. One day Derlwood took a left turn a little too fast, and all I could see was one of the barrels of water and one dog flipping end over end across the woods. The sideboard broke off, and both Pup and a barrel of water went flying. We lost fifty-five gallons of water, but the dog was fine.

That dog was a part of the family and went everywhere Derlwood did. Everybody in the area had dogs, and if one of them made a threatening gesture at Derlwood, there was a dog fight. They were hard to break up, and some of the dogs would get injured. For us, she was a great dog, but after we had her for about two years, we lost her. She got horribly sick, and Dad thought she had been poisoned. All I remember is how much she suffered and how much we missed her.

I must tell you about the wild hog and the smokehouse. Almost every farm had to have a building for smoke-curing meat. It was a small standalone building located separately from the other building. Normally it is not used for anything else but smoking meat, so you kept it clean and ready for smoke-curing meat. We had one that looked like the one in the picture.

One day a wild hog wandered onto the farm, and somehow, Dad caught him and closed him up in the smokehouse. Now a wild hog is a fighter. He is much stronger than a domestic hog and much more aggressive. They also grow a set of teeth called tusks. Their tusks develop and grow during the life of the hog and become very dangerous. The hog that Dad caught was young and not fully developed yet. He was black with very thin hair. He was dangerous because of their strength and aggressive behavior. They are hard to catch and control.

I was not home when they caught him and did not see how they got him into the smokehouse, so I did not know how strong he was.

Well, after we kept him in the smokehouse for a couple of days, Dad decided that he would turn him loose in the field with our other hogs. That created a problem because that meant we had to catch him and move him to a new location. Dad had varicose veins in his legs, and that put him at considerable risk if the hog was able to cut one of them. Derlwood volunteered to catch the hog. Well, my big brother was my hero, and he could do anything.

He stepped on the top board that was nailed across the door and jumped down into the smokehouse with the hog. I would like to say the fight was on, but that hog came after Derlwood and put him back out that door so fast I could not believe it. I was embarrassed, and everyone else was laughing. We had caught and managed bigger hogs than that one, and I did not know why he could not just grab his leg and drag him to the door.

I didn't take too long to find out. Fueled by frustration, I was pretty upset with the hog, and I decided to take action. I managed to climb to a point where I could reach over the top board and give him a good whack. I suppose I thought I could show him who was in charge.

Armed with my trusty old straw hat, I swung at him. However, in my fervor, my foot slipped off the board, and I ended up going headfirst right onto the hog. That hog, without hesitation, countered by hitting me with his nose, and the result was that I was propelled into the air. I tried to scramble back towards the door, but I suddenly felt his nose against my rear end, and he essentially guided me back out the door. It all happened so rapidly that I could hardly believe it. I had never encountered anything that was both swift and strong like that hog. And, to make matters worse, he managed to tear up my straw hat in the process.

After everybody finished laughing at me and Derlwood, everybody ganged up on the hog and caught him. We had to use our wagon to haul him to the field to turn him loose. We had a top for the wagon that let us close him up where he could not get out. Dad told us, "Don't mess with him, take him out into the field and just release him."

Derlwood and I drove the wagon out into the field, but we positioned it just a few feet from the wire fence, with the back end facing the fence. Then we banged on the sides and top of the wagon and opened the tailgate. That hog hit the ground running as fast as he could and ran right into the wire fence. It looked like he only made it halfway through the fence.

He got loose from the fence and took off. When we got back to the house, Dad asked how it went, and we told him that we drove out into the field and opened the tailgate, and he ran off across the field. Every word was the truth. The hog and smokehouse shown in the above pictures are similar to, but not the actual items.

There was another funny incident with a hog that I would like to tell you about. After we got a good start on the crops and the work settled down, we would take our little homemade boat and go to some of the fishponds in the area and do a little trotline fishing.

The boat was too heavy for one man to carry from where you had to park the truck to where you put it in the water, so Dad would take another big person with him. Derlwood and I were too small to help carry the boat through the wooded area, but we could come and make the campfire and coffee while they got the boat in the water and the trout line set up.

We would go after work, so it would be dark by the time we got set up. Derlwood and I would pick a spot in the brush close to the truck, gather some firewood, build a fire, and boil the coffee over the fire.

On one of our trips, we had the fire and the coffee going, and Dad and his helper were in the small boat out on the water setting out the trot line. Derlwood and I were sitting on each side of the campfire facing each other and watching the coffee boil and were busy eating some food that we brought with us, a big hog walked right up behind Derlwood. He was not a wild hog, just a farm-grown hog that was attracted by the fire and the smell of the coffee. We did not see or hear him until he bumped into Derlwood's backside.

Derlwood jumped up and charged right through the campfire and right over the top of me. I don't know who got scared the most, the hog, Derlwood, or me, but we cut three new trails through the brush. Our commotion was so loud that it scared Daddy, and he almost jumped out of the boat trying to run to us. I did not see the hog again, but Derlwood, me, and the coffee survived ok. That memory still makes me laugh every time I think about it.

When I got home after school, I had chores to do before I could do my homework assignments. The only light we had in the house was a couple of kerosene lamps. We had no electricity or running water. We still had the old battery-operated radio we had at Neals, but no battery. The war was over now, so we really did not listen to the news anymore, but I did miss the Grand Old Opry. Everybody was up before daybreak each day, and by dark, you were ready for bed. Looking back at that first year on Uncle Chiefs Place, I don't know how we survived.

I don't remember any time when we had a day off. Everybody worked all day, every day. I remember that Mom looked more tired than she did at Neals, but she seemed happier. I think it was just because she could get the things she needed now. I know the food was better at mealtimes. I also think I was because Dad was now a sharecropper; instead of just an hourly farm worker, it was a morale booster.

By the time we had settled in on Uncle Chief's farm, the war was winding down, and most of the intense fighting had concluded. Local men who had served in the military were returning home. I was quite young and somewhat isolated, so I don't recall much about those who were lost in the war. However, I do remember that some of the individuals who came back were left disabled, while the majority of them appeared to be in good condition.

While I still have vivid memories of the beginning of the war, I don't have any clear memories of how I learned that the war was over, only that everyone was happier, and things were better.

Some of the men who came home worked on the farms with us during harvest time. The men worked in the fields, and for the most part, the women worked at the barns and houses. The conversations that took place between the men were very exciting to this young lad.

As I remember it, moving to the new place did not change many things for me. The house was almost the same as both the others, a frame-style house with no electrical service or running water. We still had a large wood-burning stove for cooking that was similar to the one in the picture, and we also had an open fireplace that required a lot of wood.

By the time we were settled into our new location, I was getting big enough to start sharing the workload. At first, Mom was my teacher, and I had to help her with her chores like pumping water and filling those firewood boxes.

My first job was to carry the wood into the house and fill the boxes every day. In the summer, which was not bad because we did not use the fireplace, but the winter required a lot more wood. At first, I felt proud of my job, but pretty soon, it stopped being fun and became work.

Mom also had to pump water by hand and carry it by hand to use in the kitchen. She would pump it into small buckets and carry them into the kitchen. Well, a big growing lad like me could handle that, so it also became my job.

My new routine became going to school every weekday, every evening after school, filling the wood boxes, pumping, and bringing in the water, and then doing my schoolwork. I learned about responsibility then because the rest of the family depended on me to do my job so they could do theirs. That had a positive effect on the rest of my life.

The bigger I got, the harder the work became. Not only did Mom have to get the wood, the water, cook, clean and mend things. She also had to water the stock. Well, you might say that I quickly grew into that job also.

We could not afford a tractor, so we used mules, and they required a lot of drinking water. We also raised cows, hogs, and chickens, and they also had to have water every day. My brother was bigger than me, and he got to help in the fields doing what I considered Men's work.

The truth is everyone had to do everything they could, and they worked from before daybreak until after dark every day. The more work Mom and I did, the longer everyone else could work out in the fields. As I caress those old memories, I can't understand how we did all that hard work and still found time for each other, but we did.

# Chapter 7

# TOBACCO

Tobacco was our main money crop during the 1950s. The movies and the Government have made smoking famous and popular. The movies had just about all their big stars smoking cigarettes or cigars in most of their movies, and the Government was putting a pack containing four cigarettes in each K-ration food package. The military also started the saying, "Smoke them if you got them". This contributed to creating a larger demand for tobacco products by the 1950s.

Growing tobacco in those days was very labor intensive but did not require much overhead to get started. Your biggest expense was in the curing process, and that required building the tobacco barns with a controllable heating system, and that was a one-time cost.

The Government had placed acreage control on growing tobacco, and it was based mostly on the size of your farm. Smaller farms could only get from one to five-acre allotments. The larger farms, like Uncle Chief's farm, ran for five to ten acres. He had eight acres on his farm.

I remember that you could lease approved acreage from other farms, and I think you could grow it on either your property or on their property. I don't recall how that procedure was accomplished, but I recall that we picked up a small amount of additional acreage that way a couple of times. One time Uncle Chief got a couple of acres, and later, Dad got the neighbor's acreage.

The way we had to grow tobacco in those days was a lot different than the way they do today. We had to prepare a seed bed and grow our plants. First, you had to clear everything off the ground that you were going to use. Then to kill everything that might try to grow back in the seed bed, to do this, you built a big barn-type fire on the ground.

Then you plowed and raked up every bit of trash out of the ground. Then raked the ground until it became a three-inch-deep layer of soft soil. Then you build sides all around the seed bed. Normally you just use some logs for this.

To water the plant beds, we had to haul the water in barrels using a small pan to spread the water over the cheesecloth covering so it would not disturb the seed. You would have to repeat this three times a week until the plants were moved to the field.

The plants needed to grow to about ten inches tall before transferring them to the field. How big the seed beds were depended on how much acreage you had.

In preparing the field for tobacco cultivation, the process followed a typical pattern: first, the land was plowed as per usual, after which raised rows were constructed for planting the tobacco. These rows were typically around thirty-six inches wide, allowing for the placement of plants at approximately eighteen inches apart from each other.

The variety we grew, known as "Gold Dollar," was a substantial plant. It could reach a towering height of about five feet, and its leaves would extend over a span of around thirty inches.

The plants were fragile and had to be carefully planted by hand with some water and fertilizer. Any plants that died had to be replaced within a week. You were not regulated on how many plants you had, just how much ground they were on. The Government maintained strict control over the size of your tobacco patch. Each year they inspected each tobacco patch by measuring all of your authorized acreage every year in square feet.

They would cut down any plants they found on the property that was over the limit. When they inspected the patch, some of the inspectors would let you pick the place to be cut.

While the plants were growing, you had a lot of tasks to complete. There are three different plowings to accomplish, you had how each row at least two times, and you would add some fertilizer at least once. You had to put bud poising in the bud of each plant to fight the budworms. Spray the plants with poison to fight the hornworms.

When the plants reached their normal height, they would develop a seed pod at the top of the stalk, and you had to break them off by hand. At the same time that the plant was growing the seed pod, it started to grow suckers. These are small sprouts between the base of the leaf and the stalk. All these had to be broken off by hand. That procedure was called suckering tobacco.

*Tobacco starting to develop seed.*

*Tobacco plants with fully developed seed pods in bloom.*

All these tasks were important because this was when the plant was trying to grow its leaves to full size, and they were the part you sold.

The way we worked the tobacco crop back then was a lot different than they do today. After the plant was topped, suckered, and its leaves were fully developed, the leaves would start changing color from green to yellow. This started with the bottom leaves turning first. The bottom three to four leaves were called sand lugs because they were on the ground and covered with sand.

You would pick the selected leaves by hand, being careful not to damage them. Then you put the bundle under one arm to carry them as you went to each stalk until you got an arm full. You would then put them in a tobacco sled. That was called cropping tobacco. This procedure was repeated as the leaves changed color until all the leaves were collected. This would normally take 5 to 6 cropping.

My first jobs as a kid were to drive the sleds back and forth between the tobacco field and the barn.

At the barn, the tobacco was unloaded from the sled and sorted into small bundles of 3 to 4 leaves, depending on the size of the leaves, to be strung on tobacco sticks with string. This process was called stringing tobacco and was normally accomplished by the women and additional help.

The sticks of tobacco would then be moved into the barn for curing. The curing process required drying out the tobacco leaves with controlled heat provided by wood-fired furnaces. The temperature would be systematically raised until the leaves were properly dried. This would take three to four days with 24 hours of continuous monitoring and adjusting the heat inside the barn. It took a large pile of wood per barn.

*Getting ready to string the tobacco.*

Derlwood and I were responsible for cutting, hauling, and firing the wood for the furnaces most of the time. During the nights, both of us would take shifts. One of us would monitor the temperatures and adjust the fires as necessary while the other tried to catch some sleep—usually right there on the ground near the barn. We would switch positions as needed, always ready to assist when tasks required two pairs of hands.

During harvest, or what we called Picking Time, we would have to have all three barns working. When the tobacco started changing color, you did not have much time to work with it. On a lot of days, we would have to empty a barn before daylight so we could refill it the same day. The sticks of tobacco must be moved to different storage area and stacked while it is still stung on the tobacco sticks. Anytime you handle the tobacco after it is cured, you have to be careful because the curing process dries out the leaves, and they become brittle.

To prepare the tobacco for sale, you had to take it out of the stack and make sure that the leaves were moist enough to handle. Then you had to remove the leaves from the tobacco sticks, in restore enough moisture to make the leaves flexible. This is a balancing act. Too much moisture will cause the leaves to get mold on them or rot. You must remove the leaves from the tobacco sticks, in other words, you had to unstring it. It must be spread out and graded by condition and color. Then it had to be stacked in a circle on large tobacco with the leave stems pointing out. This is how you take it to the tobacco warehouse.

Here it would be auctioned off to the highest bidder based on a price per pound bid. The major tobacco companies would send the buyers to all the warehouses to buy tobacco through the bidding process.

There were different processes for accepting the bid offers. Most of the farmers had someone representing them that had the skills to get them the most money for their tobacco. These people would monitor the market and advise the farmers on the best time to sell and how to present their products. You would sort it out by grade, and it would be displayed by grade.

The cigarette companies would bid on the top grade, and the snuff companies would buy the lower grades. Your representative would do all the communication with the bidders and single you on if he felt the bid offered was good or not, and you would give him the ok signal if you wanted him to accept the bid. Once you accepted the bid, you no longer had anything to do except Sign the sales slip and pick up your check. If you did not accept the bid, then you would have to relocate your tobacco. Sometimes that was just setting it up for sale at the same warehouse, and sometimes, it meant taking it to another warehouse.

The bid was structured as a price-per-pound offer, dependent on the prevailing supply and demand conditions. When the available supply fell short of meeting the buyer's requirements, the bid amount would be increased. Throughout the season, the same tobacco could fetch different prices at various times. Hence, timing the sale correctly was crucial to securing the best possible price for your tobacco.

Uncle Chief had some good advisors, and they always got a good price for all of our tobacco crops. Each year Dad was able to buy us some more stock and better farm equipment. One year he bought us a nice pickup truck. Our best year was the last year we sharecropped Uncle Chief's place. We had eight acres of tobacco and made over five thousand dollars for our half of the sale. That was the year we bought our own farm consisting of 160 acres that was next to Uncle Chief's Place. It was the original Osteen family homestead.

## Chapter 8
# THE FARM

Dad sent Mom to the bank to get the money to pay for the property, and the bank owner, Mr. Smith, would not let Mom have it until Dad came in and said that it was ok. There was nothing wrong with the transaction, but Mr. Smith had been friends with Mom and Dad for a long time, and he knew that was everything Dad had, and Mr. Smith was not going to take any chances. Those days of trust and friendship are exceedingly rare today.

By the time Dad bought our farm, I was thirteen years old and just getting old enough to start doing the harder work. The problem was that I still was not strong enough to handle all the heavy tasks. I was growing up to be tall and skinny. I had built up good endurance for doing the lighter work like pumping and carrying water, cutting firewood, and taking care of the stock.

The problem was that I could not Lift or carry the heavy things like the large bags of seed and fertilizer or control the bigger stock like hogs and cows. I was getting big enough to start working with the mules. I could put their harness on them, hook them to the wagon and drive them. I could also do some plowing.

When we purchased the farm, it had not been lived on for a few years, and everything about it needed a major cleaning up and fixing up. That job fell to Derlwood and me.

The house on the farm had been used to store all kinds of things like seeds, hay, and broken plow parts. Before we could even start moving in, we had a couple of weeks of clearing out the trash and cleaning up. The old house, after being cleaned up, still needed a lot of fixing up, but that would have to wait until after we moved in.

We would not be working at Uncle Chief's place the next year, and he would need the house on his farm for the new workers. The first job for my brother and me was to take the wagon and move all the trash somewhere and burn it. We also needed to make a seed bed for the tobacco plants we had to grow for the next year.

The procedure for growing tobacco plants was to make a seedbed by clearing everything off a designated area and burning the ground to kill any old seeds or roots in the ground before building the plant bed. The size of the area depended on the many plants you figured you would need for the allotted acreage. There were no restrictions on how many plants you could grow, just how much land you used to grow your tobacco crop on. Most beds were around twenty to thirty feet long by fifteen to twenty feet wide.

We had found a place where the prior owners had, at some time in the past, planted their gardens and selected it for our seed bed. We did not have much acreage, so we only needed a small bed, but we had to clear a larger area to protect the bed itself.

Derlwood and I brought the wagon, a pair of mules, and some tools for cleaning the area for the bed. All the burnable things like brush, an old fence post, and weeds were piled up on the bed to be burned. Then we hauled some of the trash for the farmhouse and piled it on the pile to be burned. We were making good progress until my brother stepped into trouble.

My brother was always a very fast runner. He could chase down and catch about anything on the farm. Well, just as we were finished unloading the wagon, a small rabbit jumped up and took off. Derlwood exclaimed, 'Look at that rabbit! I bet I could catch him!' and in an instant, he took off like a flash.

They made one big circle around the clearing and headed for brush, and Derlwood was gaining on him, but at a full head of steam, he stepped in one of the postholes. His forward motion stopped instantly, and it looked something like those old road runner cartoons. His body tried to go forward but sprung back, and he fell flat on his back.

It scared me half to death, and I ran over to where he was. His right foot was still in the post hole, and his knee was sprained so bad that he could not get his foot out of the hole. He was in extreme pain, and I had to pull his leg out of the hole. He could not use his right leg at all.

I had to use the mules to back the wagon to where he was so I could load him onto the wagon to where he was and load him in the wagon. He could not sit up, so he had to lay flat on his back on the wagon floor while I drove him about a mile and a half to where Mom was. It was not a smooth ride for him. I drove him to the house where we lived, and Mom got Dad, and they moved him to the bed.

By the time we got him into bed, his right knee had swollen so big that Mama had to cut his pants leg open to get it out of his pants. There was no ambulance service where we lived, and if you wanted a doctor, you had to go find him. So, Derlwood had to recover on his own. The only thing Mom could do was keep hot towels wrapped around his knee. He was lucky that there were no broken bones. In a few days, he was walking again.

While Derlwood was recovering from his knee injury, I kept working on the cleanup project. I was starting to get along pretty well with the pair of mules that I was using. I could drive that wagon and haul anything I could load in it. I could drive them as a team to drag the larger items to where they needed to be. I think the best part was that I got to ride in the wagon or on the sled most of the time.

This was a good gentle pair of mules, which was surprising because normally, Dad would only buy a stock that nobody else liked. I think part of it was because he could get them cheaper, but he also loved a good challenge.

He had a little Texas mule we named Kilroy, which was much more my size, but he was mean, and you had to rebreak him every Monday morning. Once he got over his mean streak, he was a good, hard-working mule, and if you could keep up with him, you would get a lot done. It took me almost two years before I could handle him.

When we moved to Uncle Chief's place from Neals, we Changed School Districts. We were now in the High Springs School District, and Derlwood and I now had to go to the High Springs School. The official name of the school was The High Springs Sandspur. The school board was made up of all local people, and they adjusted the school calendar to fit the local labor needs. Things like harvesting and planting had a lot to do with the starting and ending dates of the school year.

The school suffered some major losses during World War II and had not fully recovered at that time. Well, it started the year before we finished the move-in project, and Dad sent me back to school, but he kept Derlwood home for a couple of weeks to help with the move-in. I don't think that helped me any. I did not like being in school during the day, where I did not know anybody and was just waiting to get back home.

When I did get home, I had to start back watering the stock, cutting wood, and filling the wood box, then helping Mom get supper ready. I was supposed to do some school homework, but with everything that was going on at the house, I made little to no attempt to do school homework. I had developed a bad attitude in school, and that made things worse. When I was working on the cleanup, even though the work was very hard, I felt like at least I was accomplishing something.

After we moved into our own house, things changed a little bit. Mom and Dad knew I was having trouble in school, and they sent Derlwood back to school to help me. Even though he was in a different grade, we spent a lot of time together, and that helped to get me straightened out.

When we got home in the evenings, Derlwood would have his job to do, and I would have mine. Derlwood worked very hard on the farm. Dad expected him to do as much work as he did. Even in those days, Derlwood knew that he was going to be a good mechanic, and he loved working on things, but he did not like farming. The only thing I remember wanting was a horse that I could ride.

As soon as we moved into our new place, it became evident that we had taken on more than we could handle. The house needed extensive repairs, fences had to be fixed or replaced, and we required additional farm tools, seeds, and fertilizer. On top of that, we had to construct a tobacco barn and ensure we had enough provisions for food and clothing. While we were aware that Dad had maintained good credit with Mr. Smith at the bank, the amount of money required far surpassed any previous loans we had taken.

While we were having breakfast that morning and trying to plan how to get the loan, God sent us a miracle. Harley Osteen interrupted our quiet morning with a visit to the house to give us an unrequested but very much-needed loan to help us get started.

Harley came in and joined us for a cup of coffee, then he reached into his bib overalls pocket and pulled out two thousand dollars and laid it on the kitchen table. He said that his family had talked it over and that we were a good neighbor, and they felt that we might need some help getting the things that we would need for our first year, and they wanted to help us.

Well, that sure shocked everyone. After what felt like a long time, Dad asked how he wanted it paid back, and Harley stated, "Just pay it back as you can." Then Dad said that he would get Mama to write up an agreement for him, but Harley said that he did not need it because he knew Dad was good at it. Then he thanked Mom for the coffee and headed back toward his house. Things went a lot smoother after that.

There was so much work to do that each day started before daybreak and went dark. Dad didn't believe in working on Sundays, but at that time, the workload required it. In addition to the work that our house required, there was an additional building that needed work, and it was for the working stock.

It was called a corncrib and was located in the stock pen close to the house. This small barn-type building was used to store feed for the mules. The roof extended out on each side to provide shelter, feeding stalls, and equipment storage.

One side of our crib featured four feeding stalls with grain troughs and hay feeders. Each animal was assigned its own feeding stall, and they quickly learned which one was theirs. This made feeding the mules much easier.

Various repairs were needed. We had to put up a new fence and a gate, and this job took priority over working on the house so we could move the mules from Uncle Chief's place.

After fixing the stock pen and relocating the mules to their new home, we turned our attention back to repairing our own house. The back porch was generally in good condition, but the steps leading to it needed to be rebuilt. This porch was elevated about five feet off the ground.

On the other hand, the front porch, which was only two feet high and exposed to the weather, had several boards that required replacement. The front porch lacked steps entirely, with just some stacked concrete blocks serving as makeshift entryway.

The picture is of my mom and Dad coming back from church after moving into their own first home. As for the layout of the house, it was shaped like an "L" featuring a spacious living room complete with a fireplace.

This living room was connected to the Master Bedroom, which spanned the front of the house. A second bedroom was also present, and it was shared by Derlwood and me.

The kitchen made up the backside of the house. There was a small room that could be used as a storeroom or a small single bedroom. I remember when we moved Mom's big old wood stove into the kitchen, we had to replace the flue system. The kitchen needed other things, but they had to wait. The money was going fast.

When we lived on Uncle Chief's place, we had some hogs, cows, and chickens. We had to build pens for them so they could be moved. I don't know for sure if we ever got things the way we wanted them.

Derlwood and I had both intended to transform that small room into our own private bedroom. However, that plan didn't come to fruition for quite a while.

The only other thing I remember about moving into our own house was that we could never catch up on the workload. I missed so much school that year that I had to take a setback and repeat that year. That was embarrassing, but I knew it could not be helped.

By the end of the first year on our farm, Derlwood had dropped out of school completely and had a part-time job at a welding shop in town. He was still living at home and would help Dad when he could. By the end of the first year, Mom had gotten a job with the peanut mill in High Springs. Dad was able to handle most of the fieldwork on the farm, and the rest of us had to cover everything else.

I would go to school every day I could, and when I got home, I would pump and carry water to fill all the water troughs in all the stock pens. I would also fill all the water containers in the kitchen and wash area. I would cut wood and fill all the wood boxes. Mom would take care of the house and cooking. I think this was where I really learned about handling responsibility.

Everybody had a job to do, and if you did not get your job done, everybody else was affected by your failure. Dad always checked on everything without failure and would immediately challenge you as to why you had not completed your job.

It was already in the fall of the year by the time we were able to completely move into our own house, and the weather was very hot. We still had some crops to harvest at Uncle Chief's place, and everything we were doing was always outside and in the sun.

Dad picked a calm day, and we burned it. The burn took all day and half of the night to burn down to where it was safe to leave it unattended. Normally there would not have been any high fire risk because we had completed a control burn for all the wooded areas and fields, but this farm had not been lived on for a few years, and there was a lot of burnable trash on the ground. The seedbed fire was so hot the ground stayed hot for a couple of days.

Wood fires were always a risk to people in the area, and our fire was so large that some of our neighbors came over to make sure the fire was under control. We should have notified them that we were going to burn, but we didn't take the time. The wind had laid down, so we dropped everything else and did the burn. We got it burned safely, but we sure were exhausted.

That first year of living on and farming our own land was very busy. No one had lived on the land for five years, and every fence row on the place was overgrown and had to be cleaned out and the fences repaired or replaced. We had a pump in the center of the farm for pumping water for stock. The property lines formed a one-half mile square that was divided equally into four forty-acre fields, and that pump was set at the center intersection of all four of the fields.

At one time in the past, the pump was driven by a windmill, but now only the tower remained, and the water had to be pumped by hand. We could not afford to replace the windmill, and there was not enough wind flow at that location to make it reliable, so we built a stock pen around the pump with controlled entrances from all four sections. It was a lot of work, but when we needed it, it worked well.

The property also had 20 acres that were not cultivated with some large pine trees on it. Dad got a sawmill owner to come and cut the timber into lumber for one-half of the lumber. Our part of it was enough lumber to build our tobacco barn. The area also had a lot of scrub oak trees on it, and we cut them for fence posts. Derlwood and I got the job clearing it for cultivation during that first year.

Before we could start any plowing of the fields, we had to clear off the five years of overgrowth of brush and weeds. We could clear the small stuff by running a weed cutter over it and then burning off the field. The larger brush would have to be cut by hand. You could use a turning plow to turn the top three to four inches of soil over. All of this had to be finished before anything could be planted.

Before we even started to move anything into our new house, Dad had planned out what he wanted to plant and which fields he was going to use. Mom was planning how she would manage the house and take care of us. Her first priority was food for us.

She always canned all the extra food that she had, and she had a lot of mason jars on hand and that big pressure cooker that she used to prepare the canned foods. Well, that pressure cooker got a lot of used canning blackberries.

When we started clearing out the fence rows, they had a five-year growth of briars, and they were loaded with blackberries. That kept us supplied with Blackberry Cobbler, which I loved, for that first winter.

To get the land ready for planting and the house comfortable to live in, we had to divide the workload. Dad and Derlwood got the fences and open fields, while Mom and I got the house, wood supply, and stock pens.

One of our problems with the house was the yards. There was a big yard around the house, and the large front yard had some type of grass that grew in the front yard, similar to Mongo grass, to cover the ground. The problem was that it had not been trimmed or maintained in five years and had become a fire hazard for the house and a safe haven for snakes. Mom assigned me the task of removing all that mess first.

*Our Grape Arbor | Root Simple by Unknown Author is licensed.*

Burning it in place was not an option because of the house, so I had to dig it up and move it to a safe burn area. That left just a bare dirt front yard.

On the back side of the house, there was a large Grape Arbor with large purple grapes, eight feet wide by 20 feet long, similar to the one in the picture. Our arbor had been there for several years and was very thick and ragged on top. It made a good, shaded area in the yard that was always cooler, but it also made a big mess in the yard.

Mom wanted to save the arbor, and I loved the grapes, so that got put on our to-do list. There was a metal dish-type object on a firepit that we called a sugar kettle which was used for heating water for large cleaning jobs like washing our clothes. That had to be put back in service without delay.

My everyday chores were refilling the water and firewood containers for the house, watering all the stock, and making sure all the mule pens were clean. Then I could work on our to-do list.

Mom also had her chores list of things she had to do each day before she could work on her projects. Somehow most things got completed as scheduled.

Dad and Derlwood started with cleaning out fence rows, repairing or replacing the fence. We had some cows and some hogs that had to be moved from Uncle Chief's place. They also had to relocate our chickens and their coups. All the fence on the farm was old and needed to be replaced, and most of it was beyond repair. The new fence was expensive and took money that we could not afford. Thanks to being able to share the neighbor's fence, we made it.

After a lot of pulling, digging, cutting, and burning, they got the fields ready to plow and the pasture areas set up. Mom got her large garden plowed and ready to plant and was able to find enough old fence to enclose it for her. Things for us were coming together really well, and we were able to slow down just a little bit.

The electricity company for our area was trying to get easements across the farms to run a new service for us. There had never been electricity in this part of the country, and Dad and some of the other small farm owners would not let them have easements. They did not want anybody or thing on their property. When asked about putting power poles on their property, that was an even stronger NO. To them, it was one more thing for them to have to plow around. It took the electric company a long time to get anything started.

During the spring of the year, Mom got a visit from someone in her family from Georgia. Her mother was very sick, and they needed Mon to come up and help the family. Mom went back with him, and we had to fend for ourselves for a couple of weeks. Well, I was the youngest, and I got stuck with the housework. None of us knew how to cook, and the food situation was not good. Mostly we just opened something Mon had canned and heated it up. Sometimes one of the neighbors would cook up a pot of something and bring it over.

One morning, while I was cleaning up the house, I got the idea to go hunting for some meat. We had a few squirrels and rabbits in the woods. Derlwood had an old, single-barrel 16-gauge shotgun at the house, so I took it and went hunting. The only thing I found were two young crows trying to fly out of their nest. Well, I shot and cleaned them. Cleaned and cut up, they looked a lot like a squirrel, so I fried them like I had seen Mom cook squirrels.

About the time I got finished cooking them, Derlwood came into the house to check on me. He looked at the meat and thought it was a squirrel, and I told him that it was his lunch, and he ate them. He liked them and wanted to know where I had found the squirrel, and I told him that they were young crows, and he would not believe me. I had to show him the feathers before he could believe it. That was the only time I made my brother eat crow, but he got a lot of kidding about that.

As if I did not have enough to do, Dad bought a bunch of goats. We had to build a pen for them, and I had to feed and water them. The male goat was as big as a Deer and was brown and white.

He was a little too big for me to control, and he would fight with you by standing up on his hind legs and butting you. Derlwood liked to play with him, and he would get the goat to try to butt him, and Derlwood would catch his head and wrestle with him.

Not only did he look like a deer, but he could jump like one. He was always jumping out of his pen, and one day, he went about a mile across the woods to another farm. Derlwood and I took a rope and walked over to bring him back. Derlwood made a halter out of one end of the rope and tied the rope to it and led the goat back to our farm.

Things went well until we had to cross a fence. The goat refused to jump over the fence, and we had to throw him over it. After crossing the fence, things went well until we stopped for a shot rest. Derlwood was holding the end of the rope, and he sat down on the ground.

The goat was just standing there beside Derlwood, and I noticed that our homemade halter had shifted around on the goat's head. I walked toward the goat to straighten out the halter, and suddenly, he reared up on his hind legs and struck me right in the middle of my chest with his head.

He knocked me down flat on my back so hard that my feet flew up and over my head. I was hurt and so mad that as I jumped up, I grabbed an old tree limb off the ground and hit him as hard as I could. The tree limb was rotten, and it just broke into several pieces. The speed and power of that goat took us both by surprise, and it was a good thing that limb was rotten.

There was another thing that happened while Mom was in Georgia that I would like to tell you about. We still had Dad's old car, and Derlwood was still keeping it running.

The battery was getting bad, and it didn't have enough power to make the engine turn over without some help. So, someone had to use the hand crank to start it. We had learned that if someone pushed down on the starter button while someone operated the hand crank, it would start up much easier.

No problem, I knew how to do that, and Derlwood was able to turn the crank. On one of our very hot days, Derlwood had come to the house to check on me and get some lunch. He was going to drive the old car back to where he and Dad were working. I knew that the ignition switch had to be turned on, but I had forgotten that part of the switch was bad, and the two ignition wires also had to be twisted together for the engine to start.

Derlwood asked me if I knew how to turn on the switch and operate the starter. I assured him that I did. We had done this before, and I knew what I was doing.

I got inside the car and turned the switch on and pressed the starter button. Derlwood was spinning the crank as fast as he could. The car was trying to start but just couldn't start. We tried it again, and it failed to start again.

Derlwood asked me if I was sure I had the switch on, and I turned the switch off and back on again to show him I was doing it right. He was getting so hot that he was about to get heat stroke. He tried it a couple more times but got the same results.

He came to the driver's door and showed him what you were doing. Just as I was going through the procedure again, I noticed the two bare wires that were to be twisted together, just hanging down behind the switch. I had forgotten to twist them together.

Derlwood saw it about the same time I did, and he got mad. When I saw the way he looked, I started laughing, and I could not stop. He got madder and started hitting me on my shoulder with his fist, and I could not get away, nor could I stop laughing. If he had not already got so hot and exhausted, I think he would have beaten me to death.

We spent so much time remembering and laughing about that, that his wife, Delores Barber, told me to be sure and put it in this book.

Well, Mon lost her mother, but she got back home before I destroyed the house and family. Jobs were getting sparse in this area and South Georgia.

One afternoon a friend of Dad's, John Leggett, from the Alama, Georgia, area, came up to the house to see Dad. He was looking for work. He had walked and hitchhiked all the way from Alama, looking for work without any luck.

Somehow, he had heard that Dad was working on a big farm and was hoping that Dad could help him. Mr. Leggett had a family consisting of his wife, two daughters, and a son, and they were still living in the house where he last worked but had to move now because the job had ended.

The only person Dad knew that might be able to hire him was Nash Davis, AKA Shorty, at Neals. Mr. Leggett was very tired, and road-worn and needed a good meal. He spent the night with us.

Dad went looking for Mr. Davis. Somehow Dad found out that Mr. Davis would be at Neals the next day. The next morning, Dad took Mr. Leggett, all cleaned up and rested, to Neals. Dad met Shorty and introduced him to Mr. Leggett. Dad explained Mr. Leggett's situation to Shorty and gave Mr. Leggett a good character reference.

Shorty had a new piece of property with a family-sized house on it that was still vacant. Based on Dad's recommendation, he hired Mr. Leggett and gave him the use of the house. Shorty generously loaned Mr. Leggett one of the farm trucks for his move and even provided an advance on his pay to facilitate the transition. Mr. Nash Davis was known for his kindness and generosity.

It was during that first year that I got my first horse. She was a little too small to be used for a plow horse but was just right for riding. The need for horses was being replaced by cars and tractors, so there was no market for small riding horses. Dad made a good deal on her, and I was able to pay him back the money he spent on her.

She turned out to be a great horse for me. She had a gentle disposition and a very smooth riding gait. She had a slow, easy lope and was in excellent condition. When working stock, she was quick and had moves like a Quarter Horse. I loved riding that horse, and I rode her everywhere I went.

At first, I rode her bareback because I did not have a saddle, but later I found someone who had an old saddle that he was not using anymore. It needed fixing up, and he gave it to me. I fixed it up, and to me, it was perfect.

Having a horse gave me a feeling of freedom that I had never felt before. For me, to be able to go and get a cold drink or candy bar was a three-mile trip. My horse could knock that off in no time.

To go to town was a five-mile trip each way. I could now ride my horse through the woods to the edge of town and cut off a mile each way. Now I could go to the movies on the weekend. Riding my horse became my favorite past-time.

One of my chores was to check our stock. Screw worms were a major problem for the hogs, cows, and goats. They needed to be checked daily. Normally we could check most of them when they came in for water, but if they did not show up for water, you needed to find them. The horse made that job easier and quicker.

I loved riding late in the afternoon after my work was finished. I would start at about sundown and ride for two or three hours. We had dirt roads, but they were clean and easy to ride even after dark. About once a week, on good nights, I would ride to Mr. Leggett's house at Neals and visit his girls.

We got through the first year ok and were able to pay back some of the money we owed to Harley Osteen. Dad and I even got the tobacco barn built and used it. Derlwood and Mom had gotten part-time jobs that helped with the bills.

The second year on our farm went better than the first. We did not have as much secondary work to do and had some better equipment to use. Dad's health stayed good, and he loved working on his own farm.

I got to go back to school, but I had to repeat the seventh grade. Mom had gotten a full-time job with Copulins Sausage Company, and Derlwood was working full-time as a mechanic. Each day for me was busy, but I could still find time to ride my horse and get my schoolwork done.

Dad bought a riding cultivator, which required a two-mule team, but I got a lot of plowing time with the other mule that One called Kilroy. He was still a problem, but now I could handle him. Somehow Mom got all the household work done and still worked full-time. Derlwood joined the Air Force, which had now split away from being the Army Air Corp and formed a new branch of service.

The local electric company was close to getting easements for their new service run that would include our farm. Dad still did not like the idea, but he knew it was going to happen.

I was still watering all the stock and fighting the screw worm problem. The goats were my biggest problem for screw worms, but we had gotten rid of the Billy goat, and the rest was not a problem for me.

One problem that I did have was that my horse was getting a bad leg, and I could not ride her much. Dad had found me another horse that he liked.

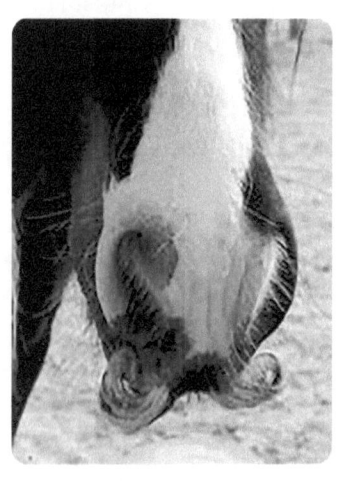

He was called a Gypsy Vanner and looked like picture. This one was bigger but not a good riding horse. Her feet were larger like a draft horse, and her back was too wide to hold a saddle well. She was a black horse with a blaze on her face that looked like a lightning bolt. She had whiskers on her lip that looked like a handlebar mustache. The blaze came down the right side of her face and split the mustache in half.

The left side was black, and the right side was white. She was a gentle horse and comfortable to ride but could not perform like a good saddle horse.

My new horse got a bad case of gang warts on her face, and in a short time, they went from her lip up the side of her face to her eye. I got our local vet to come out to treat her, but he did not have any cure for her. He had also checked my first horse's leg and said that I should just go ahead and put her down. I was not going to do that.

One day I rode the horse with warts over to the commissary at the community called Clark for soda pop and candy bar. On the way back, I met an older black gentleman that lived in the area. I knew him because I had met him a few times before and he always liked to talk about horses.

He looked at the warts on my horse's nose and asked me what I was doing about them. I explained that the Vet had told me that there was nothing I could do. He held the horse's face in his hands where he could get a good look at them and then said that I should make a poultice out of powered sulfur and molasses to cover the affected area.

I immediately went to find my dad and shared the newly learned information with him. I asked about the possibility of getting sulfur for treatment. My dad wasn't familiar with this remedy but was curious. He encouraged me to give it a try.

He sent me to the High Springs drugstore to buy sulfur and gave me the money I needed. I got on a horse, rode to town, and purchased two pounds of powdered sulfur and half a gallon of molasses. Once I finished the errand, I headed back home, covering about thirteen miles that day.

Even though I was a bit behind on my chores, I still managed to prepare the treatment before bedtime. Mixing the sulfur with molasses, I successfully applied it to the affected area on the horse's nose. I repeated this routine every day, and after just two days, I noticed the warts starting to come off. Within the next week, all the warts had disappeared completely.

The rest of the year went okay. Derlwood did not have to go to Korea and was sent to the Air Force Automotive Vehicle Maintenance school instead. He liked the school, and he wrote that it was a good school, and he was learning a lot.

I thought that was a good thing, but I sure missed him. The crops were growing well, and the livestock was looking good. The electric company had started marking out the route for their new power line, and I was doing good in school.

The electric company took a long time to install the new service line. They worked everything in phases. They would show up at the farm and need to gain access to their power easement to complete the phase they were working on at that time. Then they would disappear until they were ready to complete the next phase. After they got the power cables run, they showed up and put the wiring in the house. Between the time the house was wired, and the power was turned on was a considerable amount of time.

During the time the electric company was finishing everything so they could turn the power on, I was so busy working in the fields that I forgot all about the electricity. One day while I was finishing up one of the fields on the back side of the farm, I worked late, and it was after dark before I got home. The only light was the lamp in the kitchen. I found my way into the stock pen and got my mules taken care of and made my way to the back porch to the wash basin and got washed up. I was tired and hungry, and all I wanted to do was eat supper.

Dad was sitting at his usual spot at the end of the dining table while Mom stood by the stove, preparing our supper. The dim light for the dining table came from an old kerosene lamp. Mom directed Dad, "Turn that lamp up; I can't see what I'm doing." Her voice had a sharp edge, indicating her frustration. In response, Dad, also displaying some annoyance, turned the lamp up to its maximum brightness. However, this caused the lamp to start emitting smoke and smudging the lamp shade. Mom raised her voice, instructing Daddy to turn it down as it was filling the shade with smoke. With the situation escalating and with my primary focus being on eating, I hoped to avoid an argument. Dad got up from his seat and extinguished the lamp by blowing on it.

It was so dark you could not see anything. Then suddenly, I was blinded by the light. Mom had turned on the electric light directly overhead. It was a 150-watt bulb, and it sure lit up the room. Mom took one look around and yelled, "Turn that thing off; you can see dust and cobwebs everywhere".

The electric company had come by the house that day and checked everything and turned the power on. Mom and Dad had decided to play a trick on me, and they sure took me by surprise. We sure got a lot of good laughs over that. The house was wired to have one light bulb in each room, and they were all 150-watt bulbs. The kitchen and living room were wired with an electric outlet box.

By the end of the school year, my first horse's leg was so bad that I could not ride her, and we had never got any harness for the other horse. I still wanted a good saddle horse, and I traded both of my horses for a three-year-old Tennessee Walker.

She was only halter broken and had never had a saddle on her. She was a beautiful red strawberry color with four white stocking feet. She had a white mane and tail and a blazed face. She was a very pretty horse, but she did not have the normal flat face. She had a rounded nose; we used to call that either a Roman Nose or a Rocking chair face.

I knew that I would have to do a lot of work with her before she would become a good saddle horse. The school was out, and I would schedule a half hour a day to work with her.

She was long-legged and tall. I just knew she was going to be a great saddle horse. I was not in any hurry to try to ride her or to get thrown by her. I started getting her used to being halter and led around. I spent a lot of time brushing and touching her. I switched to a bridle and then added a saddle blanket. She did not like that, but she got used to it.

I added my old saddle without the stirrups. That took longer, and she did not like the cinch, but I stayed consistent and slowly added to the pressure until she took the complete saddle and stirrups. I did a lot of leading her around with different things on the saddle, and I would pull on the saddle horn. She settled down ok, and I got up the nerve to try that first ride.

I found part of a field that dad had just finished plowing, and the ground was soft. I brought her to the area with the soft ground and set up my first ride. I did the usual walking around and pulling on the saddle, and then I pulled myself up onto the saddle.

She was not happy about that and reacted by trying to shake me off, but I was using a mean bit with that bridle, and she calmed right down. At first, I let her go where she wanted to, and then I slowly started guiding her toward the barn.

She acted like she was scared and confused, but as soon as I got to the gate at the barn, I dismounted by easing over and sliding off. She was still a little scared, but I led her up and down the lane in front of the gate a few times and then removed the saddle and brushed her down.

I did not have a lot of time to work with her, but I did something each day. The first time I rode her off the farm, she started really testing me to see what she could get away with.

Sometimes she would only act up when I would first get on her and then be okay for a while. The first time I rode her to the Clark commissary, I met the older black gentlemen again. Boy, he liked the looks of her, but his expression changed when he saw that round face.

He said, "That sure is a pretty horse, but she is a mean one". Then he went on to say that he had never seen a horse with the type of face that was not mean. He was right about the warts, and he turned out to be right about her.

I had several problems with her but was always able to get her back under control. One time when I was riding her in the woods, she suddenly acted like she was about to fall down, then did a hard spin around and took off. She caught me by surprise and threw me off of her, but I did not lose the rain. I got her stopped and got back on and ran her as hard as I could for about a quarter mile. I always punished her when she pulled that stunt.

One Sunday afternoon, I started to take a trip to Neals. The distance to Neals was about eight miles, and then you had the same trip back. About halfway between home and Neals was my best friend's house. His name was Donald Matthews, and I was going to stop there on the way down. Well, I was all cleaned up and had a lot of Brylcreem on my hair, holding my cowlicks down, and had my newest pants and shirt on. The road was a double-wide graded dirt road that had just been graded. I stopped there to water the horse and talked with Donald and his little sister.

When I got back on the horse and tried to head on down the road to Neals, that horse pulled the same stunt she did in the woods the time she threw me off. This time she did not get me off, but she got about 50 yards down the road toward the house before I got her stopped and turned around. I got her headed in the right direction and layer the whip to her. Just as she got up to full speed and we were passing Donald's house, I felt the saddle jump and come loose. On the next jump, I was floating above the horse, and pieces of my old saddle were flying everywhere. At about 30 miles per hour, I pushed myself loose from the saddle and became a dirt dart.

I hit the dirt on my shoulder and back, flipped over on my stomach, and slid feet first through all that sand. By the time I got up on my feet, the horse had stopped and turned around and was trying to run back and pass me by going between me and the road ditch fence. I was able to run her into the fence and grab the reins and stop her.

My old saddle rigs were scattered down the road. I was using burlap bags for a saddle blanket, and Donald used them to collect all the saddle parts. My clothes and hair were full of sand, but I was not seriously injured anywhere except for my pride. Donald had a tac room out in the barn, and we took everything there to work on it. I had so much sand inside my clothes that I had to pull off everything, turn it inside out, and beat the sand out of all my clothing. I then got a tub of water and tried to take a bath. I tried to wash the sand out of my hair, but that Brylcreem was holding so much sand that my hair looked grey. Donald must have pumped 10 gallons of water on my head, and I still could not get it all out.

My saddle was the old range type and had a metal ring to hold the front cinch on, and it also held the breast strap, called the Martin Rig. The strap holding that ring was what broke. Fortunately, Donald was able to repair it and put everything back together. I put the saddle back on the horse and went to Neals. As soon as my girlfriend saw me, she asked what had happened and then said, "You got sand in your hair". She washed my hair again.

I had lost so much time at Donald's house that I had to cut the visit short and start the long ride home. The ride was long, boring, and uneventful, but that horse continued to be a problem as long as I had her.

The school term ended, and I passed to the Eight grade, but I also became an instant full-time farmhand. It was that time of the year when you had to harvest your current crops and get ready for next year. You had corn and hay to gather for stock feed for next year. You had to break each ear of corn off the stalk by hand and haul it to the barn for storage as feed. Most of our hay came from peanut vines. The peanut vines had to be plowed up with the peanuts still attached to the vine. The vines had to be stacked on specially made poles to dry. When the peanuts and vines were dried out, you ran them through a thrashing machine that separated the peanuts from the vines. You bagged up and sold the peanuts and made hay out of the vines.

You also had to butcher your meat supply for the next year and get it into cold storage. Then you had to clear the fields, repair and or replace fences and get them ready to start next year's crops.

Well, before I knew it, school started again. I started the eighth grade and was doing good. I was trying to get my mind back on school, but the weather got so dry that the land could not be plowed when we needed to start getting it ready for the crops. By the time the weather changed, Dad's health had gotten bad again. He developed circulation problems with both legs and was stuck in bed for weeks.

Dad was hardheaded and did not like doctors. He often said that if you were able to go to the doctor, you did not need him, and the doctor would not come to you anyway. For Dad to not be able to go to work was the hardest thing in the world on his pride. His habit of always working beyond his physical abilities is probably what caused his health problems to start with.

Well, I dropped out of school to help get the plowing started. After a few weeks, Dad recovered enough to assist around the house, and he attempted to resume fieldwork. At that point, I decided to go back to school, even though I knew I was significantly behind in the class. However, circumstances changed swiftly as Dad severely injured his back, rendering him unable to walk. As a result, I made the decision to permanently drop out of school. This happened when I had just turned 16 years old, putting me two years behind my classmates.

To catch up and keep up with the work, I had to work every day from daybreak until after dark. Mom and Dad both did everything they could, and some of our friends helped us with the work. Dad promised me an eighth of what we made from the crops that year. There were other considerations like feed for my horse and my room and board. I had gotten some new shoes and clothing just before I dropped out of school, and I had not left that farm since.

Dad had worked something out with our neighbor, Evie Osteen, and we were using a place on his property to grow our tobacco crop that year. Mr. Osteen had a small house and a nice-sized equipment shelter on the property, where we planted the crop. By May of that year, I had caught up on most of the work and was plowing the tobacco crop for the last time. The size of the crop was small that year, but it was really looking good. The stalks were almost shoulder high with big, long leaves. I was really proud of that crop, and I was already planning on trading my horse for a car.

It was a sunny Saturday morning, and I was feeling good. I had a couple of small tasks to do that day, and I had gotten an early start. One of the tasks required a pair of mules, and I had our best pair. They were working well. My plans were to knock out those small jobs before lunch, clean up, and go to town for the first time that year. I really wanted a hamburger, an RC Cola, and to spend some time just hanging around town and maybe seeing a movie. I was all through plowing the tobacco and headed home by 11 a.m.

Things started falling apart as I made my way back home. I was cutting across the woods as I usually did when I unexpectedly encountered a six-foot Rattlesnake.

This snake had managed to capture a full-grown rabbit and was in the process of trying to swallow it. The area was known for having numerous rattlesnakes, and our usual practice was to eliminate any we came across.

I had to first calm the mules down before I could safely leave the vicinity and deal with the snake. Fortunately, I was near a shelter, so I guided the mules there.

The challenge now was finding a suitable tool to kill the snake. The woods were regularly cleared by controlled burns to maintain the cleanliness of the area. After some searching, I discovered a hoe that I could use. Returning to where the snake was, I was surprised to find it still struggling to consume the rabbit.

With the hoe, I ended the snake's life and proceeded to bury its head. As I was doing this, I noticed my father walking in my direction.

He was walking slowly, and with two walking sticks. This was the first time he had seen the tobacco since the day we planted it. He was having one of his better days and wanted to check on how things were doing.

We went up to the shelter and looked the crop over. We were both proud of that crop. Dad needed to rest before walking back to the house, so we sat down on the porch of the little house. I could see a bad-looking black cloud to the West of us, and it was moving in our direction. I did not think Dad could make it to the house before the storm caught us, so I suggested we wait there until after the rain blew over.

The clouds were coming in fast, like a typical thunderstorm. I remember Dad saying to me, "Son, I don't like the look of those clouds because they have too much red in them". I did not know what he meant by that, but I soon found out.

First came the rain, then the wind, and then the hail. Within thirty minutes, that tobacco crop was beaten into the ground. Every plant was blown over, and a lot of the leaves knocked off the stalks. We spent the rest of that day trying to stand up what plants we could and tried to save what we could. My dream of going to town vanished, along with my hopes of buying a car. That was when I decided that I would not be a farmer.

Through the rest of that Summer, Dad's back got better, and he was able to work again. We finished gathering the crops and loaded the last of the tobacco on a truck for the auction at about the end of August.

When we finished loading the truck, I told Dad that if he could give me with thirty-five dollars for my share of the crop, feed my horse until we could sell him, I would head to the city and find myself a job.

He agreed, and I went to the house, taking my final bath in that old #3 galvanized washtub. I packed the few clothes that still fit me into an old paper shopping sack, put on a shirt for the first time in months, and hit the road.

## Chapter 9

# LEAVING HOME

I do not recall the date, but it was late August 1952 when I left the farm and headed for Gainesville. I was not just leaving the farm; I was heading to a world of new and exciting adventures. I was so excited about what I thought I would find out there in the world that I did not think about how hot the sun was as I walked down that old dirt road to the main highway to town.

To me, it was very simple; my uncle owned a restaurant called the Orange and Blue Diner, and it was located on West University Boulevard. I would walk or hitchhike until I got to it. Once I got there, I would find me a job and a place to stay. (By now, you should begin to realize just how naive this country kid really was.)

I would buy my food at the Orange and Blue, and that way, my uncle would get the trade. With thirty-five dollars in my pocket, I did not have a worry in the world.

Once I got out on the main road, I got a ride into High Springs; and then walked out to the road to Gainesville. I was used to walking, and everything seemed new and exciting to me, so time was not important.

I got a couple of more rides before being dropped off at the corner where US-441 becomes Thirteenth Street. At that time, it was the Northwest corner of town. I had made good time, and it was just past noon when I started walking down Thirteenth Street heading for West University Blvd. The last person who dropped me off had told me to stay on Thirteenth, and I would come to university; then turn left and I would find the Orange and Blue on the left side of the street.

I didn't have a clear sense of the distance; all I knew was that it would be a lengthy walk. The journey felt relatively easy, considering I only had to carry that shopping bag containing my clothes. So, I maintained a good pace.

Upon reaching the first gas station, I paused to confirm I was still headed in the right direction. At the station, there was a refreshing drinking fountain with cold water, and it tasted wonderful. Since I had left home early that morning, I hadn't taken any breaks to eat or drink.

The water and directions were free, and I was not going to eat until I reached the Orange and Blue. After a couple more stops, I arrived at West University Blvd. I turned left and after what seemed like only a short time, I was at the Orange and Blue Restaurant. It was just a small, what we now call a greasy spoon diner, but to me, it was beautiful.

The building was just wide enough for a row of three booths and an "L- shaped counter with a grille and large coffee urn. In the back corner was a jukebox. The back part of the building served as a small kitchen, storeroom, and one small bedroom. The building had two doors, one in the front that entered the customer area and one on the side for entrance to the kitchen area. There was no such thing as air conditioning, so fans and screen doors were used to keep the heat down inside the place.

I remember pulling the screen door open, walking in, and proudly asking the waitress if G. W. Bass owned the place. She gave me a strange look and answered yes, do you know him? I told her that he was my uncle, and I ordered a cheeseburger all the way with an Orange Crush soda. As I set my bag of clothing on the counter, she gave me that strange look again and asked if my uncle knew I was there. I noticed that everyone I talked to in the city was giving me that strange look. I told her no and put some money on the counter to pay for my order.

While I ate my burger, I remembered that just before I got to the diner, I passed a supermarket that really looked nice. I decided that they could use my help, and that was where I was going to work.

# Chapter 10

# MY FIRST JOB

Thank God for blessing us, dumb people. Looking back on it now, I realize that if I had not been totally dumb, I would not have made it. I asked the waitress if I could leave my bag there for a little while and left the diner.

I walked into the supermarket, which was called Winn and Lovett's back then, and asked to talk to the boss. There came that look again, and I was informed that he was the manager.

While I was waiting for him, I looked around the store. I was surprised at how cool it was in the store. Man, I was going to like working there. A couple of men came up to me, and one of them said his name was Mr. Miller, and he was the store manager. He asked how he could help me. I told him I was there to go to work.

Here came that strange look again, and he said, "Let's go to my office". (I hate to keep on about being dumb, but the thought of me being just a kid and maybe he did not need any help. It never once crossed my mind. I was an honest, hardworking guy straight from the farm. I could do anything. Anyone should be glad to get a worker like me.

He was a nice guy, and he asked me if I had any experience working in a supermarket. I proudly told him that I was raised on a farm and that I could do anything. Just tell me what you want me to do, and I will do you a good job. It took me several minutes to convince him that he needed me. I was beginning to wonder just how he had gotten to be the boss if he could not see what a good worker I would be. Finally, he threw up his hands and turned to the other person with him and said, "Get his information and let's try him." I asked if I would get one of the aprons everybody was wearing and where do I start.

He assured me that it would be ok to wait until the next morning to start. I gave the other guy my name and told him that I would bring my address the next morning, that I had just got there and did not know the address. I did not tell him that I had not yet found a place to live.

As I walked back to the diner, I could see two signs on University Blvd, and one was state theater and the other was a laundromat. That took care of all my needs except a place to live. I needed a boarding house with a room to rent.

When I got back to the diner, I asked the waitress if there was a boarding house close by. One more strange look, and she said yes, right next door, but don't let her know you have any connection to this place. She really hates our jukebox.

I picked up my bag of clothes and went next door. The elderly woman, who answered the door, didn't appear to be very friendly. I asked her, "Is this a boarding house?" to which she responded, "Yes". Then I asked, "Do you have a room for rent?" another strange look, and she slowly said, "Yes." I said, "Well, show it to me," and started toward the door. After a little longer strange look, she said OK and started down the hallway.

The room she showed me was a nice-sized room with a dresser and a closet. She said there is a bathroom down the hall, and you will share it with the other borders. The rent is $15.00 per week, then her voice rose a little louder, and she said, "In advance".

I handed her my twenty-dollar bill and said, "I will take it", and started putting my clothing in the dresser drawers. She asked two quick questions. How long do you need it and if I was employed? I told her that

I was there to stay and that I worked for Lovett's. She went and got my change, and then she told me that two meals a day, except Sundays, was included. There was some discussion about rules and not getting fed if I was not at the table on time, and she gave me a key to my room. That was the first time I ever had a key to my own room.

My mission for the day was now complete, and I went back to the diner for another cheeseburger and a big Orange Crush. When I returned to the diner, my uncle and aunt were there talking to the waitress. They greeted me and, with that strange look again, asked me what I needed. I said nothing and ordered my burger.

They had some more questions, and I explained that I had a job and a place to live and that my dad knew I was going to Gainesville. They left, and I hung out in the diner, talking to the waitress and her husband until I got tired enough to go to bed. The waitress and her husband were nice people. I do not remember their names, but I spent a lot of time hanging out in the diner with them.

I got up early the next morning and went to the store to report to work. I got there before it opened and found the parking lot full of food and stock items for the store. I just knew that someone had messed up by leaving all that stuff unattended out in the open.

I placed myself in the middle of everything so I could watch it until some of the employees got there. There were cases of freshly baked bread, stacks of canned goods, and all kinds of fresh produce. In a few minutes, someone walked by the parking lot and stopped and started picking up some of the vegetables. I called out to him to leave them alone, they belonged to the store.

He asked who I was before explaining he was the produce manager. After I finished telling him who I was and he enjoyed his little laugh, He unlocked the store, and I helped him, and some other employees bring the stock inside.

My first job was to bag and carry-out groceries. I also learned that until I was hired, all bagboys were part-time. Most of the bag boys were college students working part-time. My starting salary was thirty-two dollars and fifty cents a week. Man, that was about the same amount that I had just gotten for several months of very hard work. This was a great job.

Most of the work was inside, where it was cool, and I only worked eight hours a day plus four hours on Saturday. The problem was that I had nothing to do after I got off work. I was used to working from dawn until dark every day. So, it got very boring when I was off work.

The third day that I worked in the store, some old crabby employee that worked there stopped me as I walked across the nice, highly shined floor and pointed out that my Brogans were leaving little black streaks on the floor. Well, I got a good lecture on what type of shoes I should have before I came back to work.

At first, he was upset about the floor, but he knew that I was a new employee and spent some time explaining how to avoid getting bad foot problems from walking on a concrete floor. He had learned the hard way and wanted to help me. It was good information, and I have always used it. So, I was basically sent from work to buy a proper pair of shoes. I got a pair of shoes and some socks which took most of my spending money.

Two weeks after I started at the store, Mr. Miller gave me a raise to thirty-five dollars a week and put me in charge of the part-time bagboys. Most of them worked on Friday and Saturday because that was our busy time. This got interesting in a hurry. All the bagboys were older and had a lot more education than I did. The harder I worked trying to help them, the more work that I got stuck with.

After getting through the first weekend, the Assistant Manager called me into the office and explained that my job was to make sure the others were busy. He said that he would make money off six employees if five of them stayed busy and only one watched.

He had been watching me on Friday and Saturday and was coming to my rescue. I got some good instructions on scheduling hours and assigning work tasks. My job was to make sure that we bagged all the items sold at the cash registers, the area was cleaned and restocked with our supplies. The most unpleasant part of our job was to sweep that parking lot, and it had to be swept at the end of every day.

The store had a signup sheet for bagboys who wanted to work and what hours they could work. Each week the number to pick from would range from 12 to sometimes 20. Some could only work a couple of hours, and some could work a whole week. Most of them were good guys and would do a good job, but some had to be watched very closely.

I remember one short, fat kid was always a problem. He only wanted to work with certain cashiers, and then all he wanted was to talk to them. After having to reassign him several times because of complaints from the cashiers, I assigned him to sweep the parking lot. He reluctantly took the cleaning equipment out to the parking- lot, but when I checked on him, he had left without sweeping the area. I got another employee to help me, and we cleaned it. The following morning, I called him in and fired him. That was on Saturday, and the following Tuesday, I was in the Manager's office explaining why I fired the son of one of Gainesville's prominent citizens.

I explained something to the effect that he was lazy and would not do what he was told. I was not familiar with what we now call "politically correct, "and I am sure I said something a little more country and with fewer words. His mother started crying, and Mr. Miller asked me to explain what he was doing, and that caused me to fire him. I explained what he was and was not doing, and Mr. Miller excused me from the meeting.

After several minutes I was called back to the office. The first thing I was asked was if I would agree to give him his job back. I said no.

Then Mr. Miller backed me up and told his mother that it was my call because he depended on me to get the work accomplished. His mother explained that she was not mad at me, but she was trying to help her son and wanted me to give him a second chance. She knew he needed help and felt that after being fired, she could get him to change if we would give him another chance. I agreed to take him back, and Mr. Miller explained to his mother that if he was fired again, it would be final. Well, he came back, but it did not work out. He quit before the end of the week.

I liked working at the store and most of the people I worked with. I helped another young man about my age get a full-time job at the store. With him working full-time, my job was easier, and we became friends, but after a while, he started getting in trouble that just about got us both fired. While Mr. Miller was the Manager, things went really well, but he got reassigned. The new manager was not easy to work for, and I always felt like he did not like me.

## Chapter 11

# ORANGE AND BLUE DINER

One day in January 1953, the waitress at the Orange and Blue Diner got hurt and was not able to work. I was asked if I could work the mid-shift until she got back.

The problem was the diner sold beer until midnight, and I was underage. So, I worked hours from midnight until about six a.m. I then started my shift at eight a.m. at the store.

The work at the diner was slow most nights during that time. All I had to do was run the grill and serve coffee. Most nights, I would get some good naps on the stool in the corner behind the counter. After a busy night at the diner, the store shift would be rough.

The waitress was off work for about ninety days, and the diner was open twenty-four-seven. During that time so, all I did was work. After midnight the diner and one other small coffee shop were the only places that were open. We got all the drunks, weird people, and a few other people who worked the mid-shift.

Some of the people just did not have anywhere to go, but some were either too ignorant or just too mean to go home. I remember that I had misjudged a customer at the store once and tried not to be too quick to judge people anymore.

There was a regular customer who arrived on a motorcycle with a sidecar platform. He consistently required haircuts and never shaved. His appearance seemed unkempt, and the old green coveralls he wore only added to that perception.

He always had some dogs riding in the side car and was a regular customer. He would always get some meat and dog food by meeting with one of the managers going into the back part of the store. Most of the time, one of the employees would take the stuff out to his cycle for him. Sometimes he would come through the cash registers with the items all wrapped up. However, he always had a note for the cashier with an amount written on it, and he would always pay in cash.

I thought he was a bum, so I asked the Manager why we served him and made such a fuss over him. First off, he was a good customer who bought a considerable amount of stuff from the store. He was also worth a sizeable about of money and property.

He was retired and did not have a family, but he had a hobby. He picked up every stray dog in the area, housed, fed, and trained them. He paid for all veterinarian care for the dogs and found them a new home. He liked looking like a bum so people would not bother him.

One of the people who came into the diner almost every night was always clean, well-dressed, and had a neatly trimmed beard. He did not drink coffee but always drank hot tea. Sometimes he would order a hamburger. He would not touch salt but would cover everything with pepper.

If the jukebox was playing, he would stuff cotton in his ears and complain about the noise. He came and went like he was on a schedule. He would never sit in one of the booths. He always sat on a stool at the counter. All I knew about him was that he had some type of sleep disorder, and for the most part, he slept on park benches, and he was called Professor.

When the University had exams, the diner would fill up with college kids studying for upcoming exams. The professor would stay in the diner and go from group to group, helping the students with their studies. He really was a professor who taught at the University.

Some of the customers were real, nice people. One of our regulars was a guy who would stop in just to check on me sometimes. If there was a troublemaker in the diner, he would stay until after the troublemaker left. Sometimes I would have to call the police to handle the situation, but most of the time, one of the other customers would get the person to leave.

The police who worked in that area would also try to keep an eye on the place. I was always glad to see them come in. If I had a situation that I was concerned about, I would always get two of the large coffee mugs, fill them with coffee, and set them on the counter. That was my way of saying I might need your help. It seemed like before they would get their coffee drunk, the problem would just go away.

There was always someone trying to cheat or con you out of something, so you always had to be on guard. But there were others who would go out of their way to help you.

I remember one night. I was totally overrun with customers. I was cooking burgers as fast as I could get them on the own the grill. One of the couples that stopped in to eat pitched in and helped.

She got behind the counter and took care of getting the orders straight and collecting the money. The guy with her helped with the grill, dishes, and cleaning the counter. We ran completely out of change, and one of the customers volunteered to go get some change, and I gave him a twenty-dollar bill.

All the customers were working out ways to pay the checks, and after about two hours of that rush, I was totally exhausted, and almost everyone had left the diner. I had totally forgotten about sending the guy to get change.

Just as I was getting my first chance to sit down, some guy with a big grin came walking up to the counter. I asked him what he wanted, and he looked at me and smiled. You don't remember me, do you said as he lay the change on the counter. Then he said, "I bet you thought I was not coming back". I still did not know what he was talking about, so he reminded me that I gave him money to get change for the dinner.

He said that he was sorry it took so long, but he had been everywhere trying to find change. At that hour of the night, there was almost no place open, or that had any change. Even after all the confusion, when the dayshift waitress closed out the register, it was right on.

I met several good and interesting people at the dinner, but the funniest I met was due to an accident that I thought would cost us the dinner. The counter that ran up the center of the floor and curved around to the wall had a row of stools for the customers to sit on.

The stools were supported by a four-inch pipe that was secured at the base to the floor. The seat part of the unit was mounted on a short piece of pipe that fits into the four-inch piece. The top piece had a large square metal plate welded to the short piece of pipe.

The plate had four holes, two in the front and two in the rear to bolt the seat down. The top unit was kept in place by putting the short piece of pipe down in the bottom piece of pipe.

While this configuration made it easy to remove the seats for cleaning, it also meant they could be changed easily. Well, one of the units was broken. The two bolts that held the front of the seat were broken, and if you leaned back, the seat would tip over backward.

Well, this seat had been taken out of service, leaving a four-inch pipe sticking up in front of the counter. While we were waiting for a new one, we tried to keep it as the last stool at the rear of the counter.

Well, at about four-thirty, one warm morning, two couples came in for breakfast on their way to a day of fishing. They were really enjoying their trip. They came in and took the four stools at the end of the counter just inside the front door.

Unbeknownst to me, someone had moved the broken stool to the seat right in front of the door. One of the guys had sat there. He was laughing and talking to the group, and he tried to get something out of his pocket. As he tried to lean back, the stool flipped over backward and dumped him off the stool headfirst. He broke his fall with his hands, but that caused him to flip over backward, landing him on his stomach. This caused his feet to hit the screen door at the entrance.

To complicate matters further, in order to go from the parking lot to the interior of the diner, there were two steps that needed to be climbed. Unfortunately, due to the downward slope, he ended up flipping out of the door. So, when he tried to lean back, he took a double back flip and landed face down in the parking lot just outside the front door.

Man, I just knew he would sue us for that. But he got up and brushed himself off and really started laughing. As soon as everyone knew he was not hurt, they all had a good laugh. His comment about the incident explained what a good sense of humor he had. He said, "Man, I have been thrown out of a lot of places, but this is the only time that I have been thrown out by a bar stool."

They stayed and ate their breakfast which I tried to give them on the house, but they refused the offer. The guy who fell paid the bill and left a good tip saying that it was one of the best laughs he had ever had.

# Chapter 12

## HANK'S SONG

In the first part of March of 1953, I met one of the most interesting people that I met while working at the diner. It was about two o'clock in the morning, and no one else was in the diner. I was trying to take a nap behind the counter when he came through the door and said, "Pour me a cup of mud and burn me a burger." I had not heard anyone order anything that way before, so it took me a second to be sure what I heard.

Now calling the coffee we had there by that time of night mud would have been a nice compliment. The old type of coffee pot we used held five gallons, and to make coffee in it, you had to boil a very large pot of water on the stove that was back in the kitchen. Then you put a basket with the coffee grounds in it on the top of the pot. Then you climbed up on something so you could reach the top of the pot and poured the very hot water through the basket of coffee grounds. That was how the waitress got hurt. She was trying to pour the water into the pot and spilled it all over her chest and side. She got scalded pretty badly.

Well, we avoided making new coffee if possible. All the old pot did was keep heating the water you poured into it. By this time, the coffee had been cooking for between three and four hours and was very rank.

I poured him a cup of coffee and had just got his burger on the grill when I heard him bumping the coffee cup on the counter and saying, "Give me another cup of mud". I had my back to him at that time, and I thought he had spilled his coffee. I picked up the counter towel to clean up the counter with and turned around. To my surprise, there was no spilled coffee on the counter, and his cup was empty.

I could not believe anyone could drink coffee that hot, that quick. I refilled the cup and positioned myself where I saw how he did that. It was simple, he took the ice out of the water glass and used it to take the edge off the temperature. I watched him suck down the second cup while I cooked his burger and started the third cup. I could not believe that anyone could even drink that coffee, much less that fast.

Just as I was growing genuinely concerned about him, he looked at me and asked, "Where am I?" It was at that moment I realized something was not quite right. "You're at the Orange and Blue Diner," I replied, "and you owe me thirty cents." I had a feeling he might be attempting to play con job on me, and I was determined not to let him leave without settling his bill.

He seemed slightly agitated and inquired if I could provide more specifics by telling him the name of the town. "Gainesville," I responded, "and you owe me thirty cents." He then asked, "Gainesville, Georgia?" I corrected him, saying, "No, Gainesville, Florida." He followed up with, "How did I get here?" By now, I was pretty sure he was attempting some sort of con. It seemed like he was feigning ignorance about the state he was in, and I was not buying into it.

He looked really confused and asked for another burger. Then he asked where Winter Haven was and how he could get there. He was starting to sound normal now, and I explained how to get there and was starting to feel a little better about him.

Then he took some change out of his pocket and reached around and put a quarter in the jukebox. Without looking at the selections, he just punched in several selections. At that time, you got six plays for a quarter.

We talked for a few minutes, and he explained that he had been driving so long that he had just zoned out. He had been in Alabama helping a friend get things straightened out, and he did not stop to rest.

Just as I started to think he was okay; a song came on the jukebox. It was a new song and had only been on the jukebox for a couple of days. The song title was "Hank's Song." I had heard it, and I thought it was Hank Williams singing it. Then he scared me again. He got really mad and demanded to know who was singing it. I said that is Hank Williams, and you owe me sixty cents. Hank Williams had just died on New Year's Eve that year.

He was yelling," That was not Hank Williams," and he was trying to read the label on the record while it was playing. A check of the jukebox listing showed that the song was written by Tommy Collins and sung by Ferlin Husky. It was written as a tribute to Hank after he died and rushed into production. Tommy Collins used Hank's song titles to make a song.

The guy asked me, "You think that sounds like Hank Williams?" Now I knew what the con job was going to be. He would try to make me think he was someone important and ask me for some money to help him out.

I replied, "It sounds like Hank to me, and you owe me sixty cents." He looked at me and laughed, then put a five-dollar bill on the counter. He said that is not a tip, and it is to show you that I am not going to stiff you. Wait here while I get something out of the car.

A minute later, he came back with a loose-leaf binder that had some eight by ten photos in it. He then asked if I had ever seen Hank Williams, and when I said no, he asked if I could recognize a photo of him. I said yes, and he showed me a photo of Hank Williams standing with his band. I pointed out Hank standing in the photo, and next to Hank was the guy I was talking to. He was Sammy Pruett, who played the lead guitar in Hank's band.

Pruett stayed at the diner for a while and told me all about touring with Hank. He explained that Don Helms took care of getting them paid, the problems with Hank's ex-wife Audrey, and Hank's drinking problem. Pruett did not like Audrey, but he did like the woman Hank was married to when he died. He played some more songs on the jukebox and told me some of the stories behind the songs. When he felt he had revived enough to travel, he paid his bill and left.

When the waitress was able to come back to work, I quit working at the diner. I was still working at Lovett's and working double jobs had really worn me out. It took a few days of just working at the store to get back in the swing of things.

While I was working both jobs, some of the employees quit, and almost everything was changed around. I became aware that some of the employees had become unhappy with their jobs. The people with key positions had all been changed around, and it seemed like I got a new job assignment every day.

I was also aware the new manager did not seem to like me, but for the most part, I was just too tired to care. Someone else took over the bagboys, and I was moved to different assignments that ranged from stocking the shelves to produce, and sometimes I just worked as a cleanup clerk. At first, I felt relieved to get rid of some of the problems and just have a single task to worry about.

When I first started there, we had some real, good cashiers, and it was always fun working in the bagging area. The faster cashiers would challenge the baggers to a speed contest. I remember one day when I was trying to keep up with our fastest cashier; I picked up something alive.

One of our elderly lady customers had a pet squirrel and kept it in her big old purse. She had taken him out of the purse to get something out of it, and I grabbed him my mistake. Nothing or no one was hurt, but it sure scared the heck out of me, and just for the record, I could never keep up with that cashier. Now it seemed like no one was happy with their work anymore.

After a few days of working just one job, I began to have lots of boring time on my hands. I started looking for something else to try. I was seventeen years old now, and I could join the service. I remembered all the stories that I had heard from the guys who came back from World War II. Most of the stories that I heard did not make me want to run out and join the Army or Marines, but I was impressed with some of the stories about the Navy and Japan.

The Draft was still in effect, and we all knew that someday we would be called. If you got drafted, you did not get much choice as to which branch you got assigned to.

# Chapter 13

# CONSIDERING THE MILITARY

I went to the Navy Recruiter and checked on getting into the Navy. Since I had only heard about Japan and ships called Destroyers from the guys I had talked with, I was surprised at what they had to offer.

Since I had not graduated from high school, the recruiter told me about some of their education programs and technical training schools. He also explained the military had raised the entrance requirements and wanted you to have completed High School before entering.

They did have a quota system, but you had to go on a waiting list based on your overall scores on the entrance exam. I went ahead and took the entrance exam and got the necessary approval from my parents. I guess Dad felt that I would be safer in the Navy than running around the streets of the city. I was told that I might have to wait five or six months and that he could not guarantee that I would make it at all. So, I kept looking around for something else to do.

Someone introduced me to a tall skinny kid about my age who was from the country by the name of Richard Smith. While I was riding with him, he taught me the layout of the city. We discovered that we had lots of things in common. One day, while helping a woman change a tire on her car, we discovered that we had both gone to Bell School.

We had been in the same grade and remembered that we had been friends for a short time. We remained friends for several years after that. There was an opening at the Western Union office for a delivery boy, and with Richard's help, I got the job.

I had to borrow thirty-five dollars to buy me a brand-new Western Flyer bicycle. I quit my job at Lovett's and moved to a boarding house located on the corner of NW Third Avenue and NW Third Street. It was a big two-story house that was operated by an old couple, who never had any kids, so they took a liking to me. I had it made.

Richard had an older brother named Raymond, who was serving in the Army in the Tank Division. He was stationed in Korea at that time. Richard could not wait to get into the Army. He had just joined the National Guard in hopes of avoiding the waiting list. We stayed friends, and he was always trying to get me to join the Guard with him.

He got me permission to attend some meetings at the Armory where they trained. The National Guard had a program where, if you were an active member of the Guard, you could request to go on active duty and bypass the waiting list. Richard was playing that for all it was worth.

## Chapter 14

# WESTERN UNION

Working for Western Union was not overly exciting, but I did get to ride my bike around town and see things there that were interesting. It was getting late in the Spring, and the weather was getting hot. The only relief you could find was a long downhill grade, so you coast and create a breeze. Riding in the rain was not recommended, but we did it anyway in the summer,

Sometimes the people who received the telegrams would be happy and give us a tip, but sometimes they would get mad and yell at us for the bad news. Sometimes we would have trouble with dogs, and if we hit or kicked the dog, we would have trouble with the owner.

Richard and I worked different shifts, and a lot of times, when we did not have anything else to do, we would ride together. The worst situation I remember was one night when I was riding with Richard. He got a late delivery to a new area that was still under construction.

A few houses were completed, but only a very few had anyone living in them yet, so we had not worked in that area. By the time we found the address, it was getting dark. The house had the correct number, and we knew that the street was correct. There was a car there, but no lights were on.

We tried to get someone to come to the door by ringing the doorbell and by knocking on the door. When we failed to get anyone to come to the door, we called out that we were Western Union and had a telegram for delivery. It was a long ride to the house, and we did not want to have to come back.

No one came to the door or turned on any lights, so we gave up. We had message tags that we had to fill out and leave on the door if we could not make any contact with anyone. Richard filled out the card and hung it on the door handle, and we left.

We had only gotten about two blocks away from the house when a car caught up with us and crowded us off the street into the ditch. A large man jumped out of the car with what appeared to be a small ball bat. He was super mad and demanded to know why we were at his house spying on him.

Richard was trying to tell him we were delivering a telegram, but he did not believe that for a minute. He just kept on saying that we were lying and demanding to know what we were spying for.

When Richard could safely get the telegram out of his pouch, he read the name and address to him and asked if that was who he was. He calmed down a little but still did not believe us. Richard explained that we had left a message note on his door about the telegram and tried to give the Telegram to him.

He would not take it for a couple of minutes, and when he did take it, he just put it in his pocket without opening it. He then demanded that we show him the message, so we rode back to the house and stopped in the front yard. There was light on the front porch as we noticed the tag from the yard.

With the telegram in his pocket and the notice on the doorknob, he was still angry and ordered us to leave his property, instructing us never to return. We departed without ever discovering the reason behind his hostility.

The shift I worked was a split shift. I filled in for the other two delivery boys, two days, and two evening shifts. My fifth day was split between the day and evening shifts. I did not like those hours and could not plan anything.

I had way too much time on my hands, and the people I met were mostly the deadhead type, or they would have been working. Somehow, I managed to stay out of trouble, but I don't know how. I just kept thinking that I did not want to cause my parents any embarrassment. I started looking for another job, and I went to a wholesale hardware company called String Fellows.

# Chapter 15
# STRING FELLOWS

I found the man who did the hiring in a makeshift office. He was a large man dressed in Khaki pants and shirt. He took a long look at me, and when I told him I wanted a job, he did not show any emotion or concern at all. He asked me if I knew how hard the work was.

I had no idea how heavy or how hard the work was, but I assured him that I was used to hard work. He printed a name on a piece of paper and told me, "Take this to our Warehouseman and tell him that I said to give you a job". I did not think that I would be going to work that morning, but I had left Western Union to find a job.

I found the guy at a large warehouse that was built on a railroad siding. I handed him the note, then explained that I was to tell him to give me a job. He asked me what the guy looked like that gave me the note. After I described him, the guy I gave the note to told me to wait right there and not to do anything, and he took off. He came back in a few minutes and said, "he is not kidding". Then he told one of the employees to let me help him unload the box car of roof rocks. He looked at me and said, "Come on, Pee Wee." I was the smallest person there, and the name stuck.

We went to the box car filled with bags of marble-sized rocks. The bags weighed almost as much as I did. We had large two-wheeled carts to push them with.

I managed to get a cart full of bags, but I could not tip it over to push it. I had pushed a two-wheel cart before, but never this big or heavy. I had to stand on the tires and use all my weight and strength to tip the cart. When it tipped, it was too heavy, it fell all the way down, and I could not lift it.

The guy I was working with was also small in size but much stronger and better built. He helped me get the cart back up and took some of the bags off so I could push it. He felt sorry for me because he knew what I was going through. He was the smallest one there when he started, and he was called Pee Wee.

I spent the rest of that day moving the bags by only carrying a half cart at the time. Pee Wee told me unofficially that if I wanted the same pay as everyone else, I would have to do the same amount of work. My only comment was that I would do the best I could.

When I went back to the boarding house, I was so tired and sore that I could barely make it to the table. The lady that ran the house asked me what had happened to me, and I told her that I had a new job, and it was extremely hard work.

She said she would pack me a special lunch for the next day. At that time, I was hurting so bad that I was not sure there would be a next day. I was so sore the next morning that I could hardly get up and thought walking would be completely out of the question, but I made it.

By the time I walked to work, I was walking normally. When I walked onto the loading dock, I was greeted by a lot of disappointing looks from the employees. The only one that was glad to see me was the guy I had given the note to. Man was he happy to see me.

I learned that everyone had bet that I would not come back to work, and the foreman had covered all the bets. I never knew how much he made, but he was laughing and collecting money all day. All day long, I received complaints from the rest of the crew.

On the second day, we unloaded a box car filled with kegs of nails. The foreman sent me back to the manager's office for some gloves. He knew that I did not have any money, but they charged it to my account. I really needed them because there were one hundred pounds of nails in each keg, and the keg weighed five pounds. There was no good way that I could pick up a keg.

You could not get both hands under it, and there always seemed to be a nail somewhere that was going to stick you. At first, I could only move two kegs at a time, and the stacks you put them on were four kegs high. Setting the first keg on the bottom was hard, and I could not lift the last one on top.

I would always try to get the second and third one in the stack. That did not make my coworkers very happy. By the end of the day, I had gotten up to three kegs per trip. Still could not put the top one on the stack.

On the third day, I was assigned to help the Foreman move doors and put the glass in them. The wood doors were not shipped with the glass installed in them. That only took a couple of days to finish, and it was a job I could manage.

I got the weekend off, and then they put me on a delivery truck as a helper for the driver. The hardware company delivered to local hardware stores located within a range of seventy-five miles around Gainesville. Even working on the delivery trucks was heavier work than I was physically strong enough to do. There was almost nothing there that I was strong enough to manage, so I started looking for another job.

## Chapter 16

# ALLIS CHALMER

I do not remember how I found out about it, but an Allis Chalmers Tractor dealership on South Main Street had an opening for a mechanic. I went there and asked for a job. The owner's name was Thomas Erbb, and he was a genuinely nice man that was easy to talk to. He had a shop foreman named Hugh Carlisle. Mr. Carlisle knew my dad and my brother, and he gave a good recommendation based on my family's reputation.

I did not know how to work on tractors, but the boss gave me a chance, and everything went well. The whole operation consisted of the boss, a secretary, the foreman, an older guy who also worked as a mechanic, and me. They sold tractors and farm equipment and did repairs.

Everything at the dealership was new and clean. I started out working with shop tools and some I borrowed from the foreman. The third week I bought some tools from the S & K tool delivery man on credit. I loved the work and seemed to learn quickly.

Mr. Erbb needed me to run some errands with the company pickup truck, but I had never got a driver's license. I knew how to drive and had been driving without a license. Well, the boss took me to get a license so I would be legal.

I could manage most of the minor repair jobs, and now I could drive the flatbed truck that was set up to haul a tractor if we had to pick one up, so I started handling some of the service calls. If I did not ask for help, they would let me try to handle anything they assigned to me. They let me make a few mistakes so I could figure it out for myself.

While I was still trying to learn my way around the shop, the boss and the foreman went out of town to a seminar for four days. The other employee was off work for that period of time. That left me and the secretary. The boss left me to run the shop, and I was to check with the Secretary, if I needed anything, and she would have the final decision on things. That worked out well because she did not know anything about the shop, and I sure did not know anything about her work.

When they left for the seminar, there were no jobs pending in the shop, so I did not have repair work to do. However, we did have some new equipment, a front-end loader and a side delivery rake that needed to be assembled and checked out, so I made that my job. I had asked about the front-end loader, but no one knew anything about how to put it together or attach it to the tractor. So, I got all the paperwork on it that we had and studied it. I did the same thing with the side delivery rake and then brought them both inside the shop.

The rake looked like it would be the easiest to assemble and did not require any special hook-up. The hardest thing about assembling the rake unit was the frame. It consisted of three long heavy metal beams. They were not straight. They all were arch-shaped and required special supports so they could be assembled. I was able to make supports for both ends of the beams, where they had to be bolted together. Two of them lay flat on the supports and were easy, but the top beam had a vertical arch and had to be balanced during the assembly process.

This was where I got into trouble. While I was trying to balance the beam and get it bolted in place, it flipped over and penned my arms down, and I had to get out from under the beam. I had to call the secretary to come help lift the beam so I could get my arms free. That was really embarrassing to me, but she got a good laugh about it. I did not have any more trouble with it, but I am sure she spent the next three days worrying about what I was doing. After she had a good laugh, she agreed not to say anything about it.

The front-end loader had a lot of heavy parts, but they were shorter and easier to manage. By the end of the second day, I had the loader assembled and ready to install on a tractor. The next morning, I got the tractor that the loader was ordered for and went to work. This was the first time I had seen one, much less try to put it on a tractor, but by noon it was connected to the tractor. After lunch, I started checking and adjusting everything. By the end of that day, I had an operating unit. I had studied every nut, bolt, and adjustment on it. I had even serviced and bled the hydraulic struts.

The next day was Friday, and the boss might return sometime that evening. I wanted to operate the unit, so the following morning, I took it out to the open area behind the shop. There, I learned how to use the bucket to move dirt. After making a couple of minor adjustments and cleaning it up, I put the unit on display in the front lot. I felt really proud of myself and what I had accomplished.

The boss got back on Monday and was incredibly happy with both the loader and the rake. The foreman was out of the shop on an errand, and at about ten o'clock, a customer walked into a shop, he took one look at me and asked, "Where is the boss." I told him that I thought he was in the office and asked if I could help him. He said, "No," he was not going to deal with the dammed kid and went to the office. In just a couple of minutes, Mr. Erbb returned to the shop with the customer. Mr. Erbb said, "This is Olen, and he is our expert on the front-end loader." He adds that I was the only one who knew anything about it.

This started a long-running feud between the customer and me. The customer owned a landscaping company and was currently using Ford tractors with front-end loaders. He was not happy with them and was looking for a better unit that he could afford. The Ford tractors were smaller than the Allis Chalmers, and their loaders had buckets that would only hold a half yard of dirt, and our buckets would handle three-quarters of a yard. I took the tractor out and demonstrated it to him. He wanted to see how it worked alongside one of his Ford units. For that, I sent him back to the boss.

Mr. Erbb worked out an agreement with the customer to have me take the tractor over to the dirt pit, where he was working, and load a dump truck with it. I had an advantage in that I had better equipment to work with, but I did not have any experience with it. So, I took it back to my testing area and did some practice.

When I arrived at the pit, I encountered his driver for the test. He was an older black man who had been employed there for many years. He did not seem particularly interested in competition; he simply wanted to assess its functionality.

He took his tractor, and I took ours, and we each loaded a truck. I managed to fill my truck just before he did. We then swapped units and conducted the test again. This time, he outperformed me by roughly the same margin. As a result, the owner decided to purchase one of our units.

Within a week, he returned to the shop, extremely angry and demanding to see the boss. Unfortunately, the boss was unavailable at that moment. When I offered to assist him, he directed his anger towards me in a forceful manner. He used harsh words to describe the product he had purchased and expressed his refusal to interact with what he perceived as an inexperienced youngster.

He then proceeded to blame me for selling him the defective item. Caught off guard and struggling with a short temper, I impulsively grabbed the largest hammer within reach and began to advance toward him. My actions were driven by a loss of control, causing him to swiftly leave the shop.

I knew I was going to get fired for trying to assault one of our biggest customers. I gathered up all my tools and started cleaning them and putting them away. Mr. Erbb came up to me and looked at the toolbox, and then said it was a little early for lunch, but go ahead and hurry back, I have something I need you to do for me.

I was surprised that he had not fired me, and I knew that he had to know what had happened. I told him that I thought you were going to fire me. Then Mr. Erbb gave me some advice that I have always used. He said, "Olen, any fool can lose his temper, but it takes a good man to hold it." Then he said, "Go enjoy your lunch, cool off, and I will see you when you get back."

I did a lot of thinking during my lunch break, and when I got back, I went to the office. Mr. Erbb explained that what the customer was mad about was that both hydraulic struts had blown seals and were spraying hydraulic fluid on the driver. I was to go and either fix it or bring it back to the shop. I was not sure I wanted to chance running into the same guy that I had chased out of our shop with a hammer in his own area. Mr. Erbb had set a condition that he would not be there when I was. I would talk to the same driver that I had worked with before.

I drove out to the pit and found the unit. I checked it out, and there was a lot of fluid, but no seals were leaking. The fluid was coming from the small holes in the strut housing. I had noticed them when I was putting them together, but I could not find anything about them in the paperwork. I concluded that they must be some sort of relief port, and I showed them to Mr. Erbb, who had no idea either. I cleaned up the fluid and serviced the struts, and they worked simply fine.

The only thing I could figure out was that the unit had been overloaded, and the little holes were safety valves to protect the strut seals. I talked to the driver and asked him what they had been trying to move with the unit. He would not say anything except that he just worked there. Then he pointed to the area where the unit was and said, "I haven't been over there." I went over to the area and found some large rocks with bucket teeth marks on them.

I did not want to cause the driver any problems. I just told him that the unit was fixed, and I left. When I got back, I told Mr. Erbb what I found and that I felt sure that someone had tried to lift that heavy rock and the relief valves had dumped the fluid. He contacted the tractor company and confirmed that they were relief valves and were set to spray the fluid in the direction of the driver.

My Brother got out of the Air Force and came home after I started working at the dealership. I was still living in the boarding house, and the lady who ran it broke one of her rules and let him move into the room with me. She put two small beds in the room, and we worked out the rest. We both had busy schedules and did not spend much time in the room. I was hanging out with Richard, and some other friends we had met, and my brother started a new job. He worked for an Aero Willis dealership.

I had a Dodge truck with a big flatbed body that hauled new equipment on. One of our regular runs was to a warehouse on Peachtree Blvd in Atlanta, Georgia. The older guy that worked with us was the one who normally made the runs to pick up the new equipment. He was always complaining about how hard it was to make the trips, and it was unfair that he was always the only one they sent. I didn't know that he was a chronic complainer, and I tried to do him a favor by volunteering to take one of the trips. So, I took one of the trips to Atlanta.

The boss gave me the invoices and fifty dollars in cash to make the trip and said if I needed anything to call him. I had never driven a truck that big before or driven in heavy traffic like Atlanta had. The trip went well, and by the time I got there, I had learned how to drive the truck. By the time I found the warehouse, they had closed for the day, but I was able to park inside and sleep in the truck.

About daybreak, someone woke me and checked my invoice, then directed me to the loading dock. I was able to back the truck up to the loading dock, but I did not get close enough so they could load it.

Someone helped me by pointing out that the reason they put the rubber bumpers on the dock was so I could back up to it without damaging the truck. I was really nervous, and I guess that it showed.

They loaded the equipment and helped me strap it down. I think they wanted to get me out of there so someone else could use the dock. Anyway, I had a good trip back and turned in most of the money. Mr. Erbb was concerned that I had not paid for a motel room and got some rest. The other guy who was making the trips was mad at me for turning in the money. He considered anything that was left over as part of his salary for the trip, and he was mad at me for taking his job as the driver. He did not work there long after I started driving.

The trips were not regularly scheduled. They were made when something was needed in a hurry. It was mostly something that someone had ordered through the dealership that we did not have in stock. Most of the time, the trips were quick and easy. But the last trip I went on was a trip from hell.

I don't remember what month it was, but it was late in the Fall. I had the weekend off and needed to get away from the bunch I had been hanging out with, so I went to the farm. On that weekend, there were dances on Saturday night in both High Springs and Newberry. That weekend I went to Newberry and had a good time dancing and drinking and got home just before daybreak Sunday morning.

Mama woke me before sunrise to catch up on everything. I was tired and a little hungover, and I needed some rest. I did not have a car, so I was hitchhiking everywhere. By midmorning, I had convinced Mama that I had to get back to Gainesville, and I went back to the boardinghouse, hoping to get some rest.

I had good luck with the rides and got back around two PM. As soon as I stepped into the boarding house, the lady that ran the place told me that my boss had been trying to reach me all day and that I was to call him as soon as I got in.

I called his house, and his wife said that he had been working on something at the shop. I called the shop, and he was still there. He had an order for a harvester and had one located in Atlanta. The customer would be there to pick up the unit on Tuesday, and he needed me to make a run to Atlanta that night.

I started servicing the truck for the trip while Mr. Erbb got the invoices and money ready. I had the truck inside the shop and had finished servicing everything except for the drivetrain when Mr. Erbb got a phone call. One of our customers was getting ready to leave town for a couple of days and needed to get his tractor fixed while he was gone. I had to make a quick run to meet with a customer, and I picked up his tractor and brought it to the shop for repair.

When I got back, the truck was parked outside the shop. Mr. Erbb said the foreman had come in and finished the truck and put everything away. Mr. Erbb had made a special deal with someone at the warehouse, and I needed to meet with him as soon as they opened. I was already running late if I expected to get any rest. My plan was to get there and park at the entrance so they would have to wake me when they opened. Well, that plan fell apart when I got to Atlanta.

At the first gas stop I made; I discovered that I had no gas cap on the truck. The old guy at the station had a box of old caps and found one that fit. That only cost fifty cents, so no problem. The next problem became known when I turned on Peachtree Blvd. The truck was losing power and running rough. Then I noticed that I had no lights, so I made it to one of those new self-service types of gas stations that were open twenty-four hours a day.

The next problem was that the attendant was only there to collect money; no service was available. The attendant was a young lady dressed to please the eye of the customer. So, I got my toolbox out and pulled the generator. I had worked on them in the shop and repaired them as best I could, but with a dead battery, I could not start the truck. All I could do was wait for a local garage to open.

Just after seven, I got a ride to a garage with a customer from the gas station, and I took the generator with me. The guy who was just opening the garage was able to check out the generator, and my repair job had fixed the generator. The guy at the garage also got me a ride back to the gas station.

I put the generator back on the truck, but no one had any jumper cables. I was able to talk to the driver of the gas tanker truck delivering to the station to pull my truck so I could start it. The truck started up ok, so I pulled it up to the gas pump and filled it up. I would not shut off the truck because the battery had not charged yet. I was close to the warehouse and was only a little late getting there.

I backed the truck up to the loading dock and left the motor running while I tried to find the person I was supposed to contact. Someone went looking for him, and I got back in the cab and tried to get a nap.

After a short wait, someone came and told me that I had to go to the office for a phone call from my boss. I got to the office and learned that I had two more problems. The first thing was that the Warehouseman had been unable to get the harvester, but they had located another unit, and it was scheduled to be delivered to a warehouse in Decatur, Georgia, by five PM. The second problem was I had to get some additional equipment at Lucky's Hardware which was right downtown Atlanta.

I made it to the hardware store and got the items there, and then made it to Decatur. I had hoped to get the harvester loaded and catch a couple of hours of rest before heading back. With a little good luck, I could still make it back before closing on Tuesday. Well, that was not going to happen either.

When I got to the gate at the warehouse, a guy met me and told me that Mr. Erbb had called and that I was to go to Gainesville, Georgia, to get the harvester. Also, I had to meet the owner at the warehouse at seven AM, or I would not be able to get it. It had something to do with a meeting he had to attend. Now I knew that the plan to deliver it on Tuesday was not going to happen, but I was just too tired to care. Gainesville, Georgia, was not that far from Decatur, and I should get there, find the place, and get some sleep.

The trip was through the north Georgia mountains, and the truck still gave me problems. Sometimes it ran well, and sometimes it would start running rough and losing power. I had just gotten on the road to Gainesville when I ran into road construction. The traffic was all stop-and-go, and there was no way to change your mind. It took hours to get all the way to Gainesville.

I had no idea how to get to the warehouse, so I stopped at a gas station to get directions and gas. The guy working the night shift was nice and knew how to get there, but he thought I should wait till daylight before going into the area. I was starving, and there was a small restaurant next door to the gas station, so I parked the truck under a large tree and went to get some food. It was a place kind of like the Orange and Blue, and it also had a loud jukebox.

They had some drunks there that were still having a party. I was so tired that I was like a zombie. One of the drunks asked me where I was going, and I said Gainesville, and then he asked where I was from, and I said Gainesville, and he got really mad. I had no idea what he was mad about. Then he said that he was trying to be nice, and he thought that I was a smart aleck kid. As I was trying to explain the two Gainesville's, I remembered the night Pruett came into the diner. Now I knew how he must have felt.

It was well after midnight when I left the restaurant. I asked the guy at the station to wake me in time to make it to the warehouse by seven. The best he could do was to try to remember if he wasn't too busy. I tried to get some sleep in the cab of the truck, but I was up before six.

The next morning brought some improvement. The truck started without issues and ran smoothly. I managed to acquire the harvester as planned. However, a new challenge emerged regarding its size.

The harvester was both too wide and too high for my truck. The wheels protruded beyond my truck bed by around six inches. The discharge chute extended to such a height that it would not fit under overpasses.

The individuals who assisted me in loading the harvester used packing material to raise it above the truck's cab. They lowered the chute on top of the cab and advised me to drive cautiously, hoping it would be fine. However, their suggestion did not instill much confidence in me, considering the challenging roads I had to navigate on my way home.

Only half of each tire rested on the truck bed. I secured it as best as I could using chain dogs and returned to the gas station. After discussing the issue with the station attendant, our only viable solution was to release air from the harvester's tires, secure it with chains, and then reinflate the tires to high pressure. I proceeded to pump a hundred pounds of air into each tire. This method effectively fastened the harvester in place.

I hit the road toward home with only one more stop to make. I was to stop in Macon and pick up some silo fence. Everything started out ok, and the road conditions were good for a while. I had made good time, but then the truck started acting up again. I had a heavy load and was on a downhill grade.

I got mad at the truck, and I just stood on the gas pedal. The truck was jumping and trying to stall, but it kept going. After a little while, it suddenly smoothed out and ran perfectly. Everything settled down, and I was making good time the rest of the way down the mountain.

I was heading for Macon; I checked the gas gauge to make sure that I could make it, but the gauge showed that I only had one-third of a tank of gas left. I just thought that the truck used a lot of gas coming down that hill. I was getting very sleepy and needed to stop to get some No-Doze pills anyway, so I made the first truck stop that I came to.

I pulled up to the gas pump and started filling the tank. Suddenly everyone on the other side of the truck started yelling to shut off the gas. They said Man, you are spilling gas everywhere. Not only was my tank leaking, but it was splashing on the exhaust pipe.

My gas tank had a two-to-three-inch split in it just above the center of the tank. Someone picked up my gas cap and told me that it was a radiator cap, not a gas cap. It would not let air back into the tank as the gas level dropped causing a vacuum in the tank.

As the fuel pump tried to pump gas to the engine, it would increase the vacuum in the tank and restricting the fuel supply to the engine. This was the reason the truck would start running rough and losing power, and when I opened the gas cap, the vacuum was released, and the truck would run normally. Now finding a gas cap was not much trouble, but finding someone to weld the tank was a bigger problem.

There was an independent garage in the area, and I was told that the mechanic was the only one in the area who would weld gas tanks. I went over and gave him a sad story, but he was working on a school bus that had to be ready to pick up the school kids that afternoon and that was his top priority.

He said if I wanted to drain and pull the tank off the truck, which would save him some time. He would not work on the tank until it had been steamed out. Well, I drained the gas from the tank and removed it. As soon as he could take a break, he started the steamer, and I steamed the tank.

While I was waiting for the tank to get finished, I was having a hard time staying awake. Some young guy stopped in, looking for a ride, and

I tried to talk him into waiting for me. If he rode with me, he could help keep me awake. He could see how tired I was, and he was not about to ride with me.

I lost a lot of time getting the truck back on the road, and I knew that I was not going to make it to Macon in time to pick up the Silo Fence. The truck was so full that I would not have had room for it anyway.

I had formulated a plan to reach Fargo, Georgia, cross the state line, and find the Florida State Patrol station that was just cross the state line. They had a parking area where I could ensure the safety of the truck and get some sleep.

As I cruised down the road, I passed a parked police car on the side of the road. Taking a glance at my speed, I confirmed I was within limits. However, the police car pulled out from the side and moved ahead of me.

The officer scrutinized my truck intently as he passed by. A short distance ahead, he stationed himself in the roadway, motioning for me to stop. Anxious that I might be in trouble, I complied. Yet, to my surprise, he was only concerned about whether my truck would clear the upcoming overpass.

Inquiring about the clearance of my truck, I realized I didn't have that information. He proceeded to guide me safely beneath the overpass, closely observing to ensure I would make it through unscathed. Once I successfully navigated the clearance, he signaled me to continue on my way with a wave.

I got to Macon, and the main road was closed for construction, and you had to take a detour. I followed the signs as close as I could and got back on my route.

I drove a mile or so, and things did not look right. I continued until I found a State Route sign. It said I was northbound, and I should have been going south. I turned around and headed south again and thought that I missed something because I was so tired.

I went back through the same route and wound up back on the northbound side of the road again. I had no idea what I had done wrong. I went back, and this time, I saw a police car on the side of the road. I stopped and asked him how to get through the detour without getting turned around.

He said to follow him, and he would lead me through the detour. I followed him, and we wound up back on the northbound side of the road. Some kids had turned around some of the detour route signs. He was not happy about the prank, and I was just happy that I had not been arrested.

I was living on No-Doze pills and so tired that I really don't remember how I made it to Fargo. I remember that I was glad to get there, and I thought I would be able to get some sleep there. The last thing I remember about Fargo was that there was a ground fog. I was thinking how glad I was to not have to drive in the fog.

The next thing I remember was sitting at a red light in front of the VA Hospital in Lake City and watching the light change from green to red and back to green again. I had no idea where I was until I saw the sign that said, Slow Veteran's Hospital. I was really confused, and my eyes burned and felt like they were full of sand. I had driven about thirty miles beyond where I was planning to stop.

I do not know how many people I may have run off the road or how I had kept the truck on the road. I was only about an hour from Gainesville and home. I drove the twenty-six miles to High Springs and was still falling asleep.

I stopped, got a cold drink, and poured some of the ice water on my head. I was totally obsessed with making it home. I only remember two things about the rest of the trip. I remember turning onto University Blvd and then trying to find someplace to park the truck.

I do not remember what happened when I got back to Gainesville, but I learned later from the people I was directly involved with at the boarding house that a group of construction workers had come into town, and they had filled the boarding-house and all the parking areas around the house. I had taken the truck about three blocks away and parked it under a large streetlight.

My brother was in the room when I came in, and he said when he spoke to me, I just waved and kind of fell into the bed and was asleep. Mr. Erbb and the foreman came to get the truck and could not get me awake. They kept asking me, "Where is the truck?" and all I managed to mumble was something like, "It's outside," and I threw my pillow at them, and the keys were in the pillow. They found the truck and took it back to the shop to unload it.

Later that afternoon, I woke up and managed to get to the shop, although I still felt a bit tired. I remember most of what was said during the conversation. The Foreman got angry right away. He told me that the universal joints in the drivetrain were completely worn out, and he almost didn't make it to the shop because of that issue.

He also mentioned that he had to cut one of the chain dogs that was holding the harvester, as he could not get it to release. He thought I should be responsible for the cost of this. When he cut the chain, it flew off and nearly hit him. While he kept complaining about this, he also said, "There is no way someone as small as you could have tightened the chain dogs so tightly!"

Just then, Mr. Erbb walked over and asked if I was alright. I hadn't had a chance to say anything yet. When I explained to the Foreman that I had let the air out of the tires to secure it with chains, Mr. Erbb burst into laughter, and the Foreman started swearing before I could tell him that each tire still had a hundred pounds of air in them.

I was trying to remember that I was aware the drivetrain was starting to make noise, but I did know how bad the universal joints were. That is why we always serviced the truck before any trip, and I had serviced it but then remembered that I had not greased the drivetrain. Then I remembered that the truck was moved, and Mr. Erbb had told me the shop Foreman had finished servicing the truck.

Mr. Erbb got his laughter under control and told me to come with him, and we went to the office. I filled him in on what had happened on the trip and gave him paperwork and money that was left over. He was glad that I was ok, but he was a little upset that I had not stopped somewhere and got some rest. He gave me a ride back to the boarding house and the rest of the week off.

As I thought about the trip, I knew that I would not be making any more of them. I remembered other trips when I had driven too long and fallen asleep while driving. One time I was returning through some of the low swampy parts of Georgia, and something woke me just in time to see a bunch of cows bedded down in the road. I was driving slowly, and I managed to miss all of them. I remember that what I heard was someone yelling my name. There was not another vehicle anywhere in sight on that road, and that scared me.

I was just north of Fargo and needed some gas. Fargo had two gas stations, and both had living quarters attached to them. The one right on the route was a nice building with an apartment over the office and pumps. I woke up a young couple who were living there; they were nice, but they only rented the apartment, and the owner lived outside of town. They told me where the other station was, and that the owner lived there. I went there and woke him up. He was an angry old man and was about to shoot me. He did not care what I needed; he would not open the door for anyone after dark. He let me see that he had a shotgun and that he was threatening to shoot.

I left and went back to the first station and got directions to the owner's house. I expected to pay extra for gas, so I thought it would be ok to ask them to help me. I found the owner's house and got lucky there.

Fargo was a very small town that is known for its Turpentine operations. The people there were very poor, but this guy lived in a large, beautiful place that looked like a plantation house. The yard was full of very nice new cars, and I could not believe what I was seeing. As I pulled up in the yard, the people in the house were leaving, and they were all dressed in very fancy clothes.

A guy wearing a white dinner jacket came over to see what I needed. He was the owner, and he was having a dinner party. I felt so out of place there, and after just getting threatened with a shotgun, I wanted to run. But I told him my sad story and he agreed to come to open the station as soon as he finished saying goodbye to his guest.

I went back to the station and waited for him, and he came and turned on the pumps, and I filled the truck. All he asked for was the amount of gas, but I gave him a tip anyway.

Richard and the group we were hanging out with had rented a small house, and I had moved in to help them pay the rent. My landlady at the boarding house kept a tight rein on me, and I guess that I wanted more freedom. Richard was just about to go active and was trying to sell me on what they called the buddy system.

If two people joined at the time, they could request to be stationed together for their first assignment. In our case, which would only be through basic training. The Army was not my first choice, but if the Navy was not going to take me, I was willing to try it.

It didn't take long to realize that the group house thing was not going to work. Sometimes we would have as many as six people living there, but me and Richard were the only ones who could find a paying job. We had to pay for everything, and the food situation was getting bad. I was worried about getting in trouble because some of the guys kept trying to get me and Richard involved in their schemes, which was always bad. I did not want to chance getting in trouble, so I quit my job at the dealership and went back home.

I took a week off before looking for a job. I was planning on going to work at Copeland Sausage Company in Alachua and did put in my application, but before I got a response from them, I changed my mind. I went back to Gainesville just in time for the Christmas rush and got a seasonal job with the A&P Supermarket selling Christmas Trees.

The store put up a tree lot in the corner of their parking lot, and I worked outside in tree lot. The hours were long, and the weather was cold, but the pay was good.

I had started at the store just before they got the tree lot finished and was temporarily assigned to the produce department. The store was nice and like new. Any produce work involves water and getting wet, so by the time I started in the tree lot, I was used to working a little cold. I had to be there before they opened in the morning to get the lot ready and then close it up after they closed.

I was still in touch with Richard, and he was still trying to get me to go into the Army with him. It had been six months since I signed up for the Navy, and after checking with them and not getting any indication of when they would call me, I had given up on them.

It had been about fifteen months since I left home, and I was getting tired of that lifestyle, and I was ready for something with a future. Richard had a date to go on active duty, and it was coming up in early January. For me to get everything finished, it would be too late to go with him.

He had talked to his recruiter several times about the buddy deal and was sure that if we talked to his recruiter, he would work it out so we could go in together. I agreed to talk to his recruiter with him, but if the deal wasn't a sure thing, then I was going to consider other options.

His appointment was around the twenty-eighth or twenty-ninth of December, and my job with the store had run out.

## Chapter 17

# CHOOSING THE NAVY OVER THE ARMY

All the military recruiters were in the old Post Office building on the same floor. As we walked in, we passed the area used by the Navy Recruiter. As we passed his area, he looked at me and yelled, "Hey, aren't you Barber," he said, "I have had been looking all over for you, I could have shipped you out yesterday." Well, that was as close as I got to the Army.

On January 5th, 1954, I reported to the US Navy recruiting office in Gainesville to get my transportation to the military induction and physical examination center located in Jacksonville. I was told to be there before 8 AM to get my ticket and other papers before boarding the bus.

I had been told that the military would pay for my bus ride to Jacksonville and a room for the night and that I would be picked up on Wednesday morning to be taken to the base for my physical exam. I was also assured that I would not have any problem passing the physical. Once I had passed the exam, I would be sworn in, and the Navy would take care of everything I needed to get to my first duty station.

It was a good thing that I did not need anything because I did not have anything. I showed up at the Recruiter's office with $4.50 and seven packs of cigarettes that were borrowed. I had a small bag with less clothing than when I left home the first time. They said they would provide what I needed, and I was about to find out if that was correct. I do not recall anything unusual about the bus ride to Jacksonville, but I was surprised at how small the rooming house was. It was a private home converted into a rooming house.

The bus stopped in front of the house, on the street, and announced that this was where all the passengers for the Navy induction center were to stay. There was only one other guy that got off with me, and he introduced himself as Miller.

As we entered the house, a friendly elderly lady greeted us, checked us in, and assigned us a double room with two single beds. Miller and I shared the room. There were about five or six other people in the house who were also scheduled for their physicals the next day.

Most of them had their own plans, and only one person chose to hang out with us. I remember that he seemed lost and unsure about what to do.

After a few minutes of boredom, Miller and I decided to go for a walk. Unfamiliar with the local area, our plan was to stroll down the street and explore. Just as we were about to leave, the other guy, still appearing lost, approached us and asked, "Are you guys in the Navy?"

After explaining to him that we hoped to be, we learned that his name was Chancy, and he was from Fargo, Ga. He asked if he could hang out with us because he did not know anyone there, and this would be his first night away from home. I felt sorry for him and invited him to join us. I remembered that Fargo was a small backwoods turpentine town, and if this was his first time away from there, he would need a lot of help. Chancy turned out to be the real deal. He was wearing all the clothing he had brought with him and had his toilet articles, soap, toothpaste, and toothbrush in his pockets. If he had any money, he never showed it.

The combination of excitement about going into the Navy and the anticipation of taking a physical exam the next day that would determine if we would be accepted had us fired up and walking it off felt good. We walked around the area and found a store where we could get a big cold RC Cola. Miller bought the drinks, and the other guy bought a bunch of penny candy called kits. We all took our time drinking the RCs, but Chancy hung on to his like it was gold.

It felt good to get out of the house and just walk around. We talked about what we thought the Navy was going to be like. None of us had a real clue about what to expect. The people who had been in the Navy that I had talked with only wanted to tell sea stories about liberty in Japan or ships called destroyers. One guy had told me that you could get anything you wanted in the Navy if you fought hard enough for it. So even though I had no idea about what I wanted, in my mind, I was sure I would get it.

When we returned to the rooming house, we had a light meal for supper. I don't remember much about the meal, but I do recall how quiet everyone became as we drifted off into our own private thoughts about the upcoming day.

Although I had been assured that the Navy wouldn't reject me, the reality was that I'd be in a bit of trouble if they did. I'd find myself stranded in an unfamiliar big city, a hundred miles away from home, with no clear plan for how to get back.

I did have an aunt and Uncle who lived somewhere in Jacksonville, but I had no idea how to contact them. My uncle worked as a Baggage Master for the railroad and had taken me on his run from Jacksonville to Fort Pierce and back a few years earlier. However, that had been my only visit to Jacksonville.

Early the next morning, someone knocked on our door, and we got our notice to get ready for our ride to the examination center. Both Miller and I had trouble sleeping that night, and we were awake before the call. As soon as I stepped out of my room, Chancy was standing just outside my door, waiting for us to get up. He looked like he had been there all night.

We spoke to each other, picked up our bags, and went into the front room of the house where there was a man with a list of our names. After looking us up on the list and checking off our names, he told us there was some breakfast for us in the dining room.

I remember that it was not what I was hoping for. There was coffee, which I did not drink, some toast, fruit juice, and cereal. Miller had joined us at the table, and Chancy was asking Miller if that was all they were going to feed us. Miller told him that he thought lunch would be better because we would be in the Navy by then.

A bus with military markings on it picked us up and took us to the examination center. Everything there was strictly military, and we were getting our first taste of military rule. Everything moved on a tight schedule from the time you got off the bus until you got back on it. Yes, even the bathroom breaks.

Everything was being rushed, and directions were getting sharper and louder as we were processed through all parts of the examination process. The whole process was set up like an assembly line. They started by asking us questions about supporting America and being loyal to the service, then questions about fighting and killing people, and a lot of things I did not understand.

The next part was the part everyone talked about. They ran us all into a large room, and we had to strip off all our clothing. Then we lined up and went through a row of smaller cubicles, where they checked everything from your hair to the soles of your feet. The procedure seemed to take forever. The temperature in the room felt cold. I felt uncomfortable. However, we were all finished and ready to eat by lunch time.

We were loaded up on a bus and taken to a mess hall to eat. By now, we were being moved and directed by numbers. As you lined up, you were told to move with the line and keep your place in it. By this time, nothing sounded at all like a request, and everything was an order. I did not see

Miller or Chancy until after the meal. We had just a few minutes to talk before they yelled, "Lineup". We were taken to a large lecture hall in a different part of the center, where we were permitted to take a smoking and bathroom break.

Here I learned that the Navy referred to the bathroom as "The Head" I have no idea why that was, but I was told that I had best remember it, so I did. Before the next part got started, I got together with Miller and Chancy and got seats together for the swearing-in part of the ceremony.

The ceremony started with some high-ranking Officers who congratulated us for having passed the requirements for induction into the U.S. Navy, and that was followed by a lot of speeches about how great the Navy was and how lucky we were to be a part of it. Then some high-ranking official was introduced as the person who would conduct our Swearing-in Procedure. As he recited the oath, we raised our right hands and stated our names. At that point, we were told that we belonged to the U.S. Navy.

# Chapter 18

# THE LONG TRAIN RIDE TO BOOT CAMP

After the swearing-in, we were split up into groups to be transported to basic training, which was called Boot Camp. Miller, Chancy, and I were put into a group consisting of people from North Florida and South Georgia, to be e were sent to San Diego, California.

Our trip was scheduled to take us through Chicago, Illinois, before reaching San Diego. Chicago had a large training facility, so we asked why we weren't going there for training. We were told that the decision was based on the weather difference. Chicago's winters were much colder than what we were used to, and the weather in San Diego was more similar to that of Florida. They were concerned that the abrupt weather change could make us sick.

Although there were about ten others assigned to our group, Miller, Chancy, and I had bonded and promised to support each other through whatever challenges we faced, so we stuck together.

At the train depot, we were issued our papers, which included all our train tickets, as well as our meal tickets. Once we were issued our papers for the train, we were put in the custody of a Navy Shore Patrol Officer, who was assigned to escort us to the Naval Training Center in San Diego and held our official orders.

We had to wait about six hours before we could board the train. Our escort put us on the honor system with instructions to say our goodbyes, get something to eat, and be back there in time to board the train. We put all our personal bags in one pile and left the area.

There was a waiting area for the people who were seeing people off, and we had to walk past it to leave the boarding area. To my total surprise, my aunt and cousin were there. Mom had contacted them, and they came down to see me off. She took me to get something to eat, and we spent some time visiting. The time went by fast, but I made it back to the boarding area in plenty of time. I do not know what Miller and Chancy did while I was gone, but they were waiting at the boarding area when I got back.

Our trip was routed from Jacksonville to Chicago, Illinois, to Los Angeles, CA, and then to San Diego. It was about 8 PM when we boarded the train and were assigned a Pullman Car. By the time we got on board, I was getting tired. I had only ridden a train once before, and that was with my uncle, and that was in the baggage car. I remembered how tired I got on that trip, and it was just an overnighter. This trip was going to take a few days, but at least I had a Pullman car to ride in this time.

After getting in our assigned car, we still had about an hour before the train started moving. At first, there were a few little bumps and jerks, then a series of small jerks as the train started moving out of the station.

As I sat in a booth by the window watching the lights go by, I remember having a very strange feeling. I was sitting with Miller, Chancy and some other guy that was part of our group, but I cannot remember his name. We were all excited about starting our tour in the Navy, but we were also a little scared of what might be ahead of us. Most of our conversation was nervous chatter but some of our thoughts were questions about being able to make it through Boot Camp.

We had all heard stories about people that got thrown out of Boot Camp because they could not handle it. Sometimes it was physical, sometimes medical, sometimes it was emotional or mental. If any one of us got thrown out for any reason it would be very embarrassing. I noticed that Chancy was incredibly quiet and when I asked him if he was ok, he said "Yes, just lonesome".

When our Pullmans were ready our Shore Patrol escort came back with his list and sent us all to bed. I do not remember how long it took for my fatigue to overcome the noise and movement of the train so I could fall asleep, but it did.

My wakeup call came about 7 AM and I had a tough time clearing my mind. I was in a small space that was moving and there was not enough light to see very well. After almost tearing off the curtain to my bed space I started waking up and remembering where I was.

Someone was telling me to get dressed and report to dining car for chow. I understood the chow part, but, had no idea where the dining car was. By the time I got dressed Miller and Chancy were up and Miller led us to the dining car.

This was the first time to use meal tickets and our Escort explained what items on the menu we could order that would be covered by the Meal Tickets. We could order anything on the menu, but if it was not listed as a ticket covered item, we would have to pay for it.

The items listed under the Meal Ticket section made a good basic breakfast. coffee or juice, toast, pancakes, two eggs, bacon or sausage, a small cup of fruit or cereal. There was a little complaining, but no one refused to eat.

After we finished eating, we returned to out railcar and found that it had been converted back to booths for seating. There was a bathroom, but we could not use it if we were going through a city. In those days there were no holding tanks and the toilets flushed right down on the tracks. The conductor would come around and lock the bathrooms as we entered a city and unlock them when we pulled out.

The train did not stop at many towns, but it was not an express and there were stops and delays along the way. I had never been in this part of the country before, so I spent most of my time looking out the window.

Miller and Chancy shared a booth with me and spent a lot of time talking and making plans for things we wanted to do. Miller and I decided that the Shore Patrol thing looked like a good job, so that was what we were going to do in the Navy. Then we got a chance to talk to our escort about being a Shore Patrol Officer and learned that it was not a job, it was just a temporary assignment. So that plan was out the window.

Boredom started setting in and we found ways to amuse ourselves like playing with toilets while going through small towns when the conductor did not lock up the bathrooms. That did not last long, someone saw the streamers that the toilet paper made and came straight to our car with our escort. He did not ask if we did it, he just order us to stop it right then and we carried out our orders.

There were some stops that the train made where we could get off the train for a few minutes and look around. Most of the time we would just walk around and window shop because we did not have any money to spend. We did buy some post cards for an idea we had.

We would write a message explaining that we were service men on our way to a new base and ask anyone who found the card to write to us and tell us where they were from. We would put our names and the address of the base we were going to. The plan was to scatter a few of them in each town we passed through on our trip and see how many we got a response from. I do not remember how many we scattered, but I think we got three responses.

Each time we got off the train we noticed that the weather was getting colder. We were not used to the chilly weather and were not dressed for it. I had never seen snow and would be my first chance to see it. I don't think Miller had seen any snow and I know that Chancy hadn't.

As we got close to Chicago, we began to see small traces of snow in ditches. It had not Snowed in Chicago in a few days and most of it had melted.

When we pulled into the train station in Chicago it was late at night. First, we had to stay in the train car until after daybreak. Then we would have to stay off the car for about 6 hours while they moved our cars to another train.

Our route had been from south to north and the train line we were on, I think that it was the Eastern Seaboard. I don't know how many cars the military had contracted to move us, but I think it was more than one. We were told that we would keep the same cars and they would connect it to a different train.

We were escorted to a restaurant in the train station for breakfast then we were taken to large locker room with showers and bathrooms. The restaurant was large and very nice. They also had a meal ticket menu.

I remember that our waitress was nice, and I would guess in her forties. She was trying her best to understand our Southern drawl. She did pretty good until she tried to take Chancy's order. He did not like what he saw on the menu and wanted some grits.

She had never heard of grits and had no idea what he was trying to say. She had to ask him twice what he wanted, and he got mad at her and yelled out "Grits woman, this is breakfast and I want some grits."

The waitress was embarrassed and so was the rest of us at the table. I told Chancy that they don't eat grits up here and that really confused him. Well just what do they eat for breakfast he asked, and I told him that they eat potatoes and that really set him off. He yelled "Potatoes for breakfast, I never heard of such." Miller started talking to him and helped him place his order. I apologized to the waitress who was very happy to get away from our table.

After we had breakfast, we were cleared to move around the area while the trains were switched. We were in bad need of a shower by that time and that was our next priority. We also needed some clean underclothing. We changed what clothing we could and washed the rest as best as we could.

We hung the wet clothes anywhere we could in the locker room area to dry. We were told that we could find a laundry mat in the area, but we were short on money.

It was cold and windy, and we were not dressed for that weather. To make matters worse, part of the extra clothing we had was still drying in the locker room. My shoes were loafers and I had thin socks, shirt and pants that were too thin and a light wind breaker.

Miller and Chancy were dressed about the same but we were not going to be denied the chance to get out and look the area over. We went back to the bathroom and got a bunch of paper towels and lined the inside of our socks, shirts, and pants. With the extra insulation we went for a walk. It was cold but not too bad.

Walking around when it is cold and windy is not the most comfortable thing you can do. And even though it is a place you have never seen before, and you don't have money to spend, you quickly get tired of sightseeing. But we did kill a couple of hours before returning to the station.

We went and rounded up clothing items that were drying in locker room. We were incredibly lucky that someone had not trashed them. We took the paper towels out of our clothing and put back on all the clothing items we could and left the locker room.

Our escort came back, and we went back to the restaurant for a late lunch on meal tickets. We had a better choice of items than we did for breakfast, the lunch was pretty good. Even Chancy did not complain this time.

The rest of the afternoon was spent just hanging out in the terminal area. I was not looking forward riding a train all the way to San Diego, but I was glad we were not staying in that place. At least for the most part, the train was warm.

I don't recall much about the ride to LA except that it was a long ride. Most of the time I just watched the countryside go by. I had never seen that part of the country and it was sure interesting to see. I do remember sitting with my head leaning against the window, just zoning out and staring out the window, when another train going in the opposite direction suddenly passed within inches of my head.

I was not in any danger, but when you are touching the inside of a train window, it seems like there is only about two inches between you and the outside of the train. Trains going in opposite directions only need about twelve inches of clearance to safely pass each other and sometimes that is all the clearance they have. When both trains were traveling very fast, in opposite directions from each other, the closing speed is doubled.

I don't know how many inches apart the sides of the trains were, but on some bridges or narrow passageways, it appeared to be about 12 to 18 inches. The first time we passed that close I tried to jump out of the booth. Every time it happened it scared the living heck out of me.

I don't remember the name of the train, but I do recall that it had a big picture of an Indian Chief on the engine. When we got into the open country that old train could really run and they let it fly. There were scheduled stops along the way, but we had to make an unscheduled one.

Somewhere on an Indian reservation we hit and killed two horses. The train stopped there for over two hours. We were told that the train did not have any damage but because this was on an Indian reservation, we would have to wait until both the reservation and local police officers would have to complete their reports and they got all the required signatures before we could leave.

I don't recall any impact, but I do recall that we made a hard stop and within a few minutes the train backed up. At first, we were told to stay in our car but later we were told that we could get off and walk around a little. We were cautioned not to get in the way of the police, or they would make us stay on the train.

There was not much to see, just the two dead horses alongside of the tracks. I had never seen that part of the country and enjoyed looking at the countryside.

The most interesting experience I had was trying to walk on something that was not moving. We had become so conditioned to walking on a moving floor that we were all walking like drunks. On the first part of the trip, we had that feeling when we would get off the train but each of those rides were short compared to this one.

This was the first time that either Chancy or I had seen this type of countryside except in the movies. We spent most of the time laughing at how different it was from Fargo, Georgia and trying to figure out how they made a living.

There was not enough grass to feed a goat much less a cow and it sure did not look like farmland. We were surprised that there were no usable trees. At least by our standards. Those trees could not produce fruit, lumber, or turpentine, nor did they make a usable shade.

It seemed like a long time before we got back on the train, but it sure did feel good when we did. Once the train started moving, we traveled on to Los Angeles before changing trains again. I don't remember much about that part of the trip except that it was long and tiring. They switched us to a commuter-type train that was not comfortable. I was tired and only wanted to get that part of the trip over.

## Chapter 19

# OUR INTRODUCTION TO BOOT CAMP

After what seemed like an exceptionally long ride, we were transferred to a bus. We also got a new escort assigned to us, and I think that was the official start of our boot camp training. He was a very mean-spirited person who loved to give orders. On the bus we were told that it would be late when we arrived at the training center and even though we did not deserve anything as good as Navy Chow we would be fed. We were warned not to waste any of that "good food."

It was almost midnight when the bus arrived at the base. We were taken straight to the mess hall where we were chased off the bus and into the chow line. Now we had more than one person yelling at us to hurry up and get your tray we don't have all night.

You only got fifteen minutes to eat. We went down the food line and the mess cooks threw food on our trays as we moved past. I don't remember what the food was, or maybe I just could not recognize what it was. It was half cooked, and we had to eat too fast to taste it. While we were eating, they were yelling don't waste any of that food. After they got all of us out of the chow hall we were rushed back on the bus and driven to a different part of the base.

The next part of the base was where we got our first items issued to us. We were lined up and walked down a long table where there were items of clothing being issued to us. At each station someone would guess at what size we were and throw an item to us. A shirt, a pair of pants, a tee shirt and boxer shorts, socks, and shoes. I think the only person who asked for our size was when we got the shoes.

As we left the end of the line, we were told to take everything we had with us, including the clothes we were wearing and put in the containers provided and put on the new stuff we got. We were told we were going to our barracks, and we could shower there. It was after midnight already and we marched to the barracks which was only a short distance from where we were. It was cold but we were told that we would get the rest of our gear later.

In the barracks we were assigned a bunk number, told to make up the bunk, to get our showers and to be quick about it because the lights were going out in twenty minutes. Each bunk had a mattress, a mattress cover, one blanket and one pillow with no pillowcase. My bunk was a top bunk by the window. Some of the guys went to shower first and the rest of us made up our beds.

All the showers were running full blast, we jumped under the water and right back out and rubbed in some of the soap and rinsed off, grabbed a towel, and tried to get to our bunk before the lights went out. I don't know if we made it under twenty minutes or not, but they were yelling that we could not do even a simple task right so how did we think we could be a sailor. We were told to get in our bunks and to stay there as they turned out the lights.

I got in my bunk and covered up with the blanket, but soon realized that it was too cold. The windows next to the bunk were opened a little way from the bottom and the top. The guy in the bottom bunk was able to close the bottom half of the window without getting caught so I tried to close the top part.

The only way I could reach the top of the window was to stand on my bunk and the windowsill that was only about one inch wide. I got in position, but the window was high and hard to lift. As I was trying to lift the window up, my foot slipped off the sill, and down I came. The right side of my face struck the windowsill causing a nice bruise to my right cheek bone. I got the window closed and back in my bunk before the fire watch made his round. Note the fire watch was like a guard assigned to keep everyone safe during the night.

The next morning, we officially started our basic training by getting assigned to our company and moving into our barracks. Our company was 007 and named company seven. To help explain what happens next, I would like to describe the training center. The United States Naval Training Center, Located in San Diego, California, is a basic training unit, also known as Bootcamp.

It is the induction, primary training, and outfitting units. The purpose of the Training Center is to collect all the new inductees that are sent there for basic training and transition them from civilian to military status. This starts with getting them assigned to a training unit that is called a Company. Each Company can accommodate up to seventy recruits. Each Company is given a number for a Company name. The number is a sequential system starting each year, with the first company being 001.

Once a group is assigned to a company, all their actions are scheduled, and the person in charge of the company is called the Company Commander. He is selected from the qualified senior noncommissioned officers assigned to that training command for duty. Each Company has one Company Commander and one Assistant Company Commander. Our Company Commander was Chief Petty Officer B. C. Wall. He was older and played the father image role. I do not remember the name of his assistant; he was younger, and his role was to be the bad guy, and I might add he played the part well.

The night that we arrived by bus at the training center, the crew that met us started the transition from thinking like a civilian to the Navy way of thinking. All personal things were put in containers for either shipment back home or to be trashed out, and the choice was ours. My stuff went to the trash bin.

We were issued one uniform with socks, shoes, and underwear. The next morning, we had an early reveille with a lot of yelling and rushing around. Get your stuff and get outside and fall in. It was very confusing to everybody because no one understood what they wanted, everything we did was wrong, and the harder we tried to get it right, the bigger the mess became. Finally, we were pushed into lines starting with the tallest in the front of the line. We were in a nearby parking lot, being prepared for inspection.

There I was, standing at attention with my big black eye from falling off the windowsill the night before. The inspector took one look at my shiner and declared me to be a troublemaker. "I see you have already started the trouble, and somebody has had to straighten you out". Then he said, "We will straighten you out". I wanted to explain what happened but was not allowed to speak.

After making sure that we understood, we were to remember our line-up positions, and we were marched back to the chow hall for breakfast. At this time of day, they were serving a regular meal. The chow hall was crowded, so we got a little less harassment this time.

Next, we were marched to the barracks that we were assigned for the rest of our training. They put each one of us in front of a bunk unit and told us which bunk we were assigned to and to make sure we remembered it. Next, we were taken to the back of the barracks, where there were rolls of bedding stored. Each roll consisted of a small mattress, a mattress cover, a sheet, a pillow, a pillowcase, and two blankets. We had to pile all the bedding on the mattress, roll it up and take it to our beds. Then we were shown how to properly make-up the bed.

Some more recruits joined us at the barracks, then we all were marched back to the building where we got our initial uniform the night before. This time we got the rest of our issue.

We received a duffle bag to carry all our belongings, followed by the remainder of our uniforms, underclothing, toothpaste, toothbrush, comb, and various other items. We needed to pack everything into the duffle bag and then transport it back to our barracks, placing the bag neatly on our bunk. Looking back, the rest of that day was dedicated to learning how to stencil our names on each item and how to properly organize them in our compact lockers. We also learned how to tidy up the area.

I had the chance to speak to Miller and Chancy for the first time since we got off the bus. Miller appeared tired but was managing to figure things out. On the other hand, Chancy seemed to be facing difficulties with various tasks, and a couple of other guys were attempting to assist him. He was genuinely happy to see both Miller and me. During our conversation, we tried to reassure him that things would improve over time.

Our time was cut short when we had to assemble in formation again. This time we were instructed on how to prepare for inspections that would take place every morning. This would be our first, and we were going to meet our Company Commander. We were instructed to make sure we had a clean uniform, a shave, and a shoeshine.

We also had to make sure the barracks were perfectly clean, beds were made correctly, and our lockers were stored correctly. Note: until this year, all your clothing items had to be rolled up tightly and securely tied so everything would fit into your sea bag. Before then, you had to live out of your sea bag, but they had switched to lockers now, and that made things easier. They had changed the requirement for the wearing of leggings. Before, you had to wear them all the time. But now, only when you were on watch duty.

This was the first time I had to stand for an inspection, and I did not know what to expect, but I had heard some wild stories about how hard they were. The only thing that I was worried about was the shaving part. I had not grown any whiskers yet, just peach fuzz. There were a few of the other guys who had not started shaving yet. But we tried to shave anyway. Well, we worked long and hard that night trying to get that first shine on our new work shoes before the lights went out.

Reveille came early, and so did the inspection. We jumped out of bed, got dressed for inspection, and got in formation before we got awake. According to the inspectors, everything was wrong. We were too slow getting in formation, we did not line up correctly, and we all needed a proper shave.

Then we were called to attention and introduced to our Company Commander, his assistant, and then we were inspected by them. Chief Wall, the Company Commander, walked slowly through, looking us over and asking questions about what type of jobs we had before and offering suggestions on how to make our uniforms fit better, while his assistant constantly chewed us out for things he did not like, making comments like, "worst shoeshine I ever saw," "is this the first you ever wore clothing" and "don't you know you have to put a blade in the razor before you shave".

## Chapter 20

# BOOT CAMP COMPANY 007

After the inspection was over, the handlers that had been in charge were released, and our Company 007 was officially formed. We met our company Commander, Chief B. C. Wall. I do not remember the date, but I looked up the official date the Company started, and it was January 15, 1954. So, I left Gainesville, Florida, on January 5th and officially started training on January 15, 1954.

As soon as Chief Wall assumed command of our company, things got better. We finished the processing in part of our introduction. We got our haircuts and physical examinations. I remember that we had lost at least two of our people during that process.

I also remember that one guy had to have all his teeth pulled. He was a big healthy-looking young man but had a problem with his teeth not being strong enough to keep them from breaking. They sent him to the hospital to have the procedure done, and when he came back, he told us that it was from something he was born with. I remember that he had a great sense of humor. He said he was getting worried about being in the Navy, and he said, "First they gave me a comb, then they cut off all my hair, then they gave me a toothbrush and pulled all my teeth, and if they try to give me a jock strap, I'm going AWOL."

Part of our induction was to have a psychological exam, and that took at least one more of our company members. During the second week of training, Chancy went missing, and it was a couple of days before we knew he was really missing. To complicate things even more, it had started to rain. For the most part, it was a light rain, but it never stopped. The San Diego area has an arid climate, but the rain continued for over two weeks.

We knew that Chancy was having problems, and some of us were trying to help him through it. Both Miller and I were trying to find someone who could tell us what happened to him, but no one knew anything. I started making requests to speak with Chief Wall, but they do not like you to do that.

They think if you have a problem, you should work it out at the lowest level. But I persisted in talking with him, and finally, he met with me. I explained that I was a friend of Chancy and wanted to know what happened to him. He told me that Chancy had been sent home. I asked why and explained that some of us were trying to help him through the training.

Chief Wall explained that Chancy was a risk to everyone because he could not be depended on to carry his part of the load in an emergency. The Chief said the safety of all of us was his responsibility, and he had made the decision to send him home. I never heard anything more about him. I do not remember how many people our Company started with, but only fifty-six made it through to graduation on April 7, 1954.

Our training schedule was based on one-week periods, and the first four weeks were general military called primary training. The fifth week was service week, better known as KP- duty, and the rest was advance training. Primary training was mostly out in the field, and you had to wear the work uniform. Advanced training was mostly classroom, and you had to wear a white or blue dress type.

It rained during most of the first four weeks, and our clothes were always either wet or damp, and by the fourth week, I was fighting a case of flu. Our guard duty training advanced as we completed different levels of training during the first four weeks. During the fourth week, I was assigned to guard the base ammunition storage facility.

The facility was located away from the main area, so we were transported to and from the facility. On my last watch at the ammunition storage facility, it was a soft rainy night, and my flu symptoms were making it hard for me to keep going. At the end of my watch, our ride came by to pick us up. The driver who came to pick me up was not a part of our training staff. He was just a driver from the motor pool. He looked at me and told me to ride in the cab of the truck. It was warm and dry inside, and it really felt good.

My case of flu was making it hard for me to keep going on the training schedule, but I knew that if I missed a week of my training schedule, I would be reassigned to another company. Man, I did not want that to happen. Our company held the honor company award. That is earned by outscoring all the other companies in the most training events. We had won all but one of the contests. In addition to the pride it gave us, we also got ahead-of-the-line privileges at all scheduled events, including lines at the chow hall.

Because I had seen movies about the Army and Marines training, and they all had Obstacle course training, I thought that before we finished our training, we were also going to have some type of training like that. The driver wanted to talk, so I asked him, "When do we start the real rough training?"

He looked at me and asked if I was in my fourth week. I said yes, and he laughed and told me I had just finished the hard part. Then he asked me what training I was talking about. I explained it, and he told me I was in the wrong branch of the service for that. That made me feel better about my training schedule and the next day, I checked into the sick bay for treatment.

I spent three days in the infirmary and then was released for light duty for three days. That worked out nicely because it kept me from the week of KP duty. Instead of being sent to the chow hall for duty, I was assigned to clean the barracks.

Starting the sixth week of our training, we moved to classrooms for our training, and that did not include physical work. So, we started wearing our semi-dress uniforms, which were blue and white jumpers and trousers and the same little white cloth hat.

The classes that we attended ranged from history to job assignments. The US Navy has several divisions, and General service is geared to the ships and their support. The CB is the construction battalion, and the Aviation is the aircraft support division. During the first part of the introduction to the different parts of the Navy, we were told that the Aviation department was full and not taking any new people. Well, as soon as we heard that, Miller, me, and two other men made the decision to challenge that.

Each part of the Navy also has nicknames for people assigned to each part. Seaman for the generalship support, and Airdales for aviation. To be honest with you, I had no idea what Aviation was about, but I had been told by someone that you could get anything you wanted from the Navy if you persisted hard enough. So, we took that as a challenge.

Even though I had seen airplanes with US NAVY painted on the wings, I never made the connection. It took me a long time to learn how to pronounce the word 'aviation', and that night when I got back to the barracks, I looked up both aviation and Airedales in the dictionary, and the description of Airdale was a "large dog." I did not like the idea that I might be called a dog if I went into aviation. Each time we went to job counselors, the four of us refused to change our choices.

The bottom line is the Navy will have to fill their needs first. They ask for you to make two choices, a first and a second choice, and they will try to fill them. If they cannot fill either of your requests, they will plug you in anywhere they need a body. Miller and I both had no second choice. The truth is, neither one of us knew what we wanted to do except challenge their request for us to change our choices.

As we progressed through advanced training, things began to improve. Meeting our inspection requirements and maintaining an honorable company status led to a reduction in our physical training demands. Consequently, we gained more personal time. This allowed us to write letters home and enjoy the recreation hall, complete with a grill serving real hamburgers and Coca Colas. The presence of a jukebox allowed us to listen to the latest music.

On occasions when our families weren't around, the military provided programs for trainees like us. They connected us with local church members who graciously invited us to their homes for dinner. I recall Miller dialing a number that resulting in a pleasant visit to home of church member. The home-cooked meal was a true delight. This experience also included a visit to a nearby movie theater after dinner. On that occasion, the theater was screening the new film "The Creature from The Black Lagoon," which we had the chance to watch.

The only other big events were completing the last part of our training, getting the notification on where we were going next, and our graduation parade. When our assignments were posted, three of the four of us who requested aviation got it. Miller, I, and one other sailor were going to Norman, Oklahoma, for Airman Preparatory School. Now I was sure that persistence would work, and I kept using it every time I could. Now we just had to wait for April 7, 1954, the day we would officially complete our basic training, AKA Boot Camp, with our big parade.

On the morning of our graduation, we had already written letters or made phone calls to everyone we knew, informing them that we were on our way home. We were granted a two-week leave starting at the end of our training, with the option to begin it in San Diego or after checking into our new command. I decided to wait until I reached Norman. My chosen mode of travel was by train. Although I didn't know it then, this would be the last train ride I'd take.

On that final day, everyone woke up on time, charged with excitement and emotion. We packed our sea bags with all our belongings and bid farewell to the people we had shared so much with during our brief training period. We made promises to stay in touch, but the truth is, those promises rarely endured beyond the next duty station. It's as if everything starts anew as soon as you arrive there. Miller and I traveled together to Norman for the same training, but we lost touch shortly after our arrival.

After our graduation parade, we went back to the barracks, picked up our sea bag and finished checking out of the training center. All our orders and travel arrangements to our destinations were ready for us to pick up. I was going to Norman, Oklahoma, and then on to Gainesville, Florida, for my Boot Leave. The people handling my travel arrangements had also got me the bus tickets I would need. The military paid for travel to Norman, but I paid for the bus ride. They took the money out of my boot camp pay that I was going to receive. They also arranged military transportation for us from the base to the train station. With that, we started a brand-new adventure and all I wanted to do was leave that base.

## Chapter 21

# HEADING TO NORMAN OKLAHOMA

*I* was so excited about being on my way home that I don't remember walking and carrying that sea bag to the bus terminal. We had a few minutes before boarding the bus, so we started looking for a place to eat. A soft drink machine was all we found in the area, but that was a welcome sight.

By the time we could board the bus, I had located Miller. We got our bags stored and found a seat together and settled in for the trip to the train station. I do not remember how long it took us to get there, but it sure was not like the ride we took from the train station on our way to the training center when we arrived. I think the reality of our new freedom was starting to set in. When we arrived at the train station, the bus stopped, and the driver just said, "Everybody off the bus and make sure you got all your property." With that, we were on our own and had to find our way to the train.

I remember that once we got inside the terminal, it was crowded. We had a difficult time finding the ticket counter where we got our boarding passes for the train. Somehow, we got our sea bags checked into the luggage pickup for our train and found the correct line to board the correct train. I really cannot explain how I felt. I think that my emotions were a combination of the excitement I felt about successfully completing basic training and going home. I was fighting with my apprehension about what would happen next.

The train ride was scheduled for two days, but our tickets only got us a Pullman for one night, and I remember that I was so tired that I was ready for bed as soon as they fixed our Pullmans. Our car was the last coach on the train, and there were several other service members traveling on the same train. Like me, they were going to new duty stations or home on leave.

Somehow, we had all grouped together in our car. Everyone was excited and asking each other questions. We were laughing, talking and making too much noise. The conductor came and told us that we had to be quieter because he was getting complaints. By that time, it was dark, and the train crew was chasing us out of their way so they could set up our Pullmans.

The next morning, just like on my train ride from Florida to California, we had to get up and get dressed in some cramped space and clear the coach while the train crew pulled down the Pullmans and set up the coach. We went to the dining car for breakfast, but this time the meal was on us. No meal tickets.

The day was long, and we had a lot of time to kill. We went to the lounge car, where you could buy coffee and other drinks, but they were expensive, and I had to conserve what money I had. We were not going to get to Norman, Oklahoma, until late that night, and I still had to eat. So, all there was to do to pass the time was talk and stare out the window. It was a very long day.

It was late at night when we got into Norman. I can't remember just how I got from the train to the base, but I do remember that the last part was by bus. Miller and I were still traveling together, and we got checked into the Duty Office and the transit barracks. It was only a couple of hours until we would have to get up, so we just found someplace to lie down. We had to report back to the Duty Office at eight AM. Before we checked in at the Duty Office, we walked to the chow hall and were allowed to get breakfast for free.

We reported into the Duty Office at 8 AM and finished checking in. This way, our two weeks' leave would not start until we were signed out. The way the military handles leave is that your leave time will not start until the minute you are officially signed out, and it ends the minute you are checked in. This way, we can sign out at one minute past midnight and get the full twenty-four hours of the first day, and you can wait until one minute before midnight to check-in.

By mid-morning, we were all finished with our checking in, and all we had to do was wait until midnight to check out on leave. We also learned that a bus-line in the area had a special bus route that left from the base main gate at midnight and went to the main bus terminal in Oklahoma City. We had to catch that bus to be able to connect with the main bus lines.

We were very tired, and we went back to the transit barracks to bum the unauthorized use of a couple of bunks. The barracks were almost filled, but the person running the barracks was willing to let us use two bunks that were not assigned to anyone yet. If someone came in that required a bunk, we would be kicked out. That was great, and we got unrestricted use of the showers. We each had a small bag that was for overnight traveling that we called absent without leave (AWOL) bags that held the things we needed for our bus trip.

We were afraid that after a hot shower and getting into a warm bed, we would oversleep and miss our bus to Oklahoma City and our connection to the main bus lines, so we needed someone to make sure we did not oversleep. The barracks Firewatch agreed to wake us in time. That was great, and we now had everything covered.

However, the bunks that were available were the second and third in three bunk set. All the way through training, we had slept in a two-bunk system. Miller had slept on the lower bunk, and I had the upper bunk. Well, this was not a problem, Miller would take the second, and I would climb up to the top.

Well, that worked out just fine until the Firewatch woke us up. We were so tired from our trip that we were in deep sleep when the Firewatch awoke us by hitting the bunk with his nightstick as they did in all our bootcamp training. To make sure that we did not fall back to sleep, we developed a habit of jumping out of the bunk and holding on to the bunk frame until we could get awake.

Well, when he hit the bunk, the surprise caused us to jump out the same way we were conditioned to. Only this time, the distance to the floor was different, and we both lost our balance and crashed to the floor. It shocked the Firewatch, and he thought we were drunk.

Well, we made it to the gate, and the Duty Officer came and signed our leave papers so we could leave the base. The problem was that the special bus was scheduled to leave at midnight, and officially, we could not sign out until one minute after midnight, and we would still have to walk to the bus stop.

The Duty Officer looked at his watch and said, "I think my watch is running slow," and he signed us out ten minutes early, so we made the bus ok. When we got to the bus station in Oklahoma City, Miller and I split up. He was going to a different location, so he took a different bus.

The bus ride from Norman, Oklahoma, to Gainesville, Florida, was a long miserable ride, to say the least. The buses in those days did not have the comfort of the buses of today. One thing, I don't remember any on-board bathrooms or reclining-type seats.

As I remember it, there were two main bus companies, Greyhound and Trailways. My ride required that I use them both. I took Greyhound to Chattanooga, Tennessee, and switched to Trailways for the rest of the trip.

I do not remember all parts of the route we took. I think we went through Little Rock, Arkansas, and Memphis, Tennessee, before changing bus lines in Chattanooga, Tennessee. Prior to my train ride from Jacksonville, I had never seen any of that part of the country before. I thought it would be exciting to see all the countryside up close and personal from the bus.

At first, the excitement of being out from under the constant controlling hand of the military for the first time since leaving Jacksonville and the anticipation of getting home on leave kept me going. The first part of my ride started at midnight in Norman and was just like riding the train, all you see is the lights and darkness passing by your window.

The bus from Oklahoma City did not make many stops during the night because this was the express part of the run. As I enjoyed the ride, I had a good feeling of independence, and I felt like I had just escaped from something unpleasant. It did not take long riding in the darkness for it to become boring, and I was exhausted. I tried to sleep sitting up in the seat, but that did not work very well. I remember that the few stops during the night were short bathroom breaks, but at daybreak, we made a breakfast stop. I had my boot camp pay, but it would have to last for the whole trip, so most of what I ordered to eat was ordered off the price side of the menu. I had to stretch every dime as far as I could.

I remember that during the day, we passed through a lot of small towns that we did not stop in and some really crooked roads. One of the roads went through a mountainous area, and the bus driver told us about an elderly lady who was scared by the curves. She asked him if driving through the curves scared him. He said, "No, ma'am, I just closed my eyes"! She took what he said seriously and panicked. The driver said that she got off at the next stop and filed a complaint against him. The driver was a really nice guy and had a good sense of humor.

At one stop, as I started to disembark the bus, the driver pulled me aside and informed me that his route was transitioning from express to local at that point. He explained that another bus would take over the express route, and I had the option to switch buses there.

To make the switch, he suggested that I provide a valid reason to the ticket agent. One of his suggestions was to mention that I was uncomfortable with the other driver's conduct or driving. Holding onto my bag, I approached the ticket agent to request a transfer. He glanced at me and inquired about the reason, though he didn't seem to fully absorb my explanation. With a smile, he stamped my ticket. I signaled the alternate driver that I had secured the transfer, and he acknowledged it with a wave. Since I was in uniform, the ticket agent seemed to be aware of the situation.

The rest of the trip to Chattanooga was very tiring, and there was no way to lie down to try to rest. I was riding in one of the older buses that had a straight bench-type seat in the rear of the bus. During that time, the segregation rules were that blacks could only sit in the very back of the bus. We did not have many passengers, and there were no blacks on the bus, so I went back and stretched out on that bench seat. Just as I stretched out on the seat, somebody threw a pillow at me and said, "You might as well be comfortable". By the time my head was on the pillow, I was sound asleep.

The next thing I knew, the bus driver was waking me up, and we were not at the bus terminal, we were in the bus garage instead. The driver had unloaded all the passengers and moved the bus to the garage. He explained that he thought he was missing a passenger and checked the bus before he left it. I had no idea where I was, and I remembered that the schedule only gave me fifteen minutes to get to the Trailways bus terminal and check in to catch my connecting bus.

I panicked, thinking I was going to miss my connection. I grabbed my bag and asked the driver where the bus terminal was, and he pointed to the next building. I was still trying to wake up, and the bright sun outside was making it hard to see.

The Greyhound terminal was just across the bus parking area where they loaded and dropped off passengers. As I ran from the bus garage to the back of the bus terminal, all I could think of was that I did not have time to go looking for the Trailways bus terminal, so I would have to pay for a taxi to take me there.

I ran through the bus terminal to the taxi stand in front of the Greyhound terminal, jumped in the first taxi I found, and told him to take me to the Trailways bus terminal and to hurry. The cab driver made a U-turn and pulled up to the curb directly across the street. Man, I was embarrassed. The two bus terminals were facing each other and directly across the street. The cab ride cost me fifty cents.

To make matters worse, Greyhound had arrived early, and the Trailways bus was late. I had plenty of time to make the connection and get something to eat. I was mad about the cab driver charging me fifty cents instead of just pointing out where the bus station was, but I was too embarrassed to say anything.

The trip from Chattanooga, Tennessee, to Gainesville, Florida, was much shorter and enjoyable. I was getting closer to home, so I was passing the time looking for Georgia landmarks so I would know how close I was getting to being home again. I also remembered that when I got to the Gainesville bus station, I would still be just over thirty miles from the Farm.

Everyone knew I was coming home, even though I had no idea what time I would arrive. I was hoping that I would be able to call my brother at work, but there was no telephone at home. At that point, I did not care if I had to hitchhike or walk, I knew I would make it home. We arrived at the Gainesville, Florida bus station just before noon, and I was able to get my brother to come and pick me up.

# Chapter 22

# HOME AGAIN

When my brother arrived to pick me up at the Gainesville bus station, I was finally starting to relax. The journey had left me exhausted, and my only desire was to reach home.

Thoughts began to flood my mind about the tasks that awaited me, including calling my girlfriend. It reminded me of something we were told during our basic training orientation – that by the time we completed the training, we would feel like we had matured so significantly that our friends back home would seem dull in comparison.

This message was repeated throughout our training, even up to the chatter surrounding our release from boot camp. Though I hadn't paid much attention to it, as I held a close bond with only two individuals: my best friend Richard Smith, who was in the Army and thus distant, and Lucille Kirkland. Lucille and I had been exchanging letters, yet she still resided with her mother and lacked a phone, while I was without a car.

I had turned eighteen during my first week in bootcamp, and Lucille was just turning 18. I had met her while working at a part-time job a few weeks after my girlfriend dumped me. She was the only girl that I had dated after the breakup. I liked her because we had a lot in common.

She was raised in a very poor family, and so was I, so we both understood what it was like not to have anything. As I thought about the hard times and embarrassment I had gone through, I started feeling better about the Navy.

I knew that I needed all the education that I could get. I had learned a lot in bootcamp, and I was already going to another school. My brother was in the Air Force, and he went to some good schools while he was in. So, I started feeling better about being in the Military.

My brother got there to pick me up, and I was happy to see him again that everything else just faded away. The ride home was just a blur until I saw how happy Mom and Dad were when we pulled into the yard. She had cooked a big meal, and I tried to eat everything. I was very hungry.

We talked for a long time, and mom tried to bring me up to date on everyone we knew. They were surprised that I liked the Navy. I don't think they understood much of what I was talking about, but when I told Dad that I would be working on airplanes, he did not seem very happy.

I do remember that when I got ready to go to bed, it was the quietest that I had heard in months. I realized that this was the first time in months that I had been in a room all by myself. I can't even remember getting in bed, but boy, did I sleep that night.

The next morning, I borrowed Derlwood's car and went to visit Lucille. She was still living in her mother's house and did not have a phone, so I had to go to her house to see if she was home.

She was home and was glad to see me. I had told her in a letter that I wanted to see her when I got home but did not know just when that would be. We had dated a few times before I went into the Navy, and we liked each other. We had stayed in touch by mail while I was in bootcamp and had made plans to get together while I was on leave.

Lucille's situation was about the same as before I left for the Navy. She could not drive, and her mother required full-time assistance, so she was unable to get to work. Her family was working on getting state assistance to get her mother into a medical care facility. She met all the requirements and had been accepted and was waiting for the next bed space to become available.

Lucille was the only one of the children still staying with her mother. Her younger brother was now working and living with an older couple who were family friends. Her younger sister, whom we called the wild child, had left with her biker boyfriend – a genuinely good person who simply loved riding his Harley Davidson 74 motorcycle. The older sister was the linchpin, juggling marriage, two jobs, and providing the primary financial support for the family.

I spent as much time as I could with Lucille, and most of that was spent at home. I did not have any extra money and only a limited time before I had to return to my new base in Norman, Oklahoma. We were of legal age and decided to get married. To meet the state time requirements on a Marriage License, we had to go to Georgia, so we set up the marriage in Valdosta, Georgia.

She got a nice navy blue and white dress, and I was going to wear my winter uniform, which was navy blue with white piping. My mother and a family friend of her family were going to be the witnesses.

Derlwood let us use his car for the trip, and things started out well. But like always, I was trying not to be late and had a flat tire just before we reached the Courthouse. I had to change the tire and could not change out of my uniform. I got so dirty that I couldn't wear my dress uniform, and my only backup was my White uniform. So, I cleaned up the best I could in the courthouse restroom, and I, of all people, got married in White. We went to my parents' farm for our very short honeymoon.

# Chapter 23

# NORMAN OKLAHOMA

My boot leave ran out on Saturday, April 24, 1954, at midnight. My bus trip got me back just in time. I must have had a lot on my mind because I do not remember anything about the ride except that I could not be late checking in.

I had so many things to do when I got there. I had to find out what paperwork I would need to change my status from single to married and file for dependent pay for my wife. The military took part of your pay and added a small amount of money to it and sent it to your wife as a separate check. Since I planned to bring her to Norman, I had to find a small furnished apartment that I could rent.

Arriving on a weekend meant there wasn't much I could start until Monday. My primary concern was getting a place to sleep, store my things and get authorization to eat in the Chow Hall. The Duty Officer's Assistance got me a bunk in the transit barracks until I got my assigned barracks. A signed copy of orders was all I needed for the chow hall.

I was there for training, all classes started on Mondays, and the new class was already set up. That meant that I probably had to wait a week before getting assigned to my class. I had some time on my hands, and I tried to find my buddy Miller. My first attempts to find him failed. Later I learned that he had come back early, and he was two weeks ahead of me.

It was a few days before I got to talk to him, but we were both going in different directions. I still had no idea of what I was going to do, and he had already decided what he wanted. The fact that I was married meant that we were not going to be hanging out much. I only saw him a couple more times, and that was just in passing. I lost all track of him.

I had nothing to do on Sunday but read the bulletin boards. I did find some notices for places to rent, but none were furnished. I did see a notice about a special math class that was starting. I found that to be interesting. But the only thing I could find out was that it would be covered during the first day of our introduction, and that would be Monday, which was the next day.

The next day was a little confusing and busy. I was trying to get checked into my assigned barracks, but they needed to know which class I was going to be assigned to, and I had not been assigned yet. I had to get the forms I needed to change my status to married. I was also trying to get a lead on a furnished apartment within walking distance of the base. And I had to get to the introduction class.

The class was short and informal. There were only three of us, and the instructor was just someone assigned to help us get settled in and on a list for the next class. He was able to let me know that the first week was about testing and getting an overview of the different jobs I would be training for.

I would meet and talk with some counselors and fill out a lot more forms, and I would be taking some tests, and one of them was a math test. All jobs require a satisfactory math score to qualify based on the type of work the job requires. Then I learned about the math course, it was a two-week math refresher course designed to help students that had low math skills to improve their scores.

It was suggested that if we did not get a high score on the math test, we could apply for the two-week course. I wanted all the school I could get, and I wanted to stay in Norman as long as possible, I made sure my score was not too low or too high. So, I got extended two weeks at Norman.

This training was so much better than boot training, and I got a lot done that first week. All my marriage paperwork was in, I was in a barracks, got my first paycheck after leaving bootcamp, and was getting ready to start the math class. I had also gotten a lead on a small, furnished apartment close to the base. Everyone was nice and tried to be helpful, but still, I did not have access to the car.

When we were in training, we had to have a pass to go off the base. I was able to request and get a pass to go check on the apartment. So, my trip was to locate the apartment and find out if it was within walking distance of the base. It was only a twenty-minute walk from the main gate. It was a small house and really did not look like anything I could afford. I did not see anyone to talk to, so I made sure that I had the correct address and went back to the base to think It over.

The next morning, during our class break, I spoke to my instructor about helping me obtain a phone number for people who lived there. He took the information I had given him and said he thought he could get the number. When we returned after our lunch break, he had the number ready for me. Initially, I felt nervous about calling a stranger without being certain about what I wanted to say. However, I made the call after our class ended. I recall that the lady who answered the phone was easy to talk to. She invited me to come to see the apartment the following afternoon when her husband would also be present. We didn't discuss the price during the phone call. She was polite but expressed the desire to meet us before continuing the discussion. I explained that Lucille wasn't available at the moment, but she still agreed to meet with me.

I got another pass and went back to meet them. They turned out to be a nice old couple, and when they heard my story, they wanted to help. The space they were referring to had a large bedroom with a bath and a small table with two chairs. There was a small dresser and one closet. She offered to let us share the kitchen.

She asked me a lot of questions, and most of them were about Lucille. I remembered that during the time I was trying to answer questions about Lucille, I suddenly realized just how little I knew about her. All I really did know was that I needed to get her to Norman. The owners of the house wanted to help get Lucille to Norman, and then we could make the decision about the apartment. They would hold the apartment for us.

I do not remember the details about how we got Lucille to Norman, but she did ride the bus, and I think we borrowed the money from my family. I do remember that when she arrived in Norman, I was in class. The lady that owned the apartment had got her there by the time I got there. Even the people in the military were helping, the official that I had to request the off-base pass from. I knew I would need an overnight pass, and he left one for me.

I cannot remember the names of the couple we were renting the apartment from, but they sure were nice to us. When I got to the apartment, Lucille was already settling into the apartment. She was tired from the trip, but the landlady had made her a good meal, and she got a hot bath, so she was feeling pretty good.

The couple liked Lucille and insisted that we join them for dinner that night. The only discussion we had about the rent was them saying, "Don't worry about that for now." We engaged in conversation throughout dinner, and they asked many questions about us. Needing rest since I had to return to the base early the next morning, I borrowed an alarm clock from the landlord before heading to bed.

After what seemed like a very short night, I got up at 6 AM, so I would have time to make my class on time, and as I was trying to quietly leave the house, the landlady called to me, "Don't worry about Lucille I will take care of her". I was surprised but relieved.

I had to provide verification that I was living off-base with my wife to get my permanent off-base pass. I had that now, and the pass was approved. It costs you your barracks, bunk, and chow pass. That helps, but it will not offset your expense of living off base. Well, by the end of that day, I was legally living off base.

Living off-base offered the advantage of a permanent off-base pass and the ability to bring a personal vehicle onto the base. However, I didn't have a car at the time, though a couple of my fellow students did.

Two of these students were older and had more service experience than I did, and we became friends, primarily because of my permanent base pass. In exchange for some beer, they generously allowed me the use of their car to commute back and forth, covering all expenses, including gas. The car I used the most was a forty-nine Plymouth coupe with a spacious trunk. The owner provided written permission for me to use it, and I obtained a base pass for the vehicle. This arrangement significantly improved life for both me and Lucille.

There was a change in the Base Housing situation due to an unexplained drop in the occupancy rate. To address this, the qualifying requirements were altered in an attempt to maintain occupancy. Under the new rules, any married personnel stationed there could apply and be considered for a unit.

I submitted a request and was granted a furnished unit, which meant I needed to vacate the apartment. The couple that had been so helpful to us was genuinely disappointed, and although we felt a sense of regret about leaving, it was a more convenient arrangement for me.

Before the change in the qualification's requirements, students could not get the units. Only those who were assigned for duty could qualify, and they had to go on a waiting list for a unit. When we moved into a unit without having to wait or be base personnel. It upset some of the wives of old timers who were living in the units.

Our reception was a cold one. Lucille got some harassment from the women. No matter what she did, one of the women living there would always complain and make sure that Lucille felt unwelcome there. It got to a point where I had to go over and talk with her husband.

He was senior to me by quite a bit, so I had to be careful about how I approached him. Also, he was physically larger than me, and I was in his house. I told him our story and that we did not understand why his wife was upset with us. He said that he would talk to his wife about it and not let it upset us. I think he dealt with something like this before. We did not have any more problems to speak of.

I remember that we were flat broke all the time, and sometimes it got hard just to eat. The guy that owned the car was glad we were living on base because they could keep beer at my house, and when they wanted to go off base, it was easy, they would come over and get in the big trunk of the car, and Lucille and I would get in the car and go shopping off base.

When I got off the base, I would open the trunk, and they would get out of the trunk and into the car. They would repay us by paying all the expenses. Neither Lucille nor I drank at that time, so sometimes we would go eat with them, and a couple of times, we went to a movie. When we would start back to the base, I would stop the car, and they would jump out of the car and get back in the trunk, and I would drive home. We were lucky that they never inspected the trunk of the car.

The training was good, and it was going by fast, the two weeks of the special math course were coming to an end, and I had improved my math scores to where I could qualify for any of the "A" level schools. The next part of my schooling was to complete the four-week Airman Preparatory training that I was sent there for. After that, I would be transferred to a class "A" school to some military unit for duty.

Before this time, I had only considered becoming a mechanic. However, I guess God had other plans for me as I found myself assigned to a four-hour duty watch with someone who changed my perspective.

This young sailor was on the brink of completing his initial four-year duty and had already achieved the rank of E-6, or Petty Officer First Class. To accomplish such a feat in just four years, one needed to possess exceptional intelligence and a strong commitment to mastering the job. He served as an Aircraft Mechanic, designated by the letters 'AD,' primarily working on reciprocating engines. However, his role was transitioning to the new realm of jet engines.

This change necessitated his retraining to adapt to the new engine type for further advancement. To shift from AD to ADJ (working with jets), he undertook training, requalification, requested the switch and obtained the necessary approval.

He went on to emphasize that the most promising opportunities now lie in the field of Electronics, and he strongly recommended that I consider pursuing an electrical specialty. I found his advice impressive and felt increasingly certain that I should heed his guidance.

The next Monday, I started the Four-week course with an overview of all the different jobs that made each one appeared to be a great job. We had four main categories of jobs, and one week was assigned to each of them. On the last day of the week, we met with a counselor. He would review your scores and try to best fit you for a job. I chose either AT, Electronics, or AE, Electrician. At first, he tried to get me to consider a mechanic, but I refused that offer.

In each of the following three weeks, he kept trying to convince me to change because even though my math scores were high enough to qualify me for the class, he knew that I would have a very hard time completing the school. In my heart, I wanted to go to "AT" school, but I also knew that it was the hardest of the two schools. The AT school was located in Memphis, Tennessee, and the "AE" school was in Jacksonville, Florida.

My current situation in Norman was getting bad. I was not getting my normal pay because they were taking a part of it to send to Lucille with the part they added. We had not gotten her check, and what I had was not making the stretch. I got in touch with my mom and asked her to send me some money. By the time she got back to me, we were down to our last bit of potato soup. Lucille's check was sent to Mom's address, and Mom air-mailed it to us. By the time I got the check, I had started considering "AE" school and Jacksonville as a safer choice. The check got us through the rest of the school.

By the last meeting with the counselors, I knew that "AE" was the best choice, but I still wanted to be a radio operator, and that was in the "AT" part of the job. So, I pulled a nickel out of my pocket and called heads for AT and tails for AE, and it came up tails. I sure was relieved. Lucille had to take the bus back home, and I got to take my first flight.

## Chapter 24

# AVIATION ELECTRICIAN CLASS A SCHOOL

Upon completing the training at Norman, I got orders to go to the AE class A school in Jacksonville, Florida. Lucille had to take the bus back to my home in High Springs, Florida. The military was transporting me and three more students from Norman to AE A school at The Naval Air Station, also known as NAS, by air. This would be my first time to fly, and I sure was excited about flying.

The Naval Air Station, NAS, is divided into two parts. The operations side, NAS, and the Naval Technical Training Center side, NATTC. I was heading to the NATTC side. We were flying on an old Beechcraft-type airplane that the Navy owned. It was a small twin-engine plane called a tail dragger because the third wheel of the landing gear was under the tail of the plane. The passenger compartment was set up with four regular seats and two jump seats. We had four students and four crew, including a pilot, a copilot, one female flight attendant, and one additional male crew member. It was very crowded on the plane.

The flight was not scheduled to leave Norman until about midnight, and I think the top speed of that type of aircraft was about 80 Knots. Not only was that going to be a crowded flight, but it was also going to be a long one. And to make matters worse, it was nonstop. No commercial airlines would have got away with the conditions we had to endure.

It was dark when we took off, so all I could see was the lights below us. I was tired, and it did not take long of just looking out the window into the darkness to get bored, and I fell asleep. As soon as it turned to daylight outside and I could look down onto the countryside, I was hooked on flying.

The countryside was so beautiful with all the differently shaped farms and wooded areas. We were flying at an altitude of approximately 8,000 feet, and you see the different fields on a farm. This was my first time flying, and I had never seen the ground from that perspective. Watching all the roadways, small towns, and houses made the time go by faster. And that was good because this was a long flight.

I do not remember what time it was when we finally landed, but judging by how hungry I was, it was late in the day. We were on the ground, and now we were able to stand up, walk around, and take care of some other pressing matters. We did not go into the terminal. Instead, we just taxied around the airfield for a while. Then we were told that we had landed at the wrong airport. We were at the Jacksonville International Airport; our airport was on the opposite side of Jacksonville. We were on the North side of town, and our airfield was the Naval Air Station (NAS) which was on the South side of town. So, we took off, circled around the area, and landed on NAS. I was sure happy to see that terminal.

We were told to remain in the terminal area until transportation for us to go to the Training Center could be arranged. We had to go to the station duty office to check-in. That is required any time you are transferred from one command to another.

When we got checked in at the duty office, we were told that we would also have to check into the main barracks, then we were to go to the chow hall for a meal. After the meal, we were to report back to the main barracks for our building dorm and bed assignments.

While I was trying to get everything straightened out, things got interesting. There were three other students at the duty office waiting for us to get there. The person who was the assistant to the duty officer took a list of all our names, the list was alphabetical, and my name was the first one on the list.

He called my name and ordered me to come front and center. As I was moving to where he wanted me, I was not happy about being first on the list. He told me that I was in charge and reminded me that this was a military base, and we were to look like a military unit.

We were to form a squad arrangement and march in formation from one point to the next. Then, while I was still mad about being first on the list, he said, "I have to assign one of you to mess cook duty for thirty days", with that, he called the second name on the list and assigned him to the mess cook duty. Suddenly I did not feel so upset about being first on the list.

He then turned the squad over to me and said, "Carry out your orders."

The main barracks were about ten blocks from the duty office. I marched the squad to the main barracks and gave them a copy of our orders, so they could make all our assignments. Then we went to the chow hall and delivered to the cook in charge of the galley his new mess cook.

Then we went through the chow line for our first meal since Norman. We were all really hungry, and the chow looked good until I got to the meat. It was liver, and I did not like liver. It looked good, but to me, it tasted bad. After we ate, I marched them back to the main barracks, and that ended my assignment.

The school is scheduled for six months of forty hours per week of Electrical theory and two to four hours of homework each night. Your typical day starts with a 6 AM wakeup, breakfast at the chow hall at 7 AM, and class beginning at 8 AM. You got a mid-morning break, lunch for one hour, a mid-afternoon break, and the class was over at five PM. Chow at the chow hall at Six PM, then back to the barracks for homework and sleep.

The main difference here was the only time that you were restricted to the base was when you were on duty. The duty assignment was every fourth day and one weekend per month. You would normally be required to stand one watch each day you were on duty. Anytime you were not on duty, you were not restricted to the base.

The homework assignments were to review the material that you were scheduled to cover the next day. So long as you maintained passing grades, everything was ok. If your grades dropped below passing, you were counseled, and if you could not improve your grade, you would be dropped from the school.

Electrical Theory required a lot of math, and there was no such thing as calculators in those days, only Slide rules. Your slide rule became your best friend. I still have mine, although I have forgotten almost everything about how to use it. I have a Japanese-made Sun Hemmi Bamboo slide rule, and it is still in good condition. The slide rule is only accurate to the first two numbers in your answer. After working with it for a while, you can get really close to the third digit in your answer. The margin of accuracy in your answers compensates for this.

Most of the electrical theory questions require the use of electrical equations to find the answer. I learned very quickly why the counselors in Norman were not sure I could pass the course with my math scores. The simple problems were something like $E=IR$. The E stood for voltage, the I stood for current, and the R was for resistance. What it translates out to is that the voltage is equal to the current times the resistance. I had never heard of algebra, so I had to learn everything the hard way.

The school program was an excellent way to teach students how to be aircraft electricians. First, they teach you the theory that makes the parts work, then how they work in the aircraft and how to repair them. The bad part was that they only had six months to complete the training. The good part was they had some excellent instructors.

After I finished my check-in and briefing, I was off duty until my class started, which was the following Monday at eight AM. With almost three days off, I went home. I lived about one hundred miles from the base, and I had to hitchhike to get home and back. In those days, people were good about giving hitchhikers a ride, especially service men. So, I put on my uniform and headed home. As soon as I went out of the main gate at the base, I caught my first ride. It was with someone leaving the base headed in my direction. He dropped me at a good location to catch my next ride. I had good luck all the way home, and the trip went by really fast. My last ride dropped me off in town, where my brother worked, and I borrowed his car to go on out to the farm.

Lucille had got there about three days earlier. She had a long bus ride, but there were no problems, so she had lots of time to think. Everything had happened so fast that she had not had time to think things through. Now she had a lot of questions about what my plans for us were. So far, things had been hard.

Now she was living in one place, and I was living a hundred miles away. I did my best to give her hope that things were going to get better. Even though the salary was not much, it was dependable. In ninety days, I would have been eligible to compete for a promotion. Because I was in school, there should be no reason that I would not get it.

The bad things were that I would not be able to work part-time while I was in school. Lucille did not have any chance of finding any paying jobs while living there on the farm. However, we were living rent-free, and she was helping Mom with some of the work. With us living rent-free, we could at least buy some of the small things we needed. I was planning on checking for some furnished apartments in the area of the base that I might be able to rent. In the meantime, we would just have to tough it out.

I really enjoyed the weekend, but I was worried if I would be able to handle the classes or not. During my check-in at the base, they explained how the classes were designed and that they were hard for even the average student. Each part of the lessons was designed to teach you what you would need for the next part of the course. If you get behind, you will have difficulty understanding the next part. So, completing the homework was a must-do.

After good luck hitchhiking back to the base on Sunday, I started my first class the next morning at 8 AM. I remember that we had been told to bring a pencil and a notebook with paper for taking notes. Our dress requirements were our working uniform which was dungarees, a chambray shirt, and a white cloth hat.

We gathered outside the Administrative Office. After we got our welcome aboard speech, followed by a list of the rules for the school, we got an escort to our assigned classroom for the first phase of the course. There were tables and chairs, with a desk for the students and chalkboards for the instructors. There was no air-conditioning in those days, only big electric fans. Each room had large windows to help with the cooling and room lighting. This was Jacksonville, Florida, and this was the month of June, and it was hot.

As soon as we all got seated, the instructor passed a seating chart around, and we were told that we were to stay in our assigned seats. To make a change in where you sit, you were required to make a request to the instructor and get it approved. With that, the instructor introduced himself to us and called on each of us by reading our names from the seating chart, and we had to stand and restate our names and the name of our last assignment. After that was completed, we had a short time to ask questions, and then we got a twenty-minute break.

When we got back into the classroom, the blackboard was filled with a list of written words that I did not recognize, and I began to realize how much trouble I was in. They were all electrical terminology that we needed to learn. Our instructions were to copy them down and study them as homework. The instructor spent the rest of the morning going over the words and explaining them. Then we took a one-hour lunch break. There was no way I could get all the words written down, and I had to use part of my lunchtime to finish copying down the words.

We started the afternoon class with more information about the list of words, how to pronounce them, what the terms meant, and how we would be working with them. I was lost in the first fifteen minutes after the class started, and I think I stayed that way for the whole school.

This was my first week of school, and the duty schedule called for me to have weekend duty on my second weekend. That gave me the first weekend off, and I hitchhiked home again. It was a good trip, and things were getting better for Lucille.

She was not very happy about the news that I would have to stay on the base the next weekend. My brother had a phone, and we worked out the arrangements so that I could call her at his house. Long-distance calls in those days cost money, so we would have to keep the calls short. Being able to talk to each other made both of us feel better. We talked about the school I was attending and how important it was for me to be able to complete it. My brother was off that Sunday, so he drove me and Lucille to the base and dropped me off. I tried to study my homework, but my mind was not in it.

The next two weeks went by fast, and I got the phone call made, but I think it made Lucille feel worse. The good news was that I was able to contact my Uncle Hershel. He was married to my mother's half-sister, that lived in Jacksonville. He loved to flyfish and would always spend part of his vacation with us on the farm and go fishing with Dad. They had a boy, my first cousin, named Ivy. Ivy was a year older than me, but we spent a lot of time together when we were growing up.

When Uncle Hershel and Dad went fishing, Ivy and I would head out for a hunting session. Ivy was equipped with a 16-gauge shotgun and a .22 caliber rifle. As they leisurely drifted down the river fishing, we took to the riverbanks on foot for our hunting expedition. With the conviction of great explorers, we made our way through the river swamp, ensuring we had prearranged meeting points on the riverbank for reuniting.

We never really found any game that we could shoot, but on one of the trips down the Suwannee River, we got a rather embarrassing surprise. There was a strip of the river that went through some rough areas and then made a sharp horseshoe-type curve, which had a nice riverbank. We were to make our way to the curve and wait there for them to pick us up.

Some of the area, before we got to the curve, was very swampy, and we had a difficult time getting through it. We were tired by the time we reached a nice place on the riverbank. The place we found was a perfect place for a pickup point. The riverbank was about four feet above the river level, providing a good view of the river. We found a spot that was dry and did not have much undergrowth, just some large trees around it.

We were tired, and as soon as we could get to the clear spot, we sat down to rest. As we watched the river flowing by, we spotted a bottle floating down the river with the neck sticking up above the water. Ivy said, "I can hit that with the rifle," so I handed the rifle to him. It was not an easy shot, but Ivy took a slow, easy aim and fired.

Suddenly all heck broke loose. It sounded like a herd of wild elephants was crashing through the brush all around us. It scared the heck out of us. There was a flock of wild turkeys resting in the brush and trees behind us.

Even though we both had guns, we were too scared to even think about shooting anything. We never knew whether or not he had hit the bottle.

Ivy came to the base and picked me up one day after school, and I had dinner with them. They had a lot of questions about how and what we were doing. During the conversations, Uncle Hershel mentioned that I needed to get a car and that he might be able to help me get one. I told him that I could not afford one at that time, but he said he would keep an eye out for one. Getting off the base and seeing them was great, but I did not get back in time to do my homework.

During those two weeks, I found out that there was a small trailer park just off the base that had some old-World War II house trailers. They were small and old, but the Navy was using them for base housing. I was not able to find out anything officially, but I did hear that they were only for temporary use only.

We had our first phase test on Friday morning. When you have a phase test, that ends that phase of your training. When you complete the test and get your grades, you are off until the following Monday. When you start your next phase of training, you are clear with no homework for the weekend. I got an early start home and had good luck with rides all the way to the farm. It sure was good to be home.

I filled Lucille in on all the good news, and that brightened up her day. Now we had some plans that we could hope for. We would continue saving our money and try to get into that trailer park housing close to the base. Our income was not much, but with all the help we were getting, we did not have any bills to speak of. I still did not know if I had passed the phase test, but I felt good about it and had a good weekend.

I left the house a little early on Sunday to go back to the base. All the way back, I kept thinking about the possibility of being able to get one of the units in the trailer park close to base. I had not seen the trailer park or any of the trailers, but I had heard that they were old and small. I also remembered that they were for temporary use, and that was what I wanted them for. Being a student in a six- month long course should help me qualify for them. Anything would be better than the situation we were enduring at that time.

When I got back on the base, I started trying to find out more information about the trailers. I did not have any luck finding anyone with direct knowledge about them, but one of the guys in the barracks recommended that I talk to one of the school counselors. Their jobs were to help students. The next morning on the way to class, I stopped by the school administrative building and made an appointment to see a counselor. I also checked my test score from Friday's test. I passed it okay.

We started a new phase of our training, and it was just as difficult as the last phase. I got so involved in the training that I forgot about the counselor and the request for an appointment. When I got into class the next morning, the instructor called my name and handed me a note. One of the counselors had scheduled an appointment for 11 AM that morning. The instructor gave me permission to leave class to make the appointment but wanted to be sure that it was not something that he could handle. I told him it was about base housing and just to wish me luck.

I don't recall the name of the counselor, but he was a young man not much older than me. He was in a hurry and just wanted to know what my problem was. I remember thinking that this was going to be a waste of time. I tried to explain the situation to him, but when he looked at his watch and asked where the units were, I really felt stupid, all I would tell him was that it was close to the base. With that, he started escorting me to the door, saying that he had to run but that he thought that he knew someone who might be able to help me and that he would check with him. He was holding my request form and said he would pass it on. Man, I really felt let down after thinking I was going to get the help I needed.

The morning class period was almost over, and I did not want to go back to class, so I went on over to the mess hall. I was so upset that I couldn't tell what, if anything, I ate. I had such a bad attitude over the disappointment that I spent the rest of the lunch hour just walking it off, even though it was a hot day. When I got back to class, the instructor asked how the appointment went, and I just shook my head and said bad. I was not in any mood to talk about it.

The rest of the day I could not concentrate on the class. I did not want to look at any homework. All I wanted to do was go find the trailer park, but I did not have a car, and the weather was getting bad. For the first time since I got in the Navy, I was mad at the service. I guess I was having a good old-fashioned case of the blues.

By the time I got into class the next morning, I realized I still had a test to pass, and I was getting way behind with new study material. By mid-afternoon, I was getting back into studying, and then someone passed a message to the instructor, He looked at it and passed it on to me. It was a name that I did not recognize and a phone number.

On my afternoon break, I went to the office and called the number. Someone answered the phone, and I told him who I was and that I had a message to call. He explained that he had been contacted about helping me with a base housing issue. I explained my situation to him, and he knew about the trailer park. That sure made me feel a lot better. We talked for a couple of minutes, and he suggested that I write down his home phone and call him after I got out of class. Now I was on another high, and the Navy was great.

After I got out of class, I waited before calling him, and I wanted to give him plenty of time to get home as he had requested. I went to chow, then to the barracks. I showered, changed clothes, and even tried to study my homework, but I could not keep my mind on anything but that trailer, so I called him.

He was expecting my call and answered the phone. He explained that, for the most part, the Navy was planning on phasing out the trailer park. He knew that I had not seen the park or the trailers, so I did not know how bad they were. He said that he had driven by the park on his way home and that some of the trailers had people living in them. He suggested that I go to the park and look them over before getting my hopes up too high. He gave me directions on how to get there.

It was close to the main gate, just turn right as you exited the main gate, take the first left, cross the railroad tracks, and it would be on my left just a little way from the railroad tracks. He also explained that I would have to apply for base housing at the NAS Administrative building. He asked me to call him back after I had looked the trailers over.

With the possibility of finding a place to live near the base, things were looking up, my mood had improved. However, the lack of transportation remained an issue. Due to time constraints during my lunch hour, I couldn't visit the trailer park and return in time.

I managed to acquire the phone number for the Base Housing office, and upon calling them, they provided encouraging information. They required me to fill out a form so they could review my details. This was happening on a Thursday, and I was running out of time to complete tasks before the upcoming weekend. It was crucial not to miss my planned trip home.

Despite having a Friday quiz that I needed to perform well on, I faced a tough decision: whether to delay following up on the housing request until the following week or not. I ultimately chose to prioritize getting my schoolwork up to date. I decided to attempt a visit to the trailer park on my way home that Friday. The need for a car was becoming increasingly apparent.

Friday was a very busy day with school and the test. The morning was spent reviewing the material that he had covered, and all of us students had a lot of questions. We had our lunch break, and the instructor was late getting the test started because of more reviews before the test. It was a hard test, and I know that I would not have passed the test without all the reviews.

By the time I finished the test, I was already late getting started home. The best time to get good rides is just as the 4 PM traffic starts, and I was going to miss that. It was 5.45 pm by the time I got out the gate to start hitchhiking.

My first main route change was in the little town of Green Cove Springs. Normally my first ride would get me all the way there, but that day it took three rides. By the time I got a good ride that would get me to my main route home, I was three hours later than normal. I had done a lot more walking and thinking than normal. Now I realized that I needed to get Uncle Hershel to help me get a car.

I thought a lot about the situation without knowing how bad the living conditions may be in the trailer if I was able to get it. While I was thinking about it, first, I realized that it would be temporary, but so was what we had now, and it wasn't that great either. By the time I got home, I was so tired I did not care, I just wanted to see Lucille and get some rest.

Lucille and I talked about trying to get a car and that if we got the base housing, we would have a lot more expenses. We were starting to get a few dollars saved, but not nearly enough to cover the additional expense.

Lucille was really getting tired of the way she was living and the isolation on the farm. She was willing to take the chance, stating that it would be temporary. After all, she took the bus to Norman, Oklahoma, on a chance and with less. I promised that I would talk to Uncle Hershel about the car and request whatever housing that I could qualify for. It was quiet for the rest of the weekend, and I got some rest.

Sunday morning, I felt charged up and ready to get back to base so I could get started on my projects. As I was hitchhiking my way back to the base, I was hoping this would be the last time I would have to do this. The weather was not helping the situation, and it took longer to get rides. Normally, I could make it back in time to catch the chow hall's late meal, but not this time. When I got to Glen Cove Springs, I had to stop and get some snacks to eat.

I had planned on going by the trailer park and walking through it just to get an idea of what it was like, but the last ride I got was running late and, in a hurry, so I just went to the barracks.

I called Uncle Hershel and asked him if he could help me get a car. I remembered that he said he might be able to help me. To my surprise, he was working on it. He had located a 1950 Buick Hydro Glide that he thought he could get a good deal on. He said that he would know for sure in a few days.

I told him about the trailer park deal that I was working on and that I had not been able to see what it was like. I explained that the trailers were old and small, but they were still using them as temporary housing. He asked a few questions and suggested that he pick me up the next day so I could have dinner with him, and we could swing by and take a look at them. That was the best news I had in weeks.

Monday morning, I was able to make the arrangements to get the housing request filled out. The lady that helped me with the forms could not give me any information until after they processed my request, but she did say that students could qualify for the units. She said she would try to have an answer for me in a couple of days. Once again, I was feeling so good that I did not really care how bad they were.

After school, I changed my uniform so I could go out of the gate to meet Uncle Hershel. I had confirmed that if I did get the base housing, I would get what they called a dungaree pass. That meant that I could wear my work uniform while going back and forth to work, and that would also make things a lot easier. I was waiting outside the gate when Uncle Hershel got there, and we went to the trailer park. It was easy to find, and it was close to the main gate. We also found someone who lived in one of the units, and they let us look at the inside. The unit was small, but for just the two of us, I thought it was fine.

I had a nice visit and dinner. Uncle Hershel now had a better idea of what we needed and was going to Help. Aunt Vivian told me that if we got the unit, she would help Lucille with the things she needed to get it set up. I never liked getting helped, but in this case, I was okay with it.

I would pay off the car as soon as I could. All I could do now was study and wait for things to happen. Uncle Hershel and Aunt Vivian drove me back to the base and dropped me at the gate. I don't think that I walked back to the barracks, I think I just floated. With a new hopeful heart, I relaxed and went back to concentrating on my schoolwork. So far, I have been passing everything, but my grades needed some improvement.

I was waiting for the report from the base housing unit on my request for a unit, and Uncle Hershel was working on getting the car. I phoned my brother and relayed a message to Lucille that everything was moving along and looking good.

The next day I got an early start and reviewed my homework before class. The class started with the same hard driving pace and more new material, but somehow, I felt a lot more relaxed. This was my duty day, and I had to stay at the barracks. I also had to stand a two-hour watch in the middle of the night, but I still had a lot of time to spend on my homework.

The next two days went by without any follow-up on the housing unit or the car. Friday came, and it was not until after the Friday test that I got any news at all. When I turned in my completed test, the instructor handed me a note from the counselor's office that said the base housing office had checked on my status, and the counselors had recommended me for a unit.

After I had read the note, my instructor explained that their recommendation only meant that getting a unit should help me with my studies, not hurt them. At least I knew they were working on it, and that made me feel better. I tried to phone Uncle Hershel, but he was not home. I did not feel like hitchhiking home, but I knew that it would be better than hanging out on base, so I hit the road.

The 5 PM traffic was heavy as I cleared the gate and crossed the road. I managed to navigate through the traffic and quickly found a ride. The driver was heading down the coast and kindly took me to my cutoff at Glen Cove Springs.

I had a stroke of luck with my next ride, a friendly couple picked me up and offered to take me all the way to Starke. From the moment I got in the car, they started bombarding me with questions. They seemed genuinely curious about everything, from the military to the local area. Engaging in conversation with them was enjoyable; it helped pass the time and shifted my focus away from the situation at the base.

The remaining part of the journey home is a bit of a blur. It felt long and tedious. My mind was on a roller coaster of emotions as I contemplated various scenarios. I pondered about securing housing, unsure of whether I would get the housing unit and what the cost might be if I didn't. I tried not to entertain thoughts of failing school and being transferred to a new base. The reality was that the school days were numbered, and a transfer was imminent. Suddenly, a multitude of questions flooded my mind that needed answers.

By the time I got to the farm, it was well past supper time, but Mom had saved me a meal. She was making sure I got something to eat, and I noticed that Lucille was getting a little mad about how Mom was fussing over me. I had not seen that before, but I should have known it would happen sooner or later. Lucille was stuck in the middle of nowhere all week, and now somebody else was doing her job. I knew that somehow, I had to get her to where I was.

When I explained to Lucille that I was hopeful that we would get the housing unit, I could not tell her when. I could see the disappointment in her eyes. I changed the conversation to the car, and that did not help either. I finished my supper as soon as I could and changed out of my uniform and took her for a walk.

It was a warm night, and the walk felt good. It took a few minutes to get her to start talking about what was bothering her, but she needed to talk to someone. She was beginning to feel like a prisoner in that house, and she had lost total contact with her family. I assured her that I would borrow a car the next day, and we would go to Gainesville and visit them and do some window shopping.

The next morning, I took Dad's old truck, and we hit the road. We went to Lucille's mother's old place, but she was now in an institution. That was not a surprise. She was able to locate her older sister and learn that her brother had moved in with the people who were helping him out before Lucille left. Her younger sister, the wild one, had taken off with her boyfriend, who was a biker. I had met him when Lucille and I were getting married, and he was a nice guy, he just liked to ride his 74 Harley Davidson motorcycle.

We drove around town for a while but did not see anyone else we remembered, so we splurged a little bit and had a nice lunch. We looked in some stores and made a list of the things we knew we would need when we got our place, and Lucille bought a couple of items of clothing. By the time we got home, we both were in a better mood.

The next morning, I got an early start back to the base. The rides were fair, and it took me almost five hours to get back. I phoned Uncle Hershel and spoke to him about the car, and he had made a deal with the owner. They had agreed on Five Hundred dollars, but the owner was getting a new car and would need that car until he could pick up his new one. The dealer had promised that it would be ready soon.

Now all I had to do was study and wait for the housing unit decision. We had some coin-operated washing machines and dryers in the barracks utility room, and I got some change and did my laundry.

By Monday, things began coming together in a hurry. The base housing unit sent me a message that I had been approved for a unit and needed to sign some papers, and I would be on the list for a unit. The bad news was that I would be placed at the bottom of the list and would have to move up to the top of the list and then wait for the next available unit. The good news was that there were only a couple of people on the list ahead of me.

The clerk helping me with the papers told me that when a unit became available, they would contact the people on the list in the order of their position on the list and see if they were still interested in the unit. If they could not be located or should they turn the unit down, they would be dropped from the list, and it would go to the next qualified person.

She assured me that the list moved quickly and that I should stay in touch with the housing unit. I was hoping that Lucille was planning on what she would need for the trailer, like curtains, bedding, and dishes. I remembered all the things that we had to borrow back in Norman. We left Norman with only our suitcases, and so far, we had not started buying anything as of yet.

On Tuesday, I still had not got any word from Uncle Hershel on the car. I was hoping that I would be able to drive it home this weekend with a lot of good news. In my mind, I was starting to see us moving into our own trailer and me being able to drive to school and back.

By the end of the day, I just had to find out something about the trailer, so I called the Base housing unit and asked if they could tell me how many people were on the list for a unit. The person answering the phone went to check, and when she came back, she said, "One". With that information, I knew that I should get the next available unit. The problem was, how long would I still have to wait?

I did know that I had duty the next day, and I would still have a weekly test on Friday that I needed to pass if I still wanted to stay in school. I really liked the school, and I realized how lucky I was to get it. Not only was I learning something, but I was also getting paid to be there. After thinking about that, I switched my priorities to doing my job and passing that test and spent the rest of that day studying.

Wednesday proved to be a busy day as I juggled both school and my duty responsibilities. With the packed schedule, I couldn't spare a moment to make any follow-up calls. Then, on Thursday morning, I tried to arrive at class early. I took the opportunity to engage with the instructor before the class commenced.

I explained to him that I was waiting for information about a car that I was trying to buy, and I told him that I was first on the housing list and hoped to be able to get my car that afternoon. He said that he would help me and that I should study the handout material very thoroughly, and he got me a copy of the material. I took that to mean that our test was going to be based on that information.

About halfway through the afternoon, I got a note from the instructor that said, "Your car is here," that was all the information on the note. I took it to mean that Uncle Hershel had picked up the car and that I needed to call him. I looked at the instructor, and he nodded his head toward the door, indicating that it was ok for me to leave. I left the classroom and headed to the office, where I called Uncle Hershel.

Although I hadn't seen the car, its presence wasn't crucial; my main goal was to obtain a base pass for it. I required a bill of sale and my military ID card. Proof of insurance wasn't necessary at that time. Uncle Hershel was already prepared; he had the bill of sale made out to me so that I could register the car in my name.

He met me at the main gate, and there, I obtained a seventy-two-hour temporary pass. The security officer at the gate mentioned that since the pass would expire on Sunday, I could request an extension on that day. It was my first car, and I felt immensely proud of it. It granted me a sense of freedom, akin to being released from prison.

After we finished getting the temporary base pass, we went to Uncle Hershel's house, but he insisted that he drive. When I asked him how I had to pay him for the car, his response was that I did have to pay him his five hundred dollars, but to take care of my other problems first, starting with registration first. Then he reminded me that I had a little bride to take care of.

I knew that I would not be able to get the car registered on Friday with the school test that same day, so I planned to get it on Monday. I remembered that before Uncle Hershel would turn the car over to me, he went over the entire car with me. It had a straight eight-cylinder engine with an automatic transmission.

He had made a good selection with that car; it had good tires all around and a spare. I could tell he was proud of it, also. While he was showing me everything about the car, I remembered all those times that he would let me run the boat when we were fishing back when he would spend his vacations with us on the farm. He always treated me well, and I liked him.

On the way back to the base, I tried to get used to how the car was handled. I think it was the biggest car I had ever driven. For a car with an engine that large, you would think it would be a lot faster in acceleration. I drove through the trailer park and looked at the trailers again.

The trailers were small, and there were only a few of them left. Some looked like they were not in use. I stopped in the park for a few minutes, just trying to get some idea of how long it would be before I could move in. While I was daydreaming about how good it was going to be, I remembered that I had a test the next day that I needed to pass. I returned to the barracks and was lucky enough to find a parking space. I spent the rest of my time studying for the test.

Friday was a good day. I woke up early feeling good and made it to the chow hall for breakfast and got to class a little early. I talked to the instructor and told him about getting the car and thanked him for his help. The class covered the same material that I had studied the night before, and I was ready for the test. That was the first time I felt that good about any test.

After I finished the test, I called the housing unit for an update on the unit I was waiting for. More good news. They had a unit, and I should get it before the end of the next week. I do not remember what the total deposit was going to be, but I was not expecting to have to post a twenty-five-dollar cleaning deposit. Well, that would be more money I would have to find. At least I would get home this time with good news. Boy, it was nice riding in my own car instead of having to hitchhike.

On this trip, I had made good time getting home. Everyone was glad to hear the good news, but Derlwood, my brother, was more interested in the car. He was a good mechanic, and he really checked it out. Lucille was hoping that I was going to take her with me right then. Having to wait another week was not her first choice. We both knew that taking her to Jacksonville before we had a place to live was not possible.

She agreed to get everything ready for the move by the next weekend, and Mom was going to see what stuff she could let us have. Dad and Derlwood threw in a little money to help us with the move. I think they were getting tired of us being there.

Saturday morning, I took Lucille for a ride in our car, and we did some more shopping. She needed some personal things and some clothing. That evening we all went out to dinner and had a good meal, and it was great just to get out. Sunday morning, before I left to go back to the base, Derlwood took my car to the shop where he worked and changed the oil and greased It up and did not charge me anything. Later when I started back to the base, I noticed that he had also topped off the gas tank. It was hard to get started back to the base because it felt like I was leaving for good. I think it was the disappointment everyone felt because we had to put our plans on hold again.

I had to get back to the base early enough to get my base pass extended before it expired. I stopped at the security office to renew my pass and got into a lot of trouble with the security guard. My current pass did not expire until the next day, and he thought that I should wait until then. I explained that I was hoping to get the car registered the next day, but because I was in school, I was not sure I could get the time off that I needed. That just gave him another reason not to extend the pass. He was just being a jerk, and I was trying not to lose my temper and to stay cool. Another security guard working there just walked over and picked up my paperwork. He stamped the extension, signed it, and wished me good luck with registration. I thanked him and left the security office.

When I got back to the barracks parking lot, I learned something new about owning a car, it did not come with a parking spot. I knew that I could only park in authorized spots, or they would ticket and tow your vehicle, and you could lose your base pass.

I started driving around the area and found a spot over at the school administration building, and I took it and walked back to the barracks. The next morning, I went to school early again and met with the instructor and asked him if I could get time off to register my car.

I could tell that he was getting tired of me needing something personal, but he told me to get a request form from the office and fill it out. I got the form, and he signed it and told me how to find the closest DMV office and to come straight back. I had no idea how long it would take. To start with, I did not know the area, and I was driving In heavy traffic most of the time.

I found the place, got in line, and worried about how much it was going to cost and if I would have enough money. It took just over an hour to get to the window, and then the clerk must have thought that I had stolen the car because she started asking me questions that I did not have the answers to.

I got really embarrassed and nervous, and I'm sure that made her more suspicious. She went to her supervisor to help her out, and he asked a lot more questions that I could not answer. Then he looked me in the eyes and asked if I had purchased the car. I said "No" and that someone had bought it for me. Then he asked, "Did he get you a signed copy of the title." Then I realized that I had left it in the glove box.

I had not used it to get the visitor's pass because it was in my name. I ran back to the car and got it. It was signed correctly, and I got my new registration. I got back to the base security office and got my permanent base sticker and made the first class after lunch.

Tuesday, I called the base housing office and learned that a unit was going to be ready the next day, and I would have to meet with an inspector at 1 PM to confirm the inspection and get the keys. That made me happy, but I knew that it would not go over very well with the instructor. The material we were studying was new, and I was not going to be ready for that test on Friday. I had to pass that test, so I spent every minute studying.

Thursday morning, I put on my best work uniform and shined my shoes, and was in my seat when the instructor came in. I had the request form filled out, and very respectfully, I presented it to him. I was not still in boot camp, but this was still military, and this guy was my supervisor, and I sure did not dare get on his bad side. He signed the paper and said you better pass your test. I made the appointment and got the keys and made it back for the last class.

On Friday, I passed my test and returned home. Lucille had everything packed and ready to go. We nearly left late that night, but Mom and Dad convinced us to wait until the next morning to set off. We were up and, on our way, early the following morning. By noon, we were having lunch in the trailer, our new home.

The trailer had been cleaned before it was released to us, but we recleaned everything. I went to the barracks and cleaned out my locker of all my personal things. I would have to file for a living off-base status which would give me a few more dollars, but it would cost me my chow pass and my bunk in the barracks. On my duty nights, I would have a bunk to use if I needed one.

Monday morning, I learned a new lesson: the traffic at the main gate was very congested between 7 and 8 AM. I spent so much time in bumper-to-bumper traffic that I was almost late for class. That car seemed to burn more gas just idling than it did going down the road. Getting off the base was also a problem. The next morning, I left home at 6.30 AM and was at school at 7. AM. This gave me an extra hour to study before class, and I had no problem finding a parking spot.

Living in the small trailer was not the best living conditions, but we were happy. We had to stretch our money as far as it would go, but I had a lot more time to study. There was no television, but we did have a small cheap radio. For the most part, we just tried to stay cool during the day and took walks after it cooled off in the afternoon. The trailer park was located close to the end of the runway for the base. At first, the noise of the planes landing and taking off was a problem, but we soon got used to it.

Our next big surprise was when Lucille realized she was pregnant. We had not planned on that, but we were close to the base, and her medical requirements were free. There was also a bus service that came within walking distance of the trailer park and went onto the base. It was for the military and dependents, and it went by the infirmary, commissary, and base exchange. Lucille could not drive, so using the car was not an option.

By the time we got a due date for the baby, I realized that I would be out of school before then. That meant we would be transferred to a new base during the late part of her pregnancy, and we would lose the base housing. That was not a good thing, so I had to figure out how we would manage that. I was doing good in school now and in the last part of my training. The last part of the school was what they called "Hands-on troubleshooting the aircraft electrical systems," and in this part, you get to work more one-on-one with the instructors. During this time, I started trying to find a way to stay at the Jacksonville base so I would not lose my base housing.

When each class graduates, the Navy will send the same number of duty assignments as there are students to fill them. The list will be posted about two weeks before the graduation date, and each student will be able to request their choice wish. Prior to the posting of the list, no one knows what duty assignments there will be. By the time we graduated, and the list came out, all the instructors knew what my situation was.

There was one billet for a unit called VF-43, and it was located at NAS Jacksonville, Florida. That was just across the base from where the school was. I went to the office to get my request form, and I talked to one of the senior instructors about the billet and my chances of getting it. Without making eye contact with me, he said, "Maybe you should not request anything and just wait and see what happens." I was surprised at what he said, but I got the message to keep quiet about everything. Then later, I heard someone who was trying to get the VF-43 assignment say that it was no longer available. When the assignment list came out, I was assigned to VF-43.

# Chapter 25

# VF-43

Upon graduating from AE-A school, I was transferred to VF-43, a Navy Fighter squadron which was located on the same base as the training center. This was a lucky break for me. I got to remain in the base housing unit, and the distance from work to home was about the same. Lucille kept the same doctors. All I had to do was to check out of the Training Center and into the operations part of the base and my new squadron, VF-43, the Fighting Falcons. I also had a new promotion to pay grade E-3. I was now an AEAN which stood for Aviation Electrician's mate Airman class. It was no big deal, but it meant that I got a small raise in pay.

VF-43 was in the process of changing the type of aircraft they were flying. They had been flying propeller-driven aircraft called the Corsair. Now, they were transitioning to the newer jet type, known as the Grumman F9f-8 Cougar Jet.

This transition took about 24 months. Throughout this period, the squadron gradually phased out the old Corsair planes and received the new Cougar Jets. All pilots and maintenance support personnel had to be assigned to and trained for the new aircraft. The entire unit was given 24 months to complete this transition and be ready for duty. During this time, the squadron remained on shore duty, which meant they were not deployed to sea or overseas for assignments.

My first assignment with the squadron was general maintenance which meant you would be used to fill in anywhere needed, which included mess cooking and compartment cleaning. Mess cooking was by far the most undesired job.

All operating units assigned to NAS had to provide help to the station personnel to operate the mess hall and barracks. When I checked in to the training center, one person in the group had to pull Mess Hall duty, and I missed the assignment because I was first on the list and was picked to be the leader.

My first week with the unit I was assigned to maintenance, which included cleanup. The second week the squadron had to send someone to mess cooking and to do compartment cleaning. Because I was married and living off base, they decided to put me in compartment cleaning for two months.

This was a temporary assignment, and it worked out well for me. The Navy had a home study program you could get for free, and through their program, you could earn all the continuing education credits required for your next promotion qualifications.

I signed up for it and had a lot of time to work on it both on the job and at home. I was enjoying the assignment, but after about six weeks, they transferred me back to the squadron. I was assigned the duty of operating the ground power units for starting the aircraft. The mobile power units were Jeeps with a portable power generating system built on the rear part of the Jeep. It was called an NC-5 unit.

I would drive it to where the aircraft was parked, back it up to the aircraft, plug the power cable into the aircraft, and when the pilot was ready, bring the generating system up to speed and turn on the power. It was tiring work because the power cable was large and heavy, and you had to hook up to all the different aircraft.

Things at the trailer park were going great. Lucille was doing great, and each day, we had some time to enjoy together. I always left the house at 6.30 each morning and was at work by seven. This worked out well because that meant I could get the morning preflight done on all the aircraft before the pilots were ready to fly. My boss had let me change my hours, so I got off an hour earlier every day, and that let me miss the heavy traffic both ways.

One morning I got up and did not feel good, but I went to work anyway. While I was trying to finish the preflight work, I got a call to go see the maintenance chief. Every morning at 8 AM, we all had to fall in for muster. (The military term for roll call and daily inspection) If I had aircraft to service, I was excused from muster. I thought it was because I had missed roll call, but by the time I got to where the chief was, my stomach was going crazy.

Instead of reporting to him, I turned and ran to the bathroom. A younger chief petty officer chased after me yelling orders for me to stop. By the time I got to the stall in the bathroom, I was vomiting my stomach out all over the place. Someone was still yelling at me to report back to where I was told to go.

Then the maintenance chief told the other guy, "Can't you see he is sick." The maintenance Chief stayed there and helped me get stable. Then he took me straight to the infirmary at the sick bay. I had a bad case of food poisoning.

I thought of Lucille and her condition. We had eaten the same thing, and I did not think she could survive what I just went through. The chief took me back to the hangar and sent me home to check on her and to recover. I had no way to contact her except to go to where she was. All the way, I was afraid of what I might find when I got home. I jerked the front door open, and she was ok. She was cleaning up the trailer and was happy as a lark. Whatever it was that made me sick had no effect on her.

Working on the aircraft at VF-43 was a great experience. My first assignment after I got there was running the NC-5 Power units. I was taking the home study courses that the Navy provided, and they gave me more information on how to troubleshoot and make repairs. So, the work and study went hand and hand.

The pilots were working just as hard to learn the aircraft and its different systems, so you got to know your pilots, and they got to know and depend on you. Some of the pilots were great people who liked to play jokes with each other.

Shortly after I got started working the line where the pilots hung out between flights, I watched two of the pilots kidding each other about which one was the best at being able to get lost from another pilot while flying and which one was best at finding the other pilot. One of the pilots kept looking at the weather, and we had a low overcast but good ground visibility. One of them bet the other one that with just the length of the runway for a head start that the other guy could not catch him within thirty minutes.

Well, the challenge was on, and some money bet. The rules were that they would both take their planes to the end of the runway, and the chase plane could not start rolling down the runway until the first plane got off the ground.

I operated the NC-5 to initiate aircraft start-up while additional ground personnel assisted in maneuvering the planes onto the taxiway. The pilots took the planes to the end of the runway and aligned them up. The first pilot got as much speed as possible and then pulled his plane straight up. The second plane followed as fast as he could, but by the time he was leaving the runway, the first plane had already gone out of sight in the overcast.

Almost as soon as the chase plane got into the overcast, the first plane dropped out of the overcast over the end of the runway. He made a normal landing and taxied back to the Line. By the time the chase plane gave up the chase and got back to the line, the first pilot had already showered, changed clothes, and was waiting to collect his bet.

The pilots had to learn all types of flying skills and combat tactics. I remember hearing the pilots talking about their low-level flying over Jacksonville Beach so they could watch the sunbathers. I remember that sometimes when they returned for some of their low-level training, we would find grass in the engine intake screens. One time I found some leaves and tips of limbs in the intake. On that same flight, the plane captain found scratch marks in the polish on the underside of the wing. I don't recall ever finding any physical damage to any of the planes.

One of our young pilots, Ensign Conrad, had a bit of a daring streak. He had a girlfriend residing in South Georgia, merely a few miles away from Jacksonville, on her father's farm. Ensign Conrad would take his designated aircraft and perform a low pass near her house to indicate when he was about to take off, giving her the signal to come and meet him.

Despite her being of legal age (over 21), her father held a strong disapproval of Conrad. This did not deter them, as they had developed an effective signaling system. However, during one of his flights to signal her, it appeared that no one was present at the house. He buzzed the house a couple of times, and no one came out. Then he made a good low run that would almost suck the roof off the house, and still no one came out.

Conrad thought that they must have gone to town, so he flew over the small town looking for her father's truck; not having any luck there, he came back to the farm to get a better look for their truck.

This time his girlfriend, her father, and her mother came out of the house together. Conrad made the mistake of thinking they were no longer mad at him and put on a little air show for them, and they waved back at him. As soon as he returned to the base, he had a message to report to the Fleet Air Detachment Duty Officer (FADDO), which was the administrative supervisor and support service for our air group.

Someone had told the father of Conrad's girlfriend how to look for the number on the aircraft that identified the aircraft and the military command it belonged to. He filed a complaint against Conrad, and he got grounded for two weeks.

The Air Force had a special command called the Strategic Air Command, SAC for short. Their job was to locate targets that posed a threat to the country and destroy them with bombs. The job of the fighter groups is to stop them from bombing your area. They conduct training drills with the fighter unit so they both get the training they need. They will schedule an air raid, and the fighter unit will try to stop them.

No shots were fired, or bombs dropped. Fighter groups were supposed to fly their planes between the bombers and the target before they got in position to drop their bombs. That simulates air-to-air engagement. Well, we knew they were planning an exercise, and we were planning to intercept them. On the day the exercise was scheduled, they flew over the target before our pilots even got dressed. That was certainly a major embarrassment. SAC was very well trained and almost always won those Exercises.

Lucille was getting late into her pregnancy, and everything was going well. She was active and always doing her work around the trailer. One evening when I was home from work, she had washed all the laundry and was hanging it out on the clothes line.

We were going to have dinner with Uncle Hershel and Aunt Vivian. Lucille was happy that she didn't have to cook, and she really liked them. We had a nice visit, and after dinner, Aunt Vivian turned to me and said, "You get this girl home and get her bag packed. She is going to have that baby tonight."

I asked what made her think that. She explained that it was the way she looked, all the energy she had, and the amount of dinner she had eaten. Lucille laughed at her and said that she was fine. We stayed a little longer before going home. Lucille had already packed her bag but was not concerned about it. At about 3 AM, we were on our way to the hospital.

They admitted her into the hospital, but it would be a few hours before the baby would be born, and they showed me the waiting room. At 7 AM, I checked on her, and she was resting in her room, so I went to the Squadron to let them know and get some time off. I returned to the hospital shortly after 8 AM, and to my surprise, my mother was there. I don't remember just how she found out or how she got there, but I was glad to see her.

I had always thought of the baby as a boy and Lucille, and I had picked out the name for a boy. While Mom and I were waiting, Mom kept telling me that it might be a girl. I had always kidded with Mom about things, and I told her that I had not ordered a girl, so it would have to be a boy.

Mom was getting more upset with my kidding her about the baby. Then the nurse came into the waiting room and called me and said you have a baby girl. I was just delighted that she was ok, but Mom kept trying to make sure I was going to be ok with a girl. There was no one in the room with us at that time, and I could not resist picking at Mom a little more, so I said, "Maybe I can find someone with a boy and make a trade." My mother got so mad at me that I thought she was going to chase me out of the hospital.

After Pat was born, things went great, she was healthy, and Lucille did not have any complications, I was back to work in no time. I was trying to learn every electrical system in the aircraft. Most of the systems had been covered in AE school, and some in the home study material I was studying. Our planes were new, and there were a few systems that were new; however, I could not find good information on them.

One of the systems was the fuel capacity system. It was a new type of system for measuring the amount of fuel remaining in the fuel tanks and calculating how much remaining flight time the pilot would have. It was a complicated system based on a new concept of reading and calculating the remaining fuel. It was called the Capacitron system, I am not sure of the correct spelling, but instead of using old mechanical units, it used a capacitor-type sending unit. This system required special test and calibration equipment.

All aircraft have preventative-type maintenance schedules based on hours of flight time. Every aircraft's schedule can be different depending on the manufacturer's requirements, but every aircraft has one, and it is to be strictly followed. I was working my way down the inspection list, and when I came to the fuel system, I was stumped. There was a requirement to test and calibrate the system but no instructions on how to accomplish it. The only instructions were to see the manufacturer's recommendations and the name of the test equipment to use.

I put that on the list of things to do and moved on through the checklist. Next, I started asking the other guys in the shop about how to check and calibrate the system. No one knew how to do it. One of the senior people said that it was done at the manufacturer. Somehow that did not sound right to me. I learned the FADDO controlled the test equipment, and I could check with them.

A few days later, I had a weekend duty and some time on my hands, so I contacted the test equipment section of FADDO, and he gave me his name and said he would show me the tester and how to use it. He suggested that I come on a weekend because that was when he would have the time to spend with me.

The next day I went to the test equipment unit to find him. Because of it being a weekend, there were not many people there. I found the equipment check-out office, and there was a chief petty officer by the name of Baker there. I explained that I had an appointment with someone who was going to show me how to use the test equipment for the fuel system.

Chief Baker was very nice and told me that because it was a slow day, he had let the person that I came to see off for the rest of the day, but he would be glad to help me. This new equipment was still classified. He checked to make sure that I was qualified to work with the test equipment and took me into the check-out room where the equipment was.

He checked the equipment checkout list to see if anyone from VP-43 had checked it out. There was no one listed from the squadron on the list. He showed me the equipment and how to operate it. But I really needed to operate it on a real system to understand it.

I asked my shop supervisor if I could be trained on it. He gave me the brush off and was told that it was about my pay grade. I was the junior person in the shop, so I just let it go.

During the next few weeks, everyone at the squadron was busy getting the pilots ready for aerial gunnery practice. All fighter pilots have to learn how to fly and shoot at the same time. Before you can do live fire with the aircraft, there is a lot of training without ammunition.

We were busy with that training when something happened. One day while I was working on one of the aircraft in the hangar, someone brought me a message to report to the Executive officer's office. I had no idea what it was about, but normally, anytime you get ordered to that office, you are in trouble.

I went straight to the office, and when told to enter, I saw my division offer, the XO, and sitting behind the door that I opened was Chief Baker. I spoke to him, and then I turned and came to attention. After being told to stand at ease, the XO asked if he knew the chief, and I said yes sir, he helped me with some test equipment. Then the XO told me to explain what I had just said, and I explained it and was asked which piece of test equipment that was, and I said the Capacitron tester and calibration unit. With that, I was dismissed, and as I turned to leave, I noticed that Chief Baker was holding the equipment logbook for the test equipment room.

I did not know what happened, but I could tell that someone was in trouble. A short time later, Chief Baker walked over to where I was, and he was smiling. He greeted me and said thanks. I asked him what was going on, and he explained that the XO had called him and was very upset because he had not provided us with proper support equipment for our aircraft.

One of our aircraft made a normal landing, then ran out of fuel and flamed out (the term for a jet engine shutting down) on the runway with a fuel gauge that showed 18 minutes of fuel remaining. Someone had told the XO that FADDO did not have the required test equipment.

He had brought the test equipment check-out log to show that the equipment was available. The logbook showed that I was the person from VP-43 that had requested the unit. The XO had called me to verify his story. Little did I know at the time that we would meet again, and he would return the favor. As a result of what happened, all our aircraft were grounded until they were tested and calibrated.

Shortly after the incident with the plane running out of fuel, I completed my requirements for promotion and got my advancement to Petty Officer Third Class, Paygrade E-4. I don't know who or how much punishment they got, but no one bothered me.

We completed the practice training and got ready for the live ammunition training. That training required a special area where the pilots could shoot, and no one was in danger. The training area we got was Guantanamo, Cuba. We were to deploy for two weeks for the training.

Lucille decided to go back home with our baby, where she would have help if she needed it. We all got some time off to make our arrangements to deploy, and I took them home.

We had made the arrangements with the Naval base at GITMO for some of the equipment that we would need and had shipped the rest. We were to fly to the Leeward point side of the GITMO Naval base, where gunnery training would be conducted. This was in the year 1955, and that was before Castro took control of Cuba.

## Chapter 26

# GITMO

The flight from Jacksonville to GITMO Cuba was much better than my flight From Norman, Oklahoma, to Jacksonville. There were more of us on the plane, which was larger and more comfortable.

We arrived at the main base at Gitmo and then had to take the ferry across the bay to Leeward Point which was set up for fighter squadrons to train in live Ariel gunnery. There were no special comforts on the point, just the essential requirements.

We had barracks to house the crew and a BOQ for the officers. There was a small hanger for working on the aircraft and a chow hall. For recreation, there was an open-air beer garden with a loud jukebox and a Cuban Beer called Hatuey. The beer had a profile picture of an Indian on the label, so you could only see one eye. We referred to him as the one-eyed Indian.

The beer was not a good beer. When you drank it, sometimes it would be like drinking water, but the next time it would knock your hat off. We used to joke that when the Indian winked at you, you best quit drinking right then.

There was also an outdoor movie screen set up so we could watch movies. But the projector was the only thing that had a roof over it. It rained almost every night.

We were here to work, and work we did. We started early and worked late every day. The pilots not only had to learn how to fly and shoot, but they also had to qualify. To accomplish this, they had to shoot at a flying target. That required that we build some 8-by-24-foot banners that could be towed by an aircraft.

The banner was made from a nylon screen-type material that was either white or silver in color. Each banner required a metal rod that was 8 feet long and strong enough to support weight and stress on the banner caused by the flight maneuvers.

The plane assigned to tow the target had to have the tailhook removed and a special hookup for the cable installed that would pull the target. The cable had to be long enough to keep the target a safe distance behind the plane. You would have to lay the target out straight on the runway and fold up the cable so it would not tangle when pulled by the plane.

The plane would get in the takeoff position, and we hook to cable to the special hookup. The plane would drag the cable and target down the runway and lift off the ground while pulling the target up with him. At the end of the flight, the plane would line up with the runway and fly low, then release the target from the plane. We would have to chase the target and retrieve it from the runway so the planes could land.

Each shop would have to help the other shops with their work during the rush times. It took a lot of work on everybody's part to get the training done. The ordinance shop had the biggest workload. They had to handle all the requirements for live ammo, which started with getting the ammo safely to the ammo prep building. Here it had to be transferred to containers and shipped to where it could be inspected. Then it had to be belted. Each plane had to have 100 rounds, and it had to have the projectors painted the correct color for that plane.

This task had to be finished right before the flight because the paint would dry, and it had to still be wet when used. All the pilots would shoot at the same target. Each plane had a different color bullet, and when they hit the target, they would leave a hole with the color of the bullet. That way, you could count the number of hits by each pilot.

At the end of each flight, the pilots could review the banners to see how they did. Some days they would make four training flights in a day. On bad weather days, if the pilots could find an area that had a satisfactory spot, they would take off and fly to the spot and run their training. The training program required maximum team effort on everybody's part.

You got to know each pilot and how they were doing, and you gave them all the encouragement you could. When they had a bad day, you felt it also, when they had a good day, you shared the excitement. This was the first time the pilots had flown aerial gunnery training in this plane, and for most of them, it was their first time to fly aerial gunnery.

Leeward Point was set up for the older propeller-driven aircraft, and the runway was a little shorter than the length normally used by jets. We had the F9F cougar jets, and they were a small sweptwing type and did not require the longer runways to be able to land and take off.

Leeward Point was like an island with a point at one end. The runway started on the tip of the point and ran parallel to the beach. At the end of the runway was a large sign that had the word WHEELS painted on it in large letters. That was to remind the pilots when they were coming for a landing to be sure and check their landing gear.

For our safety, we operated more like an aircraft carrier and posted a landing signal officer on the end of the runway with the signal flags. The point had a good elevation above sea level, and the water was very deep in that part of the island. Working on the end of the runway, in some ways, felt like being on a carrier deck.

Flying aerial gunnery off that runway also required that one person be posted there to hook up and retrieve the target banners. So, two people were always stationed at that position during gunnery operations. There were no shady areas to rest in, but the sign was a large sign that was set to slope back at the top to provide a better view for the pilots. It also provided a small amount of shade, but it was on the blind side of the approaching planes.

We took some old parachute material and made a home-made hammock to use when we had no traffic. The ordinance person assigned to hook up and retrieve the targets got the most use of it. One day I was assigned as the signal officer, and Freddie Bowman from the ordinance shop was handling the targets. I saw the plane pulling the target that made his approach for landing, and he was too low and off course.

I yelled for Freddie, "Watch Out! He is too low." I signaled the pilot that he was too low, but he was closing in too fast. He was off to my right side of the runway and drifting across to my left. The best path to safety was to veer to the right and avoid the trajectory of the target. I kept my eyes on the target and passed just beneath it. The target collided with the sign, ripping off the section where the "W" was painted, transforming it to read "HEELS." When I shouted to Freddie, he reacted promptly, swiftly moving away from the sign and successfully clearing it in time.

At the time all this was going on, the Duty Officer was in the control room watching. From his point of view, it looked like the target had hit me. When the target hit the sign, things flew everywhere. He sent everything he had to help us, including an ambulance for me. Nobody was hurt, and the plane also survived just fine. I never saw what the target looked like after hitting the sign. All I had to do was pick up the pieces of the sign and clear the runway.

Just before we finished our training, we got to go to Guantanamo City on Liberty. We were the first group to be allowed off the base since Fulgencio Batista restricted the military for some type of embarrassment caused by a military group before us. This was in 1955, before Fidel Castro took over Cuba.

Any time the military allows a group of its people to temporarily visit a populated area like a city, they form a Shore Patrol to send with them to keep them under control. The number of people to act as shore patrol is determined by the size of the group. When the group consists of multiple commands, each command must provide some people based on the size of the group. VP-43 was a small group, and I was the only one assigned from our squadron. At that time, I was a young skinny kid that had no idea what he was getting into. Thank God that I was assigned to work with someone who was older, more intelligent, and I should note, larger in stature.

The trip to Guantanamo was something else. I had to take the ferry across the bay to join the rest of the group that was going. Then we took a long boat ride up the river to a place called the barn. I would estimate that it was halfway between the base and the city. There we switched from the river boats to an old narrow gage train for the last part of the trip into the city. There was a large floating dock for the boats to offload everybody and a large building that looked like a barn for us to wait for the train. It was a beer garden with a limited amount of food. You might say the party started there.

The train was an old narrow gage steam locomotive that looked like something right out of an old western movie. The ride was anything but smooth. When we were going down the track, the cars rocked back and forth so much it would make a sailor seasick.

When we got to the depot and opened the flood gates, all the liberty group headed for the closest bar that was not already overfilled. The officer in charge of the Shore Patrol unit called us all together and paired us up. I was lucky the partner I got was an older person with a lot of experience working as a Shore Patrol. He was a family man and always used the Shore Patrol assignments as a free way of getting to go places and see things that he could not afford otherwise.

My partner was explaining things to me, and we went into a nicer-looking place to sit down and get something to drink when we got our first problem. As my partner was explaining how to watch for trouble, he spotted it. A sailor was sitting with a girl and buying her drinks, and a civilian was slowly circling their table with an angered look. He was also keeping one hand out of sight.

My partner moved between the table and the civilian. With an almost unseen and short flip of his nightstick, he caused the guy to drop the switchblade knife, it was open, and my partner stepped on the blade and picked it up by the handle, breaking the blade. He then calmly handed it back to the civilian and said, "I think you dropped this."

The girl at the table got up and got the guy out of there. I don't think the sailor ever knew what happened. We stayed there for a little while and did not have any more problems there. Most everything else was just small arguments and not a problem.

I only had two more situations to deal with while I was there. The first one was when we were trying to get everyone back to the train to go home. We saw a group of civilians surrounding five sailors and yelling at them. We got to the crowd and had to work our way inside the group to find out what it was about.

The tallest of the sailors was trying to hide three-quart bottles of whisky under his uniform jumper. All were different but good brands. One of the civilians was the liquor store owner, and he said they had not paid for the liquor and wanted them to return it to him. Several of the Civilians were confirming the store owner's statement. The owner showed us the cash register list showing the charges. The sailors did not remember for sure what they paid for it.

The crowd was getting larger, and the sailors were too drunk to realize that they were not going to get in that crowd with the whisky. If they did get it out, they could not take the whiskey back with them.

The train was loading by the time we had to get them on the train. The sailors refused to give it back, and the Civilians refused to let them go without paying. My partner got close enough to the guy hiding the whiskey to touch his jumper and told him that he could not carry it back with him anyway and tried to get him to give it up. The sailor refused and tried to fight with my partner, and he hit one of the bottles and broke it under the sailor's jumper. The sailor dropped the remaining two bottles, and the crowd grabbed them. Everybody left without any more trouble.

Oh yes, I said I said there were two. The last one was at the train station. We were running out of time to get everyone on the train. The largest of the Shore Patrol was grabbing the drunks and throwing them into the train box car. I was helping to push the drunks up to where the big guys could grab them, and a very large cook did not see my armband and picked me up and threw me into the box car. As he was doing so, he saw the armband, and then he reached in and pulled me back out and apologized.

The only other issue I remember occurred when someone was assisting a drunken individual from the dock onto the boat. Unfortunately, the drunk person fell between the dock and the boat, ending up in the water. Although they got wet, fortunately, no injuries were sustained. The following day, I heard that some individuals were mistakenly sent to the wrong ship on Sunday, despite it being a no-fly day after the liberty party. Certain planes required minor maintenance work, and additional ordinances had to be set up, but on the whole, it was a relatively light workday.

However, Monday marked a return to a heavy workload for both the pilots and the ground crew. By the end of the first week, the pilots began to exhibit improvements in their accuracy, hitting the targets, but they were still far from qualifying. In the initial flights, not every pilot managed to hit the target, but by week's end, all pilots were registering some hits. Each pilot consistently used projectiles of the same color during every flight. After laying out the targets at the end of the flight, we were able to assess each pilot's performance. Our fondness for all the pilots grew, and we always aimed to provide them with encouragement or congratulations.

Over the last days of this training period, all the pilots were improving their gunnery scores, some more than others. Two of the pilots showed some real promise. For the squadron to qualify for deployment as part of the Air Group, all of the pilots would have to qualify. So, we knew that we would have to come back for additional training.

The squadron was in a two-year retraining period because of getting new aircraft and personnel. Aerial Gunnery was only one of the many things we had to qualify for to be able to deploy with an air group. We still had just over one year to complete all our qualifications and get our ORI, Operational Readiness Inspection.

As we closed up our operations for this training session, we were tired from the exhausting pace of the work but pleased at what we had accomplished and looking forward to getting back home. We made the necessary arrangements to ship all our equipment, and we got on a plane and flew back to NAS Jacksonville.

After returning home from the first Aerial Gunnery training, we started preparing for our next major project, to get prepared for our Operational Readiness Training for operating from an Aircraft Carrier.

Our unit, VF-43, had just switched over to a new type of Aircraft and gotten all new pilots. All but three of them were young Ensigns fresh out of Flight School. Our Commanding Officer held the rank of a US Navy Commander, our Executive Officer was a Lieutenant Commander, and our Operations Officer held the rank of a US Navy Lieutenant. They were the only experienced officers in the unit when it started with the new aircraft. The unit was in a two-year transition period when I got assigned to it.

We were now in the last phases of the Transition period. All our pilots were qualified to fly the new planes but in Carrier operations and some other special operations that were required of a Fighter Squadron.

Before we could be fully qualified, we had to complete the required carrier take-off and landings training, more Aerial Gunnery, and then successfully complete the Operational Ready Inspection, called the ORI.

Our Aerial Gunnery training was initially scheduled for two training sessions, so we had to return to Gitmo for Aerial Gunnery training, but first, the pilots had to complete the carrier landing and take-off training. They also had other special flight training that would also sharpen their flying skills.

Every part of the squadron had made special plans to be ready to operate from a carrier. The main problem was about the small amount of room that would be available to the Squadron on the carrier. This restricted everything that you could bring on board the carrier. This included the number of planes and personnel. You had to select your best aircraft and trained personnel.

We had extra personnel in the squadron and in my shop. Some of the people wanted to make the cruise, and others did not. The choice would not be made until just before we boarded the carrier, so we didn't worry about that.

I had reached the point where I could reenlist early if I wanted to. The advantages were the reenlistment bonus, and it would help you to qualify for special training programs that required you to have the obligated time you needed to qualify. I was making plans to get as much school as possible and to go to college when I could.

I was still living in the base housing trailer and wanted my own house or house trailer. So, I reenlisted for six years. I was having good luck in the Navy, and I was enjoying it. I had completed Class A school which qualified me to be an Aircraft Electrician, and I wanted to go to Class B school.

It was basically a one-year advanced Electrical school. I had the basic qualification but needed a waiver on time in grade to fully qualify, but I could request that through the Personnel Division.

I found a good deal on a new twenty-nine-foot Buckeye house trailer and purchased it. There was a small private trailer court in the same area as where I was living, I rented a spot there and moved in. I kept the same car I had and was able to buy the things we needed for the trailer.

Lucille and I took the baby and went for a visit back to the farm to share our good news with the family. I was the only one in our family to consider a career in the military.

I got a big surprise from Dad. He had made plans for me and my family to move back on the farm when I got out of the Navy. Our neighbor, Evy Osteen, was retiring from farming and moving out of his house on his farm to a new house he was building by the main road. Dad wanted to lease his farm and move me into his old house, and then we would share both farms.

He never considered that I might have other plans. I did not want to move back to the farm. Especially the same one where my last crop had been beaten into the ground by hail. That did not turn out to be a good trip.

The pilots started their carrier landing and takeoff practices at a small military base in the Jacksonville area named Mayport. It had a training area with runways where the pilots could practice their approaches, landings, and take-offs. The runways were painted to look like a carrier deck.

On the carrier, there is a large cable that runs across the deck to catch the tailhook on the plane to stop it. The trick to a carrier landing is to get the tailhook to touch the ground just before it reaches that cable so the cable will be able to stop the plane before it runs off the edge of the ship; however, if the cable fails to catch the tailhook, you had to be able to take off again.

On the carriers, that all happened in a very short distance, so you had to have full power on the plane to keep the plane flying. Two problems:

first, you need to slow down the plane and allow it to touch down before the tailhook reaches the cable. Then, you must quickly return to full power in case the hook misses the cable.

The second problem is there's a slight delay for the engine to reach full power. To accomplish this, the pilot must learn when to pull the power off the engine so that the plane will drop at just the correct spot for the hook to catch the cable and reapply the power to full throttle. The key lies in timing.

During your approach, you decrease the power, allowing the plane to descend for landing. Right before it touches down, you ramp up to maximum power. The time delay to reach maximum power is shorter for a reciprocating engine compared to a jet engine. In our case, we were using jets, so power needed to be applied earlier.

The runways had a painted line to represent the tailhook cable and a line to represent what would have been the edge of the ship. During the training exercises, the pilots would make their approach, touch down and take off, do a fly-around, and then repeat everything. The observers on the ground would watch his approach, landing, and take off and communicate with the pilot with radios about how he was doing on each fly-by. This would give the pilot live time updates on any corrections he needed to make. Carrier landing is only one of the flying skills that the pilots had to learn, but each skill helped them improve their overall aircraft handling ability.

After a few weeks of special training, we packed up and headed back to Gitmo for more aerial gunnery training. This time we did things a little better. Now we had a better idea of what we needed. Somehow our pilots got a

twin-engine Beechcroft aircraft plane to take with us. It was similar to the one in the photograph.

With this plane, we made liberty runs in some of the larger cities in Cuba. Three times a week, they would fly four of us to a city for a twenty-four-hour liberty run and pick us up the next day.

The aerial gunnery training was about the same, except the pilots did a lot better on their shooting scores. It appears that the special flight training had helped them to line up with their targets better.

It did not take long for all of the pilots to qualify, and two of them did exceptionally well. I remember that one of them got 98 hits out of 100 bullets. Our CO was kidding him and asked what he had done with the other two bullets and came right back with, "I shot a seagull."

As we finished up at Gitmo and made ready to return home, we were very proud of our guys and how much they had improved. We felt like we had the best pilots in the fleet.

Shortly after we returned to Jacksonville, our two top-scoring pilots were selected to go to the National Aerial Gunnery Competition on the West Coast (Now Called Top Gun). But on the way out, a tragedy struck. We sent the two young Ensigns with our Operations Supervisor, Lieutenant Lake.

Lieutenant Lake, who was an older and more seasoned officer and highly respected by everyone, was killed when his plane crashed while in route to the West Coast. The group encountered a severe thunderstorm and tried to fly over it. The two younger pilots successfully navigated through the storm, but LT Lake's plane crashed, resulting in his death. I recall hearing that the other two pilots made it safely, but I have no recollection of how they performed in the competition.

By the time we got back home, we had to start thinking about the upcoming cruise. We still had a lot of things to do to get ready, and we still had too many people to take on board the ship. I was hoping that I would be one of the people left behind.

Normally deploying squadrons leave a small detachment back at the home base to take care of equipment left at the base and do any support work that might be required. Normally it would only be one or two people; everyone else would be transferred to another unit. But that decision would not come until just before we left.

I still wanted to request a waiver for Class B school, so I contacted one of our personnel clerks and requested his help. He promised to look into it and complete the required forms.

After a couple of weeks, I walked into my shop one day, and the clerk was talking with a couple of people in the shop. One of the people he was talking to was David Corbin. Corbin and I were both of the same rank. We got assigned to the shop at about the same time as AEANs and got promoted to AE3s at the same time.

The clerk was trying to get Corbin to volunteer for an assignment that sounded like some type of joke. Somebody was always trying to pull a joke on someone. I did not catch the whole story, but it had something to do with going to an Air Force Command for a tour of duty. Thinking it was just a joke, I decided to play along with it and said, "Sign me up, coach, I don't smoke." That statement was always used to respond to a common joke in those days. With that comment, I walked out of the shop and did not think about it anymore.

After a couple of weeks had passed, the squadron was nearly prepared for their upcoming cruise. However, I had not seen the list of personnel going on the cruise, and there had been no follow-up regarding my request for a waiver for B school.

Frustrated by this, I decided to visit the personnel office to inquire about it. Upon entering the office, I approached the clerk and inquired about the status of my waiver request. He gave me an odd look and asked, 'What request?'

I reminded him about the waiver and felt a tinge of annoyance that he hadn't taken any action on it. He seemed puzzled, and in response to my question, he asked "Why are you here" he said, "You were supposed to be at McGuire Air Force Base." He retrieved my personnel file from the cabinets, opened it, and studied it for a moment. Then, he exclaimed, "How did this happen?"

It turned out that all my orders and the necessary check-out forms had been completed but left in my file. The original request had come from a US Navy squadron named VR-6, which was seeking two AE3s for a two-year assignment. Apparently, he had taken my casual comment in the shop as a serious volunteering effort.

He had gone ahead and processed all the paperwork without informing me. As for Corbin, I couldn't recall exactly what happened to him during that time, but I do remember that he was dealing with some kind of emergency. The clerk informed me that I needed to hurry as I was already supposed to have checked in at McGuire.

I was now in a state of shock. I had just walked into the personnel office, kind of bored, thinking that I was probably going on the cruise and needed to get the wife and child situated where they could take care of themselves while I was gone. Then suddenly, I found out that I had been transferred to another command and was already AWOL.

I would need advance pay to make the trip. The personnel clerk got the forms ready for me to take to Disbursing to get advance pay for travel. He was also sending a request to VR-6 for additional time to report in. But I still had a lot of things to get done.

I was going to pull my house trailer with my old Buick and had to buy and install a trailer hitch on the car. I did not have a phone at the trailer where Lucille was, so I could not tell her what was going on until I got home.

I did call the place where I bought the trailer, and they only had one hitch. The one they had was a new type of trailer hitch called the Glide Ride, and it was a little more expensive than I wanted to pay, but they assured me that it would work well on my car with my trailer. They added the cost to my current balance owed on the trailer. They did not have anyone who could install it for me, and it was so heavy I had to have help loading it in the trunk of the car.

By the time I got home that night, I was all checked out from the base and legally enroute to my new duty station. I had left early that morning for a routine day at work, and now I was no longer assigned to that base.

It was getting late, and I had to go to High Springs to get my brother to help me mount the trailer hitch. I also had to let everybody know that I was leaving for two years. Everybody was shocked and tried to help.

We spent the night at Dad's house, and early the next morning, I took the car to the garage where Derlwood worked. He was working for the garage, where we had to work between customers to figure out how to install the hitch. It was a new type and complicated. It had to mount to the rear axle housing and the rear bumper.

The hitch was made so you could adjust the tongue weight of the trailer to the rear axle. Well, we did not know how to adjust the hitch, and it had to have the trailer connected to be adjusted. Once the hitch was installed, the weight of the hitch made the rear of the car ride low. Derlwood jumped up and down on the hitch, and with just his weight, he could cause the suspension to bottom out. Everyone in the shop got a good laugh at my hitch.

We thought that there was no way I could tow the trailer. I had no choice but to take it back to where the trailer was. I trusted the people that I bought the hitch from who had assured me that it would work well on my car with my trailer. Well, about then, I had my doubts.

On the drive back to Jacksonville, I tried to drive carefully, but a couple of times, I felt the suspension bottom out. When I got to our trailer, I backed the car up to it in order to hook it up. It was just a little pasted noon, and I wanted to get on the road. I had to go to Trenton, New Jersey, all I had was a map, and I had never been anywhere near there before, nor had I ever pulled a trailer on the highways.

Lucille worked on getting things inside the trailer ready to travel. A couple of neighbors came over to help. They got everything inside and tied down, including our small Washing Machine. The guy helped me hook up and adjust the trailer hitch, and to my very pleasant surprise, the adjustment worked perfectly. Fully ready to ride, and the car and trailer were level.

It was hot, and we were working on the sandy ground and had sweat and sand all over us. The back seat of the car was fixed up for Lucille and the baby to ride as best as they could. Everything was going great, and I had got my nerve up and wanted to get on the road.

We all got in the car and started it. shifted it into drive, checked everything for the last time, and pressed the accelerator. Nothing happened. The car strained, and I could feel the rear end of the car try to rise up, but the car would not move. I tried forward and backward, and no movement.

The neighbor and I checked everything, including the trailer. He got a jack from his house and jacked up the wheels on both sides of the trailer. They were free and clear. In so much as I had been driving the car and it was fine, it was the last thing we checked.

The brake on the right rear wheel was locked. We had to jack up the car, get under it and adjust the brake shoe. My neighbor was able to get the brake released and tried readjusting the brake. It was now well past midafternoon, and the evening traffic was already building. Late, tired, and sweaty, I got everyone in the car and started it again. This time, everything went smoothly, and I pulled the trailer onto the highway, heading north just before the rush hour traffic started.

Pulling the trailer added some new complications. There was no power brake system, and the old system was not strong enough to efficiently handle the additional weight of the trailer. The trailer had an electrical brake system and it helped but it still required more distance to stop the unit. In heavy traffic it was difficult to maintain a safe distance between you and the vehicle in front of you.

Even though I was tired by the time I got on the road, the stress of the driving conditions kept me awake. It was close to midnight before I had to make a stop to rest. Lucille had the baby in good shape, and she was asleep on the back seat. But Lucille needed a break. I pulled into a gas station to service the car and stretch my legs. I noticed that my headlights did not appear to be working. I checked them and they were very dim. I was parked at the gas pump and had shut off the engine. I knew it would not start without jumping the battery.

While Lucille went looking for the bath facilities and some snacks, I gassed up the car and checked the old 6-Volt battery. The water level was good, it just appeared to be discharged which indicated that the generator was bad.

I contacted the service station attendant for some help. He was a very nice young man, and he had a unit for charging and jump-starting vehicles, but it was midnight and there were no auto parts stores open. He hooked the charger up to the car and started it charging while I took a break and helped Lucille getting the baby ready for bed.

The service station attendant had a friend who worked the midnight shift as the duty tow truck driver for an Auto Salvage yard in the area. We contacted him and he was at the office and had a used generator that would work on my car. He said he would help me replace the generator and he would take my generator as part of the cost if I could get the car over there. He also explained that if he got a call I would have to wait until he was clear. I agreed and we got my car started and drove it to the salvage yard. The guy knew my situation and only charged me five dollars.

I drove to the Washington D. C. area before stopping again. I did not want to drive through that area during rush hour. About 5 PM I found a hardware store with a nice parking lot and contacted the owner about parking my rig there and getting some rest. I told him my situation and he came out to the car and looked us over. He was a nice guy and showed me where I could park close to the building and let me hook up to a water faucet to get fresh water into the trailer. He said, be sure to turn off the spigot and don't leave a mess.

I parked the trailer and hooked up the water hose to the trailer so Lucille could clean up the baby's things that we needed. While she was getting herself and the baby ready to travel, I laid down on the bed and slept until about 7 PM. I remember that it was about 8 PM when we pulled back on the road. The traffic was still heavy, but somehow, we found our route and we just followed the traffic through the city.

Somehow, we made it to McGuire Air Force Base and went looking for a Trailer Park, where I could park the trailer. We found a small town close to the base called Wrightstown. In the center of town was small trailer park with only 4 usable spaces. It was very crowded and looked like it could have one space, and I did not think I could get my trailer in it. I talked with the owner of the trailer park, and he had one space that he kept covered up until he was sure who was trying to rent it. He cleared the space and with his help I got the trailer in the spot.

My top priority was to get checked onto the base and hope that I would not be charged with being late. I disconnected the car from the trailer while the park owner hooked everything up. Lucille and Pat stayed with the trailer and I went to the base and checked in. I was so tired that all I wanted to do was sleep.

This place was a lot different from the other commands I had been in. Here everybody was easy-going and relaxed. Someone came over to me and asked if I was checking in. I said yes and I was all prepared to give him my sad story of why I was late. He checked his papers and said, "Oh, yes, I got a paper that says someone from VF-43 is being transferred to us for duty. Is that you?" I said yes and he said good. Then he said, "You are authorized some time to get settled in, are married and is your family with you?" I said yes and he asked if three days would be enough time. This took me by surprise, and I asked him, when I was supposed to be here? He looked at his paper and said, all it says is that you will be transferred, no reporting time is given. I asked for the three days, and he gave a reporting date, and I left the office.

All the way back to the trailer park my emotions were switching from being relieved that I was not in trouble for being late to being angry that I had risked everything by pushing so hard trying to get there on time. When I got in the trailer, Lucille and the baby were asleep on the bed and all I did was join them.

## Chapter 27

# LIFE AT MCGUIRE

Duty in VR-6 at McGuire Air Force Base was a lot different than duty in VF-43 at Jacksonville. My new squadron, VR-6, was a Military Transport squadron that moved military troops and their dependents. They had the large four engine aircraft called the R6D by the military.

In the 1950s, the government used the military to move troops from one military base to another all around the world. The Navy called their system NATS for Naval Air Transport, and the Air Force called its Operation MATS for Military Air Transport. The Air Force was created after World War I as a new branch of the military called the US Air Force, by changing the name of the Army Air Core to the US Air Force.

While my last squadron was a newly formed operation and was all about getting their new people trained for a new operation, VR-6 was an old squadron just doing its job. Everything was more laid back and easy going. I came into the Duty Office on Tuesday morning just before eight AM and was greeted with a friendly welcome and was asked if I was checking in. I gave him a copy of my orders and said yes, sir.

He looked at my orders, smiled, and said, "Welcome aboard." Then he said, give me a couple of minutes, then offered me a cup of coffee while I was waiting. I was still worried about being late checking in.

After a few minutes, one of the personnel clerks came in and asked if I was the new guy checking in. He had a copy of my orders and a check-in form. He gave his name and said that he had been assigned to help me get checked in. This had never happened in all my military experience before. He asked me some questions and started filling out the check-in form. Next, he stood up and said let's go, and I will show you around.

First, he drove me around the base and gave me a map of the base, and then we went back to the squadron to turn me over to my work supervisor. I was very pleased about the royal treatment, but I had to find out about being late checking in, so I asked him about it. He looked at his papers and said, "All this says is that you will be reporting in, that's all." I was relieved but a little mad about all the worry I had gone through about being late reporting in.

The first few weeks at work went well. The planes were big, and I had a lot of systems to learn, but there were a lot more people to do the work. One of the things about this squadron that I liked was that when you had a difficult job to accomplish, you could also spend more time learning the systems. You could also fly on the planes for test and training flights. They also had a special flight training program that you could qualify for, and it paid you a little extra money called flight pay.

The trailer park that we were in was not working out very well. Everything was much too crowded. I met some other people who were living in a bigger trailer park that offered better living conditions. To get a parking spot there, I had to go on a waiting list. It was getting late in the fall before I got moved into the new trailer park. The park and the neighbors were very nice.

The weather was getting colder, and I had a fuel heater in the trailer, but I had never used it. The heater was set up to connect with an outside fuel tank. I got a tank and connected it up, but I did not know how to operate it. The first cold night we had, I got out the instructions and attempted to light it. It was a small free-standing type of unit, and it took several attempts to get it lit. Then I found a new problem. By the time I got it to light, it had flooded. It started getting too hot, and I tried to turn it down, but it just kept getting hotter. I shut off the fuel supply to the heater, but by then, it had gotten red hot.

All the walls in the trailer had a heavy coat of varnish on them, and they were close to the heater. I thought they were going to catch fire before the heater would finish burning up the excess fuel in it. We got some water and towels and started wiping down the walls around the heater. We were lucky, the heater started to slowly cool down, but it took a long time to get it to a safe level. The next day I got a neighbor to help me light it again. This time it worked correctly.

After about six months, I got transferred to a different building to work. The unit was called the Engine Buildup Unit, EBU, and our job was to take the new engines out of the shipping crates and put all their accessories on them. Then we mounted them on the frame that would attach them to a special mobile machine where the new engine would be started up and tested. After it passed all the inspections, it would be transferred to the new frame that would be used for mounting it to the aircraft.

When we finished, the engine was ready to mount on the plane. We worked regular day shift hours there. The trailer park was about five miles from the base, and some of the people went home for lunch. On the Air Force Base, we did not have to change clothing to go on and off the base like we did at a Navy base. Another advantage we had was that we did not have to have a pass to enter or leave the base. Life was a lot simpler. My old Buick needed some repair, and I bought an old Cushman Motor scooter to ride back and forth to the base. It was the one that looked like a box with small wheels. You could not ride it as fast as you could travel in a car, but for short distance runs, it was ok, and it used very little gas.

One day, as I left the shop for lunch, I was riding my scooter and following a truck they called a Six-by. We were cruising at around thirty-five miles per hour when a car coming from the opposite direction suddenly made a left turn right in front of me.

My scooter's front wheel collided with the right rear tire of the car. The impact propelled me over the car and onto the ground on the other side. Despite the ordeal, I ended up with just bruises and scrapes, luckily no broken bones. Interestingly, the axle from my scooter's front wheel punctured a hole in the car's rear tire and also bent the rim. Speaking of my scooter, recovering it required a large shovel and basket – that's how dire the damage was. Needless to say, my lunch plans were completely derailed.

When I returned to the shop, my supervisor directed me to the infirmary and then sent me home. Taking the following day off, I began searching for a solution to the transmission fluid leak in my old Buick car. However, the cost of pulling out the transmission and fixing the issue equaled the value of the car itself.

I decided to trade it in. In exchange, I acquired a 1951 Ford two-door Coupe, resembling the one shown in the picture below. The new vehicle ran smoothly, albeit lacking a rear seat due to its prior owner – a salesman who had removed it for carrying sample cases. Equipped with a standard shift and a straight six-cylinder engine, I made the trade under the condition that the dealership would service it before I picked it up the next day.

To my dismay, upon arriving for pickup, I discovered that someone from the dealership had backed another vehicle into the driver's door. Despite causing minor damage, the door was easily repairable. They provided me with the necessary paint to fix it, as well as a fresh set of white sidewall tires.

The base featured a pleasant hobby auto repair shop, motivating me to embark on creating a hot rod. Given the six-cylinder engine, the hot rod's transformation would be mostly aesthetic.

My vision was to give it a subdued black primer appearance, lower the rear, and attach full fender skirts. Financial constraints limited my options, but the allure of the 1951 Ford design persisted. Customizing a car was an uncharted territory for me, introducing a new challenge.

One of the bad things about the military is you can work overtime, but you cannot get paid for it. I had reached a time in my life where work and learning were the only things I wanted to do.

I was getting off to a good start in my military career. I had just turned twenty, and I was getting promoted to AE-2, which is paygrade E-5 or Staff Sergeant. I found myself going through a time when I felt like I could do anything I wanted but could not decide what type of work I wanted to do. I did not want to waste time doing something now and not use it later. It took many years for me to learn that it was the challenge that appealed to me, not the job itself.

I would work at the shop on the base until the end of my shift, then go to the hobby shop until it closed. I was creating a problem at home and did not recognize it. Lucille was home taking care of the baby and hanging out with some of the other wives in the trailer park.

She was also twenty years old, and I am sure she was getting bored. Financially we were struggling just to make our payments, so we had no money for anything else. There were no bank accounts or credit cards, just a couple of stores where you could get some credit.

I had to take advance pay to make the transfer from Jacksonville, and now that was being taken out of my pay. By the time I got the car finished and the advance pay paid off, our marriage was not going well.

I finished my assignment to the Engine Buildup unit and was transferred back to the flightline maintenance crew. I was now eligible for training for the Flight Pay program, and I signed up for it. For the training that was required, I did it during my normal work shift.

The required hours of flight time had to be accomplished on an available basis, in addition to getting the extra 30 or 40 dollars per month's pay. You could also qualify for some of the transport trips as a trainee. The big trip that most of us wanted was a combination of troop transport and training flight for the pilots to Europe.

This trip would take between one and two weeks to complete and went to multiple places in Europe. For the pilots, it was for familiarization training of all the airports in the area and their mission services. For the flight crew, it was a chance to see some of the cities in Europe.

For our fully qualified Air Crew members, it was a regular assignment, but for us trainees, it took months to get a seat on one of the flights and special permission from the officer in charge of your assigned maintenance unit. In my case, it took me six months to be assigned to a trip, and while most of the expenses of the trip were paid for as part of the operation by the military, you had to have some extra money if you wanted to see or do anything. So, after I was assigned to a trip, I had to get a loan to cover what I would need.

Just before the day of the flight, one of the biggest miracles in my life happened. I did not think it was a miracle at the time, but I thought it was one of the worst things that had happened to me. Two days before the flight, a Chief Petty Officer from outside our squadron came up to ask me if he could have my spot on the fight.

Well, I was not going to give that seat to anyone. I told him that I worked for six months to get that seat and didn't know if I would ever get another chance, so I would not let him have it. He explained that he was retiring, and he and his wife had spent a lot of time in Europe. He needed to buy some things for their retirement home. I still refused to give up my seat. Then he told me that he would have to go over my head, but he really needed to be on the flight.

The next day I got a call that my Department Head wanted to see me. I reported to his office, and he told me that he was pulling me off the flight and assigning someone else. The Supervisor sent me home to cool off. He also gave me a disciplinary warning. I didn't know what a blessing I had received at the time, but as the flight was returning home with a full load of passengers, it crashed at sea, killing everyone on the plane.

The crash of that plane caused the biggest investigation I ever saw. The plane was transporting some of the top officers from one of the United States Air Force's SAC commands, and the plane had disappeared somewhere off the Azores with no communications about having any problems.

Starting as soon as the news about the crash came out, we started getting a large amount of new people assigned to the squadron. They infiltrated all the different sections of the Squadron. Because I had been pulled off the flight line the day before the flight left, and the fact that I was so mad about it that I was given disciplinary action, I got a full investigation.

I got a new helper assigned to me to train. It was so obvious that they were undercover investigators that we were laughing at them. They did not know anything about the job, and all had brand-new uniforms. After a few days, they all suddenly got transferred out of the squadron.

The Navy was searching for the wreckage and was able to find and confirm enough wreckage of the plane to legally declare the people who disappeared with the plane to be dead.

After things settled down from the plane crash, things got worse between Lucille and me. We split up, and she took the child and went back to Florida. My attitude at work wasn't getting any better, and I needed some time away from everything that was going on there, so I took a two-week leave.

A friend of mine stationed at McGuire, Staff Sergeant Lester Hill, was planning a trip back to his home in South Dakota. His wife had just dumped him, and now he, too, was getting into financial trouble. He had a trailer and a one-year-old Buick Roadmaster car that was costing him more than he could afford.

I had gotten to know him through work, and he lived in the same trailer park. He was working on a hardship discharge from the Air Force and needed to go home to work on his qualifications for his hardship, and I agreed to go with him and help drive.

I used my two weeks leave from the Navy, we loaded up and took off. We knew that we didn't have enough money to handle an emergency if one came up, but the car was in good condition, and He had just put a new set of recapped tires on, so we were not worried. He was sure that we would be able to get some work while we were there, and that would help. Lester also had some copper cable that was cleaned up, and copper had been bringing in a good price. Lester was planning on copper being worth more in South Dakota, so we took it all the way with us.

The trip was good overall. We switched back and forth between driving and sleeping in the car. Somewhere during the trip, while I was driving, one of the rear tires burst. I was driving at about sixty MPH, and let me tell you, I had my hands full trying to keep the car on the road until I could come to a stop. Unfortunately, the tire was not repairable, so we drove on the spare the rest of the way.

I don't know how many saloons out West are named the Silver Dollar Saloon, but we stopped at one of them. The bar had been covered in silver dollars at one time, but now everything in reach of the customers had been stolen, but they had a stuffed Jackalope on display. I was looking it over, and Lester and the bartender were explaining how rare they were. I did not think it was real, and they told me how it was made. I guess that practical jokes were a way of life out there.

It was after dark when we got to his dad's ranch house. They were aware of our arrival but had already gone to bed by the time we reached there. Nevertheless, everyone woke up to greet and welcome us. They were really great people. Before we went to bed, we went back outside the house, and I saw the most beautiful sky I had ever seen. There were millions of stars, and it looked like we were walking through them. I was spellbound and asked Lester, "What is that." He just looked at me and asked if I had ever seen the Milky Way before. The truth is that I had never seen a sky that beautiful before or since.

The next morning everyone was up by daybreak. There was a large breakfast on the table consisting of three platters of fried eggs. There was bacon, sausage, and ham for meat and a pile of freshly baked biscuits. There was also gravy and butter. I was skinny in those days, and to the old people, it meant that I was not eating enough. After Mr. Hill, Lester's father, explained the eggs in terms of hard, soft, or half raw, I took a couple of eggs and a couple of slices of bacon with a biscuit, and Mr. Hill said in a loud voice, "No wonder you are skinny, you don't eat enough," and with that, he put three more eggs and a bunch more bacon on my plate. I got the message that when they cook food for you, you eat heartily. I really enjoyed the Hill family.

I met Lester's older brother, who lived on a different part of the ranch. He introduced me to canned Buffalo meat. He got up one morning and went to his kitchen table to have a cup of coffee and saw a wild Buffalo just outside the window. He picked up his rifle and shot him through the window. That was illegal, and he had to get him cleaned and cooked in a hurry. He had several jars of canned buffalo in his house. I ate a small piece of it, but to me, it did not taste good, and it was too stringy. I spent most of the morning with Lester's brother and really enjoyed the visit.

As I mentioned earlier, the people of South Dakota enjoyed practical jokes. Lester and his brother wasted no time in setting up a major prank on me. They started telling me about the customs out west and that it was taken as an insult to refuse a drink if someone offered it to you. Well, I did not have any problem believing that.

Then they started telling how kind and goodhearted the people around there were. Lester then got a serious look on his face, and he asked his brother if Tiny was still around. Then everything got serious, and he said Oh yes, and I forgot about him. Then they cautioned me to be wary of him, describing him as an exceptionally large person who could become aggressive when drinking. However, they reassured me that encountering him was unlikely. After giving me this warning, they didn't elaborate further on the topic.

Later that afternoon, we picked up Lester's oldest sister, and we all went to the only place in the area where you could buy a beer or soft drink, and it was a building with one large room. The room had a pool table, a small bar with four stools, and a cold drink box with only two brands of beer and about three brands of soft drinks.

The only snacks you could get were Sunflower seeds, Peanuts, and some crackers. They carried four brands of cigarettes and some chewing tobacco. Oh, and they also had a small jukebox in one corner of the room. Outside, they had a single gas pump and a garage for repairing tractors.

They called that place Isabel, South Dakota, and it was the only place for several miles. Well, we went inside for a couple of beers, and Lester's sister and I played pool. There were only seven of us, but that made the room feel crowded.

After we had been there a few minutes, I saw the largest person I had ever seen. He was trying to squeeze through the front door. He was taller and wider than the door, and I knew that he had to be the one they called Tiny.

He went over to the bar and sat on two of the bar stools. Everyone in the room was laughing and talking with him, and everything seemed ok, so I went on playing pool. I went to a new location at the table to make a shot, and when I stepped back, I bumped into him. He had stood up from the bar and moved to a new location. I apologized and moved around the table to make sure I was out of his way. I lined up for my next shot, and when I pulled the pool cue back to make the shot, I jabbed him with the cue.

I knew that Tiny was getting in the way on purpose, so I put the pool cue on the table and said that I quit. I heard an unfriendly response; you don't quit in the middle of a game with a lady. Well, I knew that I was being set up by someone, but I was not sure who it was.

I knew that there was no way I was going to even try to fight with anyone as big as Tiny. I knew that I was faster than he was, and all I had to do was get out the door before he caught me.

As I positioned myself between Tiny and the door, he started laughing and telling me that I was being set up for a joke by these guys, and he pointed toward Lester and his brother. Then he sat back down at the bar and asked me to come over to the bar and have a beer.

I still was not sure what would be next, so I told him, no thanks, I'll just stay over here, I know I can outrun you. Tiny laughed and said that they were always playing that joke on people because he was large. Then he said that he really was a nice guy that loved everyone. I went over and took the beer and talked with him. Tiny was a really nice guy with a great sense of humor.

He really got a kick of how small I was and said he wanted to show me to his wife. I asked why he wanted to do that, and he said that his wife would get a kick out of how small I was and that she would want to make me into a mascot for the ranch.

Tiny had grown up with and was best friends with an Indian from the Indian Reservation close to Isabel. The Indian was a professional wrestler by the name of Don Eagle. I had seen him wrestle on TV with another Indian who was known as Big Chief.

Lester had told me about how Tiny and Don Eagle used to wrestle each other for beers at the same place we were in. Tiny confirmed that and said that because he was always much larger than Don, he could overpower him and win. Then he said, "But man, is he getting so tricky now? He is hard to handle." Well, I didn't get to see Don Eagle, but I sure enjoyed the evening.

The second day we were there, Lester's younger brother got us a job hauling hay on one of the ranches. They only had square bails in those days, and all the bails had to be moved by hand. I was much too small to handle work that heavy. I was twenty years old and only weighed 130 pounds at best. Lester's younger brother was just Sixteen years old and weighed close to 180 pounds, and he was not fat. They kept me on the easier parts of the job and covered what I could not handle.

One of the biggest problems we had was with the ground. They had a type of clay out there they called GUMBO. It would stick to the truck tires and build up so thick the wheel could not turn. But at the same time, it was so slick that the truck could not get good traction.

This made it difficult to drive the truck, the wheels would start spinning, and the back end of the truck would slide around. We needed the money, and it took five long hard days to get all the hay from the field to the storage shelters. It was late Sunday evening when we finished everything and got paid.

Lester was trying to get a hardship discharge from the Air Force and had requested a two-week extension on his leave from his command. They approved it. That left me to find my own way back to Trenton, New Jersey.

I didn't think I had enough money to get a bus ticket for the whole trip, so I decided to save what money I had and hitchhike back. I had my uniforms with me, and in those days, people were good about helping our servicemen who were hitchhiking rides. I had hitchhiked a lot back in AE-A school.

I remember that early the next morning, Lester took me to the main route East, and we wished each other good luck and said our last goodbyes. I never knew what happened to him after that. He never returned to the base.

I was blessed with good weather and got my first ride in just a few minutes. I remember how tired I was from hauling that hay, and it sure felt good just to sit back and ride. Unlike most of my other hitchhiking trips, these rides were long, and I could sleep a lot. Most of the people who gave me rides would also take me to a good spot to catch rides to drop me off. I did not get many requests to help with the driving, and only one time was I asked to help pay for the gas.

One of my drop-offs was at a truck stop and restaurant. I got a ride with a nice elderly guy, and we talked a lot about the Military because he had served in the Second World War. He went out of his way to take me to that restaurant, and he bought lunch for us. Before I left the restaurant, I saw a couple of other military people come in. One was wearing an Army uniform, and the other one was wearing an Air Force uniform. I went over to their table and learned they were heading East. I got a ride with them and agreed to help pay for the gas.

The only problem was they were riding in a convertible with the top down. I got in the back seat, and the wind just about beat me to death. I don't know if there was something wrong with the top or if they just liked the open air. I kept adjusting my position until I could live with the wind and tried to get some sleep.

We made one gas stop, and it cost me only two dollars for my part. I do remember that it was a long ride, and I was sure happy when I got my next ride, it was nice and warm. I got comfortable, and I think I fell asleep almost immediately. I don't remember any more problems until we got to Chicago, Illinois.

I got dropped off in a bad part of town and had no idea where I was. There was a small hotdog stand close to where I was. I got a couple of hotdogs and watched some hot rods drag racing in the street. There was a small bar close by where I used the restroom and tried to clean up a little. I could see that I did not want to be in that place, and I made a quick exit.

I walked a couple of blocks to where there was a city bus stop with a bench to sit on, and I took a seat. There were no buses in the area, only a couple of drunks. One wanted me to give him some money so he could buy us a drink. I refused his offer, and the other guy was mad about being thrown out of a bar and wanted me to help him fight the bad guys. Well, I would not agree with that either. I realized that there were not only no buses in the area but also no police officers around.

It was getting dark, and I did not have any idea which way to go to find a bus station where I could catch a bus out of town. After what seemed like a very long time, I saw a military patrol unit go by. They did not stop, but I could see them watching me. The unit was a Shore Patrol paddy wagon type with two Shore Patrol officers in it. I really did not want them to see me up close because my uniform was a mess from all the traveling I had been doing. I had just got my promotion to E-5, and I was supposed to be setting a good example when in public. I was afraid that if they arrested me, I would lose my promotion.

Well, after about an hour, they came back and parked close to me and just watched me for a while. I knew they were my only help, and when they headed my way, I was happy they were coming. The petty officer in charge of the unit was also an E-5 and really checked out all my papers and ID before talking to me. His first words were, "Do you know where you are"? I told him that I thought I was in Chicago, and that was not what he wanted to hear. Then he asked where I was going, and I told him New Jersey, and that did not help either.

He looked at me and said that I was in the worst part of town and asked what I was doing. I explained that I was trying to get to the main bus station to catch a bus to New Jersey. Then he said that there would not be any buses running where I was until sometime late tomorrow. Then he said if I left you here till then, he was afraid that I would be dead. The problem was that he was on duty and was not authorized to give me a ride. He went back to the paddy wagon and spent a few minutes talking to his partner, then walked around the back of the unit and opened the door, and motioned to me to get in.

He took me to one of the main stations for a bus line and let me out. The only things he said were that you can catch a bus here, and you owe me big time. I went to the ticket counter and talked with the clerk. He figured out how to get me the best place on the main route East and sold me a ticket. I think the ticket cost me about ten dollars, and in about an hour, I was on a big bus headed out of Chicago. I told the driver that I had to find a good route East and asked him to drop me as close as he could, and he agreed. He got me within about three blocks and told me how to get to the main route.

It was late at night when I got to the route, and traffic was slow. It took longer than usual for someone to pick me up. I remember that the first ride only got me a short way out of Chicago, but it did get me on a better route. The rest of the trip went okay, but I was so tired that all I wanted to do was sleep. I remember thinking that I might never get back to the base and my barracks.

I returned to the base one day before my two weeks leave was over. I checked in okay, but I was so worn out that I overslept on the morning I was supposed to return to work, and that did not go over well.

I had taken the trip to get away from everything that was causing me to have a bad attitude, and two weeks later, I failed to show up for work on time, and when I did get there, I needed a haircut, and my uniform needed attention.

I had good reasons for it, and under normal conditions, it would have been overlooked, but my prior conduct made this incident look like a red flag to my supervisors. I had just received my last promotion, and I was not living up to their expectations. I got some extra assignments of unpleasant duties instead of official disciplinary action, so my military record was not damaged.

Lucille was still back in Florida, and I knew she was not coming back. I still had my 1951 Ford and the trailer, but I was in the process of getting the trailer repossessed and had moved back on the base.

After my trip to South Dakota, I got a bad start with my Supervisors at VR-6. I was going through a lot of personal losses, and I had developed a bad attitude. These problems had nothing to do with VR-6, but I started taking them to work with me.

My trailer was repossessed, and that took the pressure off those payments as well as the trailer park rent, and that helped. With part of my pay going to Lucille each month, I did not have much pay left, and I still had the car to finish and some other small debts to pay. I had moved back on the base and managed to cut my living expenses to the bare essentials. I knew that it was going to be rough for a while, but I had no choice.

While the car was nothing to brag about, it ran well and was my only transportation. I restricted my lifestyle to the base, barracks, work assignments, and hobby shop. I finished all the work on my car, and it turned out okay. I got a dull black primer paint job finished, and then I got the two-inch lowering blocks installed, and put full fender skirts on the car. It looked good, and then I customized the door handles by replacing them with electric solenoids.

To activate the solenoids, I installed push button switches, one under each running board, so that you could activate them with your foot. Then I put two push-button switches under the dash where I could operate them from the driver's position. I also installed flat coil springs in door jams to kick the door to an ajar position so you could catch the door and pull by hand. I filled in all the holes left by removing the door handles, and the paint hid everything else.

I settled into my new lifestyle and went back to learning more about the job and career field and working on getting better qualified for AE class B school.

I tried to follow up with my friend, Lester Hill, and the only thing I learned was that his trailer had been repossessed, and he was no longer assigned to McGuire Air Force Base. I also found out that his ex-wife was listed as AWOL, along with her friend.

I had too much time on my hands, and I created probably the most unsafe car on the road. In the case of a serious wreck, I would have had to be removed from the vehicle through the window. I did hide an external electrical hookup where I could open the doors if the battery failed.

The promotion I had gotten had me eligible for a temporary assignment as Mess Deck Master at Arms. That was a six-month assignment and that was about all the time I had left on my tour of duty at McGuire. I was in charge of the mess cooks assigned to the mess hall. It had nothing to do with my career field, but it did give me more time off. So, I started concentrating on my career and pushing for a transfer to AE- B school.

While working at the mess hall, I got interested in motorcycles. The guy who had the milk delivery to the mess hall had just purchased a new model 74 Harley Davison motorcycle. He delivered fresh milk to the mess hall three days a week, and I had to inspect and sign for each delivery, so I got to know him.

We talked a lot, and he really enjoyed motorcycle riding. On one of his days off, he brought his new bike by to show it off. It had all the new features and was bright red with a lot of chrome trim, and it sure was a pretty motorcycle. I was getting off work, and he took me for a nice ride around the area, and I was hooked on motorcycles.

Living my new restrictive-type lifestyle had helped get my debts under control, and now I could afford to go off base once in a while, and I had started dating a girl in the area. Her name was Elizabeth Overbeck, but she went by the name of Betty. We both liked Country Music and wanted to go see the show in wheeling, West Virginia, and planned on making a trip there. However, we had conflicting work hours. She had a good job at the telephone company and was serious about her career.

While we were trying to work out the schedule for our trip, I bought an old ex-police motorcycle and started trying to fix it up. It was a model 74 Harley Davidson, and it was heavy. It would start ok, but for me to kick it over, I would have to stand on the start pedal with both feet and jump down with all my weight. When it started, it was okay, but if it kicked back, it would throw me off the bike. Betty and I had ridden the motorcycle several times, and we both enjoyed riding it.

# Chapter 28

# WHEELING, WEST VIRGINIA

Betty and I finally got our days off scheduled so that we could take the trip to Wheeling, West Virginia, that we had been planning on. She was scheduled to work a split shift the day before her time off started, and she had someone to cover the late half of the shift, which allowed her to get an early start. We both had five days off scheduled and planned to leave after work on our last day before the break started. We planned that I would meet Betty at a garage where she was dropping off her favorite antique car for service and maintenance while she was gone and go from there.

The weather was fantastic, with clear skies and warm sunshine on the day we were leaving. It was so great that I had washed and checked out my old motorcycle and was thinking about riding it. Just before I was ready to leave to go pick Betty up at the garage, she called to let me know she was on schedule.

I asked her if she would like us to take the motorcycle instead of the car. She liked riding the bike, and the trip should have been a nice ride. She said she did not think that was a good idea based on the weather report she had seen. So, I drove my fifty-one Ford, and when I pulled into the garage parking lot, I saw the first clouds. They were black and threatening, and it started snowing the largest, heaviest snowflakes I had ever seen. The temperature was still warm, and the snowflakes just left big wet spots on the ground and windshield.

Betty was driving when we left the garage because she knew where we needed to go to get on the main route we were taking. Everything was going okay, and I was in the back seat sleeping. In what seemed like a short time, she pulled the car over to the side of the road and told me that she could not drive any farther. I got up to find out what was going on. It was already dark outside the car, and we were in what they call a whiteout. The snow had changed to a smaller, more frozen type that was blowing across the road so thick you could not see how to drive. It was the worst condition that I had ever seen. The snow was blowing so hard that it made a flat horizontal drift that you could not see through. The horizontal movement of the snow messed up your sense of direction and made you want to turn the car instead of going straight.

I had to drive slowly to avoid the temptation of steering the car off the road. It took what seemed like a very long time before we got back to normal driving conditions, but the snowfall never let up all the way to Wheeling. We had to constantly switch off driving duties all the way.

We pulled into the parking lot of the first motel we came to. The average snow accumulation was eight to ten inches. We were lucky that they had a vacancy, so we got a room. We were tired and hungry, so as soon as we got warm and cleaned up, we went looking for a restaurant. Our luck held up, and we found one nearby that was open. There were only three people in the restaurant, so we were able to get some good information on Wheeling and the live radio show we wanted to see.

The next morning it was still snowing. My car had new tires, but no snow chains, and the snow in the parking lot is now about twelve inches deep. The streets had been plowed and were ok to drive on. We went back to the same restaurant to eat and get more instructions. Our waitress called the radio station and confirmed that it was open. The biggest concern that we had was getting there.

At that time, Wheeling was still shipping out a lot of coal, and there were about ten sets of tracks that ran through the middle of town, and we had to cross over them on a bridge. The bridge was a long bridge with a high arch that caused a high hill in the middle to drive over. The roadway over the bridge had a steep elevation, and in snowy weather, the roads were very slick.

Wheeling is the only place where I saw this type of operation, but in bad weather, there were four men on each side of the bridge with special logging boots. The traffic over the bridge was controlled by clearing the road and sending one car over at a time. The car would get a running start in the parking area at the foot of the bridge and try to make it to the top of the bridge. Most cars would only make it about two-thirds of the way up before losing traction on the slippery surface of the roadway. Two of the men would catch a side of the vehicle and push it up to the top of the bridge. Then the downhill side of the street would be cleared of traffic, and you could coast downhill with plenty of room to stop.

As I went up the hill, a group of men came out to help me push my car to the top. However, there was a problem – I had removed the door handles. One of the men started running alongside the car, attempting to grab onto something that wasn't there. I worried that he might accidentally scratch the paint on the door. I was relieved that I couldn't hear what he was shouting at me.

By the time we got to the parking lot for the show, the snow was causing some bad drifts. I found a spot along the side of the building and backed my car into it. We saw the show and really enjoyed it. By the time we returned to the parking area, it was completely covered in a snowbank. The only thing that was visible was the tips of the radio antennas.

We went to the place where we thought our car was, and there was a well-dressed gentleman wearing a topcoat and gloves trying to dig his way through the snowbank to the driver's door. I told Betty that I thought he was digging out our car, and we waited and watched. When he reached the driver's door, he realized that it was not his car. He made several comments that we couldn't understand and backed out of the snowbank. I said that I thought it was my car and I would move it out of the way so he could get to his.

I walked to my car and popped the driver's door open, and drove straight forward, moving a pile of the snowbank with me. His car was backed in next to mine. We both had a good laugh about it as we finished clearing off our cars. We got back to the motel okay, but we had to go back over the bridge and the car pushers still had trouble with my car.

By the next morning, the snowfall had almost stopped, but it was very cold. I stepped outside to unlock the driver's door and to warm up the car. However, getting the door open turned out to be a challenge. I had to use the blade of my knife to carefully pry it open due to it being frozen shut. Additionally, there was a 1957 Chevrolet parked in front of my car, and its door lock and key slots were also frozen and filled with ice, making it impossible to insert the key. Our solution was to melt the ice in the lock by holding the key against it and heating the key using our cigarette lighters.

We each had a lighter, and we used all the lighter fluid to get the key in the driver's door lock. It was bitterly cold out there in the parking lot, and it took a long time just to get the key in the lock. Fortunately for the owner, he was able to get the driver's door unlocked, and we pulled the door open.

The delay caused us to get started a little later than we had planned. The traffic was slow, but the roads were drivable, and we made it to the entrance of the toll-road. As we approached the toll booth, the operator was trying to listen to something on the phone, so without paying attention to us, he punched a toll card and handed it to us. We got on our way, and there was very little traffic.

The road surface was covered with snow and ice, and part of the time, we drove by keeping between the marker signs on each side of the roadway. Every vehicle was having trouble except for the Volkswagens, and they were flying down the road with little to no problem. Trucks were having the most trouble sliding off the road, and so were regular cars. For some reason, my little car was doing good.

The Toll roads were using a company called Howard Johnsons for all their rest stops. They had food, rooms, and gas pumps at each stop. We stopped at one when I needed fuel and when we pulled off the road into their parking lot. Almost everything was blocked off, including the driveway to the pumps, with a ridge of snow across the roadway. I pulled up to the pumps by crossing one of their little snow ridges. It took a few minutes, but some guy came out to pumps, and asked what I thought I was doing? He was not happy. I told him that we were traveling and needed gas.

My car was covered in snow and had two little places in the windshield where I saw out. He asked where we were coming from, and when I said wheeling West Virginia, he was surprised and told me that the turnpike was closed and had been all morning. Then he said it has been on the radio all morning. I told him that I was sorry, but my radio didn't work.

Then he said we would need to turn around and get to the office; they don't have any more rooms, but they will find a place inside, where it is warm, and where we could get some rest. I said OK, but can I go ahead and gas up while I am here. That way, we will be ready to go when the road opens. Reluctantly he turned on the pumps and let me fill up. I paid him, and he walked back to the office.

Betty said that she did not want to stay there. I observed that the snowbank blocking the drive was the only thing keeping us from getting back to the road and pulled my car in gear and drove right over the bank and back to the roadway. We did not know that the toll road had been closed, but that had to be the message the tollgate attendant was trying to receive when we came through his booth.

We didn't get anything to eat, but we had a lot of snacks in the car to munch on. There were no real problems on the rest of the way to where we were supposed to get off the toll road. Betty lived a little less than two miles from that toll booth.

When I pulled up to the window, the attendant was sleeping in the chair, and I had to blow the horn to get him up. He came to the window and looked confused. I tried to hand him my toll card so he could stamp me out, and he would not take it. At first, he said that the road was closed and that he could not let anyone on it. Then I said I don't want to get on, I want to get off. I was trying to hand him my card, and then he repeated that the road was closed, and he could not let anyone off.

Betty was getting a little mad about this time and said, "We have traveled from Wheeling, West Virginia, and I'm tired, and I can see my house from here, and you are telling me I can't go home?" Then he said something like it could not be because the road had been closed all day.

With that response, I handed him my card again and told him to check it. The only stamp on the card was when we entered the road, and that seemed to confuse him more. Then he repeated that the road had been closed all day and wanted to know how we got there. Then he looked at us and the car and checked the card again. Then he said that we were the only people that he had seen on his shift. Then he said, "I don't know how to handle this, I am not supposed to let anyone through."

Betty used a more direct approach; she said just figure the toll from Wheeling to here so we can pay it and then open your gate before we drive through it. She followed that with a strong "I'm going Home" statement. He gave us the amount, we paid it, he opened the exit gate, and we exited the toll road.

The streets had not been plowed, and we almost did not make it to her house. I was only able to make it halfway up her driveway before getting completely stuck. That snowstorm was so bad everybody was snowed in. It took me five days to make it back to my base.

# Chapter 29

## LEAVING MCGUIRE

I restricted my lifestyle to the base, barracks, work assignments, and riding my motorcycle. I went back to learning more about the job and career field and working on getting better qualified for AE class B school.

I had too much time on my hands, and I created probably the most unsafe car on the road. In the case of a serious wreck, I would have had to be removed from the vehicle through the window. I did hide an external electrical hookup where I could open the doors if the battery failed.

I was now riding the motorcycle everywhere and not using the car. One of the guys in my barracks wanted buy the car so I made him an offer he agreed to. He needed to take a trip home to get the money. I held all the paperwork on the car until he returned with the money and let him take the car. That was the last I saw of him, my car, or any money. Later I learned that the car had been parted out and sold to a wrecking yard.

After a couple of weeks of riding every chance I got, I was talked into going on a trip from New Jersey to North Carolina with my friend, who had the new Harley, and a friend who lived in North Carolina. I had an account with the Harley Davidson dealership where I had bought the motorcycle and got some nice riding clothes. With a full set of Leathers, a nice heavy matching shirt, and trousers with my little motorcycle cap, I was ready to hit the road.

We got a very early start on the first day of our four-day break. The weather was cool but very nice, and the sun was coming up and promising to be a beautiful day for riding. I remember that it was a really enjoyable ride. I had a full-size windshield to block most of the wind, warm clothing, and we had good traffic, and we were making good time.

By mid-afternoon, it started to get cloudy and cool off some. I had developed a problem with the throttle control on my bike, it had developed a bine at just about cruising speed. If I needed to speed up or slow down, I would have to force the throttle through the spot that was binding. For a little time, it was not a problem because I could go just over the speed limit for a distance and then drop just below the limit for a while, but that changed.

It started raining, and there was no place to get out of the rain. To make matters worse, we were getting close to the city of Roanoke, Virginia, and the traffic was getting heavier. We had to constantly change our speed to stay with the traffic, and it didn't help my hand at all. For a while, my leathers held off the cold, but they were getting drenched in the rain.

As the sun set, a dense ground fog began to roll in. We found ourselves in the Bent Mountain area, where traffic was moving slowly due to the ongoing rain. My clothes were completely soaked, and I was shivering uncontrollably, to the point that my shaking was affecting the bike.

I recall having to tilt my gaze almost downward to discern the white line on the road, a guide to staying within our traffic lane. The fog was so thick that we were only able to maintain a speed of thirty to forty miles per hour. I focused on tracing the inner white line to prevent veering off the road.

A rabbit ran across the road, and I ran over him with my front tire. As my front tire ran over him, his sideways movement caused my direction of travel to move my front tire to the right, and I almost lost all control of my bike. I was all over the road, but I did not fall or run off the road. I thank my Guardian angel for that.

We all stopped on the road while I checked my bike. I was so cold I thought I was going to freeze to death. Someone said that he thought there was a truck stop about thirty miles ahead of us, but I was sure I would not make it before I froze to death. Somehow, we made it to the truck stop and into a building where there was some warmth.

They had big heater units mounted on the ceiling with the warm air blowing straight down to the floor. We grouped up under the heater and tried to get warm, but none of us could stop shaking. The guy who was working there came in and told us that if we ever expected to get warm, we would have to pull off our wet clothes. He was right, but when you're freezing, the last thing you want to do is pull off your clothes. After we took off all of our outer clothing, we did warm up, and we all fell asleep while our clothing dried. We were all so exhausted from the cold and stress that we just collapsed.

It took some three or four hours for our clothing to dry. The leathers took the longest, but we were so tired that we didn't care. It was after daylight before we got started, but we rode the rest of the way to where our friend lived. It was somewhere in the hills, and that is all I remember.

I think everyone was making moonshine because that was all they talked about. Somebody made me a bed on the floor, and I went to sleep until we had to leave. My right hand and wrist were so sore that it hurt to operate the throttle. Before we left, we tried to fix the throttle by putting some oil inside the cable assembly and in the hand grip itself. I think it helped, but it did not fix the problem. The ride back was a lot better, but it sure was a long one.

# Chapter 30
## MOTORCYCLE

Close to the end of my tour of duty at McGuire Air Force base at Trenton, New Jersey, I had to go home for an emergency. My motorcycle was the only transportation I had at the time, and I enjoyed riding, so I took off on a two-week trip.

The weather was great for riding and the bike was running good. I stuffed my two large leather saddle bags with a supply of clean clothing and other things I might need and hit the road. When I bought the bike, it was dressed up with full windshield and a set of chrome crash bars that wrapped around the engine and provided two more positions to rest your feet. It had a large buddy seat for riding two people and was comfortable.

I got an early start and things were going great. The traffic was a little heavy but moving good and I was enjoying the ride. I had lost track of time, but it was about midafternoon, and I had covered a good distance. I was just moving with the traffic following a station wagon with a couple of small kids in the back. They were playing and waving at me, so I was watching and waving back at them when suddenly something hit me in my right eye.

I felt like I had been shot with a BB. With my full windshield as the only eye protection, I also wore my Aviator Sunglasses. The pain in my right eye caused my left eye to close also. I was blinded and going about fifty miles per hour on a motorcycle with traffic all around me.

I started slowing down while moving the bike to the right side of road and trying to use my sense of feel to find the edge without running off the surface of the road. I had the old foot operated clutch and hand gear shift.

Somehow, I managed to get the bike stopped and I could feel the road surface with both of my feet, so I thought I was still in the traffic. I could hear and feel the wind from the traffic whizzing by my left side. I tried as hard as I could to get my eyes open but neither one would open. I remember putting the bike kickstand down. It was on the left side of the bike so the bike would lean toward the traffic. I was afraid of getting hit by a passing vehicle if I got off the bike on the left side because that put me in front of the oncoming traffic, and I could hear a steady flow of it. I do remember wondering why no one seemed to slow down or stop. My eye was hurting so bad that I had to do something.

I slowly leaned the bike over on the kickstand and nothing happened, so I got off the bike. While holding pressure on my right eye I moved around to the right side of the bike. It took a few minutes before I could get my left eye to see anything. I had to get one of my T shirts out of my saddle bag and press it against my right eye to get my left eye to clear up enough to see anything. The first thing I was able to see was that I was just about five feet off the road on a short asphalt covered pull off. Now I know that it had to be God who got me off that road. It took about an hour to be able to keep my left eye open and then only if I kept constant pressure on my right eye.

Finally, I was able to see well enough to try to ride to a service station where I could get some help. It was difficult riding in my condition and my depth perception was affecting my vision. I remember finding a service facility that had a large garage and I stopped there hoping to get some help for my eye.

The guy who came over to see what I wanted was not the most helpful person I had ever met, but he did give me some aspirin, and did check my eye. His first response was that I should go to a hospital. I rejected that offer and asked him if I could use his restroom to clean up and get out of the bright light for a while. He acted like he was not happy about that idea so I told him that just needed a place where I could rest my eyes for a while. He kind of grumbled a little and said it was okay, but only for a little while, and I would have to move my bike. I moved the bike and went inside. I tried to check my injured eye in the bathroom mirror. It looked horrible. It was so bloodshot that it looked like it was bleeding inside.

When the guy working at the station came back, he had a small tube of some kind of ointment and told me that I needed to put some of it in my eye. I did even though I didn't know what it was, it made my eye feel better. I asked if I could rest there in the shop for a while. He let me for a short time. I got the feeling that he did not like bikers, and I had not brought any of my military uniforms with me.

I was able to lay down on a bench in the back of the garage for a couple of hours. The pain in my eye was easing off and I was able to doze off for part of the time, but I could hear comments being made by some of the people in the shop.

One asked, who is the bum passed out back there. Another one who sounded like the person running the shop saying, "He is about to get moved out." I pretended I had not heard the comments, got up and checked my eye and went to the restroom to wash my face and I was starting to feel a little better so I left. But before I left the garage, I thanked the guy who ran the place for letting me get some rest and told him I was feeling better. I got me a soda pop and some little thing to eat, gassed up the bike and headed south.

I don't remember much about the next part of the ride except that I had made a lot of stops along the way. My eye had started hurting again and it was harder to keep riding. I also started having trouble with the clutch slipping and it was getting harder for me to see.

I arrived in a small community that I remember as being called Rebel, South Carolina or the name could have had two parts like Rebel-Something. I do remember that it was a pretty little town.

I found a service station and pulled my bike up in front of a service stall and waited for the attendant. I was rubbing my eye when he came over and asked if he could help me. He looked at me and asked if I was okay. Then he took a long look at my bike. I told him that I needed someone to adjust my clutch and I needed to rest my eye for a while.

The first thing he did was to go over to bike and check it out. He said that he could fix it; however, he was busy and could not do it right then. He also said he had owned one just like mine and he was familiar with it. Then he said that I would need to move it inside the garage.

He could see that I was hurting and asked if I wanted him to move the bike inside the shop and I said yes. He started it up and checked the clutch and rode it into the shop. He looked at me with that, I've got bad news and said, "Yes, the clutch needs work but you also need a battery". I explained that I was on my way to Florida and would be gone for about five or six days so he would have time to get the bike fixed. I don't remember any conversation about how much It would cost or how I would pay for it.

A customer had pulled up to one of the gas pumps and he had to go take care of them. I checked the battery box on the bike, and I could see the battery acid had leaked out. I knew that the battery case was busted and the acid would damage the paint but I was too tired and hurting too much to care.

When the station attendant returned, he had another person with him. He introduced me to the other guy and told me that he was a truck driver and that he was heading south, so he asked him if he could give me a ride. The driver looked at my eye and said that all I had was "Sleep eye." He was a take care kind of person and as I tried to tell him that something had hit me in the eye, he just repeated that all I had was sleep eye and for me to get in the sleeper and get some sleep and I would be okay. I climbed into the sleeper and slept all the way to where he dropped me off close to home.

I don't recall any particular problems with getting home but I did get a good night's sleep and I truly enjoyed that. I had come home to help mom work through some family problems and by the time those were finished, it was time for me to head back to New Jersey.

I had to hitch a ride back through Rebel, South Carolina to pick up my motorcycle. My brother has taken me to the main route going north through that area. We got an early start so he could get back to work on time and that was a good thing because rides were slow. I did not have my military uniform and people were not as good about picking up bikers, but I got a couple good long rides and made it back to Rebel by midday.

I remember that it was only a few blocks from where I was dropped off to the shop where my bike was. I still remember how pretty the little town was. As I was walking to the shop I stopped off at a small diner and got a meal. I remember there was something about the town of Rebel that made me feel good.

I walked to the garage to get my bike. It was all cleaned up and ready to go. When the attendant came into the shop, he was limping a little on his right leg. I could see that he still had some bandages on the leg just above the ankle. I asked what happened and his first response was, "Your bike did that." Then he explained it was his fault because after adjusting the clutch, he had not reinstalled the guard cover over the clutch before testing it. The bolts in the clutch assembly had snagged his pants leg and hit his leg. His leg had some scrapes but no serious injuries.

He said he had also replated the battery. He had enjoyed riding the bike and it was ready for the road. I repacked my saddle bags, gassed the bike and hit the road. I was blessed with another great day for a ride, and it sure felt good to be riding instead of walking.

The roads were in good shape, and the traffic was light, so I made a good time. Somewhere in North Carolina, I saw a large buck deer with a fantastic set of antlers running across the road ahead of me. He was a sight to see, but it reminded me of what would happen if I had hit him. I realized that I was getting too relaxed on the bike, but I was thoroughly enjoying the ride.

Well, it wasn't long before I got a good wake-up call. I was a little too tired and a little too comfortable and fell asleep. I heard a loud noise that sounded like a gunshot that got my attention. I had crossed the oncoming traffic lane and was heading for a ditch. I stopped the bike on the side of the road before running off into the ditch and then looked to see if I could see what had made the noise. It was dark, and I was the only thing on the road that I could see. I thought that it must have been a tire that had blown out, but both tires were fine. Then I thought that the motorcycle had backfired, but the motor was running as smoothly as it could be. I checked the bike for anything that might be broken, and it was perfect. As I started back down the road, I decided that it was time to find a motel and get some sleep.

After some much-needed rest, I got back on the road to New Jersey. It was another good day for riding. I was making good time and thought I was only about a hundred and fifty miles from Trenton, New Jerey, when there was a hard jerk in the forward motion of the bike, then no forward power at all. The motor was running fine, but it would not engage with the transmission. The primary drive chain was broken, and all connections between the motor and the transmission stopped.

There was a service facility just up the road a short distance, but it was uphill, and I could just barely push that bike on level ground. This time I was stalled in the traffic lane, and as good luck would have it, a large gentleman got out of his car and grabbed the rear end of the bike, and we pushed it all the way to a service facility. I was stuck there until the bike could be fixed. I thought I was closer to home than I was, and my best option was to go home and have the dealership send their truck down and haul it back. After making arrangements with the repair facility to store and leave my bike there, I got ready to start hitchhiking again.

There was a restaurant at the service center, and when I checked it out, I saw someone wearing Air Force-type clothing having lunch there. I went over and introduced myself to him and asked if he was headed to McGuire Air Force Base. He was not going there, but he was heading in that general direction.

He was traveling alone and agreed to give me a ride as far as he could. He had been traveling a long way and was very tired. I agreed to do some of the driving, and we took off. He was driving a late-model Plymouth station wagon, and I started driving when we left.

He was being transferred to a new duty assignment and had a very interesting story about what happened during his trip, and we spent a lot of time talking about that. When we arrived at the crossroads where I needed to exit, I realized that I had overestimated how close we were to home. I had to take a connecting road to another route to get to Trenton.

When I got off the road, I realized that it was a bad location to try to hitchhike. It was a smaller road with less traffic and was too dark for people to get a good look at you before deciding if they wanted to give you a ride. It was already after dark, and I was stuck.

Still thinking that I was closer than I was to where I could get some assistance, I started walking. I was looking for a place where I could call my girlfriend or get a ride. Thank God it was a good night for a walk because I had to walk all night and then some.

There was no traffic on that road. I could have made me a bed in the middle of the road and been perfectly safe. Once I started walking, I just kept going. I walked until mid-morning before I found a phone where I could call Betty.

When she figured out where I really was, she was not happy. She had to borrow a car and miss part of her shift at work. I was to stay on that road until she found me, so I just kept walking. There were no ride offers anyway, and as nasty as I looked, I was not surprised.

It took Betty over two hours to find me, and she was not happy. We were closer to her house than the base, so she took me to her house. I explained everything the best I could to her and showed her the name and address of where I left the motorcycle. I got a hot shower and some clean clothes and crashed into the guest bed.

# Chapter 31

# AE-B SCHOOL

When I was transferred from McGuire Air Force Base in Trenton, New Jersey, to NATTC Jacksonville, Florida, I did not have any vehicles. My orders authorized me to travel POV, which stood for Privately Owned Vehicle. At this time, I do not remember how I traveled. I do know that I did not hitchhike, and I think I traveled by bus.

I remember that my cousin, Ivy Capps, who was living in the Jacksonville area, picked me up. When I got there, he took me to the base to check-in. However, we did a lot of partying before I got to the base. I do remember checking in with the Duty Officer and getting my barracks assignment. That was all I was required to do at that time, and it was a good thing because I don't think I would have been able to do anything else. Ivy dropped me off at the barracks to my assigned room and I crashed. The quarters for Petty Officers were modules with four rooms, a study area, and bathroom facilities.

The next morning, I finished checking in with the base. Then I started checking in at the school administrative building. All I had to do at the school was drop off a copy of my orders, then check back with them the following Monday morning at 8 AM for my class assignment. This was the same base that I was stationed at prior to going to New Jersey, so I was familiar with it. The squadron I was assigned to when I left, VF-43, had been relocated and was no longer stationed there. The training center where I went through AE-A School had made some changes to accommodate some expansions to the schools, but for the most part, everything looked the same.

I had a three-day weekend break, so I put on a uniform and started hitchhiking home. I had plenty of time, and the rides were good. I missed my bike and my car, but I still enjoyed the trip home. I knew when school started, I would not be making many trips because of heavy work requirements, and I still had some debts to clear up before I could consider buying anything. I got to spend some time with my parents and my brother, but I was looking forward to getting started in the new school. I got back to the base just past noon and spent the rest of the time getting my uniforms ready for school.

On Monday morning, I checked in and got my class assignment. The first module of our training was mathematics, and we were the first class not to have to take the two-week Calculus course. That was a good break for me, for I had no prior schooling on that level of math. The only real training with mathematics I had was from the military school in Norman, Oklahoma, and in AE-A school.

The study of electronics is all based on a theory that is proven by math. The math we were taught was Algebra, referred to as electronic equation formulas and Trigonometry. We had expressions for voltage shown as E and current shown as I or resistance shown as R. The expressions were written as $E=I \times R$, $I=E/R$, or $R=E/I$. To the student with the proper prior schooling in mathematics, this was simple algebra, but to me, it was like some magic thing that only worked in electronics. It was years before I made the real connection between electronic formulas and Algebra.

All of our instructors were military personnel, but they were good instructors. The main problem was the intensity of the curriculum. What the average college would have taught in a two-year curriculum, the military taught in a nine-month course. Each day was eight hours of theory, followed by up to four hours of homework each night. Even the layout of our barracks was designed so that we would be in groups of four that were studying the same material. On weekends you did not have class, but most weekends, you got between three and five hours of homework. It was very difficult to do or even think about anything else.

I did not have the proper background for the course, but I was determined to get everything I could out of the training. The one good thing about the school was that it took my mind off my other problems.

Almost everything was based on a two-week cycle. Your tests were scheduled every other Friday, and course topics were changed for four-week cycles, with only two that were six weeks.

At the end of each topic, you would not get any homework, and that would be a free weekend. Two of the guys in our group had cars, and on our free weekends, we would all pool our resources and try to do something off the base. I was the only one who lived in the area, and at first, we would load up in one vehicle and go to where I lived. The guys would be on their best behavior around my parents, and my parents liked them. We would take in the local dances and blow off a little steam.

One of the strange things that happened to me while I was in B school was on one of our free weekends. I remember that the guys I ran around with had found out about a big dance at one of the VFW halls in the Jacksonville area on Saturday night, and we were planning on going to it. We had our test early on Friday morning, and I finished it in just a few minutes and was off the rest of the weekend.

I went back to the barracks and changed into my dress uniform. I was the only one in the barracks and suddenly felt lost. I had time on my hands and nothing to do with it. The last thing I wanted to do at that time was to go home. I remembered that Lucille and I were getting our divorce finalized at that time, and she was living in Gainesville, where she was recovering from being accidentally struck by a car, leaving her with a badly broken right leg.

I had some papers that I needed her to sign, and I had to serve her a copy of them. We also had a bus service that ran from the base to the Bus Station in Jacksonville. My plans were to get to the bus station and check on the cost and schedule of trips to Gainesville. I got the papers out of my locker and checked them over, and for some reason, I stuck them in my pocket. I had no intention of going to Gainesville to try to deliver them at that time.

There was a pawn shop next to the bus station, and I had seen a pair of cuff links there that was made in the shape of my initials. I decided to catch the bus to Jacksonville and check on the schedule and the pawn shop.

I got to the base bus stop just in time to jump on the bus to Jacksonville. I got to the bus station in Jacksonville in a short time and made a quick check of the pawn shop. I found nothing I wanted, and I went to the ticket office and asked about the cost and schedule to Gainesville. He told me that the bus to Gainesville was loading, but he could get me on it if I hurried.

The driver was just closing the baggage compartment, and the ticket agent asked him to wait for one more and grabbed my ticket. I realized that I had the papers with me, and I paid for the ticket and jumped on the bus. I remember thinking that as early as it was, I could get papers to her and get back to the base in time to hang out with the guys.

I took a seat close to the driver and talked to him about dropping me off before he went all to way to the bus station. Lucille was at a place close to 301 and what we called the Waldo Loop on the Northeast edge of town. He was able to drop me off about six blocks from her house.

She was home, and we had a nice but short visit, and in no time, I was on my way back to the 301 and Waldo intersection. That was a good place to hitchhike back to the base. There was a nice service station there, and I stopped and got a big RC cola and what we called a moon pie.

While I was there, the two guys running the service were playing a couple of guitars and singing some country music songs between customers. I loved country music, and I was really enjoying it, but they got busy and had to stop.

Just as I started to walk away, a customer who was gassing up his car called me by my name. I was surprised to learn that I had worked with him when I lived in Gainesville. He told me to get in the car, I am going your way, and I'll give you a lift. Well, he thought I was going to High Springs and took me to the intersection of Sixth and Thirteenth and dropped me off.

I was a little frustrated by this, as I still had no intention of going home; my desire was to return to Jacksonville. As I stood there, contemplating whether to cross the street and head back, another car pulled up in front of me. The driver offered to give me a lift to High Springs. I was taken aback by the offer, but without much thought, I got into the car and continued on to High Springs.

At High Springs, I made a stop at a place they called the "Curb Diner," the final stop on my way to the farm. I was aware that if my mom found out I was in town and didn't come home, she would be angry. So, when someone offered me a ride, I accepted it and proceeded out to the farm.

I had planned to return to Jacksonville in time to attend a dance at the VFW hall. However, when I woke up the next morning, which was a Saturday, my mom informed me that my brother needed help replacing a light fixture in his house. Additionally, my daughter Pat was there.

After completing the light fixture task, it was already noon, so I took Pat to a local diner owned by people named Dunn, whom I knew. Toni, the daughter of the owners, and one of her female friends were also at the diner. I had met them at one of the dances I had attended with my buddies from the base where I had crashed. Well, to make a long story short, I didn't manage to get back to Jacksonville until Sunday.

During my time at B-School, I became good friends with Jim, one of the guys in our group. Jim owned a 1957 Chevrolet, which was quite fast, and we spent most of our free weekends in the High Springs area. We had met a couple of local girls and ended up dating them for the remainder of our time at B school.

I had a good friend in my class who was getting close to being able to retire and he needed a promotion, and I was helping him study for the exam. He also needed some verification of his qualifications to qualify for the exam from his last command. They could not provide them, and he had requested a waiver from the school Administration.

On Friday of the weekend before the promotion exam, after our last class, we stopped by the examination center to see if he had gotten his waver. But when we stopped by examination center, I got a surprise.

While the supervisor of the center was confirming that my friend had gotten a promotion exam, he looked at my name on my shirt and said that he also had my exam. I was sure he had made a mistake because I had not requested one. He confirmed my name and rechecked the exam packets and confirmed that I had an exam packet.

When asked who had ordered me to take an exam, I learned that Chief Baker, who I had met while I was stationed in VF-43 was now in charge of the promotion center. He had seen my name on the eligibility list and had ordered me one. It was his way of returning the favor. I took the exam and both my friend, and I were part of the nine for AE-B school who were promoted, I was number nine, but I got it.

## Chapter 32

# TRANSITION TO HAWAII

The year 1959 was a very busy year for me. I finished all I could of AE-B School and earned an unexpected promotion to Petty Officer First Class, AE1, which is Pay Grade E-6. I had turned twenty-three years old, got a divorce and transferred custody of my daughter to my parents, and got a three-year military assignment to the island of Hawaii. I was broke, and in debt, but free.

My transfer orders were issued in May of 1959, and I was still in pay grade E-5, but I had received my orders to be promoted with an effective date of June 1, 1959. With my travel time and personal leave time, I was not scheduled to report to San Francisco until July.

I had orders to travel by POV to San Francisco for further transfer to Hawaii. Well, I had to change the rank insignia on all of my uniforms. I purchased them at the base before leaving Jacksonville. I had people with sewing machines who could do that for me at no cost, so I got all my uniforms correctly upgraded.

While I was still in High Springs, I met an independent trucker who was getting a load of fresh watermelons to take to the New York area. I helped him with some contacts in the area, and he offered me a ride to Pennsylvania with him. I planned to stop in Pennsylvania to see my girlfriend, who lived there.

His route would bring me where she could meet me. That saved me some money, and I really enjoyed the ride. Betty picked me up, and I got to spend three days with her before catching the bus to San Francisco.

The bus ride from Pennsylvania to San Francisco is a long and boring trip. I had a lot of time to think and sleep while sitting up. The only surprise I got was Cheyenne, Wyoming.

We pulled into Cheyenne at noon and stopped for a lunch break, and I was looking out the bus window at all the western wear everyone was wearing. It was noon, the first of July, and everybody was wearing some type of leather jacket with fancy trim. While I was still on the bus, I thought that was ridiculous. However, when I stepped out the bus door, I changed my mind.

I was wearing a short sleeve shirt, lightweight pants, and what we called penny loafers. I was hit by a strong cold wind that sent me running for cover. That wind was so cold that when I got seated inside the restaurant, my teeth were chattering so bad I had trouble ordering my meal. The only other time I had been in that part of the country was on my way to bootcamp on a train in January.

One thing that kept me motivated on that long trip was that I kept feeling like I was starting my Military career over. I was now thinking of the Navy as a career instead of just a job. I was also nervous about what I was getting into. I kept remembering what I had heard about Hawaii.

Just before I checked out of the barracks, two new students came in for AE-B school, and they had just left Air Barron Pac, the same squadron I was being transferred to. They were happy about getting out of Hawaii. They were not happy about the way they were treated there and how expensive everything was.

All they said about the aircraft was that they were large and had a lot of different systems to maintain. My aircraft maintenance experience was limited to two types of aircraft with a lot fewer systems. To make matters worse, now I would be in a supervisor category. The planes were called Willie Victors by the Navy and EC 121s by the Air Force. The picture below is of one of the Navy types that I would be working and flying on.

By the time I got to San Francisco, I was worn out. I was glad to get off that bus looking forward to a hot shower and a bed. I was able to change clothes in the restroom at the bus station and put on a clean uniform. I also learned how to get the shuttle from the bus station to the transit base.

I got to the check-in desk at the transit barracks, and the second class that was on duty was trying to give me the third degree. He kept on checking and rechecking my orders and giving me a look of distrust. All I wanted was a shower, a bed, and some rest. I got aggravated and confronted him about what he thought he was doing. Then pointed out that my orders listed me as a Second-Class Petty Officer, but my uniform insignia was of a First-Class Petty Officer. I told him that I had gotten my promotion after my orders were typed, and I was an E-6.

The problem was that the barracks had separate quarters for the First-Class Petty officers, and he was older than I was, and he thought I looked too young to be a First Class. He assigned me a room and said that he was going to check on me.

I had time to get some rest and to do my laundry before getting a passage to Hawaii on an old Military R-5 transport plane. The plane was older than the ones I had at McGuire. We had R6Ds there. The plane ride to Hawaii was a long and uncomfortable flight.

I had to clear customs and find a way to get to my base at Barber's Point. The Hawaiian bus system at that time provided only limited coverage to places outside the established tourist routes, and military bases had limited service.

We landed at the Honolulu International Airport, and I had to take a bus to the Honolulu bus station and wait for a bus to the base. I got to the base, and it seemed like everything was a mile apart from each other. It was hot, and I was dragging my big old sea bag and a small overnight bag. I finally made it to the Squadron Duty Office and checked in. I got my temporary meal pass and ride to my barracks. I was able to get a good meal at the mess hall. It was the first good food since I left San Francisco.

The next morning, I got a ride from the barracks to the shop I where I would be working. When I checked in, the shop supervisor was surprised to see me. The squadron had been notified when I would be arriving and assigned someone to meet and escort me around. I had three days off to get settled in. There were two mistakes in my orders, I was an E6, and I was not traveling with a family. My escort was at the airport when I arrived but did not find me.

After getting the required schools and training to qualify for flight status, I got assigned to an aircraft. The purpose of the squadron was to maintain airborne radar surveillance from Midway Island to the Aleutian Islands aka the Aleutian chain. The personnel on flying status were assigned to an aircraft, and you maintained it and flew on it. And for the most part, you stayed with the same plane and crew. I wound up as Electronic Crew Chief on a crew of five technicians, and we found out that four of the five had ties to Florida, so we named our crew the Flying Floridians. Our aircraft number was 007.

Our support facility was NAS Barber's Point, but our surveillance operation was operated out of Midway Island. We would move the aircraft and crew midway through each operation. For each operation, we could complete approximately 100 hours of flying. The normal time span was about thirty days. Each flight took off from Midway and landed back at Midway fourteen-and-a-half hours later. The entire flight was over water with only areas to land, Midway Island or Alaska. We always kept five planes airborne, four were on station, and one was either enroute to the station or on the way back to Midway.

The point of no return is when it is closer to continuing to Alaska than trying to return to Midway Island. Should you have to ditch, and everything works prefect, and you do not get wet, you had a small chance. If you got wet, you had nine minutes to live. When you are flying over the north Pacific Ocean, ditching isn't really an option because the sea is always too rough for a safe landing.

I am happy to say that we never lost a plane at sea. Before I got to Hawaii, they lost one plane on a training flight at Hawaii. The pilot lost too much altitude on his approach and when he made his turn to line up with the runway, he dipped the wing tip in the water. That was a disaster to start with, but the sharks got some of the ones that would have been survivors. That was strictly a pilot error.

We had one pilot error crash on Midway Island when the pilot approached the landing strip was too low, and both of his props on the left side of the plane hit the sea wall. We lost eleven of the crew and two men in the crash truck that the plane hit.

We had one plane crash due to parts failure. The plane was taking off for a mission, and as the plane lifted off the runway, the right main landing gear fell off the plane, and it flipped up and sheared off the right horizon stabilizer and one-third of the rudder system. The pilot got the plane off the ground and was able to maintain control of it. The crew on board chose to ride it in for a crash landing, and no one was seriously injured. I was not on that plane, but I witnessed it.

They calculated that the total mileage flown by that squadron would have four trips to the moon and back. But in February of 1962, the Air Force opened a new radar system in Adak, Alaska, that made our operation obsolete. They could pick up our planes on take-off and track us all around our flight path. But that system did not come without some problems.

I was flying on the day they put it into operation. I remember that we were getting all kinds of warnings of an incoming target. The target looked like an incoming missile. They went into full alert, and it was a few hours before they discovered that the target they were tracking was an echo of their signal bouncing off the moon. They discovered that the closing speed of the target was the same as the rotation speed of the Earth.

Shortly after the system was put into operation, the moon came in line of site with the Radar beam. The radar operates by bouncing the signal off a solid objective and reading the return echo. Distance and speed are calculated by how much time it takes the signal to return. In this case, they got speed, but the distance was out of range.

My tour of duty in Hawaii lasted just over three years. I got there in July of 1959 and left in November 1962. A lot of things happened to and for me while I was there. Hawaii became a state, and we had to quit referring to it as overseas. Now everything in the rest of the United States was referred to as "The Mainland." There were a few things that I really enjoyed about Hawaii, but I never liked being there.

I loved Country Music, and one area of Honolulu called Hotel Street had a few bars where they played it. The best spot was a bar named the Anchor Club. A couple by the names of Howard and Patty Jerald played there and they were very professional. I got to know them and got interested in trying to learn how to play.

I met some other guys who could play, and one of them offered to teach me how to play the guitar. His name was Frank Hampton, a young man from Texas, who was being transferred to Midway Island for a year of duty on the island. I spent most of my time on Midway because that was our base of operations for all our missions.

I bought a guitar and started learning to play. In a short time, we were joined by other guys who could play and sing, and we started a small band. We were not good, but on Midway Island, there wasn't much to do, so we became a hit. There was an Enlisted Men's club, and the person in charge of the club sponsored us. I was the senior military member of the band, and I became the band leader.

My enlistment was ending in 1962, and I was considering getting out of the Navy. I had an offer to go to Boston, Massachusetts, for a management school. I was not very keen on that idea, but I was keeping my options open.

I was happy on Midway and spent as much time as I could there. At Barber's point, they were trying to get their senior electricians off Flight Crew assignments and into the shop. When I got the message that they wanted to reassign me, I started looking for a way to avoid going back to Barber's point.

Just before my plane was scheduled to return, the Electronic Crew Chief of a different crew had an emergency and was not going to able to make his deployment. I was advised of this by the Maintenance Department Head for Midway, and I volunteered to stay over and fill in for him. That was approved, and I got a thirty-day extension on Midway; at the end of that one, I requested reassignment to my regular plane, which was on its way back for another tour. That was approved, and with that, I had been on Midway for just over 90 days and passed the time when I was to be reassigned.

My enlistment was about to end in a month. I returned to Barber's Point, having earned two weeks of downtime, which I promptly took.

Feeling confident and with little time left, I was quite cocky. However, a big surprise awaited me.

After my downtime, I visited the shop, where the Shop Chief asked which shift I wanted to work. I casually responded that it didn't matter since I had less than thirty days left. The Chief looked surprised and inquired whether I had been keeping up with the news. I admitted I hadn't, and he proceeded to inform me about the Cuban Missile Crisis. Due to this crisis, all essential personnel were put on hold until further notice. To my ego's dismay, I fell into that category. It was a shocking revelation.

Well, I went on the day shift to ride out the involuntary tour of duty. I went to check on my friends, Howard, and Patty, and learned that they were no longer together and not at the Anchor Club. It was closed for remodeling. One of their band members, Bill Spiliard, was working at a place called Hoffman's Bar and Grill on Hotel Street. He was able to let me play rhythm guitar with him and his drummer.

My enlistment had run out, and I had not renewed my Military ID card. Upon returning to base one morning at about two AM, the marine security guard on the main gate caught it and refused to let me onto the base. I just backed my car out of the entrance lane. Put my beach hat over my eyes and went to sleep.

In a short time, the base Duty Officer woke me up, and I explained that I was on an involuntary extension and my command had not issued me a new ID card. He checked with my command and confirmed that I was legal to enter and sent me to my headquarters to get an ID card.

While I was getting a temporary ID, I was informed that I was being reassigned. I had a Top-Secret Clearance, and the project was classified at that time. I was assigned to a support group for the Johnson Island Nuclear Bomb Test.

The squadron had to provide three of our aircraft to function and airborne traffic controllers for the operation. I was assigned to one of the planes. I had to make sure the plane and flight crew were ready to stand by. It was a long-drawn-out operation with constant delays; as soon as the mission was canceled, I would secure the plane until the next morning.

Almost every night, when I got ready to leave the bar after work, I would see one of our young personnel Yeomans waiting for a ride back to the base, and I would give him a ride. He would come into town and do his drinking and then catch a ride back with me. I did not know how valuable that would be to me until he showed up sober one night.

He came up and asked if I would give him a ride back to the base. We started talking about things that were going on, and while we were talking, he asked me if I had reenlisted. I told him that I had not. He asked where I wanted to be stationed and explained the person on the assignment desk in Washington was a friend of his father and that he could check with him and see what I could get. I told him that the only place that I wanted to see was Japan.

He explained that the Government had installed a hot phone line connection in Hawaii for the Johnson Island bomb test and that his office had access to it.

What he wanted to do was not authorized, but the next morning, he placed the call and reached the person we needed to talk to. They chatted for a couple of minutes, during which his contact collected all of my information and requested that I call back the next morning, promising to have an answer for us.

The next morning, I made the call, and he informed me that I needed to fulfill the required time obligation. Not only did I meet that requirement, but I also had no obligated time available. Then he mentioned that an assignment in Japan could be arranged for me, but with the condition that I re-enlist first.

He proceeded to ask me where in Japan I wanted to go. At that point, my knowledge of Japan was limited; all I knew was that someone from our group had been stationed at a place called Tachikawa. Interestingly, I wasn't even aware that Tachikawa was an Air Force base.

With the Cuban missile crisis and bomb test coming to an end, I decided to go ahead and reenlist. I finished that and requested to be assigned to duty in Japan. Now all I could do was wait.

My plane flew the last two days before the successful detonation of the bomb. On the first of the last two days, the missile was destroyed on the launch pad, the second was blown up directly ahead of us at about 10,000 feet. I was off the next day, and the test was successful. It was an airburst at 30,000 feet, and it was 850 miles away from us, and it lit up the area. I don't ever want to see another one.

In November of 1962, I got my orders and was transferred to VR7 in Tachikawa, Japan. It was a long three years and four months in Hawaii, and a lot of things happened, but one of the biggest surprises was when I got involved with a recruit by the name of Fuzzy Furr.

Furr had been a professional bull rider and had been stationed at one of the Navy bases in Texas that sponsored a rodeo event, and Furr was a team member. After one of the events, a new Commanding Officer was assigned to the base. While he was making his in-section tour of the base, he visited the base hospital after a rodeo event and saw all the injured people from the event, and he issued an order to shut down the event.

Well, Furr was raised on a ranch adjoining Lyndon Johnson's, so he called Lyndon about the situation, and the new base commander received a letter from Lyndon Johnson congratulating him on his new command and praising him for supporting the all-American sport of Rodeo Riding. Well, two things happened in rapid succession. The Base Commander withdrew his order to discontinue the Rodeo Team, and Furr was immediately transferred to AirBarronPac at Barber's Point, Hawaii.

In Texas, both Fuzzy and his wife made extra money riding in the local rodeos, and they needed that additional income for their living expenses. Now the cost of living was much higher, and Furr's wife was expecting.

They could not cover their rent on an E2's salary, and their electricity and gas had been cut off. Some of us were trying to keep them going, but they needed more help than we could afford. Fuzzy was in trouble trying to survive in Hawaii and needed a hardship discharge.

I had got to know Fuzzy and his wife, and one night he came to my house he needed to use my phone. Phones were expensive and hard to get in Hawaii, and I did not want anybody to run up my phone bill. I asked Fuzzy who he needed to call, and he said, "Lyndon Johnson, the Vice President of the United States." I told him there was no way he was going to use my phone for that.

Then He Said, "I am calling him collect". Fuzzy was serious, and I knew he needed more help than we could give, but I did not want a phone bill for an overseas call. He assured me that he knew what he was doing, and I let him try to make a collect call that I was sure would never go through. It took a while, and he had to fight with several telephone company supervisors, but he got to talk with Vice President Lyndon Johnson on the phone.

Just a couple of days later, I got sent to the office of the Squadron Personnel Officer. When I got there, he was holding a letter in his hand, and he was not very happy. The letter was addressed to Airman Apprentice Fuzzy Furr, in the care of the squadron personnel office.

The commander was mad that he could not contact Fuzzy, and someone had told him that I was friends with Fuzzy. He then looked at me and stated, "This is one the biggest and most important units in the military, and the highest correspondence we get is for an E2.

After explaining that I knew who Fuzzy Furr was and that he did not have a phone, I agreed to find him and bring him to the office. I brought Fuzzy to the office and left him there, and in about a week, Fuzzy was discharged and off the Island.

# Chapter 33

# TACHIKAWA JAPAN

In November of 1962, I was transferred from Barber's Point, Hawaii, to Tachikawa, Japan. Tachikawa City is in the suburbs of Tokyo, Japan, and it is the location of an Airforce Base by its' same name. I was assigned to US Navy Squadron VR-7, which had four R7V super constellations, as shown in the picture below, and it has the same fuselage as the Willy Victor/EC121.

Our mission in Japan was Inter Theater Air Evacuation. The advantage of the R7V aka Connie, was for medical air evacuation. We could support the Iron Lung setup, and we could maintain 72 degrees temperature inside the aircraft and sea level pressure over all the mountain ranges. It could also be set up for a full load of passengers. Tachikawa Base is an Air Force base, and our squadron was assigned to the Air Force. At the time I was transferred there, there was only one other Aircraft Electrician that had any experience on that type of plane, and he had also been transferred there from Air Barron Pac.

Well, my trip started with a long, slow, and uncomfortable ride. The plane was a very old R5D. That was the same type and possibly the same plane I flew to Hawaii on. I used to kid people by telling them that I had flown from The United States to Japan on and R5D aircraft, and it took me three years and four months to get there.

I had always wanted to see Japan, and I sure was glad to get there. I think that traveling is very educational, but when you are traveling alone and cannot speak the language of the place you are going, it can get interesting. I landed at Tachikawa with no knowledge of the language or currency. I did know that it was called Yen.

The exchange rate was 360 yen to one dollar American. I also knew that the military required all currency to be converted to Military Script. The Tachikawa base is also a port of entry, so you can change your currency as soon as you get off the plane.

I knew the guy who was there from Hawaii and was planning to hit the town with him as soon as I arrived, and he knew I was coming. I got checked in by leaving a copy of my orders with the duty officer and got my barracks assignment, it was cold when I arrived at Tachikawa, and the only winter clothing I had was my winter uniform. You do not need winter clothing in Hawaii.

I was ready to go to town and called my friend. Well, it was around 8 PM, and I wanted to get started, but he was already in bed. He was scheduled for a flight physical at 0800 the next morning, and he had already failed two attempts for high blood pressure and would lose his flight status if he could not pass this one.

Well, that left me in a mess, I was dressed in my best uniform and a pocket full of Yen, and I was going to town. I got the phone number for the Base Taxi service and gave them my address. Without delay, a taxi arrived, driven by a friendly Japanese driver who didn't speak any English.

I continued to tell him, "Town," but he seemed confused. So, I resorted to using hand signals, which still left him puzzled until I pretended to take sip of a drink. Then smiled and looked at my uniform and counted my stripes and took off. It was only a short ride before he whipped into the parking lot at the NCO Club.

Well, when I refused to get out there, he was confused again. I tried several other attempts to say, "Take me to town," and then he took off again and drove me to the security stop at the main gate. He motioned to the guard, and he came over.

This guy could speak both English and Japanese. When I explained to the guard that I wanted to go to town, he pointed to the buildings across the street and said that it was the town, and the first two blocks were all bars and places where you could eat. I paid the driver for the cab fare by giving him a large Yen bill and waiting for my change. I got my change, gave the driver a tip, and walked into the city of Tachikawa, Japan.

As I walked toward the bright neon lights, I could see a large neon sign with the name "New Yorker Club," so I headed toward it. I realized that I was in a foreign country and that I was alone, but somehow, I felt relaxed even though I had no idea what might happen next.

I entered the bar, and it was a slow night, and not many people were in the place. I looked around at the people as I slowly made my way to the bar. Everyone was friendly. I took a seat at the bar, and a Japanese woman, who was working behind it, approached me. Her English was a bit broken, but it was an improvement from the Taxi Driver, who spoke no English at all.

While I could understand her, I wasn't sure if she would understand me. I ordered a beer, but she seemed a little unsure. So, I specifically asked for a Budweiser. Her next response served as a wake-up call. She appeared puzzled and mentioned that they did have some American beer, but it was kept in a separate cooler and in limited supply. She said she would check for it but couldn't quite pronounce "Budweiser".

She then pointed to some Japanese beer on the bar and mentioned that Japan had good beer. At that moment, a realization dawned on me. I understood that I was merely a guest in their country, and their purpose wasn't solely to cater to me. I should choose from what they had to offer.

They had several brands of great beer, but my two favorites were Kirin and Sapporo. I ordered a Kirin beer and settled back to enjoy it and the pleasant company of the bartender.

No one asked for the money for the beer, and I noticed that she picked up a small pad of paper and wrote something on it. I did not want to start any kind of a bar tab, so I took some yen out of my pocket and laid it on the bar. The woman that was waiting on me asked me how long I had been in Japan. I explained that I had just got there, and she said, "Oh," and then said let me help you.

She started with the money. She picked up the money I had laid on the bar, picked out the largest bill, and handed it back to me while saying something to the effect of being too much. Then she pointed to the beer and picked up one of the smaller bills and handed it to the guy handling the cash. He took the bill and gave me back some change.

We talked, and she answered my questions as best she could, based on her understanding of what I was asking. One thing I wanted was some Japanese food. So, we went to a small restaurant close by and had an excellent meal. I had learned to eat with chopsticks in Hawaii at a Japanese restaurant there, so I had no problem eating in Japan. That night was the only time I ever saw her, but I sure enjoyed my first night in Japan.

The next day, I completed the check-in process and familiarized myself with important locations like the barracks, NCO club, and chow hall. It became evident that our command didn't hold the Chow Hall in high regard; they offered everyone the choice between receiving separate ration pay or obtaining a meal pass for the Chow Hall.

I had another Petty Officer First Class who acted as my guide. He lived in the same NCO quarters as I did and owned a car. When I attempted to pay for the gas for his car, I discovered that gasoline on the base was priced at 11 cents per gallon, whereas the cost was considerably higher off the base. In Hawaii, the cost of gas on base was about the same price as in downtown Tokyo. Without any increase in pay, my standard of living went up over 100 percent.

I was the only AE1 in the squadron, and there was only one other AE who had experience with the R7V aircraft. We had one of the old versions, the R7V at Air Barron Pac, and I had done a lot of work on that one. It was very old and needed a complete overhaul. A team of four of us back at Barber's Point had the plane taken out of service and thought for sure I would never see that problem again, but that was not correct. For the most part, the maintenance was about the same on the Willy Victors.

The weather was cold when I arrived at Tachikawa, and then it started raining a lot. For the first four days, I was there, I not only worked on the plane I was assigned to, but I helped the other three crews with their planes. All the work was either in the open hangar bay or outside on the Flight Line.

On the fifth morning, it was a clear and sunny morning. My room was on the third floor of an old WWII wood frame-type building. Each floor was built with an outside stairwell-type entrance. You exited the building by walking out onto a landing to access the stairs. On that first clear morning, I saw something that was so beautiful it took my breath away. It was Mount Fuji in all its glory.

***30. Japan: Mount Fuji – My World Fridge Magnets by Unknown Author is licensed under CC BY-NC-ND***

The early morning sun had the snow cap shining like gold. I stopped on the landing and asked, "What is that?"

A guy I was riding to and from work with said, "Haven't you ever seen Mount Fuji?" Not only had I not seen it, but I had also not heard of it. That was a view I would never forget.

It was just a couple of days later when I got another big shock. The workload for the first week was very demanding, and I had caught a bad cold. I was worn out, and when I got a day off, I expected to sleep for at least 24 hours without being disturbed. I got a good hot shower and went to bed.

Just as I was dropping off to sleep, I felt what I thought was, someone shaking my bed. At first, I just ignored it, then the bed shook harder. I was mad and I sat up in the bed to give that person a piece of my mind. There was no one in the room and my bed seemed to be walking across the room. We were having an earthquake.

That old wooden frame building was really shaking. That was the first earthquake that I had felt. They had two small ones when I was in Hawaii, but I was flying both times, so I did not feel either one of them. This time I was there, and it scared the daylights out of me.

Our main mission was medical Airborne evacuation, and Vietnam was the main area we serviced. We were part of the Canto Plain region, which covers the Tokyo area of Japan. We were only one unit that was part of that operation. All our operations, assignments and support came from the Air Force.

With four aircraft, we were flying five scheduled flights per week to Kempo Korea to move troops to and from Korea and two flights per week to Clark Air Force Base in the Philippines located in Angeles City. One flight would be to Clark and back, and the second was a three-day flight.

On the three-day flight, the first day was to Clark, the second would be to in-country Vietnam, and we flew in and out of all the small bases that we needed to pick up someone and move them to Clark. The third day would be the return trip from Clark to Tachikawa. Clark was the staging area for bringing wounded soldiers out of Vietnam as soon as they were medically stabilized and could be safely moved. They were airlifted to Clark for further medical treatment and further transport.

Tachikawa was the second staging area for medical treatment prior to movement to the Tripler Army medical center in Honolulu, Hawaii. Our work schedule was based on the maintenance condition of our aircraft and its schedule. When the aircraft was on the ground at Tachikawa, we worked until it was ready to fly. When it was scheduled, we worked until it was airborne. One of the crew flew with the aircraft on all scheduled flights.

Sometimes, in addition to our regular scheduled duties, we would be assigned emergency calls to pick up and transport someone with a medical emergency in other parts of Japan. That means that the crew has to be called back to work because you are between scheduled flights, and that is your off time. It costs a lot of money to fly that big plane. Most of the time, it is justifiable.

However, I recall one that I never thought was justified. I don't remember what the name of the base was, but it was a small base in the northern part of Japan. It was in the winter, and the base that we were going to had gotten a heavy snowfall. When we got there, the runaways and the narrow taxiways had been plowed. The accumulated snow was about four feet, but the plowed snowbanks averaged six to seven feet.

Even under normal conditions, the base would have been considered small for our plane. The runways were short, and with the frozen ground conditions, breaking the plane was more difficult, and the plowed snowbanks were close to the sides of the runway. You cannot let a turning propeller blade hit the snow because that would destroy the engine and the prop. So, the snowbanks had to be avoided at all costs.

Our propellers were the variable pitch type, and you could use reverse pitch to help stop or turn the aircraft. To turn the aircraft around at the end of the runway, you had to put the engines on one side into reverse pitch and the other two forward thrust. That way, you can spin the plane around in its own tracks. The pilots had to use that after we landed so we could taxi back to the turn-off ramp.

Before we could taxi on the ramps, we shut off the two outside engines and feathered the props. Feathering the propeller is turning the blade so that the edges of the blades are lined up with the direction of plane movement. As we taxied to the terminal, our two outside engines were over the snowbank, and the prop blades were dragging through the snow.

When we stopped at the terminal to pick up our passenger, due to the lack of a snow-cleared area available to us, we had to shut down the engine on the passenger entrance side of the plane and wait for our passenger to come aboard. The ground crew put a boarding ramp up to the plane, and a lady walked out of the terminal and stopped to talk to some people before boarding the plane. We waited 15 to 20 minutes while she talked to them, then walked unassisted up the ramp and onto the plane. She had asthma and had an attack earlier that morning, and for some reason, someone had decided to send her to a medical facility in the Tokyo area for a checkup. We had to start one engine and turn the plane around, and taxi back to the runaway, dragging our outside prop blades through the snow to the runway, get the plane aligned for take-off, start the other two engines, and take off for home.

We also had several other flights that took passengers to different places outside of Japan. We flew several flights to Bangkok and Hong Kong, both of which required an overnight stay. This meant staying at a hotel for the night in those locations. For the most part, it was paid for by the government. Sometimes our flights would be in assistance to other agencies, and they would cover the expense of the crew members.

I remember that on one of our Hong Kong trips, we were treated to a special Chinese dinner at one of the top-rated restaurants in Hong Kong.

On that trip, our plane was parked right next to a Russian plane, and we were told not to take pictures of it or go near it. One of our passengers was a US Army soldier. I was walking next to him, and as soon as he got close enough to see the Russian plane, he pulled his camera out of his handbag and started taking pictures as fast as he could. I asked him, "Are you taking pictures?"

He replied, "Yes, mind your own business; nobody's gonna tell me I can't take pictures." I told him that I was just wondering how you were doing that without removing the dust cover. Boy, he got mad, but by then, we had passed the plane.

At the hotel, we were requested to wear our dress uniforms as we were being treated to a formal Chinese dinner. The restaurant was the most elaborate one I had ever seen. The table was adorned with very expensive dishes and linen, and we were seated by our own escort. Next to my plate on the linen, there lay a pair of chopsticks that appeared to be made of real ivory. Having used chopsticks in both Hawaii and Japan, I was curious whether they were made of plastic or genuine ivory. I picked up one to test it, holding both ends and applying a slight upward pressure to the middle of the stick to assess its flexibility; however, to my surprise, it snapped instantly like a piece of glass. My waiter seemed displeased and promptly replaced my broken chopsticks with a cheap wooden set. The embarrassment was overwhelming, and I could feel my face turning red. Despite my blunder, the restaurant, meal, and service remained outstanding.

Our flights to Kempo, Korea were all round trips, and you were only on the ground long enough to off-load your passengers, Gas and service the plane, and reload. In the summer it was okay, but in the winter, it was miserable. Korea has a very bitter cold and damp climate. The part I hated the most was refueling the aircraft. We did not have a pressure fueling system on our planes, and I had to go up on top of the wing, which is about 25 to 30 feet above the concrete ramp with a heavy, pressurized fuel hose, and drag it all the way to the tip of the wing. You had to fill each fuel tank while standing on a slick surface, in the cold and sometimes strong wind, while wrestling that heavy fuel hose. I would try so hard to turn my feet into suction cups that they would hurt.

Takeoffs and landings were always risky, but in Korea, it seems like the Korean pilots did not get the same approach and landing instructions as we did. I recall that on one of our takeoffs, we almost had a midair collision with a Korean plane that was coming in for a landing in the wrong direction. We had just lifted off the runway and started our climb when we suddenly met a small Korean plane that was on its final approach for landing. The plane came so close to hitting us that both our pilot and copilot gripped the yoke at the same time and made a hard left turn. That flipped our plane on its left side, which is not a normal flying configuration for our large plane.

I was looking out a window on the left side of the plane, and realized I was looking straight down at the ground. We missed the Korean plane and recovered our plane with only a little loss of altitude which you don't have much of during a takeoff operation.

We were an all-navy crew on what was thought of as an Air Force Plane. We were primarily moving Army soldiers and their dependents, and when they got on the plane and saw only Navy uniforms running the plane, they got a little nervous.

We would play games with them during the flight to keep them nervous. We teamed up and we walked down the center isle of the plane, looking like we were worried and looking for something, stopping at the seat of someone seated over the wing and looking around him at the wing. All the time, we would assure the passenger that everything was ok. Then while looking out the window at the two engines on that wing, act a little surprised and motion to our partner to come over. He would hurry over, take a look out the window, give a serious nod and hurry away in the direction of the cockpit. Then we would reassure the passenger that there was nothing to worry about and leave in a different direction. Sometimes the passenger would stop us later and ask what the problem was, and we would just say nothing.

I don't recall having any flight problems in the Philippines, but some of the conditions in Viet Nam were different. Some of the fields we had to land on to pick up injured people were a challenge. One that I remember was at the base of the mountain. The approach to the landing strip was a nice low-level approach over some farmland and toward the mountain. The problem was that the Vietcong had control of that; they liked shooting at low-flying aircraft. Our approach was over the mountain, and we dived for the runway. On takeoff, we had to fly toward that mountain and fly around it. We never had any accidents or bullet holes in our plane.

We landed in Taipei for an overnight stop, and when we inspected the plane, we found that a small caliber bullet had hit the back side of the propeller on our number three engine. It made a small indentation in the center of the propeller blade. Normally that would send the plane into maintenance, but we decided that if it had flown us into Taipei, it would fly us out. We watched it closely, but it did not get reported until we returned to Tachikawa.

I enjoyed Japan so much that I extended my two-year tour of duty for an additional year. As soon as we got the maintenance on our plane under control, I started enjoying my liberty time. The clubs on base were Tachikawa East, which was a large, enlisted club, and the NCO Club. Both clubs had bands playing live country music. It was at Tachikawa East that I met Little Jimmy Dickens. He appeared there shortly after I got settled in, and little did I know that I would be working with him on his next three trips through Japan.

One of the military people that also played music there was a guy called Shorty Danes. Somehow, he found out that I played and asked me to join his band. I had only played rhythm guitar before, and my plans were to learn to play bass guitar while I was in Japan. I started playing in his band while learning the electric bass. The military work schedule always came first and sometimes you would have to miss a show. I met several people who played music and they taught me how to play the electric bass in country-style music.

Country Music was big in Japan and a lot of Japanese played the music. Japan's number-one country singer was a guy by the name of Jimmy Takata. I met Jimmy and became good friends with him. He was one month younger than me, and we both had been married, had a daughter and were divorced. The top Japanese country music band was called the Wagon Aces and the band leader's name was Peewee Hiruta. They were a great band. The only drawback was that the Japanese learned the music by copying each song. Somewhat like we learn a foreign language.

On the other hand, we were raised with the music and could adlib the basic parts of the music and the singer sing anything without a lot of rehearsal. Some professional country music singers like Rose Maddox would perform their show based on a list of songs. They would send Peewee a copy of their show in advance of their arrival, and his band would have every song ready just like it was recorded.

I loved the music and worked very hard at learning how to play the bass. There was a person in the Air Force by the name of Dewey Jones who played the fiddle and sang. Dewey was trying to start his own band and had some good ideas about what he wanted and how to get jobs. He was trying to get me to switch bands and work for him. I was still just learning my way around and was not ready to change.

Shorty had us booked on an Army base by the name of Fort Smith in Tokyo and when we took our break, a solider by the name of John Hines came over an introduced himself as a professional bass player. He also asked Shorty if he needed a bass player and shorty told him that I was his bass player, but if he was looking for work and wanted to audition, and if it was okay with me, he could sit in with us for his audition.

I did not like his approach, but I agreed to let him use my very cheap rig, and he was a professional bass player. He got sounds out of my rig that I could only dream about. He had played on the Nashville circuit and was in Ray Price's band. I thought he would be perfect for Dewey's band, so I made plans to introduce him to Dewey. I met with John and learned that he had gotten into some trouble and a Judge had given him an option of two years in the Military or two years in jail.

Dewey was a family man and Christian, but at that time, I did not know much about him and made the mistake of having a couple of drinks before going to his house. Dewey let us in and listened to what we had to say but turned down John's offer. He pulled me aside and expressed his dislike of me coming to his home drinking, and he also told me that I was who he wanted to play in his band. I liked Dewey's professional approach, and I gave John my spot in Shorty's band, and I went with Dewey.

Dewey put together a good band and got us booked into all the bigger clubs, then carried out the rest of his plan. He found out who in Tokyo handled the booking of the country stars when they came to Japan on tour and got them to let him help them book them in the military clubs. That little trick got us the job of backing all the stars that came through Tokyo except for the ones who made prior arrangements Peewee.

We were great for the older stars that liked to do the show as they felt like it. Some entertainers brought their own bands with them, and we played as the house band, and they were the floorshow. I remember Roy Acuff came through with his band and played Tachi East with us. Marty Robbins and his band, Jim Ed Brown with Chet Atkins and the group he called the Nashville sound also came through. All these artists were great people to work with. There were more artists than I can remember at this time. Some of them we only saw once, and some made as many and four trips through Japan while I was there.

Hank Snow came through Tokyo, and I went to see him at a large concert hall in Tokyo and met the band that came with him. Hank and his band, The Rainbow Ranch Boys, had retired. Hank was in bad health and his recording of the song I've Been Everywhere hit the top of the charts and he had to come out of retirement to promote it. Hank had Buddy Spiker playing fiddle and Jimmy Crawford on steel and I got to meet them.

To get around Tokyo, I had to ride their train system and, on my way back, I met a couple of Japanese guys who became my best friends. On the long train ride back to Tachikawa, a young Japanese came up to me and asked if I had just been to see Hank Snow's show. He introduced himself as Nick Hickey. That was the American name he liked to use. Nick and his friend played country music. Nick played the steel guitar, and his friend played the drums. I knew that Dewey was still looking for musicians and I took their names and phone numbers. Nick and I started a friendship that lasted for several years. I got Nick and his friend an interview with Dewey, and he hired them. Nick and I became best friends and worked together for the rest of the time I was in Japan.

Shortly after Hank Snow played his concert in Tokyo, he came to an Air Force based named Yokota. It was close to Tachikawa. I had played there with Shorty Danes, and there is also a Veterans of Foreign Wars (VFW) club there that we played at. John Hines called me and asked if I could fill in for him at the VFW club that night. That was one of my few nights off and I had other plans, but he said that he knew the members of Hank's band and he was going to get them to jam with us after their show at Yokota. I agreed and sure enough, John came back with Buddy Spiker, Jimmy Crawford and Jimmy Takata and their instruments.

They hit the stage playing, and they played the best music I had heard. We shut down at four AM to get something to eat. One of the customers owned a small restaurant just off the base and she volunteered to open her place and cook us some food. Buddy and Jimmy had to wait until about seven AM to catch their transportation back to Tokyo. All they had to do was grab their things and go to the Airport for a long flight back to the states. I sat there and talked with Buddy about the music and how he got started until about seven AM. I really enjoyed that night.

One of the biggest events that I was a part of was a program called Better Communication Through Music. The two-star general that was in charge of the Kanto Plains area at that time had come up with that idea. He wanted to portray the military to the public as ordinary people instead of a military unit. Each of us was to do our performance in proper dress or costume for the type of music that we were playing and then be introduced to the audience in our dress uniforms. It would start with solo acts and end up with the fifth Airforce Jazz band playing a medley of Benny Goodman music. Dewey, and a guy for the Army and I were chosen to represent country music. We played several shows in the area, and they were mostly for dignitaries. The highest person that I recall was the Prince of Japan.

To Be able to make the shows for the program, I needed a special work assignment that let me make all the shows. One of our senior Chiefs had got me assigned to a new project in the Squadron called the First Lieutenant division. This unit was responsible for the general upkeep of the squadron spaces and equipment. It was supported by sending all the new recruits that were not designated to one of the divisions to the unit to work. The squadron was facing an Operational Ready Inspection and we needed to get everything ready for it. The inspectors were coming from the states to conduct the inspection and the overall credibility of your unit depended on the score you received.

I tried to get painting and maintenance on our assigned buildings and spaces done by the base, but they would not supply anything because the base was preparing to be shut down. So, I had to apply the old Navy Can Do attitude of finding a way to get it done. Most of the personnel that were sent to me were more interested in finding a way to get out of work than doing the job. But one of the guys had completed his first tour of duty in the Air Force, got out for a while, and decided to try the Navy. He was a good worker and knew how to find the things he needed. Well, he went out and found us an Air Force pickup truck.

The base color scheme for the building was soft cream with darker trim. Since I could not get the paint I needed from the Air Force, I went to the navy base at Yokosuka for some help. Well, all they had was a lot of white paint and some black. I loaded up a few five-gallon cans of white and some of the black and came back and made some pretty Navy Gray. The next day we found a portable air compressor and just borrowed it for a few days. We got some large tarpaulins and hung them up where they were painting to protect the environment from paint overspray. Behind those tarps, we painted our barracks, which just happened to be straight across the street from the NCO Club, a very nice Battleship Gray with black trim. We had a Navy Destroyer's anchor and about thirty feet of anchor chain that we painted white.

About the time I thought I had gotten away with it, I got called to my commander's office to explain why I had not followed the Air Force base color code. There was the chief that got me that assignment, an Air Force Colonel, and my Squadron Commander. I explained that I had tried to get the paint from the Air Force, but they refused to let me have any and had to go to the Navy, and they only had white and Black, so I had to use that.

Shortly after the music project was completed, I got an invitation to the General's house for a barbeque in appreciation for the work we had done on his project. The invitation was on a nice card with his two stars on the card. I just put it in the basket because I had no intention of going. At about that same time, a young LTJG was assigned the duties of overseeing my unit. He was constantly coming in and out of the office I had built for the unit, asking me questions, and trying to make some changes to how we were doing things. Finally, I said, "Sir, there is something you could help me with," and I handed him my invitation card with the two stars and told him, "I don't have time to go to this and it won't help me anyway. Could you attend this for me?" He gave me a look of anger and laid the card down on my desk and walked out of the office. After the ORI was over and we did get a good score, I was sent back to my flight crew.

I really enjoyed the three years I spent in Japan, and I tried to live each day to its fullest. One of the bars just outside the base was named Hillbilly Heaven and had the very best collection of country music in Japan. They were great people, and they took good care of us GIs. Their policies were that if we could name a valid country song that they did not have, our beer was free. The GIs would challenge them and if they did not have the song, then the GI would write home and have a copy sent to them.

At that time 45 records were common and they had shelf after shelf of them in their music closet and they owned one of the best sound systems in Japan. I found out that their favorite country artist was little Jimmy Dickens, but they had never seen him. We had a show scheduled with him at Tachikawa East and I invited them to the show as my guest. They were surprised and excited.

The night we did the show, I picked them up at the main gate and escorted them to the club. They were very well dressed, so happy, and I had a table reserved for them. I got them the best service I could get. I asked Jimmy for a favor and explained what I was doing and asked him to let me introduce him to them. He said sure, and I showed him where they were. I took Jimmy over to their table and sat down and talked to them for the whole break. He also thanked them for helping our service men. I have never seen happier people than they were.

There were a lot of military clubs in Tokyo, Japan that played country music and I played in most of them. While I have a lot of special memories of them, one that will always stand out above the rest is the Green Park Enlisted Men's Club. That is where I met a lady named Keiko Kuramochi and she changed my life forever.

They had a country band that was playing there, but most of their people were being transferred out and we were scheduled to audition there. I got a call from their bass player, and he had shipped his equipment home and needed me to fill in for him. I was scheduled to be there anyway, so I played in both bands the first time I was there. One of our flight mechanics, Doc Denton and his wife lived in one of the units. Doc and I had flown a lot of trips together and were friends. On that night, he and his wife had brought a Japanese girl by the name of Keiko Kuramochi as their guest. I had brought a guy that was new to the squadron by the last name of Black. He had played upright bass in a different type of music and wanted to hear us play.

One of the clubs we played in was a large housing unit called Green Park. During WWII, it was a Japanese aircraft factory. It was large and had everything a housing unit needed. It had five sections that were all connected in the middle, each section had two wings, one on each side of the connection, and each wing had three floors and a basement. The schedule was for the old band to play the first set and our band would play the second for our audition. I needed to eat something and the only way I had time to was to order it and have the waitress have it ready when I went on break. My band had to set up during the break and I was already set up, so that gave me a few extra minutes. The first problem was when Doc's wife insisted that I join them at their table. I wanted to eat at my table, and the food was already delivered; just as I got my first bite, an arm reached over my shoulder and grabbed my plate and away it went to Doc's table. The picture below is of Green Park during the 1950s.

## Chapter 34

# WHEN OLEN MET KEIKO

*Keiko Kuramochi 1963*

I moved over to their table and sat next to Doc on his left side and Black sat next to me on my left side. Keiko was sitting on Doc's right side, and he was telling her what a great guy Black was and talking around me. I tried to get Doc to introduce me to Keiko and then my only introduction was, oh, and this is Olen, and he kept talking about Black. While Doc was still building up Black, I got up and walked around Doc and took Keiko out on the dance floor. The song on the jukebox was ending and my band was getting ready to start when I noticed that the other bass player was signaling to me that he would take my place on the first song. I stayed on the dance floor for the next song and talked Keiko into going on a date with me. Little did I know that she would be with me for the next 34 years.

Japan had an outstanding train transportation system. But it was for transporting people, and it was crowded. During rush hours, the longest time you had to wait for your train was 15 minutes. If you got to the station and found your boarding platform, and if your train was leaving as you stepped onto the platform, your next train would be loading in 15 minutes. They had people called packers that would push you onto the train so the doors could close. It would be so crowded on some of the trains that you would be standing up, and if you were to pass out, you could not fall to the floor. You could find a train station within walking distance of almost anywhere. But you could not bring any large packages with you. No Guitars, amplifiers, or drums. So, I bought an old car to haul the equipment in, it was a 1952 Mercury, and it cost me fifteen dollars.

None of the Japanese playing in our band had a car. The property situation in Japan was so bad that only the wealthy had a room on their property to park a car. To get a driver's license, you had to prove that you had a space to park a car, even though all you wanted was a license to drive. I found a GI that had the old Mercury, and the good thing I could say about the car was that it ran. It had a standard transmission and only the second and third gear worked. There were no reverse or first gear. There had been so much bodywork done that it was mostly Bondo that held it together. All the paint was just primer and all the fabric inside the car was gone and only a few strings were left. I had to drive the car back to the base without backing up or stalling the car. It was very tricky, but somehow, I made it.

I got a good surprise when I was trying to find the transmission gear that I needed. Someone told me about a Japanese junkyard that would have the part. This was an American-made car, and I noted that a Japanese junkyard would have what I needed. My friend took me to the junkyard, and I told the owner that I needed first and reverse gears for a 1952 Mercury, and he took off through his highly organized junk yard and went straight to the box where the gear was. It cost about two dollars.

After repairing the transmission, the car ran great. It had a spacious trunk, and I even removed the rear seat to create ample room for storing and hauling the band equipment. However, when I picked up Keiko for our first date, which was also one of our shows, she appeared very embarrassed.

While I was still with the Dewey Jones band, we backed up a young actor and singer by the name of Johnny Western. Johnny had written and sung the theme song for the TV show "Have Gun Will Travel". He had also written and recorded several western ballads and toured and opened for Johnny Cash. Johnny had a fabulous voice, and he was an accomplished guitar player.

On our second show with him, we were playing a military club by the name of the Johnson NCO Club. It was a good-sized club and one of our regular clubs, and he asked Dewey if I could go with him to a second show, he had that night. Well, I had a car, and Keiko was with me, so I agreed. With Keiko as our navigator, we found the club, and it was another NCO Club. Some of the people were fans of Johnny's and requested some of his Western Ballads. Johnny and I were doing the show by ourselves. Since I could read his chords on the guitar, I could follow him on the bass, so he switched over to some of his songs. Johnny was a very talented artist and did a great show.

Johnny was also a western fast-draw artist and wore a pearl-handled Colt 45 single-action pistol and gun belt as a part of his stage dress. Part of his act was to start talking about writing a song named Have Gun; at that time, he would fire that pistol with a blank cartridge, then say oops, sorry about that, then start singing the song.

The report of that gun is the same as that of a real .45 caliber bullet. You could not resist jumping when that sound hit you. Well, I thought we were in big trouble that night when he fired it. First, there was a lady wearing a very nice white dress and drinking a green-colored drink called a grasshopper. That green drink went all down the front of that dress. There was also a Japanese waiter carrying a full tray of empty bottles, and he dove for the floor sending bottles flying everywhere.

While the crowd was laughing at the lady with the now green and white dress, the waiter was not amused. He slowly got up to a kneeling position, and one by one, he slowly picked up a bottle. I was directly in front of him, and he was staring at us with a mad expression on his face. He would hold each bottle for a few moments as he was making up his mind if he should throw the bottle or put it on the tray. After the show, Johnny tried to pay for the cleaning of the dress, but her husband would not agree to that, saying that he had never had such a good laugh in his life. Everybody enjoyed the show, including the lady with the drink.

Johnny asked me to play bass for him on the rest of the shows in Tokyo, and I did. I spent a little over a week with Johnny, and we had a show booked each day, and on some days, we played two shows. One of the two-show days started with an afternoon show at an Officer's club. While we were setting up our gear, the club manager came up to us and told us that the last country band that played there was shut down in the middle of the show and asked us to leave. That really made me mad, and I had a couple of words with the manager. If you think there may be trouble with a band or their music, you always tell them before booking them so they can make the decision before making the trip to the club.

Johnny called me aside and told me not to worry about it because he never did a bad show. Then he said to trust him because he knew how to work with officers. By that time, we were ready to start the show, and I got another surprise. Johnny was playing a Fender Stratocaster Guitar which had become the accepted symbol for Rock and Roll music. He turned the tone on the guitar to a real trashy sound and made a horrible sound and said in a real redneck accent, "We gonna play y'all some country music cause we're country".

I just wanted to go hide, but Johnny reset his guitar to a beautiful sound and sang the most outstanding version of Wayward Wind that I had ever heard. When he made that horrible sound, everyone stopped talking and gave us a disgusted look, but as soon as he started singing, their expressions turned to shock. At the end of the song, the crowd gave us a good round of applause. I learned from Johnny that when playing at the Officer's Club, you need to find out where the most senior officer is sitting. The crowd takes the lead for that person, and if he likes you, the crowd will like you. Well, Johnny gave an outstanding performance, and we did three encores.

While we were playing our show at the Officer's Club, someone contacted the Enlisted Club, and they requested that we go directly over there and do a show. Johnny agreed, and they sent a vehicle and helper to move our equipment and held the club open for us. We had a great crowd, and Johnny did an excellent show.

The Navy Base at Yokosuka held an all-day event called The Show of Stars. They took a large warehouse and cleared it out, then built a large stage with dressing rooms at one end of the building and filled it with folding chairs. All the musical entertainment acts in the area were invited, and Johnny was booked in the early afternoon. During his act, he fired his gun, and the marine security force went nuts trying to find where the shot came from. By the time they got to our end of the building, Johnny had holstered his gun and was singing Have Gun Will Travel.

A group called The Ink Spots was booked to perform after us, but they were running late. Johnny was asked if he would fill in until they arrived. He was requested to do something using the gun he had fired earlier, like a fast draw demonstration. Johnny had a routine where he would demonstrate the art of drawing and firing the gun, and it went over really well. I don't remember all the acts that were there, but I did have the opportunity to meet The Canadian Sweethearts, Bob Regan and Lucille Starr, and spend some time with them. Both Johnny and The Canadian Sweethearts were also booked for a late afternoon show at other clubs on the same base, so we had time to kill between shows.

During Johnny's second show, we were at the Enlisted Club, which had a large crowd. One guy in the audience was very drunk and disruptive and constantly heckling Johnny. He was sitting directly in front of Johnny at a table of five people about thirty feet from the stage. I got a message to the bouncer to take care of it, but he never went to the table. Finally, as Johnny was ending a song and the drunk was making a howling sound, Johnny said something like I've had enough of you. He drew, fired a blank shot toward the table, and the guy froze in total shock. He turned pale and did not even blink his eyes.

When the security people lifted him out of his chair, he remained in a sitting position. He could not straighten his legs. I watched as they carried him out of the room, and he still could not straighten his legs. Johnny was worried that he would get sued over that, but the crowd was laughing, and the music went on.

During the time I got to work with Johnny on his tour, we developed a friendship that I still cherish today. He is now retired and living in Arizona with his family.

# Chapter 35

# SINGER TOMMY DUNCAN

Thanks to being able to play country music in Japan, I had the opportunity to work with and become friends with some great entertainers. One particularly special friend was Tommy Duncan. I remember the first time I saw him was right after I started working with Dewey Jones at the Johnson NCO Club. It was during our family night event, and Tommy was the main attraction. On family night the club sets up a special table for the wives or special guests of the band. Tommy managed to enter the club without being noticed and approached the family table to ask if they were with the band, introducing himself. He mentioned that he was supposed to sing with the band later and asked if he could join them. Dewey's wife recognized him and invited him to their table. The assistant club manager hurried over to the table to greet Tommy and asked what the club could buy him to drink. Tommy responded, "Man, I sure do need a drink. Could I have a double shot of black coffee?" This surprised the club manager, as he couldn't believe that, with all the drink options available, coffee was Tommy's preferred choice.

Tommy Had retired from working with Bob Wills and the Texas Playboys, where he had thirteen major hits and was enjoying being a solo act. He was known for his signature white Stetson hat that he wore while doing his show. He carried it in a big guitar case, and I asked him why. He told me that if he carried it in a hat box while traveling on commercial flights, it would always get messed up, but in a guitar case, nobody would mess with it. I played on all his shows in the Tokyo area until I left Japan in November of 1965. By that time, I had my own band.

I had the pleasure of getting to know a special couple named Joe and Rose Lee Maphis. They were both accomplished in their respective careers, with Rose Lee being a singer and Joe gaining popularity for his exceptional guitar playing. Initially, Joe was hired as the lead guitarist for Rose Lee's performances, and their professional collaboration eventually led to them falling in love and getting married. Together, they formed a successful musical duo.

Joe Maphis earned a reputation as the fastest guitarist alive, and his skills were so impressive that the Mosrite Guitar company even created a custom double-neck guitar for him. Our paths crossed when they joined us on a tour in Tokyo. However, during their next trip, they encountered an unexpected issue with their work Visa, which resulted in them being stuck in Tokyo. The problem arose from a glitch in their Visa status – they had been sent on a Visitor Visa, which was only valid for five days. Their agency was supposed to send them the necessary paperwork for a work Visa, but due to a booking conflict involving another artist, Merle Travis, the paperwork was never sent.

Merle Travis, though unwell at the time, had not officially canceled his participation in the tour. This led to complications that took nearly two weeks to resolve, leaving Joe and Rose Lee without the ability to earn income while stranded in Tokyo. Fortunately, Dewey, who lived in base housing, had a spare room, and graciously offered it to Joe and Rose Lee during their unexpected stay. While they were waiting for the Visa situation to be sorted out, Rose Lee spent time with Dewey's wife, engaging in activities like shopping. Meanwhile, Joe spent time with Dewey and the band, forging connections and enjoying each other's company. Throughout this challenging period, we continued to support

Joe and Rose Lee by backing up their performances until 1965, when my time in Japan came to an end.

In 1964, I was requested by the band that Shorty Danes had to come take over the band. Dewey's band was beginning to have some internal problems, so I took the other band and named them Top Hands. Nick Hickey, Vernon Denny, Tom Cox, and Herb Bettive followed me and joined the band. I also hired an Air Force guy who played an accordion and was an amazing musician. In Japan was that you were not restricted by how many members you had in your band, if they liked your band, they paid every member the same. I had a really good band and got all the jobs I could handle.

In April of 1964, Keiko and I got married at the American Embassy in Tokyo, Japan, and had to rush back to Tachikawa to play our last show with Little Jimmy Dickens. Keiko and I had been together for several months. By that time, she was well-liked by everyone in the band. On the last set we played, I asked to be excused so I could dance with my wife, and by the time I got to the edge of the stage, somebody yelled, "Wife? Did I hear you say wife?" Then I heard, "It's about time!" By the time we got off the dance floor, we had been moved to a special table with a bottle of champagne. The band and the workers at the club threw us a big celebration party.

I got all the marriage papers filed with the Military and filed for another year extension of duty, but that request was denied when they discovered that I had not been back to the continental United States since July of 1959; therefore, they said I was going back home.

My current tour of duty was scheduled to end in November of that year. To get ready for a change in Duty Stations, I had to prepare a request for my choice of Duty Assignments. I had blown off all the promotion tests because I was really happy with where I was. Now that I was married again, I found myself reconsidering certain matters. To excel in promotional tests, staying current with the new equipment and aircraft you'd be in charge of was crucial. I had not worked on anything but old obsolete planes since I was VF-43. So, I wanted to get assigned to one of the experimental squadrons. VX1 was on the east coast, and VX2 was in the Los Angeles area. I requested them as my first two choices.

By this time, I replaced that old 1952 Mercury with a 1958 Chevrolet Belair that I had bought from the base salvage yard for twenty-five dollars. It had always been a base taxicab. It had come from the factory a bright copper color but had been painted black with the worst paint I had ever seen. It was peeling so bad it looked like someone with a very bad sunburn. Even though Keiko had gotten over the embarrassment of the mercury, she was not happy about this one either. I also had a lot of work to do before I got it okay for even a slower speed. It had only been driven at slow speeds and ran rough at faster speeds. With the rear seat removed, it also made a good vehicle for storing and moving band equipment. I was not planning on taking it with me when I left Japan. I would just sell it to someone on the base. I continued to play music, and my band was sounding really good.

My orders came in, and they were for VX2. I was very happy about that assignment and started getting ready for the move. We did not have a lot of furniture, and the military was shipping it for us. To get your shipping done on time, you needed to ship it a month early. Otherwise, you have to wait for it at your new location.

There was a guy in my squadron that said he wanted to buy the car, but he would not have the money for a week. I agreed to hold it for him. I stopped trying to sell it. The car had three new tires but needed one more, and I had included the new tire in the sales agreement. So, I took the car over to the hobby shop and replaced the tire when things started to go bad.

The supervisor of the hobby shop came up to me and said that I had a call from my duty officer, and he needed to speak to you. I took the call. He told me that I had new orders and needed to come to the duty office and get them. I told him that I had just gotten my orders and asked if he was sure, these were new. He confirmed that there was a change in my original orders, and this set was sending me VP31A in San Diego. I knew about that squadron, and they had older plans than the ones I was currently working on.

I returned to the duty office to collect my new orders; my frustration evident as I intended to challenge this unexpected change. With the Duty Officer's assistance, we calculated the time difference between Japan and Washington, D.C., and began setting up a call through the military Watts line.

Recalling that I had previously secured my orders to Japan by contacting the chief petty officer at the assignment desk, I managed to establish the call successfully. However, instead of the Chief, a Navy Commander answered the phone. I swiftly outlined my confusion regarding the change in orders and my need for clarification. I asked him to retrieve and review my orders for the changes as to why they were changed.

The Commander, offering a brief lesson, corrected me. He told me that my orders were not for VP31, but was VP31A, which was the host for the Alpha detachment, overseen by the Commander of Naval Air Operations Pacific. This Commander held significant authority as one of the two Three Star Admirals who commanded all Naval Air Commands. Evidently, I was being directed to serve on his personal Aircraft Crew. He posed the question of whether I wanted him to inform the Admiral about my reluctance to join his personal crew. Responding respectfully, I declined, stating, "NO SIR."

He elaborated that my recommendation had come from AE1 Jerry Davis, a colleague I had worked with in Hawaii. With a gracious expression of gratitude for his assistance, I concluded the conversation and hung up the phone. All that remained was to collect my new orders and handle the logistics of shipping my belongings and finding accommodations after my furniture was picked up.

The person who was supposed to buy my car didn't show up with the money as agreed. Instead, he offered only $50.00 for it. By this point, it was too late to arrange shipping. I was infuriated by his deception. After a heated exchange of words, I even went as far as saying I would rather burn the car than let him have it at any price.

Thankfully, I had a good friend named Chief Thomas Brown, who was part of the military club management system and stationed near where the cars were being shipped from. I called him to inquire about potential shipping solutions. He promised to look into it and get back to me. About an hour later, he called with good news. They were in the process of loading a ship that very night, and he knew someone on the night shift. If I could get the car to the loading area before dark, he could slip it into the shipment for me.

The task was a rush, but I managed to make it happen. I drove the car onto the lot where vehicles for shipment were stored. I left the keys in the glove box, along with five copies of my orders and a bottle of good whisky, under the driver's seat, as instructed. Chief Thomas Brown ensured that my car got loaded onto the ship. However, due to the timing, the car wouldn't reach Oakland until two weeks after my own arrival there.

Keiko and I moved in with a member of the band that lived in base housing until our flight back to the States was ready. Our stuff, including my bass and amp, was packed up. However, the band was booked at the Tachi East Club that night, and they insisted that we go to the club.

When I got to the club, the band was setting everything up on the stage to play the show. Then I noticed that something was on the stage where I normally set up, and it was covered with a sheet. It was my bass and amp. Somehow, they had gotten it out of storage and brought it to the club. They planned a going away party for us.

One of our fans and his wife, who had followed us for months and had become good friends, worked in the shipping division of the base, and he had helped some of the band members to get my equipment out of storage and later put it back.

He also came to our rescue when we were loading the plane to go home. We had about 80 pounds of personal luggage, too much for our limit. He found a way to get it on the plane, so we did not have to ship it at our expense.

My friend, Chief Brown, was booked on the same flight we were on, and he lived in Napa Valley, California. We were to stay with him until our car got to Oakland.

## Chapter 36

# KEIKO'S INTRODUCTION TO AMERICA

In November of 1965, we left Japan on our way to Oakland California. This was Keiko's first trip out of Japan, all of her ideas about what America would look like was based on old movies. She thought that everybody either lived in the glamourous New York City or on a big ranch out west. On one of our shows in Japan, Eddy Dean was the headliner and she got to meet him and get a picture of him that he signed for her. She had seen him in his singing cowboy role. She had a vision in her mind of how she wanted America to be and she did not want anyone to change that.

We came back on the same plane with Chief Brown and he was going to his home in Napa, California. His people were going to meet us in Oakland and would go home with them until our car arrived.

It was a long flight and we landed in Hawaii for our port of entry and a delay there of about three hours and it was hot there. I did not care to try to contact anyone there because it had been three years since I was there.

Everybody was tired and hungry so we ate and just hung out till we could board our plane again. Our next stop was at Travis Air Force Base in Oakland. Chief Brown's people were waiting for us with two vehicles: a station wagon, and a small car. We packed both vehicles with luggage and then we squeezed in. Looking something like the Beverly Hillbillies, we headed to Napa.

Chief Brown had a nice little house and we filled it up. I remember falling asleep while waiting for our turn for the shower. The next day the women were lined up for the washer and dryer. Chief Brown had a hobby of catching Abalone, which was a good food to eat, and the inside of the shell is beautiful. See pictures below.

After a couple of days rest, Keiko and I got bored and decided to take the bus to San Diego and see where we were going. Keiko got her first hard look at reality when we arrived at the San Francisco bus station. The midnight crew was on duty by the time we got into the terminal, they had a small coffee counter open, and we went in to get some refreshments while we waited for our next bus. They only had one person working there and she was the biggest and meanest looking woman I had seen, and she was not friendly to anyone.

The coffee was horrible and served in a coffee mug, the mug I got still had bright lipstick on it from a prior customer. Keiko was so upset that she would not even physically touch anything. I tried to explain to her that after midnight they got mostly drunks and derelicts in there and they needed someone who could handle them, and that woman sure looked like she could. Keiko's vision of what she thought all coffee shops in America would look like just got shattered and she was mad.

The next part of our bus ride was long, but quiet. When we got to San Diego, we found a hotel close to bus station. I did not like the hotel and there were only a few choices for rooms. I had to take one on the eighth floor and had to wait to check in. I reserved the room and we started looking for Coronado. I was going to be stationed at NAS North Island in a small town called Coronado.

It was a long trip from Napa, but we had rested some on the last leg of the trip. We got a city bus to the ferry that connects north island to San Diego. Coronado is a nice little town, and we spent some time asking questions and one of the places we stopped was a service station and there we got lucky. He knew of a small attendant's house that was being rented out. But at that time, it was still being remodeled. It was unfurnished and priced where we could afford it. It would be just what we needed, and we would not need it for a month. I worked out an agreement with the guy and we took off back to our hotel. The next day we caught a bus back to Napa.

By the time we got back to Chief Brown's house, things had settled down some. A couple of the people that were there had moved on and it was not quite as crowded. I felt good about what I had learned and about having an agreement on a place to live. Now all I had to do was wait for the car to arrive.

We had a nice visit and got some much-needed rest, but by the time my car arrived in Oakland we were getting restless to get started on our journey. I had been told that when cars were only driven at a slow speed, they would build up a thin carbon ring at the upper limits of each piston cylinder. I was also told that I would need to slowly increase the speed until the engine started to run rough and then hold that speed until the engine smoothed out. Repeating that in small degrees should allow the piston scraper ring to slowly cut away carbon buildup to allow the engine to run normally. I took the bus to Oakland and retrieved my car.

An elderly black man with a special cart was sent to help me recover my vehicle. We confirmed the paperwork and he took me to my car. I had forgotten how bad the paint on that car made it look. Just looking at it with all that dust and grime from being shipped across the ocean, I did not think it would make it to San Diego much less Florida. When it was shipped, they had to empty all the gas from the vehicle, the guy with the cart was able to start it ok with just a little priming and some gas. He had a small carwash area where we could clean up the car and it looked a lot better after that.

The elderly gentleman with the cart was getting ready to put two gallons of gas in the car, which was all he was allowed to do, he said. Then the con job started. He asked me how far I had to go and I told him, and he said there were some gas stations out there on the road and he hoped that I would make it. Then he said that he had some extra gas, but it cost him money to buy it. I knew what the con was, for a good tip he would give me some more gas. I gave him ten dollars and he filled my tank.

Driving for me was a problem because for the last three years I had been driving on the Left side of the road or what Americans called the wrong side of the road. A second problem was that these roads were called interstates and had something new to me that is called a right only exit. I would have to drive slowly and keep to the right lane. The traffic was heavy and I kept getting pushed off the road and had to find my way back onto the road. Also making right turns were worst because of having driven on left side of the road for so long, a right turn, from force of habit, would swing you into the oncoming traffic lane.

When I got out on a straight road, I could test the procedure to clean the cylinders of the carbon ring, I could ease the speed up only slightly before it would start running rough. I also noticed that I had blue smoke behind me. The procedure was working and I could keep slowly increasing the speed and by my first stop I could keep up with the slow traffic, I needed a quart and a half of engine oil. I made it on into Napa and stopped for service. My hopes for making my trip were getting better. I stopped at a Texaco service station and got the car serviced.

I didn't know when the car was serviced last, and the station attendant was having trouble. I still had my Japanese tags on the car and he asked how far I was going. When I told him Florida, he shook his head and wished me lots of luck. I did not think the car would make it all the way and my plans were to sign the titles to car, leave them on the dash for the tow truck, and catch a plane on home.

To service the car, he had to replace several grease fittings, change the oil and filter, check everything, and rotate the tires. When he was finished, it was ready for the next road test. I drove it to Chief Brown's house and got cleaned up. They were cooking a big supper for all of us that were still in the area. Keiko was getting tired of waiting and wanted to leave and make our own way. I also wanted to see if the car was going to keep getting better or blow up. We decided to stay for the supper they were planning and leave afterwards. Keiko had everything packed and we loaded the car and explained that we would to head toward San Diego. The plan was to try to make Needles and stop there, If the car was having trouble, we would head to San Diego but if was still running ok, we would turn East.

I remember that it was a clear cool night with a big moon and some beautiful countryside. I kept working on getting the car to increase speed without running rough. By the time I got to Needles I was driving 60 to 65 with no problems and not having to add any more oil. We stayed at a nice motel, and I fell in love with the desert. The weather was perfect and the countryside with that moonlight was simply beautiful. We were starting to really enjoy our freedom and the trip. We knew that we were on a very long trip, but we took it one day at a time.

The next morning, we had breakfast and still got an early start for Phoenix. Everything went great and at about noon time we picked up a young man in a Navy uniform that was heading to Phoenix. He was a lot of fun and had been to Japan. He had a good time kidding with Keiko. He knew the area roads in that part of the country and was good navigator.

I had stopped at a service center with a gift shop. They had a comedy type post card with a picture of a cowboy riding a Jack rabbit. The rabbit was shown as being larger than a horse. Keiko had looked at it and threw it on the dashboard of the car with some other papers. She had never seen so much open countryside in her life. She could not understand how America would waste that land and she kidded about claiming it for Japan.

The Navy guy told me about a shortcut that saved me about 80 miles but cautioned that it was an isolated road without service and not much traffic. I had just serviced the car and it was running well, so I took the chance. Keiko got to see about 100 miles of nothing and was getting a little worried.

The Navy guy had seen the postcard on the dash and told Keiko that she needed to help look for giant jackrabbits because they would hide behind big rocks and jump on passing cars thinking they were something to play with. Keiko believed him and that kept her occupied for a while. There were no problems on the trip, but just as it was starting to get dark, Keiko let out a scream that scared the heck out of me. It was the first light or sign she had seen for hours. She had seen a billboard a long way down the road and thought we were back in civilization.

I don't remember how many hours we traveled on during that part of the trip, but we decided to swing by the guy's house and take advantage of the local gas war that was going on. We filled up with gas priced at 10 cents per gallon. We dropped him off and took the first motel on our route out of Phoenix.

After some rest we drove to Las Cruces, New Mexico, spent the night, and rose at 5 AM and headed for El Paso, Texas. Back then Route US 90 was the best route East. West Texas was very sparsely populated and once you left El Paso it was a long way between towns.

Traffic was almost nonexistent, and you needed to make sure you did not miss a gas station. After a long and lonesome drive, I saw a car on the side of road with a young woman flagging me down. It was a couple with a flat tire. They were stuck because the spare was also bad. I checked and their tire was the same size as the ones on my car so I decided to let them use my spare to get on into town.

They were very nice and only about 20 years old at best. We put my tire on their car and headed toward the next town. I was following them and shortly after we started, they accelerated real fast and I knew that I could not catch them. I figured that my tire had just been stolen and kept on driving. It was about 30 miles before the next town came in sight and I was hoping I could buy a replacement tire. Just as I got to the first service station, there was that young woman flagging me down again.

I stopped and the young man was bringing my tire back to the car. They were trying to keep us from being delayed. They put the tire back in the trunk for me, thanked me and asked what they owed me. I was relieved, but more importantly my faith in people had been restored.

When I married Keiko, I expected to get some resentment from prejudice people and I was on guard for it, so when I would see people staring at her I would assume that they would say something about it.

After recovering my tire, I drove on through town and made a gas stop at a station that was being run by another young couple. The girl was filling my car and staring through the car window at Keiko. Then asked me where she was from and I said Tokyo, Japan and she turned around and yelled at the young man working with her, "I told you she was not a (blankety blank) Indian." By the tone in her voice and choice of words, I guessed that Japanese were ok but not Indians. The truth is that we never had any problems with discrimination anywhere.

I asked about a good place to eat, and they gave a good recommendation: a restaurant that had the best sausage in the world and it was just a few blocks away. We went there and they did have great sausage which I really enjoyed, but Keiko did not eat much meat and no greasy foods. The lady who owned the restaurant went out of her way to fix Keiko something special that she wanted and tried to send us off with more of her sausage to take with us. Everyone we met in Texas was very nice to us.

We drove all day and all-night crossing Texas, and I kept promising to stop at the first motel on the right side of the road after Houston. I found one just across the Louisiana state line and it looked like a scene form an Albert Hitchcock Murder Mystery movie.

It was a small four room unit and the owners were just opening it up for the season. I was just too tired to go any farther without some sleep. It was the worst place I ever saw. The yard was overgrown with weeds, it was surrounded by trees full of moss, and on a small creek that stunk really bad was just a few feet from the side of the unit.

The bed had something for a mattress but it looked and felt more like a large sack of corn shucks. I lay down on top of the bed and just passed out from exhaustion. After about four hours, Keiko got me awake enough to get up and she had not got any sleep at all. She locked herself inside the room and sat on the corner of the bed until she could wake me up. She would not touch and thing in that room. I tried to wash up but the water stunk so bad I could not take a bath.

I managed to get in the car and drive to the first restaurant I came to and that was a mistake. I ordered a cup of coffee and got the waitress fill my thermos. We ordered something to eat and when the coffee came, I could not drink it. We managed to eat some of the food and washed it down with a cola.

I got back in the car and headed east. I tried to sip some of coffee in my thermos and could not stand it or the smell of my thermos. I found a restaurant that looked nice and stopped there. I asked the waitress about the coffee and explained about what I had just gone through. She was very helpful and explained about the water and that they used only bottled water for cooking and coffee. I asked how I could clean my thermos and she said that I would have to steam clean it but she would clean if for me. The meal and the coffee were great.

I don't remember where we stopped next but I do remember a gas stop in Alabama. While serving in the Military people are always asking you if you knew their son. Most of the time the person was not the same branch as you and even if they were, the odds would be about a hundred thousand to one. While in the Navy I must have been asked a thousand times and never did know any of them.

While at the small gas station in Alabama, an elderly gentleman wearing blue bib overalls, a brown shirt, brogan shoes, a straw hat with a large red handkerchief sticking out of his pocket was pumping gas in my car. He kept staring at Keiko in the car and I just waited for his question.

Finally, in a soft and emotional tone asked if she was Japanese. I said yes and he lit up like a child at Christmas time. His son's best friend's wife was living in the community and he really wanted us to spend some time with her. He explained that she was the only Japanese living there and she was so lonely. Well, we did not have the time, and Keiko did not feel up to it. He asked if I was in the navy and if I knew his son.

While I was trying not to hurt his feelings by explaining that the odds of knowing his son was impossible, he explained that his son had been stationed in Japan with his best friend, but now they were overseas at different locations. I asked where else he had been stationed and then he said Hawaii and that he had been flying in some kind of patrol unit. I was shocked. I was with the largest patrol unit there.

He said if you saw him, you would remember him for he is a nice-looking boy except for a bad burn on the right side of his face. With that information I realized that I did know him. We were doing the same job but on different air crews working out of the same shop. I remembered him by the burn scar, and he was a nice-looking young man. That is the only time in twenty years of service that ever happened.

We got back on the road and my next biggest concern was getting through Mobile, Alabama. I had never been in that part of the country before. I knew that I was getting close to Florida, but I had no conception of just how far I still was from that little farm in High Springs.

I remember that the traffic in Mobile was heavy and I had trouble driving and trying to find my way through the city. I had looked at the maps and tried to remember the correct routes to get me to the Florida state line. Keiko could not read the route signs and was not able to help me with the correct lane changes.

Somehow by the grace of God we made it into the tunnels and after that I could only hope for the best. It took what seemed like forever to get to the state line and I thought that I had gotten lost. Then suddenly there it was, the Welcome to the State of Florida sign. I felt so relieved that I had made it home again. It had been just over seven years since I caught that ride on that Semi truck out of Florida.

I was reassuring Keiko that we were in my home state and that we would be home soon, I did not know how wrong I was. She started making plans to stop at a beauty shop before going to the house. Well, that was money that I did not think we should spend at that time. I thought that we would get a motel in or close to High Springs and get some rest and clean up there before going on out to the farm.

I had never been across the panhandle of Florida and had no idea how far it was from Mobile to High Springs. By the time we finally got to where I was able to see a sign for Tallahassee, I was thinking we would be getting home, but the sign said Tallahassee was still over a hundred miles.

I did not want to believe the sign but then I remembered that I had never been to Tallahassee before. But I just kept driving and thinking about getting home to where my daughter Pat, my parents and brother were. That would be our safe heaven and any assistance we might need.

We got through Tallahassee but still no sign for High Springs, but there was a sign for Perry. I was remembering Perry and being a straight shot West of High Springs. The problem was that Perry was still a long way from where we were.

Keiko was really getting tired and grouchy. How much longer were her only new words and I could tell she did not trust me anymore.

I kept driving one town at a time. I was still planning on stopping at a motel for the night when we got close to High Springs but all I could do now was just keep driving and looking.

Finally, we got through Perry, and it was well past midnight, and I was not sure of anything. We headed East out of Perry and kept thinking High Springs was just down the road. Well, I got on US19 somehow and wound up in Chiefland before I knew it.

Now it was after daylight, and I still had a way to go. It turned out that I was closer to the farm than I was to a motel. This was Keiko's introduction to my family and she wanted to look her best. I had explained to her many times that we lived on a dirt farm, not some Hollywood movie ranch. But she had hung on to her vision.

Another complication was that I had not told my mother when we would be coming home because I knew that she would be doing was continuously looking for us and cleaning the house. Since I did not know when we would be arriving, I did not even tell her that we were coming home.

Well about 10:30 that morning Keiko got another major shock. When I pulled up in front of the house, everybody was in the middle of their annual hog killing.

Momma came around the side of the house to see who had driven up wearing some dirty clothing and a bloody white butcher's coat. They were in the middle of the hog killing and butchering process and everything and everybody were a mess.

I have no idea what was going through Keiko's mind but she was in total shock. Her big welcome to America was definably not been anything like what she had thought and hoped it would be. I think she was so tired that she really did not care.

Once you start the process of killing hogs, you are dealing with fresh neat and it has to get processed or you lose it. Everybody was so busy with work that could not be stopped, and we needed rest so when the shock wore off, we managed to lay down and get some rest.

They worked and we rested and everything got better. By the time we got up Mom had a room set up for us and things had slowed down. Even though it was my fault for showing up when I did, mom kept apologizing for everything being in a mess.

When we had time to sit and talk for a while and everybody got to meet Keiko, they all liked her. We had a big supper with lots of fresh meat, vegetables, and fresh baked bread. Keiko was not big on the meat, but she went after those fresh vegetables and bread.

After supper I got a tour of what changes Dad had made to the place. We went to take care of the stock and I got a surprise. He had more hogs than we used to be able take care of. When I was still on the farm, the stock had so much trouble with screwworms that every head of stock had to have attention every day. I asked how he managed all the screwworm cases and he laughed and said, "Son you have been gone for a long time. There has not been a case of screwworms here in years".

I remembered that before I left the farm and right after we got electricity, the power company was trying to get farmers to let them hang something on the power polls and several of the farmers, including Dad did not want any changes. They wanted to install a system on each pole that consisted of a yellow light, a bug zapper screen and bottle of toxic chemicals under the screen. The light would draw the bugs to it and the vapors from the chemicals would knock them out and they would fall into the bug zapper.

Well, that worked very well and in a couple of cycles the screwworms were gone. Dad had also replaced me and the mules with a tractor. We had running water now and that little room that I had used for my bedroom was now a bathroom.

One thing about a farm is that it is quiet at night. After traveling as much as we did and hearing a constant noise, we could not sleep. We went to bed, and it was so quiet that we could hear our own hearts beating. We got up and went to our car to talk for a while. Mom came out to ask what was wrong and we told her that it was just too quiet. After we were able to adjust to the change we went back to bed.

The next morning, I took the car into town and my brother, who always worked on everything, looked at it and asked, "How much is this going to cost?" I told him that the engine was running good and not to worry about it.

Then he said, "Well then we are going to paint this ugly thing". He Checked it over and did a complete service on it. He called a friend of his who worked for a paint company for a recommendation on the paint to use. The company had just finished a test run on a new mixture. He said that it was the brightest red that he had ever seen. He gave us enough to paint the car.

The first problem we had was that the paint used in Japan to put that Black coat on, was so bad that any kind of a Lacquer based paint would not cover it. Anywhere the Lacquer paint tried to cover the Black paint, the black paint would just melt and bubble up. Every speck of that black paint had to be completely removed.

We sanded that car till there was no skin left on our fingers. When we got the car ready, we had to get a space ready to paint it and we took one of the maintenance stalls in the garage where he worked for the Jim Douglas Chevrolet company. We tried to cover everything to protect it from the overspray paint and spent all night spray painting that car. Man was it a bright red. The second problem was that in spite of our best attempt, we had a lot of overspray everywhere. Well, we had to clean that up also.

While Derlwood and I worked on painting the car, The family got to know Keiko and Dad really liked her. He never attempted to pronounce her name, he just referred to her as that little girl. I think Mom was a little jealous, but everything went well. We spent a few days just visiting and resting up before we had to start back. The car really looked better with its new paint job, but I was warned to stay away from Bermuda bulls with that red car.

After our visit we packed up and hit the road West early in the morning. Everything went well until we were just past Tallahassee. I was pulled over by a State Patrol Officer. I was in Florida in a bright red car with Japanese tags, and a Hawaiian driver's license. I also had a military driver's License, Military ID card and my orders to California.

Because I was in the military and under orders, I was legal to go to my new duty station before having to change my License plates. I thought that going from Japan to California by way of Florida was not going to be the problem, but the officer asked me a question that made me stop and think. If we were in a serious accident and unconscious, how was he going to know who we were or who he should call to get us assistance, He told me that we would be going through a county seat just down the road and I was to stop there to get a temporary tag so I would be in the system. Then he went his way and I went to California.

The rest of the trip went well and we arrived safely in Coronado, California.

# Chapter 37

# NAS NORTH ISLAND

It was getting late in November by the time we arrived at Coronado, California, to check into my new Duty Assignment. It was located at NAS North Island, the northernmost tip of the land referred to as the Silver Strand on the West side of San Diego Bay.

The military base is the North Island Naval Air Station. I was assigned to serve as one of the personnel assigned to Commander, Naval Air Pacific (ComNavAirPac), currently under the command of Three Star Admiral Conley. The unit was named VP31Alpha, and the unit VP31 was strictly for the accountability of his aircraft. The entire Naval Air Command is divided into two halves, ComNavAirPac and Conversant. Each side is commanded by a Three Star Admiral.

While waiting for our car to arrive in Oakland, I made contact with someone who helped us locate a house to rent. We had entered into an advance agreement to rent the house. The location of the house was 440 C Ave Coronado, and it was a small caretaker house behind the owner's house and was projected to be ready for us by the time we completed our trip.

It was about midmorning when we arrived back at the gas station where our contact worked. I was expecting to be delayed a day or two before being able to move in. But our contact had forgotten about us and the agreement. A little later, when he finally remembered us, he contacted the owner and explained what had happened. The house was still available, and all the remodeling was finished, but it had not been released for rent. We went and met with the lady who owned it, and after some discussion, she agreed to let us go ahead and move in. That was a Godsend miracle, and there was a bed, refrigerator, dining table, and chairs. Everything we needed to get started.

We unloaded the car, and I was trying to figure out how we would make it until I got checked into my unit and could collect my back pay. Somehow, I used more money than I could account for. When we unpacked our suitcases, I found a packet of Travelers Checks packed in our clothing. That was the money I could not account for, and it also meant that we could eat until I got my back pay. We were able to get a bath and sleep in our own place, and we did sleep.

The next morning, we made a quick run to the local grocery store, Keiko started setting up the house, and I started my check-in procedure with my new assignment at North Island Naval Air Station.

The first problem I ran into was getting a pass to the base with Japanese tags on my car. I could only get a very limited temporary pass until I got a state license tag, and in my case, that was a California tag. Then I found where VP31 was and got checked in and started my request for my back pay.

VP31 held our personnel records and processed our paperwork but did not have any control over us. They did not like that very well, but with our boss being their boss's boss, they took care of us.

I got the dispersing form for my back pay, and I took it to the paymaster and got my back pay. Then I found where The Admirals plane was kept and maintained. It was a separate facility from VP31. It was a small, secured place with some office space and a lounge area.

When I got there, the plane and crew were gone on a flight, but one member of the crew was doing some work at the office. I introduced myself to him, and he filled me in on the plane and the crew.

He needed a phone number for me, and I did not have one at the time, so he told me to make that a priority because we always had to be on call. He took my address down and gave me his number for me to call to get updates until I could get my own number. The plane was not scheduled to return from the trip it was on for two days, so I had two more days off to finish checking in.

My first task was to get a new tag. I finally found the DMV, and the tag cost me more than I had paid for the car. Then I started the request for a phone at the residence. There was a waiting list, and I requested an emergency installation which cost more, but I got the phone in just over two days. I was to get our address to the people shipping our furniture and give a quick delivery, and things were going well.

On the third day, I met the plane and the crew. That was when I got a big shock. The plane was that same old R7Y aircraft that I had helped get removed from flight status when I was in Hawaii. It had been taken out of service and sent to a Japanese overhaul facility and converted to a VIP Plane with a personal stateroom for the Admiral.

I went aboard the aircraft and talked to one of the four flight engineers about the plane, and he assured me that it could not be the same plane because everything had been replaced. Right by his right leg was the 260 panel, where I had made a wiring repair by replacing part of three wires with extensions. Extensions could only be used for a temporary Repair. The entire length of the wires had to be replaced to be a permanent repair, and that would have required hundreds of hours of work and downtime for the plane.

I made the repair by soldering the connections and did not report it as a temporary repair because the plane was being taken out of service. After telling the Flight Engineer what was behind that panel, He handed me a screwdriver to pull the panel with and said to prove it. I pulled the panel, and there was my repair job just like I left it. He shook my hand and said, "Well, I guess you do know this plane, welcome aboard."

The crew were excellent people, and the plane was in excellent condition. I went through the prior maintenance records, and there had not been any big electrical problems of any type reported. We had three days before the Admiral was scheduled to go anywhere, and that gave us plenty of time to check the plane over. After my inspection of the plane, I felt good about it.

The Admiral's next trip was one of his regular trips to the Pentagon, and we would fly him into Alexandria, Virginia, stay overnight, and return the next day.

When you have a flag with three stars flying from your plane, you do not have to wait in lines, and you get everything you need. All we had to do was to check and refuel the plane. We would secure the plane, and they would transport us to our quarters for the night. Sometimes that would be a motel just off the base, and sometimes it would be on base. The gas truck and our transportation were waiting for us at the plane before we were ready. The next morning your ride back to the plane will be on time also.

We had rigged the engines on the plane so that we could start two at the same time. When the Admiral left the terminal door, we would start both engines on the right wing at the same time. Since everybody boarded the plane on the left side, we started both the left-wing engines when the Admiral entered the door of the plane. By the time he got to sit down in his stateroom, his personal chef would have a drink in his hand of whatever he wanted, and the plane would be moving.

The plane would never be late, and neither would we. If we were late, we missed the flight, and we would have to pay our own way to the next stop and face disciplinary action. Any other time you needed something, everyone would try to help you.

Our senior pilot was Commander Scott, who was a great pilot and had been flying VIP planes most of his career. Commander Scott would talk to the Admiral if you had a request that was within reason, and the

Admiral would almost always allow it. On one of our trips back from Alexandria, Virginia, the terminal dispatcher asked if we could give a ride to an E2 fresh out of training. He was trying to get home to California on emergency leave, and they did not have anything else for him. We already had some of the admiral's staff on the plane and were taxiing out to the runway when we received the call.

The Admiral approved it, and Scott turned the plane around and taxied back to the terminal and picked the young sailor up. When the young man realized where he was, I thought he was going to faint.

He was so frozen at attention that he would not even blink his eyes. Everyone on the plane was trying to help him and get him to relax. One of the Admiral's staff was a full Navy Captain, and he cleared some of his stuff out of the seat next to him and told the kid to sit there. It took a little coaxing to get him to sit down and a lot more to get him to relax.

The plane took off and was still climbing out when a Navy Lieutenant got up and turned to a young man and said, do you want a drink? And the young man stuttered and tried to say, "I don't know, Sir." The Lieutenant smiled and said, "Well, I think I do, and I will get you something." I think it was soda pop. One by one, different people would ask him a personal question and talk with him and he did relax a little by the time we got to North Island.

When the Admiral had special guests on the plane, we would handle their luggage, and it seemed like everyone played golf. Somehow, we always seemed to land at the places with the most popular Golf courses. But we also made a lot of good stops.

On one of our trips, Admiral Connelly brought a second Admiral with us. I don't remember who he was, but none of the crew liked him. He brought a bunch of junk with him and one big old Red Parrot that we had to babysit for three days while everybody else took in the town. We watched parrot in shifts and tried our best to teach that old bird how to talk. We constantly told him three words to say, and I don't think he ever repeated them because we were never court marshaled or thrown out of the Navy.

Shortly after I got to Coronado, Herb Bettive, who played lead guitar for me in Japan, had gotten out of the Navy and was living in Alexandria. He had left the special guitar that was given to him by Moon Mullican with the band. They knew that I was flying back and forth to Alexandria, and they shipped it to me. On our next flight to Alexandria, I took the guitar and spent the night with Herb. I caught the plane the next morning at the terminal and went home.

On one of our trips, we were scheduled to go to Alexandria and then down to Miami. We would be in Miami for a week for some military operation that the Admiral had to be there for and then return to Alexandria for a meeting before returning to Coronado. I had bought a large setting of China for Mom just before we left Japan and had it shipped with our personnel things when we left Japan, and I needed to get it to High Springs. I asked Commander Scott to see if I could drop it off in Jacksonville. I knew that it was a long shot, but I had to try. Commander Scott thought about it and suggested that I also request to take five days' leave while the plane was in Miami. He would schedule a stop and go to Cecil Field so he could drop me off. He scheduled the same thing on the way back to Alexandria. Cecil Field was still a Naval Air Station, and I was small and would not attract much attention.

We landed and taxied up to the cargo terminal and stopped the plane just long enough for me to exit the plane on the escape rope, and everybody on the crew jumped in to help, one followed me down the escape rope, and the rest quickly lowered the boxes on straps. We grabbed the boxes and moved them out of the way, and the guy on the ground grabbed the rope, and the crew pulled him back on board, and the plane was gone in about ten minutes.

I was able to get the boxes on the side of the pickup area where I could see the Main Gate and waited for my brother to show up. He was running late, and I walked over to the gate and explained to the guard what I was waiting for, and I was able to make a call to check on when he would be there. I found out that he was not going to make it but had someone else on the way. Finally, he showed up and told the guard who he was looking for. The guard let him enter and pick me and the boxes up.

I enjoyed the week off and was back at the same pickup point when that big old plane rolled to a stop. This time they did not even shut the engines down; they just opened the door and dropped the rope. All I had to do was grab the rope and hang on, they pulled me on board, and we were gone before I could sit down. When we got back to our base, I asked if I needed a leave request to cover the time off, and Commander Scott said you were off work, and I don't care what you did on your own time. Then asked if my mom liked the dishes.

Once we were airborne, there was very little for us to do if we were not manning a flight station; we played a lot of three-handed pinochle. The older guys on the crew were card sharks, and I always lost at that game. The radio system we had in that plane was an excellent system made by the Collins Radio company. While sitting on the ground at Nas North Island, our radio operator could book our hotel rooms in Hong Kong. Our operator always kept a list of the people that each one of us wanted to call, and he would scan for ham operators with phone patch capabilities; when he would connect with one in your area, he would set up a call. I would call my brother and let him know where I was.

When the Admiral would go on an inspection tour of some of the facilities under his command, we would fly him to a central point in the area, and we would wait for him, and his local units would handle his local transportation. That sent us to Hong Kong on a regular basis. We would normally stay at the Astor Hotel if we were there for four days or longer.

Hong Kong was a nice place to visit on our earlier trips, but then our Viet Nam forces started sending troops there for R and R. We were just finishing up a four-day stopover when the first bunch hit. We had just checked out of the Astor Hotel at about 10:30 AM and were outside waiting for our transportation to our plane when the first bus load pulled in. They came running out of the bus, yelling, and waving hands full of Hong Kong money.

*Hong Kong Money / Currency Notes and Coins | Flickr - Photo Sharing! by Unknown Author is licensed under CC BY-SA-NC*

Overnight all the nice quality bars and clubs around that area were changed to wild money grabbing dives.

Most of Admiral Connelly's inspection trips were uneventful, and he was a good boss to work for. However, you didn't want to make him mad. On one of the trips, while flying just above the cloud cover, between inspection stops, one of our fighter planes shot straight up through the clouds and just missed hitting our plane. Commander Scott swerved the plane hard to the right to miss the fighter.

Admiral Connelly was in his stateroom, and I am not sure what he was doing, but he came out of his stateroom and went straight to the cockpit and asked what was going on, and when Scott told him, he told the radio operator to find out who the pilot was. It only took a few minutes for the operator to have the information on the pilot flying the fighter plane. Then Admiral Connelly had the radio operator put out a call to the fighter pilot's commander and ordered him grounded until further notice. I had never seen the Admiral mad before, and based on the comments being made like he must have spilled his favorite drink, I don't think the rest of the crew had either.

The most frightening thing that happened while flying on the Admiral's Plane was on one of the last inspection trips that I went on. It started at North Island when we were getting the plane ready for the trip. One of our engines was close to what is called High Time and would go over the high time limit before the trip was over.

High Time is when the engine must be changed for overhaul because it has reached its maximum number of flying hours that is considered safe to operate. The rules were if the engine was performing satisfactorily but had not exceeded its safe time, you could extend its fling hours until the trip was over. Your other option was to change it before its time ran out.

The problem with that idea was that a new engine could not be flown over the ocean until it had completed its break-in time. And for us, that would put us too late to make our scheduled trip. We made the decision to go with the old engine.

We gave it a good runup test, and it showed no sign of any problem, but shortly after shutting it down, it had a heavy oil leak. Our mechanics found that it was the Oil Scavenger pump.

We were now into our scheduled rest time before starting our trip, but we got a new pump, and the mechanics changed it. They also changed the oil in the engine and did a hard test run of the engine. At the end of the test run, one of the oil filters detected metal in the filter. When I pulled the filter, I found a metal washer stuck to the filter that had come off the Scavenger pump that did not get flushed out of the engine when we changed the oil.

We retested the engine, and it checked out ok. The mechanics were sure the old engine would make the trip ok, but some of the rest of the crew was not sure it would make the whole trip. We started a pool betting on when the engine would fail.

The trip went ok until we stopped in Hong Kong. We stayed at the same hotel, but nothing was the same. Now when you walked in the front door of any of the bars, they would shove you into a booth with a bunch of women, and someone set a cheap bottle of Champagne on the table and try to collect 30 dollars before ever asking you what you wanted. I had made several trips to Hong Kong and loved the city but not that place anymore.

We left Hong Kong and started working our way back and stayed overnight in Japan. I was able to make phone contact with some of the old band members and have a phone conversation with them.

We went to the Kaneohe Marine base in Hawaii. We were staying overnight and were scheduled for a 9:00 AM departure. One of our radio operators was going to get some sleep, and he was staying on the plane. After servicing and checking the plane, we went to the NCO club for supper. That was the first mistake. They got a party going with the Marines and closed up the club. That was the second mistake.

We made it back to the plane, and got aboard, and went to sleep. It seemed we had just got to sleep when we heard someone banging on the plane. It was the pilot, and he was getting ready to start the plane and get ready for the Admiral. That was our third mistake because we had not conducted a preflight on the plane.

Well, as it turned out, our departure time had been moved up to 7 AM, and a message was sent to the plane by the messenger. When he could not find anyone to give the message to, he wrote it on a sheet of paper and taped it on the nose wheel of the aircraft. We had completely missed it when we came to the aircraft from the club. By the time we got our eyes opened to where we could see, our pilot, Commander Scott, was getting in the cockpit. We did a complete preflight of a large four-engine plane in 30 seconds by running around to the plane as we pulled the chocks. I am sure that we kicked at least one of the tires, so we were ready on time.

All the engines started, including the High Time Engine, and we were moving for the runway as soon as the Admiral got to his stateroom, as always. Still hungover, we settled in for the long flight back to California.

Our off-duty Flight Engineer and off-duty radio operator were sitting at the crew table with me, and as we made our climb out to 10,000 feet, it happened. There was a pop in the cabin air and an unusual noise that sounded like a run-a-way propeller. Then all four engines lost power at the same time, and the plane started to drop. The two guys at the table jumped up and ran to the cockpit, and after the longest 15 to 20 seconds in history, the engines started picking up power, and the plane leveled off. The first thing that went through my mind was not checking the fuel tanks for moisture. And when I was stationed in Hawaii, we had a lot of trouble with that. Right then, that was one time in my flying career that I was scared.

What happened was not a very bad thing. At 10,000 feet, we have to shift the engine intake air system to High Blower. To accomplish that, you pull the power off the engine and manually shift the blower control to the high position and push the throttle forward to increase the engine power.

Normally you do this one engine at a time, and the passengers don't even notice it. But two things happened at the same time. At lower altitudes, you leave engine ram air doors open, and that pulls the outside air directly into the engine carburetor. This time we hit a freak ice condition, and it was being sucked directly into the carburetors and causing the engines to try to shut down.

To fix this, you push and hold all four of the switches controlling ram air doors until all the doors are closed. That forces all the intake air to be pulled across the warm engine, warming it up before it gets to the carburetor. The noise I heard was from the drive shaft for the cabin air compressor that supplies half of the cabin air. You have one each of the outboard engines. The one on the number 4 engine had broken, and it had to be disconnected.

The flight engineer on the station had done all this in about 20 seconds, and the only thing we lost was one of the cabin air compressors and my nerve. We landed back at North Island with all four engines running, and the Mechanics won the bet on the High Time engine.

We spent a lot of time on trips and away from home, but we also got a considerable amount of time off when we were not on the trips. Shortly after I moved to Coronado, I had to drive into San Diego. The trip required that you drive around San Diego Bay.

On the south end of the bay is the city of Imperial Beach and a business called the Bonanza Club. As I passed the club, I observed that their Marquis Sign advertised that Tommy Duncan appeared there that night. Well, I had played backup music for him on four of his tours and had become friends with him. When I was returning from San Diego, I stopped and checked with the bartender and confirmed that it was the same person. Later that evening, I returned to the Bonanza to see Tommy.

When I entered the club, I had to stop so my eyes could adjust to the light. There were only three people in the bar, the bartender, a large person, and Tommy Duncan. I walked up to Tommy, and he laughed, stuck out his hand, and said, "Man, you are a long way from home, the last time I saw you was in Japan." Then he introduced me to the Bud as the best band leader that he had worked with in Japan. The big man's name was Bud Estes, the owner of the Bonanza Club, and the bartender I had met earlier was Charlie. Little did I know at that time that we would have a two-year friendship.

Bud and Tommy were talking about problems finding dependable band leaders, and that was why Tommy gave me such a great introduction. I had not considered forming another band at that time, I was still getting settled in a new assignment and a new area.

Within a month of getting settled into North Island, I was approached by someone who knew that I had played music. I don't know how he knew that I played music, but he wanted me to help a young man who played guitar and was trying to find someone to play with. The young man's name was Clint Finley.

Well, I agreed to talk to Clint, who was from Wichita Falls, Texas, and had been playing lead guitar in a band his brothers had. Clint had joined the Navy and was now stationed at North Island and wanted to try to start a small band and play on the weekend. After talking to him, I agreed to try to help him if he could find a Country music singer. Little did I know that we would develop a friendship that lasted until his death in 2019.

Clint found an older guy that played rhythm guitar. He was a good country music singer for a one-night-a-week job. The job was on Saturday night, and I played the bass if I was not flying. At first, that was not a problem because it was rare that we would have trips over the weekends. But the job soon went to Friday and Saturday nights and made things a little harder, but I still worked it out ok.

The guy who was doing the singing started having health problems and had to quit. We got a younger guy by the name of Vernon Lancaster, who was in a Navy Seabee unit in the area. We added a drummer and started getting more and more work.

Admiral Connelly was setting up his retirement and was replaced by Admiral Sheen. Shortly after Admiral Sheen took over, I was transferred to VP31 and assigned to training a special squadron that was being formed.

The squadron was a Top-Secret operation, and only four of us enlisted personnel, and one Navy Lieutenant from VP31 were authorized to work on it. It did not have a name at that time, and we could not talk to anyone about it. All the people that were being assigned to it were being ordered to VP31 for unspecified training and reassignment.

The people that would be forming the unit were reporting in, and our first priority was to find housing for them. Some of them had families that were being relocated also, and that was an additional hardship for the troops. All we could tell them was to trust us and when and where the roll call would be.

As we were setting up training for our assigned specialty areas, we would receive information about all special training required and where to find it. There were other people working in different locations on the same project, and we had very limited contact with them.

Finally, we got the official word that we would be recycling older P2V type aircraft from the military desert aircraft storage facility, called the Graveyard. They were to be restored and reconfigured with special protective armor for the crew. Then on one of our lieutenant's returns from Washington D.C. he told us that they had named the unit and it was VO67. I said oh, Fixed Wing observation, and the lieutenant when into a panic.

He demanded to know how I knew that. It was Top Secret, and I was not supposed to know that. It took a while before I got him to understand that all I did was to explain what the name of the unit stood for. V is the designation for V fixed wing aircraft and O was the designation for observation type operations, and the year was 1967. However, their mission was not going to be observation.

One of the disturbing directives we got was to prepare for a casualty replacement rate of one plane and crew per month. I am happy to report that during the entire operation, they only lost two planes; however, one and one-half crews were lost.

We finally got information that the unit was going to be housed at the Moffett Field base for their base of operations. Before we were released to pass the information on to the crews that were going there, a Navy Captain at Moffett did a press release about the whole project. That made every one of us mad, and it must have upset the Chief of Naval Operations also because within two weeks of the news release, that Captain retired from the Navy.

As we were finishing up our work with VO67, some of the people in the unit thought I had been assigned to the unit and would be deploying with them. One was the Skipper of VO67, and he came into my assigned office to welcome me aboard. I was not assigned to the unit, and my enlistment was ending in a few months, and I did not have the required time to be transferred, which I am happy about. VO67 deployed, and I was reassigned to temporary duty as the assistant VP31 Duty Officer. This was a straight day shift job with all weekend off, and our band was now playing every night, Tuesday through Saturday.

I had bought a house in Chula Vista and had to drive around the strand to North Island each morning in the rush hour traffic with my bright red, twenty-five-dollar 1958 Chevy.

# Chapter 38

# IMPERIAL BEACH

While working my straight dayshift assignment as the assistant Duty Officer, I was able to put a lot more time into working with the band. Vernon Lancaster was doing a good job as the lead singer, and Clint helped out some, but we needed a second voice in the group. Vernon Denny, who was my best friend in Japan and worked in my band, had gotten out of the Air Force and came to San Diego to join our band there. Denny was an excellent country music singer and rhythm Guitarist. I converted him to bass, and I started on the drums.

We now had two guys named Vernon. Well, Vernon Denny became Denny. Vernon Lancaster was Vern. He sang and played rhythm guitar, Clint played lead guitar, and Denny played bass and sang while I played the drums. The music was rough at first, but Clint's lead guitar and the singers carried the sound.

We started full-time at a bar called the Diamond Horseshoe Bar in National City, CA. We took the place of a very professional three-piece trio group that moved to Springe Valley Bar called the Valley Crossroads. We played at the Diamond Horseshoe bar for three months, and that gave us time for me to learn how to carry a beat on the drums and Denny to learn his way around the bass.

I stayed in touch with Bud Estes at Bonanza Club, and when he had an opening on our nights off, we would fill in for them. I found myself working so many hours, some mornings I would get to work and could not remember how I got there or where I had parked my car. After three months, the trio at the Valley Crossroads landed a gig in Las Vegas, and we moved to the Valley Crossroads.

The Valley Crossroads was bigger than the Horseshoe Bar and was located in the middle of a large housing area in Spring Valley, CA. We had a good crowd of wonderful people there as soon as we started, and they were more of a family type of people that loved to dance. One of the customers there, Sandy Bain, and I became close friends, and we are still caressing those old memories today.

We fit in there and started to try to dress up a little. We were all struggling to get by and could not afford to buy high-quality matching uniforms. But did get matching Jackets and ties. We played Wednesday through Sunday at the Crossroads, and Bud Estes hired us to play on Mondays and Tuesdays at the Bonanza Club.

The Bonanza Club was a Musician's Union club, and I was not in the Union, and I already had a serious run-in with the person in charge of the San Diego chapter.

His name was Smith, and when I first got to San Diego from Japan, the guys in my old band asked me to check on working opportunities there and consider regrouping the band there when they got out of the service. I assumed that we would become Union members because we were looking at it as a career.

When I called the union office, I got Mr. Smith's secretary on the phone and told her that I needed to know what the country music opportunities were because some musicians that were in the Navy wanted to come there after they got out. The first thing she said was, "Are you in the service?" When I said yes, she abruptly interrupted me by saying, "If you are in the Military Service, you can't work here," and hung up the phone. I thought that she just failed to understand that I only wanted information and we would be joining the union. I waited a few minutes for me to cool off before I called back.

I put the same call through, and she answered the phone, and I said, "I just called you, and I think we had a misunderstanding." At that point, she cut in and said, "I told you that you cannot work here if you are in the service," and hung up the phone again. Well, that made me very mad. I knew some people that could swing a lot of influence with processing my complaint if I asked them to, and I was extremely rude when I called her back.

When she answered the phone, I gave her some very direct instructions, which I can't repeat here, and one of them was to put Mr. Smith on that phone. That part she did. I told Mr. Smith the same thing I tried to tell her, and he did not have any problem understanding me. He was nice and gave me an overview of the country music situation in the San Diego area. There was a lot of work, but unreliable management of the country band hurt the credibility of the bands. I thanked him for his help, and we parted on neutral grounds.

When we started playing the two nights at the Bonanza Club, most people did not know that the band was not union. Bud knew that we were not union, but he hated the union anyway. Some union members got mad at Bud and slipped a minor into the club through the back door, and an inspector caught him before the waitress spotted him. That cost Bud 500 dollars and the waitress 500 dollars, which Bud paid. There were other pranks pulled by union members that caused Bud other problems.

We had good luck at the Bonanza Club. Vernon had made friends with a local Country Music Disk Jockey, and Merle Haggard was at the top of the hit list, and we were playing his new songs as fast as they came out. The DJ gave Vern and the Bonanza Club a lot of free advertisements by announcing the new Merle Haggard songs. He would announce them by saying, "Hey, folks. Merle has a new hit, and I can't wait to hear Vern do this at the Bonanza Club, and I am going to play it for you right after this special request. Vern would learn the song before he came to work that night and tell us which other Haggard songs it was like and what the difference was, we played it three or four times that night.

Through the Bonanza Club, we got a 30-minute TV show on Sunday afternoons on Channel Six at their TV Station, which was in Tijuana, Mexico. Now, in addition to shows at The Crossroads and the Bonanza Club, we had loaded our equipment and gone into Mexico. I was still driving that same red 30-dollar Chevy from Japan for all my own transportation and to haul the band equipment from one show to another. Driving that car, with the back seat removed and loaded with band equipment and the trunk full of more equipment and three people in the front seat, I got inspections quite often.

Clint decided he wanted to play the steel guitar, and he wanted to practice on stage at the Valley Crossroads, and I would not agree to that because we were being paid to play for the customers. This led to some conflict, and Clint left the band, and two weeks later, we left the Valley Crossroads. I talked to Bud Estes, and he hired us as the full-time Bonanza Club band. I hired a female drummer that also sang, and I went back on bass, and Denny went back on rhythm guitar. Vernon played the lead guitar, but we let the vocalists carry the show.

The drummer worked a day job as a telephone operator, and she ran with a crazy bunch of female workers. They tuned out to support her and got to know all the staff at the club. They all knew that beyond Bud's big and mean-looking exterior, he was a softhearted guy. This crazy bunch decided to play a joke on Bud.

One of the people that worked with them at the phone company was a 42-year-old female midget that was barely two feet tall. They dressed her up to look like a small girl child, and on a busy night, the crazy group charged the door like a bunch of drunks crashing a party. One of the adults was holding the hand of the midget, who was behaving like a young child. She wore a child's bonnet that obscured her head, and she consistently kept her head down, making it impossible to see her face.

They were blocking the door and causing a disturbance, and when Bud went to the door to see what was going on, the little girl broke loose from the adult holding her and ran right between Bud's legs and through the crowd toward the bandstand. The room was crowded, and Bud tried to catch her, but she was running around and under places; a large person like Bud could not go without running over people.

When she got to the edge of the bandstand, Bud was able to catch her. He picked her up like she was a child and raised her to get a look at her. She grabbed Bud by his ears and kissed him. At first, he went ballistic and almost dropped her, but he recovered, and when he realized that it was a joke being played on him, he tried to act mad. The crowd now knew what was going on, and they all were laughing. Then Bud started laughing, and then he carried her like a child on his arm to the bar and bought her and the crazy group a drink.

We had several special guests that would be booked for one- or two-night specials. One was Tommy Duncan, and he was a good friend and mentor. I was still planning on regrouping my old band and getting Tommy to be our manager. Tommy did not want another band but was considering helping us get started. Just before we left Japan, I had backed him up with my band and knew everybody in the band. Some of us had backed him up on four of his tours in Japan.

Tommy and his wife had a lot of songs they had written over the years, and he thought that if we came to his place for six weeks of training, two weeks of which would be with a professional A and R person (arrangement and recording expert), we could record some of his songs and be a completive band. Also, he was working on buying his own recording studio.

Tommy was a good friend and was aware that I would be leaving a good Military career and advised me against that. He wanted me to finish my career before launching my music career. As things turned out, that is what happened. Tommy did a two-night show with us, and after the Sunday night show, he went to his motel room, and during the night, he suffered a fatal heart attack. That was a hard shock for me because as well as I knew Tommy, I had no idea that he had a heart problem.

Gary and Jack both hated the union because all they did was pay dues and get nothing back for the union. They were prepared to resign if Mr. Smith showed up and challenged them. They would give him their union cards and express their opinions about the lack of benefits they had received as members of his union.

Well, Mr. Smith called Bud and set up a meeting between him, Bud, and me. We were playing when Mr. Smith came in, and Gary and Jack had their membership cards in their shirt pockets. Bud took Mr. Smith to a booth and waited for me to take a break, and I joined them. It was a good meeting, and as it turned out, it was the Sunday TV show that was causing Mr. Smith the biggest problem. Well, that was easy to fix because it was more trouble for us than it was worth, and we wanted to shut it down anyway. Bud was the main sponsor of the show, and he also wanted to discontinue it. Bud agreed to shut it down, and Mr. Smith agreed to overlook the two nonunion members in the band. There was no picketing of the club.

My enlistment ran out, but I had an option to take up to six months off before I would lose anything career wise like time in grade or service. All I had to do was make sure I reenlisted before the time ran out. I set it up with the local Navy Recruiter to make sure I got reenlisted before the time ran out and some time off.

I knew that I would get assigned to the first sea duty assignment they needed to fill but I needed a break for the military, so I took the time. I worked some part time jobs and played every night, but I was spending more than I was making. I reenlisted and got orders to Long Beach to be assigned to the USS Enterprise.

# Chapter 39

# USS HANCOCK

The first problem was that I got orders to the USS Enterprise Aircraft Carrier in San Francisco, California. It would be coming into Drydock for a repair cycle, and I would be assigned to Ships company for a three-year tour of duty. Keiko did not drive, and that was a problem because she would not have any transportation. We had neighbors across the street, and she got along well with them. They both worked and wanted her to move into their spare room so she could help them with the housework. She agreed, and I got a property management company to handle the renting and or leasing of the house so we would not have to sell it.

I did not like the idea of going on the Enterprise and sitting in drydock for a year. I started trying to get my orders changed. Clint had gotten stationed on the Hancock Aircraft Carrier with my friend Jerry Davis at Alameda, California, and they were getting ready to deploy to the Tonkin Gulf in Vietnam. I had no experience with intermediate-level maintenance, and now I was getting to be a senior paygrade E-6 which could be in charge of a work center.

My reenlistment orders were to report to the Long Beach Naval Base for further transfer to the Enterprise. I was working with the personnel assignment office on getting my orders changed. I learned that the priority for filling the requirements for ships was from people who had taken a break in their service. That was the reason for getting shipboard duty, and that ships going to the war zone had priority over those returning to the States. I knew Davis would be finishing his tour on the Hancock soon, so I worked on that angle and got my orders changed. That turned out to be a good thing because the deal with Keiko was not working out, and I had to get her an apartment in Alameda.

While I was assigned to Long Beach, I was commuting from my house in Chula Vista and finishing up my agreement with Bud at the Bonanza club. That did not leave me much time to sleep. Sleep was mostly just napping anywhere I could. Most of my time was spent in office waiting rooms waiting for something and on my own time.

I was working on getting my orders changed to the Hancock and doing odd little supervision assignments while waiting for the results and off duty early most of the time. When my change of orders came in, they were to report directly to the USS Hancock Aircraft Carrier, CV19, at the Alameda, California Naval Base.

I had everything in San Diego set up so I could leave. I had storage space for my household items. My car was sold, and all I needed was my clothing, and personal items and they were packed.

At that time, Keiko was moving into the neighbor's house across the street. I caught a PSA flight to San Francisco Airport and made my way to my new base and reported for duty on board the USS Hancock for a three-year tour of duty. My first task was to find my bunk and sleep for the next twelve hours.

I had changed squadrons and bases a few times before, but this time, it was different. Previously, I had moved to various squadrons on different bases. This time, however, I was headed to a base within a base. The ship itself is entirely self-contained. The only thing the Naval base provides is a dock to which the ship is tied for supply and service deliveries. Once you step aboard the ship, it's comparable to being in prison. Everything you need is confined within the ship's premises.

I was so tired when I reported on board that I don't remember much about checking in, just finding my assigned bunk. The berthing compartments are assigned by your work location and pay grade for Ship's Company personnel. My berthing compartment had the bunks stacked four high, and I had the third bunk. The vertical space between the bunks was about twenty-four inches. If the person above you was a heavy person, you could not turn over without hitting the bunk above you with your shoulder. Each bunk was about thirty-six inches wide and joined the next tier with only about six inches between the mattresses. You had one small locker to hold all your personnel items.

I remember waking up after a few hours of sleep and trying to figure out where I was. I felt like I was coming out of a bad hangover. I started to remember that I was on the ship but did not know where I was.

There were a few people in the compartment, but nobody that I knew. I had to ask someone where the shower was. After I got cleaned up and awake and got a uniform on that was presentable, I set out to find out where to go to finish checking in.

I knew that I was assigned to AIMD, which is Aviation Intermediate Maintenance Department, which was on the rear end of the ship, known as the fantail. I found work center 620, which was the shop I should be assigned to, and entered, hoping to see either Davis or Finley. They were both off the ship. I introduced myself and explained that I was not familiar with the ship and that someone could show me where to go to get checked in.

I was at the right shop, and in a few minutes, I would most likely be the supervisor, and that scared me back to reality. I was in a lot of trouble. I had no idea about intermediate level maintenance or what it required. I had always worked line-level maintenance. I pulled and replaced the parts and sent them off to be repaired. This was where the parts got repaired and sent back.

One of the guys showed me around and introduced me to the division commander. Lieutenant Commander Pollard. He welcomed me aboard and said that I would be working with Jerry Davis, who was the current shop supervisor. I explained that I knew Davis and had worked with him before in another command. I did not know that the commander was not very happy with Davis, and I did not let him know that I was senior to Davis.

After leaving the administration offices for AIMD, I went to the ship's personnel office and finished checking in and then found the chow hall. I was so hungry that I did not care what was being served; I was going to eat.

The rest of that day was spent learning where and how to find where I needed to go and where and when I could smoke. I had to learn where the Ship's Store was and when it would be open. I need some things like toilet articles, cigarettes, and uniform articles.

The first day on the ship was short but busy. I was lost without anyone I knew to fill me in on what I needed to know. We were scheduled to leave port on a nine-month cruise to a war zone in just a few days, and I had no idea what I needed, much less what I had.

We had an easy-to-understand work schedule at sea. Everybody worked 12-hour shifts 7 days a week. You either started at 12.00 noon and got off at 12.00 midnight or worked the other shift. In port, you had a different schedule, and that depended on watch assignments to cover the duties that were required.

On the second day, I set out to find out what I needed to get accomplished before we left port. I was told to go to a place called Data Processing. I was not familiar with that name, but I found it. It was a small room with one person, a large printer, and a 3 by 5-inch card sorting machine. I told him who I was and that I had just come on board, and I had work center 620 and needed to know what I needed to be ready for the cruise.

To my surprise, he said, "OK, but that he would need a few minutes to get it ready, and I should go to lunch, and he would have it ready when I got back." Well, I went to the mess hall and was able to get some food even though it was not a regular mealtime. I also learned that there was a small lounge for paygrade E6 to use. It was small but had a grill and a couple of refrigerators.

When I returned to the Data Processing room, the guy handed me a large folder filled with green and white colored fanfold paper and said here is everything you need. I looked at the folder and had no idea what it was. I got a little mad at the guy because I was hoping for something I could understand. I said to him, "Unless I am going to have a very bad case of Diarrhea, I don't know what good this is going to do for me". Then he said, "Oh, you don't know how to read this; you need to go to the IMRL office and told me to find it. It was in the AIMD administrative section."

I took that big heavy folder up to a very small space with IMRL on the door. If the room had been a little larger, it could have been a broom closet. There was only room for a small desk, the same size as the folder, and one chair.

In the room was a skinny little guy with horn-rimmed glasses smoking a pipe. I told him that I was told that he could help me with this, and I handed him the folder. He looked at it and asked if I had work center 620. I explained my situation, and he went through the list page by page at a speed that I could not follow. Mostly all I heard was yes, yes, and ok. Then he handed me the folder back and said you are in good shape. Everything you need is on board, but three pieces of test equipment and two of those are in calibration labs and are scheduled to be on board before we leave. One of the testers is still at the factory and will be shipped to you as soon as it becomes available.

He explained how all that paperwork we had been cussing and filling out for years had now provided enough data that the computer could determine every part I would need for every aircraft I was responsible for. What test equipment and even skill levels that my workers would need to repair and calibrate the parts? He also went over the technical library I would be using to get the factory information that I needed. With that list, he could confirm that I had every manual and every update that was available. Man, that was when I fell in love with computers.

After a couple of days, Davis and Clint came back to the shop, and I talked to Davis and found out that a chief was ordered to report in, and he would be the Shop supervisor. That took some of the pressure off me for a short time. He came on board as ordered but knew he was not staying, and three days after reporting on board, he received a change in orders. I got Davis to stay on the day shift, and I took over the night shift until I could learn my way around.

The Navy was now using a manhour accounting system called the 3M system. The three Ms stood for Maintenance, Material, and Manhour accounting. I had never used the system before, and I had to study the system. It was the Work Center supervisor's responsibility to complete and verify the reports. With Davis continuing as the Work Center supervisor, I had plenty of time to study that task. As we were getting ready to leave on our cruise, things were really busy, and I don't remember how we got it done, but we made it.

Leaving the dock was emotional, to say the least. We were leaving everything we loved behind to go halfway around the world to fight a war for their freedom. As we steamed out of San Francisco Bay, we went under the Golden Gate Bridge, and there on the bridge was a sendoff party of demonstrators. They held all kinds of derogatory signs and bags of garbage, which they dumped on the ship as we went under the bridge. The deck crews washed off the decks with fire hoses, and we made a promise to remember them when we returned.

When you leave or enter a harbor, you will cross the Ground Swells. On a small craft, they can get rough, but on a large craft like an Aircraft Carrier, they are not a problem. Once you reach open water, it gets really nice. The ship steams at a steady speed and makes very few turns, and walking around on the ship does not create any problems. You can always feel the motion of the ship and hear some noise, but you become used to it, and subconsciously, you start to treat it like a safety net. As long as you hear and feel it, you know everything is ok. Later I will tell you what it is like when you don't feel or hear the ship.

By the time we reached Hawaii, I had settled into my new routine, was learning my new job, and getting a lot of sleep. We had a short layover at Pearl Harbor before moving on, and I went down to my old stomping grounds on Hotel Street, but everything had changed. The old Anchor Club was closed for reconstruction, and I did not know any of the people now at any of the other places. After a short liberty and a good meal, I returned to the ship.

The next day we got a mail call, and that was good. Everything was going well. Keiko was all settled into her apartment in Alameda, and she was learning how to use the city bus system to get around. I also got a letter from Mom, and everybody was ok there. I was getting my pay straightened out, and all the bills were getting paid. I was starting to like not having to drive to work and not having to take care of everybody else's problems.

I don't remember much about leaving Pearl Harbor, but on the second day out, we discovered that a member of the ship's crew was missing. They turned the ship around and went back to search for him for a couple of days. Some of his crew members said that he had gotten a Dear John letter from his girlfriend while in port and was not taking it well. He was last seen the night he went missing standing in an open area on the side, and they concluded that he had committed suicide by jumping over the side of the ship after it got dark. All his personal stuff was still on the ship, and his body was never found.

Our next stop was in Subic Bay in the Philippines, which was our main supply base while on deployment to Viet Nam. Olongapo was the city at Subic Bay and was a wild place when the fleet was in. The Navy Base was on one side of a river, and Olongapo was on the other side. They had taken WW-II jeeps and turned them into colorful vehicles called Jitneys. They were your main source of transportation in the Philippine cities. They were fast and cheap, and each one was a business for the owner, and they took pride in them. When I was flying in and out of Clark Air Force Base and the three years I served on the Hancock, I took a lot of rides in them and always got where I was going safely.

After a few days of resupply and liberty, we headed for Tonkin Gulf for our first operations. For the most part, my work and duties were about the same, but the ship was involved in launching air strikes to support the ground troops. For every plane you launch, you must also recover it. The deck crews had the most physical labor part of those operations. The pilots were taking off and landing on the ship, sometimes three or four trips per day. When supplying support coverage, you operate around the clock. Everything is on a need-to-know basis, and for the most part, you only find out what you did and that is after the fact.

One of the first operations we were involved in took about three months to complete. Our intelligence department had discovered a mountain that was being used for an ammunition storage location. They watched the base of the mountain being tunneled out, and then a constant line of ammunition-carrying trucks delivered load after load to the mountain and left empty. When trucks stopped hauling the ammunition into the mountain, we sent two planes out with walleye missiles and put one missile down each of the entrance tunnels. The report stated that the base of the mountain blew up for two days, and the height of the mountain dropped by over 100 feet.

At the beginning of our first Tonkin Gulf tour, I continued to work the night shift in the shop, and Davis was the work center supervisor. We had a Chief Warrant Officer by the name of Frank Durbin assigned to the division and an LTJG officer. I don't recall his name.

The Aviation Intermediate Maintenance Department (AIMD) Commander was a Lieutenant Commander by the name of Pollard. I had met LTCDR Pollard when I checked in but had avoided any further contact with him. Pollard was not an easy person to get along with, and I had no idea that there was a conflict between him and Davis. One day, just a few days into our Tonkin Gulf operation, I was summoned to Pollard's office. Everything from my point of view was going well. I knew Davis was getting close to the end of his tour of duty on the Hancock and thought that perhaps that was what the meeting was about.

When I entered Pollard's office, he was really mad about something. He started my chewing out by asking me if I was senior to Davis. I replied by saying yes, but only for six months. His response was, you are senior, and you are not handling your responsibility and you are letting him be your supervisor? It did not matter what my response was, he was not going to accept it. He expressed his dissatisfaction with my actions by telling me that if I was planning on getting advanced to the rank of Chief

Petty Officer, I could forget it because he would see to it that it didn't happen. Then he dismissed me by saying he had some decisions to make.

I located Davis and asked him what the problem with Pollard was and he said he had never gotten along with him. I asked Davis if he was getting ready to leave the ship and he said not yet because he still had some time on this tour and had not requested any orders. I knew that something was going to happen and two days later I got reassigned to a temporary duty as the Mess Deck Master at Arms supervisor.

I don't know what happened with Davis, but he stayed in charge of the work center. I did know that each division has to supply people to assist in food service and I had got that assignment before when I was at McGuire Air Force Base. When I checked into the Food Services Division, I was told that they had requested that AIMD supply one of their E6 level Supervisors to assist with them with the supervision of their Mess Cook section.

I was aware of a lot of complaints about the food service. There were always delays during scheduled mealtimes. There was no ice and standard beverage was Kool-Aid and the cups to drink out of were always still hot. Drinking warm Cool-Aid seemed to be the center of the complaints which also included things like appearance, attitudes and cleanliness of the tables and servicing utensils. I was not aware of how deep the problems went.

I met my first problem when I entered my office. There are E-4s and E-5s assigned to the food service section on a temporary assignment and they supervise the Mess Cooks on each of the shifts. One of the E-5s was sitting in my chair wearing a work uniform that was ragged and worn out beyond any acceptable standard. He was the dayshift supervisor. It was obvious that there was a need for discipline. I introduced myself to him and gave him one hour to get into a proper uniform, and I explained where he should not park his lower extremities while in my office.

While the E5 was changing his uniform, I went through the papers on my desk and created a roster of the mess cooks and their shift and job assignments. When the E5 returned, we went on an inspection tour of the Mess Hall. There were several problem areas that needed attention.

The galley was equipped with two dishwashing machines and one of them was broken. These machines are designed to meet the health sanitation requirements and require very hot water. The galley was feeding close to 3,000 people and one machine just could not keep up with the rush hour demands, so there was not enough cooling-off time before the cups were put back in service. There was an ice machine that could supply enough ice, but it was broken. It would start making ice but within fifteen minutes, it would start flooding the room with water from the drain system.

The Supply department would not allow the galley any additional cups by saying that they did not have any more in stock. The request for repairs on the dishwasher was rejected because it was supposed to be pulled and sent off the ship for repair. It was a large and complex machine. When I did a follow-up on the request to repair the ice machine, I found that they went to the Engineering Division, and they had checked the machine and it worked according to their report.

The problem with the cleanliness of the tables was just a matter of enforcing the proper cleaning procedures. The other problems would require a new approach. Within the first couple of days of my new assignment, the word got out that I was trying to make things better and I started getting help and suggestions from different people. One of the people assigned to mess cook duties knew all the ins and outs of the supply department. One of the E4s, that was now an electronic fire control technician, used to be a machinist. With their help and my own unorthodox skills in getting things done, we put together a plan.

We had our weekly inspection of our spaces coming up and it was conducted by the Ship Captain and the division commanders. I got my guy, the expert in the Supply Division, to locate the Cups we needed and get me the Stock Numbers for the cups, the exact location, and the number in stock. I double-checked the ice machine to make sure I was not missing anything and waited for the inspection.

The ship's Captain conducted the inspection right on schedule and with the supply and engineering division commanders. He always addressed the complaints during the inspection and this time I was ready. He asked how we were doing with the problem of the warm cool aid and hot cups. I responded by asking him to let me show him the problems we were having, and he said to go ahead.

I showed him the two dishwashers we were trying to work with and explained one was broken and we could not get it fixed, which meant we were working with only half the equipment we needed to meet our work requirements, then I explained with only one machine to wash all the dining utensils we needed and the temperature they had to wash at, the cups did not have time to cool off. If we had additional cups, we could create a longer cooling period which would give us cooler cups to help the situation.

I also told him that we had ordered additional cups, but the supply had rejected the order because they did not have any additional cups in stock. The supply division commander cut into the conversation with a distraction saying that we had enough cups, but everyone was using them for their personal coffee cups, and we had other ways of cooling them down.

That was my chance to get another advantage, and I replied, "Yes sir, if I could get the ice machine fixed, we could use ice to cool the cups and the drink". This brought the response that I needed for the Engineering Division Commander. We have checked the machine, and it works. My response was that I would like to demonstrate that problem after the cup problem is cleared up.

With that, the captain asked the supply commander if they were out of cups. He attempted to say that he did not have enough to restock our supply and that they cost too much to keep wasting them. At that point, I said to my guy, "I asked you to go and check on the cups in stock, what did you find?" He read off the Navy Stock Number for the cups, the location and bin number where they were stored, how many cases there were, and how many cups per case. At that point, I knew that I had the ear of the captain.

The captain asked the supply commander how much he paid for the cups, and he gave a number of over six dollars per cup. The captain challenged that with, "My wife was buying them at Walmart for .80 cents a cup".

The captain moved the subject back to the ice machine. I told the captain that if he could give me 15 minutes, I could show him the problem with the machine. He responded that he had 20 minutes for me to start the machine.

I turned the machine on and said that it would start making ice, but within fifteen minutes, it would leak so much water that it would be running over his shoes. I had the best situation I could ask for to run this test. We had a large roof with a flat floor and the ship had a slow roll. First the ice cubes started to drop right on schedule and after ten minutes the water drain started backing up with the water dumping it on the floor. In about ten minutes I had an inch of water on the floor and the roll of the ship was washing it back and forth across the captain's shoes.

The captain thanked me for the information and turned to the Supply Division Commander and directed him to provide the cups ASAP and to use an emergency order if he needed to. Then he had a few more questions for the Engineering Division Commander about what special equipment and parts he would need to repair the ice machine. He then directed him to contact our next supply port and arrange to have the items he needed to repair the ice machine ready when we docked. The captain further directed the commander to make the repairs a top priority because his division would remain on the ship until it was repaired. I returned to my office, and I should mention that I did not go near the side of the ship for several days.

I did not have an official authorization to repair the broken dishwasher, but I did have someone assigned to me that was a machinist before coming into the Navy. He had examined the machine and was sure he could fix it. The problem was a broken gear and if he could remove the gear for a closer inspection, he was confident he could make a new one.

I authorized him to work on the machine. After he removed the gear, I set up a meeting with my counterpart in the ship's Machine Shop. I took my guy that was going to make the gear with me. The E6 in the Machine Shop was very helpful, and they worked on how to produce the special gear we needed with my guy operating the machine to make the gear. His idea worked and he had the dishwasher running within two weeks.

One additional problem that I encountered was that there were three Chiefs assigned to the Food Service Division. One of the Chiefs was finishing his tour of duty and was scheduled to leave the ship in a couple of months. one of them was in the middle of his tour of duty and the third one was just starting his tour. The problem was they all felt like they should be running things. I was getting directives from all three of them and they did not agree with each other on what needed to be done. Each time I would try to point out that there was a conflict between their directives. Each one of them would say, "Don't pay any attention to him, I am running this Division." My attempts to talk to each of them had failed to help dissolve the problem. I set up a meeting between each of them and the Lieutenant in charge of the Division.

I went to the Meeting Room and sat in a corner with my paperwork and waited for everyone to come in. One by one they all showed up and started talking to each other about everything except business. After a few minutes of bragging about what they were doing, someone asked who called this meeting and they were looking at the Lieutenant who thought that one of them had called for the meeting. I stood up and said that I had called it. I was the lowest ranking person in the meeting.

Well, that caused tempers to rise among the three Chiefs. They wanted to know where I got the authority to call a meeting. I explained that I was getting orders from each of the Chiefs that they were in conflict with each other and I only needed to know which one of them was in charge. That caused an instant argument among them, and the Lieutenant stepped in and told me to go back to taking care of my job, and he would handle that. After that, things got a lot smoother.

Things went well for a while, and I was enjoying my job, but Davis got his end-of-the-tour transfer orders, and I was reassigned to Work Center 620 as the supervisor.

There were many things that happened on that cruise that were interesting, but I remember one that involved a Russian spy ship called a Trawler. The Russians took fishing boats and converted them into spy ships. They looked like fishing boats, but instead of having fishing equipment, they had antennas.

The Russians had them stationed in the Tonkin Gulf to spy on our operations and they were always trying to stay close to our ships. When we launched or retrieved planes, we had to head into the wind to get enough wind across the deck for safe operations. On one of our operations, we were operating in a calm condition, and we had to find an air current to get any help from the wind.

We had launched some planes on a mission and needed to recover them. We found a small breeze and aligned the ship into the wind and set up for recovery. Even With the Carrier running at full speed and the breeze, we were at the low end of a safe landing condition, and our planes were getting low on fuel. As we reached full speed, a Russian Trawler cut in front of the carrier, trying to make us have to cut speed or divert to miss them. The captain stayed at full throttle and hit the collision alarm, charging straight ahead toward the Trawler. The game of chicken was on, and the Trawler hit full throttle and just barely missed getting cut in half by the bow of the carrier.

He was so close to the carrier that he came under the overhang of the flight deck and our deck crew threw everything they could get their hands on, on top of the Trawler. I don't know if he scratched the paint on the side of the carrier, but he sure hugged the side of the carrier all the way past the fantail. We made our recovery and never looked back.

All of our contacts with the Russians were not bad. When we were recovering planes, we kept one of our destroyers directly behind and close to the ship in case someone falls overboard or had to eject during a landing. We have a gentlemen's agreement with the recovery vessel that if they pick up one of our people, we will give them 5 gallons of ice cream. Well, the Russians had their ships operation in the same area and on one of our recovery operations our destroyers were diverted to provide a screening alert. Our planes were already in route to land and a Russian Destroyer came up behind us and signaled the captain to continue his recovery and that he would cover the recovery position. He also said that if he recovered anyone, he was expecting the 5 gallons of ice cream. He did a good job but did not earn or receive the ice cream.

We did have a couple of disasters on the cruise, and one was when we lost one of our F8 fighter planes and the pilot. The second was when we lost our Helicopter, but all the crew was ok. The F8 crashed alongside the ship due to pilot error.

He attempted to do a fly-by with a straight-up vertical climb out, but he let the plane get into a bad position and it flamed out. The plane stalled and nosed over and came straight back down into the water with the pilot still inside the cockpit. We watched the crash from the side of the ship. Nothing was recovered.

The Helicopter was flying just above the level of the flight deck, and it lost power and dropped straight down to the water. It floated long enough for the pilot and crew to escape from and swim away from the plane. The plane had flotation devices, and it slowly flipped over and floated upside down, and we were able to hook the ship's crane to it and lift it onto the ship. The wreckage was offloaded and sent to salvage.

When you are operating at sea and need to restock your supplies, you use an operation called UNREP which stands for Underway Replenishment.

In August of 1968, we had an accident while taking on supplies from the USS Camden involving both ships. I needed to get some fresh air and clear my head. I had walked out on the hangar deck, and I had just gone to the side of my ship and saw that the two ships were closer together than normal. I went back to my work center and told the guys that if they wanted some good pictures of the Camden, now would be a great time because we were so close enough that we could talk to each other.

Suddenly the gap between the two ships closed, and the two ships bumped together. I remember that I had braced myself for the shock of the impact, but to my surprise, I did not feel any impact. The extremely high level of energy stored up in the ships observed the impact without even a bump being felt. We were in the middle of taking on supplies that included ammunition and fuel, and they were stacked shoulder-high all over the hangar deck.

To separate the ships, the Hancock pulled straight forward, and the Camden dropped back. We were receiving fuel through four pressurized pumping stations through four-inch fuel lines. That ripped out all the fueling stations and let fuel go everywhere. The heavy cables that carried all the supplies from ship to ship broke off and got tangled around two of our aircraft. One was an F8 Cougar Jet fighter and the other on was our Twin Engine Cod.

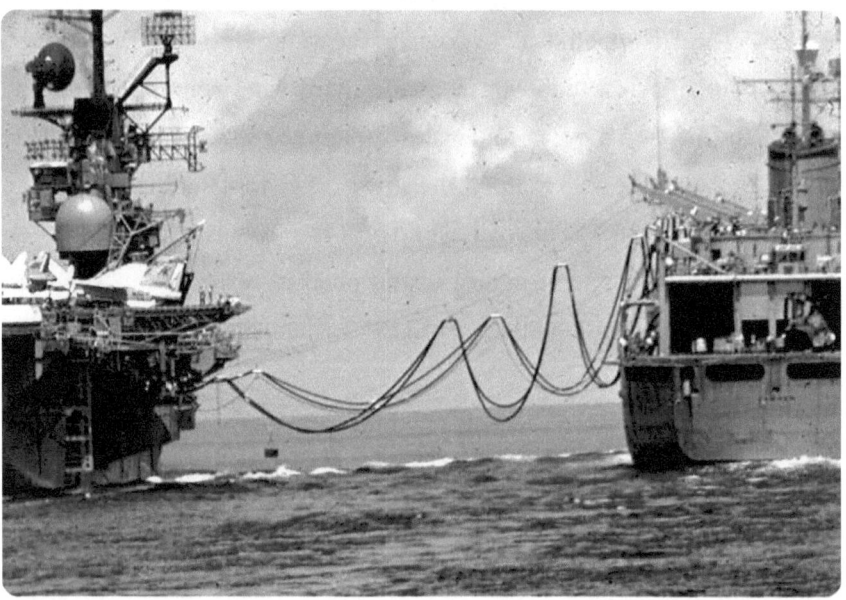

Both were pulled off the Hancock and fell on top of the Camden. I also had a hole torn in the left side of the Camden that was about 30 feet long. I knew that with all that fuel and ammunition, if a fire started, we would be blown to pieces, so we cleared the area and went to the Fantail of the ship. That would have been our only ditching station if it was necessary to abandon the ship. Thank God no fire was started, and no one was hurt.

In April of 1969, the ship was in Subic Bay for our turnaround from Tonkin Gulf, and our stay got cut short by everyone being recalled to ship for an emergency departure. We were rounded up and delivered to the ship by the Shore Patrol. We did not know what the emergency was, but the old ship was steaming as fast as she could go as we cleared the harbor. Nothing was told to us about where or why we were going until we got on the open seas. The first thing that happened was that all the nuclear unit was called out, and we were all locked down. Then we learned that we were headed to North Korea because they had shot down one of our aircraft. We were on full nuclear alert. That old ship was trying to shake itself to pieces, but it held together and steamed at full speed all the way.

When we got to our destination, it was cold, and we had to break out our winter parkas to be outside. Some of the restrictions were lifted, and we went to an open area on the starboard side of the ship close to my work center. Ray Ross was really drunk when they brought him aboard the ship, and he slept through the whole trip. He had just gotten up and came out in jeans and a tee shirt. He walked over to the side of the ship and lit a cigarette. Then began to realize how cold it was outside. He had gotten drunk in the Philippines and woke up in North Korea.

We were told that some very high-ranking people, including America's Secretary of defense, were coming on board for a meeting to determine what action we were going to take. We waited, then everybody left, and we were told to stand down and return to our scheduled duties. As it turned out, on April 15, 1969, a US Navy EC121 was shot down by North Korea. A special task force was formed, but no actions were ever taken.

After we left Korea, we seemed to bounce around a lot. We would operate in Tonkin Gulf and go to different ports. Sometimes we would go back to Subic Bay and then we would hit Japan or Hong Kong. One of our trips took us to Singapore, and that one was special. That was when I survived an initiation and went from being a pollywog to becoming a Shellback. What is shellback? It is a sailor who has crossed the Equator. It is also called a rite of passage for a sailor who has been tested for his seaworthiness. Now I have earned the right to wear one gold earring in the right ear. I think it is time for a history lesson.

In the days of sailing ships, men were hired by their ability to do hard work. Ship owners or masters were not interested in how smart you were because they could do all the easy jobs; they wanted workers for the hard jobs. The trouble was being able to know who you were because most people could not write and, in a lot of cases, did not speak the same language as the boss. So, the body of the person being considered for the job becomes their resume. They first looked at your size and then your hands. If you had calloused hands, that meant that you were used to hard work. Then they looked at your tattoos to where all you had sailed. Each seaport would have a tattoo artist with a special tattoo that he was known for. Each sailor would get a tattoo in each port he visited and would show them to prove his experience. If he had a gold earring in the right ear, he had crossed the Equator. The Navy sill honors that tradition.

The rest of the tour went well until we got back to San Francisco harbor. As we approached the Golden Gate Bridge, we had a welcome-back group of demonstrators that appeared to be the same group that gave us our sendoff, complete with all the garbage. It would appear that our skipper had forgotten that you could not clear the ship's stacks in the harbor, but he got all four of them cleared just as we were passing under the bridge. He did get them cleared before we entered the harbor. I don't think our welcoming party was very happy about it, but the last thing I saw was them disappearing in the smoke.

# Chapter 40

# U.S.S. HANCOCK SECOND CRUISE

When we returned from my first cruise our dependents and friends met us as the dock. The base had set up a safe area for them close to the dock so they could watch us, and we could see them. Everyone who was not working an assigned job on the ship was on deck looking for their visitors and the visitors were trying to see us.

Docking an Aircraft Carrier is a slow process and requires a lot of precision work. The ship has two ramps of entering and exiting the ship. The first thing was to let the crew that was departing the ship to exit first and then the dependents were allowed to enter the ship to visit with the personnel who were on duty.

Keiko met me at the dock with some of the other dependents. I learned that while the ship was gone, some of the dependents formed a group to help the other dependents in the area. That was a great thing in Keiko's case, and I got to meet some of them, and we became friends.

There was a nice family type restaurant just outside the gate and within walking distance of the dock. Keiko and I, along with her group of friends, went there and had a good meal. The restaurant was set up as a welcome home spot for the returning troops and provided excellent service.

At the restaurant, I learned how stressed out the crew from the Hancock was. The waitress was trying to open the expansion leaves in the table and one side slammed down with a loud bang. I jumped to my feet. As I looked around at the customers, I could see that everyone standing was from the Hancock. The rest of the customers were relaxing and enjoying their meal. The young waitress was embarrassed and apologized to everyone. I guess we were all pretty stressed out.

Keiko had a small apartment close to the Main Gate at the base. For most of our needs we could walk or catch a city bus. When we needed a vehicle, I rented a car which was a lot cheaper than owning one. My first cruise helped us financially because I was getting combat pay and a tax-free salary. That and the cutback in our cost-of-living expense had us out of debt. Keiko missed our house but was happy in her own little apartment and we were looking at two more cruises on this tour of duty.

While at the Alameda Naval Base we shared dock space with the USS Coral Sea Aircraft carrier. Alameda was the home base for the Coral Sea, and she was nicknamed "San Francisco's Own. When they were in port, they proudly displayed their large banner on the side of their ship.

Well just as we were getting ready for our second cruise some of our people, and no I was not one of them, snuck on board the Coral Sea and stole their banner. On the day we were leaving to go on our cruise to the Tonkin Gulf, the Coral Sea was returning from their Dependent's Day Cruise, and we passed right by them displaying their banner on our ship.

We took it to Pearl Harbor, Hawaii and sent it back to them on a US Submarine that was returning to the San Francisco area. It was all in fun and a good challenge.

I don't recall any major problems on our trip to our supply port in the Philippines. We did a lot of training operations with our smaller support ships. We did some damage control and firefighting training. We also had training on ABC warfare, which is Atomic, Biological and Chemical. We had a Nuclear Weapons Unit on board along with some nuclear weapons. Each division had to have personnel with Top Secret Clearance to assist with additional security requirements any time there was any movement or training involving them.

We made our first short stop in the Philippines for supplies and recreation and headed for the Tonkin Gulf. There were a lot of changes going on in Viet Nam at that time, and mission assignments had changed from our last tour. We now had the USS New Jersey Battleship operating in the area and the USS Long Beach guided missel cruisier. They both were getting all the attention.

We had a joint training session with them, and it was scheduled to 07:00 hours and we were all in position together in a close group, which I though was a bad idea, just off our starboard side was the Long Beach and just off their starboard side was the New Jersey. The clock hit 07:00 and at 07:02 two missiles for the Long Beach flew across our flight deck. That was our first problem with the Long Beach. The rest of the training secession was to show off the fire power of the New Jersey.

A few days later during one of our missions, one of our fighter pilots who only needed one more confirmed kill to become an ACE, had a Mig Fighter Jet in his sights that was trying to escape by crossing the border. Our pilot was yelling on the radio that he had the Mig and was getting ready shoot him when the Long Beach took him right out of our pilot's sights with a missile.

We had a very mad pilot who was declaring war on the Long Beach. He had to be physically restrained and kept from taking another plane after the destroyer, the Long Beach. The report read that the Long Beach missile had traveled 90 miles to hit the Mig that was directly in front of our plane. We did not think very highly of the Long Beach after that.

We returned to our duties in the Tonkin Gulf and had a rough tour. On one of our missions one of our planes returned for a landing with a 1,000-pound bomb that failed to release from the plane on a bombing run. Upon hitting the deck during its landing, the front end of the bomb broke loose from the bomb release rack and the nose hit the deck damaging the Fuse part of the bomb. The bomb was safely removed from the plane but because of the fuse damage it could not be safely defused. That left us having to store the bomb until it could be safely dumped off the ship.

The ship was old and needed a lot of small repairs. We were constantly having electrical fires and problems with one of our boilers. The fire alarm is sounded by a series of dings on a bell and the ship is separated in three sections. The bow is the front of the ship and identified by one single ding. The mid-section by two dings and the fantail by three dings. You get so used to hearing the fire alarm that you just wait to hear which part of the ship it is in and if it is not in your section, you go right back to sleep.

On a moving ship you always feel the movement of the ship and you get used to it. There is also always noise and some of that is what you accept as normal, and you begin to listen for those sounds to reassure yourself that everything is ok.

Well one night I woke up to complete silence and no movement. Also, there was total darkness in the compartment, and I could not even see my finger when I touched my eyelid. Then suddenly heard a low voice calling out "Hey, what's going on? Is anybody alive out there?" Now I was out of my bunk and trying to find my way out of the compartment along with several others.

It was pitch black inside, and the only movement was the slow dead roll of the ship. Slowly all that training we had been given on how to find our way out of a smoke-filled compartment started kicking in. We had also been told to practice finding our way out of our compartment by learning where everything was between you and the door. Now I remembered that I had practiced that. Hold onto your bunk until you find your lockers and are sure of that before you change your reference. I remembered that I could reach my locker while still holding onto the end of my bunk. The lockers formed a wall to the next walkway through the compartment. I had to keep everything on my right side and work my way around all obstacles, and I would be in the walkway to the compartment exit.

Once I was out of the compartment, I had to work my way to the hangar deck. That was no problem because the passageway was now full of people heading that way, and all I could do was go with the traffic. Once we got to the hangar deck, we had some help from the natural night light from outside the ship. Also, some of the workers had battery-operated lights.

We were on calm seas, and the skipper had the decision to take advantage of these conditions to get rid of the fuse-damaged bomb and make some repairs at the same time. The Ship's boilers needed to be shut down for some quick repairs, and the electrical crew needed to kill all the electrical power to replace some items. This was a very unusual procedure, and I have no way of knowing what other safeguards he had in place, but it all worked very smoothly.

We also had several good things happen on that cruise. We got a new Commander in charge of the AIMD division by the name of Rush, and I got along well with him. We had an E8 by the name of Clayton Saylor, who was assigned to the Division Administration. He and I had the same birthdate, except I was one year older than him. He and his family, and Keiko and I became friends and stayed friends until his death in 2014.

We also formed a study group for the Chief Petty Officer's promotional exam. We started with four people, but one got transferred. The other two were from the same squadron on the ship. We continued studying together until the exam, and all three of us got our promotions.

This was a busy cruise, but there was always time for me to embarrass myself. The Tonkin Gulf is one of the breeding places for Sea Snakes. I remember when I was in Hawaii, I could not believe that there were no snakes on the land there.

I had forgotten about the dead sea snake that washed up on the beach in Hawaii. After we were on station for a while, some of the guys started talking about watching for Sea Snakes and saying things like, we are in their area now, and the weather is just right for them. Well, there are always jokes being played on the new guys, like Sea Bats and mail buoys, so I was not going to fall for that. Then one afternoon, I just had to get out of the shop for a few minutes, and I went to our favorite smoking area on the side of the ship.

You can stand on the overhang and watch the water flow under you and see for miles. I saw what I thought was a piece of rope about four feet long drifting just below where I was standing. It is against the rules to throw things over the side of the ship when it is moving. I was looking alongside the ship to see who was throwing things. I did not see anyone but just a few minutes later I saw three more pieces float by. Now felt like I had better put a stop to that before he caused some problems with the rope getting sucked into or tangled around something on the ship. I was really looking hard to see who was causing the problem when some more came floating by, but I saw one of them trying to swim away from the ship and it was about seven feet long.

Suddenly I realized that they were Sea Snakes, and they were real. My first reaction was to rush back to the shop and tell everyone about them, but I realized how foolish I had been and slowly strolled back into the shop and quietly said, the Sea Snakes are out if you want to see them. Then I heard somebody say, yes, we know they have been out for some time now. That embarrassed me even more.

During my military career, I went to Hong Kong several times. I enjoyed Hong Kong, and it was a great place to buy clothing. The tailor shops always had free drinks and snacks. You could visit the shop early in the morning, pick out a suit and get fitted for it while you were getting free food and drinks and they would have the suit ready for you to pick up by closing time the same day, and they always did good work.

Hong Kong also had some great places to eat all kinds of food. The restaurants would be named after the part of the world that the food was from, and it would be prepared like the original food. Well on one of our trips to Hong Kong we were getting ready to leave the ship to go eat. Man, I was hungry for a big meal. Someone in the bunch said that he wanted some Russian Borscht, a soup made with beets. Someone else agreed and we were off. I had heard the name several times but did not have a clue what it was and didn't care as long as there was a lot of it.

We went to a nice Russian Restaurant and were seated in a very nice setting, and someone ordered Borscht for everyone. They quickly came back with a bowl of soup. I ate mine, and it was good, but there was no salad or anything else to follow up with. Man, I was embarrassed when I learned that Borscht was just a soup.

One other time when I was in Hong Kong, I was embarrassed but so was the whole crew. Milk is always a problem overseas because it goes bad so fast. We had taken on supplies somewhere before we reached Hong Kong, and the milk went bad as soon as we reached the harbor. We got the ship secured and the next morning we were sitting in a big circle of milk.

There was no milk anywhere else in the harbor. I don't know how it got there or why the water or air currents had not moved or spread it out. I do know that harbor inspectors were not happy with us. I also don't have any idea how much that cost the government, but they did not eject us from the harbor.

We got back to Tonkin Gulf for our operations and got what we thought was a bad outbreak of the flu. We all got too sick to work. I was bedridden for almost two weeks. I could not eat or stay up. I had headaches that felt like I had a train running around in my head. One by one, everyone in the shop wound up in bed but one guy. He was able to fight it off until one of the first guys to get sick was able to return to work.

They estimated that 90 percent of the crew was sick. The pilots, as well as the deck hands, were too sick to work, but somehow, they got the job done. The pilots would make a short flight, and the plane captain would have to wash out the cockpit before he could get back inside it.

Everybody that could stay up would just lay down anywhere they were and sleep every minute they could. I can still remember the first thing I could eat when I was able to get up. I went to our little First-Class mess and fried an egg and made a sandwich out of it and it tasted like a million bucks.

I talked to the senior corpsman in the infirmary about what happened. We had all taken our regular flu shot just before we got sick, and the corpsman told me that we had been poisoned by a bad vaccine.

I think the biggest operation happened when one of the pilots got shot down in the mountains of Vietnam. He was able to safely eject and came down on top of one of the mountains. He got his emergency radios working, and our rescue pilots located him. He was in a good spot for a chopper rescue, but he warned them not to try because Charlie, the Vietcong, were all around the mountain just waiting for rescue plans and crew.

We waited until it was getting dark, and we loaded up our attack bombers with Napalm bombs and started launching a plane every minute. They would fly around the mountain just below the level of the pilot and roll the Napalm down the side of the mountain. This went on all night and just after daybreak, our chopper and crew flew in and picked him up with no problems. I have no idea of how many bombs were used but I heard some pretty high numbers.

The other two AE1s that studied with me for the Chief's promotion test, and I all took the promotion test and, despite the small number of promotions authorized that cycle, all three of us on the same ship got promoted. I was one of the last to get promoted but I was just as proud as anyone else.

One other thing we did differently on this cruise was to send what would be needed on the ship after it came to port on advance leave so they could meet the ship. I was one of the four in my group. We loaded onto the ship's cod and were launched off the ship behind a group of fighters going on a mission in the Danang area. We flew into Danang and bummed a ride from there to Clark Airforce Base in the Philippines. There were no authorized passenger flights leaving Danang.

There was a C130 cargo flight going to Clark. We talked to the C130 pilot, but he could not legally fly passengers on a cargo flight and told us that he did everything by the book. Then he always followed a routine to make sure no passengers were on his plane. He went on to tell us what his procedure was, and it left us an opportunity to sneak on the plane and we did. Sneaking off the plane in Clark was no problem because the pilot was normally the last one to depart the plane.

At Clark, we learned that there were no flights to the states scheduled out. We were stuck at the base for four days before anything became available. One of the guys had a big wedding planned and was on a tight schedule and he went to Manila Philippines International Airport and bought a ticket home.

Another one from my group went with him and bought a ticket to Hawaii to try to get a connecting Military flight to California. When we got our flight from Clark to San Francisco, we changed flights in Hawaii, and Ross, who was the guy who had flown commercially from Manila, got the same plane out of Hawaii as we did.

Keiko and I flew to my home in High Springs for our vacation. While there, I bought a 1965 Ford Thunderbird through Jim Douglas Chevrolet dealership where my brother worked. He knew all about the car, and he checked it out completely and helped me get a good deal on it, and we drove it back to Alameda.

I met the ship when it came in and started getting it ready for a trip to Hunters Point for some Dry Dock repairs. I was able to get temporary base housing in one of Quonset huts while the ship was undergoing repairs. We rented what furniture we needed and made do with it.

I requested and got a temporary duty assignment to the Shore Patrol unit in San Francisco. The group called The Black Panthers was causing a lot of problems in the area, and after dark, you could not get a bus or taxicab to come into the area. So, I would catch a bus to work and have a Shore Patrol unit bring me back to Quonset Hut at night.

I was planning to go into Law Enforcement when I retired, and this was good training. I was assigned to the Bar and Establishment Unit and worked undercover in the downtown San Francisco area. That was a very interesting assignment, and we were backed up by the San Francisco Police Department.

We had no arrest power over any civilian, but we had an SFPD call box key, and we would call them if they were needed for anything. Downtown San Francisco after dark was a wild place. It was amazing how many joints would get shut down one day and open right back up under new Management almost the next day. They were restricted to only serving coffee, beer, or wine after midnight, and that would not pay the bills.

Most of the ones we worked on had a system with an outside lookout and an alarm system inside the bar. Late at night everybody wore some type of coat with big pockets and the lookouts would carry a remote unit to set off the alarm in his pocket. When he saw the police coming, he would set off the alarm inside the bar, and all non-legal drinks were immediately dumped. We did not drink any alcoholic drinks on duty, and for the most part, the patrons knew who we were, and we would just remain seated at our table with our cups of coffee during the police raids.

The ship finished the repairs and went back to Alameda for preparation for ORI inspection and Keiko and I moved out of the Quonset Hut and back to her apartment. While we were getting ship ready for its Operational Ready Inspection (ORI), my advancement to Chief Petty Officer orders came through. I got my promotion and initiation while at sea on one of our short cruises. That was an experience that I will not forget.

# Chapter 41

# U.S.S. HANCOCK LAST CRUISE

In late October 1970, I started my last cruise on the Hancock. I was now a Chief Petty Officer, and this cruise would take me to the end of my Sea Duty requirements. I knew I would be getting my orders for my next Shore Duty assignment, and that would fulfill my requirement for my retirement.

I requested orders to the continental United States. Now that Hawaii had become a state, it, along with Alaska, were now considered to be shore duty. To exclude them from your request, you had to state within the continental United States. I had also requested either the San Diego area on the west coast or Jacksonville, Florida, on the East Coast as my first and second choices.

I was still assigned to the AIMD division, but the division was being rearranged, and a new unit was created called Quality Assurance. The unit consisted of three Chiefs, one was an E8, and his name was Clark, two were E7s, and that was Chief Strickland and me.

Our duties were to oversee all the Quality inspectors and inspectors in the division. I had everything to do with electronics, and Strickland had ordinance and powerplants. Clark was the supervisor for the unit and all other special needs.

Each work center had personnel assigned to handle the Quality inspections of the jobs completed in their work centers, and we supervised them. We assisted them with questionable procedures or instructions and developed any new procedures required.

The first part of the cruise was spent reviewing and updating the current procedures and communicating with the manufacturers of the parts in question. After we got everything reviewed, we were mostly just problem-solving.

Our Division Commander, CDR Rush, had come on board during the last cruise and had some medical problems that required some surgery, but he was back now fully recovered. He considered his strong point to be a problem solver. If you told him that everything was fine, he would think you were hiding something from him.

We had a Chief on board, which was a real problem because he would keep CMD Rush fired up, and he would come down on us. The Chief would come in and out of the work centers acting really friendly with the workers and find out what they had been working on. When they would tell him they had a problem with something he would use that to his advantage.

He knew the CDR's routine, and every morning, he would just happen to cross his path as he went to his office. The Chief blew up the problem that he had just heard. But it would have solved the problem just in time to save the day. Rush would enter his office happy that he knew about the problem and chew us out because we did not handle it. At first, we would have no idea what he was talking about and waste a bunch of our time chasing down the reported problem.

A lot of the complaints were from the electronic shops, and I would get the chewing out. Well, it did not take long for us to figure out what the source of the problem was and who it involved.

Chief Clark started watching him, and I confirmed the information through the shop personnel. I set up the Chief, by creating a fake problem and using my people to give him the bait. I wrote out a fake problem with a non-existing piece of equipment and gave the worker instructions on exactly how to give them to the Chief, making sure he told him that the problem was fixed.

The Chief showed up on schedule and met Commander Rush on his way to his office. Chief Clark witnessed the meeting and then came to our office.

Right on schedule Commander Rush yelled at me to come to his office. Our plan was working great. Rush stated, chewing me out, and Chief Clark walked into Commander Rush's office without knocking and interrupted the meeting. The Commander was mad at Clark, but Clark was my supervisor, and Rush had not followed the proper procedure by not going through him.

Chief Clark took control of the meeting, chased me out of the office, and explained the situation to Commander Rush, then verified everything by showing him the written plan and calling the worker in to show and confirm his copy. I never heard anything from Rush, but I did get briefed by Chief Clark.

On our next time in port, we were in Subic Bay, and Chief Clark and our problem Chief, along with two other Chiefs, went to the Chief's Club for a few drinks. When they returned, they came back in the same taxicab.

The cab pulled up to the main loading ramp for the ship, and all four doors on the cab flew open and four Chiefs came flying out of the cab, and all you see was a cloud of dust with Chief's hats flying everywhere and fist flying.

All four of them hit the ground in one pile, and Duty Officer came running down the ramp with the security guards. By the time they got there, all the Chiefs were standing up and brushing off their uniforms.

The Duty Officer yelled, "What's going on here", and Chief Clark responded with, "Just a non-scheduled athletic event, sir". They all came aboard the ship, and that ended our problem with the one Chief.

We returned to Tonkin Gulf, and as soon as we got on station, I got a message to report to personnel, and I was given my orders for my next tour of duty, and they were for Hawaii. That was the one spot I was definitely trying to avoid. I talked to the personnel clerk that handled the processing of orders through the Personnel division, and he refused to help me try to get a change in orders request.

He was an E6, and he was in charge of all matters involving transfer orders; my orders were clear, and he had a departure date for me and would not have time to change anything. We were at sea, and that limited my options for any way to get them changed.

Our skipper had told us that we were under consideration for orders to come back to the States through Sidney, Australia, to fill in for the USS Coral Sea. Each Year there was a battle of the Coral Sea celebration, and normally the Coral Sea would attend, but she had scheduled repairs and might not be able to make it this time. Nothing for us had been confirmed, but our schedule could make us available for it, and I did want to go to Sidney.

We had stopped in Hong Kong earlier on this cruise, and I met an Australian sailor there by the name of John Champion, who was serving on their Carrier named the Melbourne. We had developed a friendship and I had stayed in contact with him. He knew that I might be scheduled to visit Sydney while he was still there. He was going to show me around.

According to the Yeomen, I was scheduled to offload in Subic Bay and transfer to Hawaii. Well, I did not have a phone on the ship that I could use to call Washington, D.C. on, to talk to someone about changing my orders on, so I waited until we arrived in Subic Point.

I avoided the directives from personnel to pick up my check-out papers and offload from the Ship. I went to the Chief's Club on base to try to find some help on getting in touch with the Navy Personnel Division of Navy to request a change is orders.

Someone at the club got me in touch with the Chief that ran the military radio system that handled the phone lines to the States. I could not get through that day, and we set up a meeting for the next day during normal business hours for the Washington D. C. area.

The next morning, again, I avoided responding to my directive to report to personnel and went to the radio station for my phone call. This time I got through to the Bureau of Personnel, and a Commander answered the phone. I was able to explain that I was trying to reach the assignment desk about a problem with my orders, and he was very nice and helpful. He took my information and looked up a copy of my orders and knew what the problem was.

He explained that a Chief Petty Officer by the name of Martinez had been assigned to run the desk, but he was really mad about having to be there and was intentionally sending everyone to the wrong choice of places. He also said that there was no reason to send me there because there was no request for anyone from where I had been sent. Then he transferred me somewhere else to assist me.

When the new person came on the phone, he asked me why San Diego and I told him that a I had a house there and was going to retire soon. Then he asked me where the house was. I told him the address was in Chula Vista. He knew right where the house was. He had lived in that area also and suggested that I consider Imperial Beach.

He asked me how long it had been since I had been there, and I told him Three years, and he said that a lot had changed and told me about it. Ream Field was a Navy Helicopter base, and they asked if I knew where it was, and I told him yes. He told me how much closer that was to my house than anywhere else in San Diego.

I asked him to give me that assignment, and he agreed. He said he would get the orders out as soon as he could. Man, I was happy about that change. I admit that I stopped by the Chief's Club for a few drinks on the way back to the ship.

At muster the next morning, the Skipper said that he was unable to get to Washington to find out where we were going because the phone line was tied up. I sure hoped it was not me that caused the delay.

I did report to personnel to tell the Yeoman that I had a change in orders coming and that I would not be leaving the ship. He was mad and did not believe me. Then he threatened to have security physically remove me if I did not have the new orders in hand when the ship departed. Well, the skipper was finally able to get through and got a verbal confirmation to start preparing for the trip to Sydney. As it turned out, my new orders came in the day before we left, and I went to Australia.

The trip to Australia meant that we would cross the equator and have another Shellback Initiation. This time I would be handing it out instead of receiving it. The problem was not that there were not enough Shellbacks, and we got the worst end of it, but we made it to Sydney Harbor, and what a sight that was. We had a close-up view of the Opera House.

I had let John know when we would be arriving, and of course, he knew by other means. He had given me his home phone number to call when I arrived.

When I called his house, I got his sister, who was home waiting for me to call so she could give me his location and new number to call. He was at a Veterans club which is popular down there. I called him, and he gave me instructions on the cab and address, and I was having trouble understanding him. I learned a new but good lesson when I told him to slow down because I was having trouble with his accent. He told me, "I don't have an accent yank, you do".

That was when I learned that when you are in someone else's country, they don't talk funny, it is their language, and your language sounds funny to them.

I went to the club and met part of his family there for a night out with dinner and drinks. The club was very nice, and the cost was only a fraction of the same thing it would cost in parts of Sydney. Private and membership clubs are for the locals, and the Pubs in Sydney are for the rich tourist.

I enjoyed our stay and met some really good people there. I met a group of the old timers that had survived the war. What I did not know was that England cut off their support and could not send them any military support when Japan was advancing on them to capture the island.

They did not have enough able-bodied men to put up a strong defense, so they sent the women and kids to the back side of the country to buy them as much time as possible, and men dug in along the beach to try to slow the invasion down a little more. Each one of them knew that they would not be alive come daylight after the invasion. They knew where the landing invasion would come ashore, and they dug foxholes and carried only what guns and ammo they had and little water to drink while they waited to be killed.

American ships engaged the Japanese in an open sea battle and did enough damage to their ships that the invasion was called off by the Japanese, and all of the last standers survived. That is why they used to have so much respect for America, and they celebrated the battle of the Coral Sea.

Australia is below the Equator, and everything is reversed from America. January 1st is the middle of summer, and July is the middle of the winter. They say that when you flush a toilet it spins in a reverse direction. Now that was something that I did not check. But there must be at least a million interesting things about the history of that little country.

Well, that is about all I remember about that cruise because I knew I would be leaving the Hancock shortly after we got home, and that was the only thing I was interested in.

# Chapter 42

# NAS IMPERIAL BEACH

Once the Hancock docked from the last cruise, I had to start getting ready for my transfer to Imperial Beach, California. My house, which was located at 1627 Oleander Ave Chula Vista, was under contractual agreement with a property management company, and I had let them know when I needed to move back into the house. I had written them with the approximate date I would need so they could start getting the house vacated. I called them, and there was no problem with the house being ready. I also had to get my T-bird out of storage and make arrangements to ship Keiko's furniture from the apartment. Then I would reclaim the rest of our stuff from storage in San Diego.

By the time I had everything ready to move, it was time to check out. We did not take any leave time when we transferred, and we just used the allotted travel time. I had completed my checkout from the Hancock, except for dropping off the paperwork and getting the required papers time-stamped and signed. I checked out early, and we went directly from the ship to the San Diego area and got a motel. The next day we picked up our keys from the management company and went to the house. It needed a good cleaning, but the damage was minor, and the management company had collected a cleaning fee which covered the cleaning supplies we needed, and a couple of our neighbors who still lived there helped Keiko with the cleaning.

I made the arrangements and moved our stored stuff into our garage and got ready to check in with my new command the next day. While checking in to the base, I learned that Chief Knapp, who worked with me training VO67, was in charge of the shop I was assigned to. The Base Master Chief (E9) Stanton from the Hancock was the senior Chief of the base. The person running the work center I was assigned to was also an AEC, and to avoid any conflict with supervision, like I had with LTCD Pollard when I checked into work center 620 on the Hancock, I took over the swing shift.

The first couple of days were spent just getting checked in everywhere and getting the rest of our furniture into the house and shopping. Going to work was a little different because, for the first time in three years, I had to drive to work again. It turned out to be an easy drive like the guy at the assignment in Washington D.C. had told me it would be.

The Aircraft that we supported here were all Helicopters, so I had a lot to learn about them. I got some surprises right off the bat. I got a request for an AC battery, and I was thinking current, and I knew that all batteries were DC. Well, the request turned out to be for an Aircraft Battery, and they used a shortcut by calling it an AC battery.

It was only a few days before I got another surprise. I got a work order that the battery in one of the Choppers needed tuning. Since a battery neither transmits nor receives a signal, it has no way of being tuned. Well, I got another lesson in their language. In Choppers, there are a lot of vibrations, and they affect the cockpit equipment, and the pilot will feel the vibrations in either his hands or feet. The higher-pitch vibrations will be felt in his hands and the lower ones in his feet. To help fix this problem, they use the physical battery as a shock absorber. You adjust this by adjusting the amount of torque you apply to hold-down mounting bolts for the battery.

The next big surprise I got was when I got a notice from the Security Department to appear in base traffic court for a traffic violation. The offense was running the gate. Well, I did not intentionally violate any laws and if I did, I would find out what I did and pay the fine. I didn't normally contest it. But when I called security to find out about it, I got a third degree about what I had done and what all they could do for me for it and that included kicking my car off the base for a year. All they would tell me about what happened was that they had the evidence, and if I did not show up in their traffic court, they would impound my car and remove it from the base.

Well, that made me feel like I was being unjustly bullied around and I could not let that stand. I went to the traffic court and challenged the charge. They were not prepared to defend the charge and when they had to produce their evidence, all they had was the officer's report which was mostly based on his opinion.

They did have a security camera on the gate, and I requested that they pull the film and present it. We passed my case until the last one so the film could be shown. The film showed my car going through the gate just as the guard was starting to signal my line to stop. I just passed the guard as he was completing the signal. There was nothing indicating that I intentionally disobeyed his order. The car behind me stopped ok and there was no disruption of traffic. The case was dismissed, but I was not pleased with the actions of the security people, including the traffic court judge. The person assigned as the judge made it clear that he did not like his job.

I left the traffic court and went to work, and there were a lot of people who had complaints about that court. I just listened to what they said and passed it off. The next day when I came to work, I had a note from Chief Knapp asking me if I would act as traffic court judge for the next hearing. I came in early the next day and met with Chief Knapp and learned that he had been receiving a lot of complaints, and after my case, the other person who was the judge was going to be replaced. After talking with Knapp, I agreed to handle the next court.

Before I left Hancock, I had talked with my friend, Ray Ross, about wanting to try a career in law enforcement after I retired. At first, he did not want anything to do with any civil service type jobs. However, after he went home to Denver on leave just before his retirement, he changed his mind.

He found that his best friend that he had worked with Recruiting duty, was now working for the Arapahoe County Sheriff's Department, and loving it. When Ross came back off his leave, he told me that he had a job for me and Keiko in Denver, Colorado. He was all fired up about it.

I was not sure that I wanted to live in that cold place and told him I would have to think about it. I had told Chief Knapp about my plans to get into law enforcement and I was interested in any training if could get it.

I thought that running the traffic court would give me a better idea of how-to right and present my cases to the judge. I only got to run one court date, but I did get a much different view of it. I could tell the court had not been fairly conducted in the past.

Before the next traffic court was scheduled, I was asked if I would consider transferring to the Security Department on the base. I wanted to know why Chief Knapp was wanting me to consider that and he explained that it would give me some training and that the Security Department needed some help with their supervision. I gave it serious thought before agreeing to try it.

They had a Lieutenant Commander and a Chief Petty officer running the Security Division, they also had a civilian guard unit with twenty guards and a civilian Captain of the guard. I asked about the Chief that was there. All I got from Chief Knapp was that his name was Gooden, and he was being sent away for extended training. Chief Knapp got my transfer approved with the help of Master Chief Stanton.

I went over the next morning and met with the officer in charge, and he gave me a hardy welcome on board. I told him that I would like an agreement for me to be able to work on all the different assignments for the learning experience. He stated his concerns about me working a starting position as a Chief when the positions are for the lower ranks. He started to say something about Chief Gooden but changed his mind before finishing his thought.

Then looked at me as if he was thinking about what he wanted to say and then said, "Chief Gooden was just shipped off to a long school and he probably will not return to this base." Then said, "Try to keep your training short." I explained that I would try to get my training by filling in for people who missed their shifts. He agreed to that and asked me to take Chief Gooden's place.

Well, I was getting the feeling that something was wrong in this division and decided to just float around and see what I could find out. I went into the Captain of Guard's office and introduced myself to him as Chief Gooden's replacement. The captain was an older man probably in his sixties. He looked at me and said I have something for you. He pulled his desk drawer open and handed me the registrations of nineteen of the guards and explained that the other one was already serving out his notice and had a new job.

Well, I was shocked, and I asked him what was going on and he told me that the guards did not like Chief Gooden and did not think they could trust him. He went on to tell me that he was advised that a new Chief would be replacing Gooden and the Captain had asked all the guards to hold off until I got on board.

I asked to borrow the captain's office and to assist me in meeting with each one of guards. The captain discreetly got all the guards for the next shift to report early and come to his office and for the off-going guards to come in after their shift. He also suggested that he show me around where I could see everybody and what was going on.

The Security Pass office was the center of everything. It is the first place you go to conduct any business you have with the base. Therefore, your first impression of the base comes from how you are treated and what you see. So far, my impression of the security division was not satisfactory. I saw some things that I did not like but opted to wait until the next day to start working on them.

I met and talked with all the Swing shift guards and they agreed to stay on and to help get midnight shift to meet with me before they left the base. After the meeting, I went home and got a quick nap and a shower and came back early the next morning. By noon I had met with all the guards, and I had only one guard that was committed to a better job and could not change his resignation.

The Security Department also had an armed security section that was manned by military and qualified civilian personnel. At this time there was only one armed civilian and the rest was all military.

I also interviewed them, and they were all upset about problems they were having with Chief Gooden. They each had a particular example of his actions or lack of that they considered unfair treatment. The basis of the problems was around traffic tickets and the way they were processed.

When it was time for traffic court some of the original copies could not be found and there was no accountability for them. I had conducted each interview privately between each of the military personnel and me, and yet each of them expressed that they felt that Gooden would not support them if the complaint involved a military officer.

I returned to the base Security Office to check on the traffic ticket filing situation. When I entered the business office, I found that it was being manned by two young female recruits and they had a radio playing loud music and they were practicing their latest dance steps. I walked over and pulled the plug on the radio and picked it up and asked who owned the radio. I got told that it was private property, and I had no right to mess with it.

Well, I felt that it was time to start applying some military discipline. I explained that I was in charge and that the radio was not authorized to be in the office and if the owner wanted it, they had best remove it or they were going to need a dustpan to pick up the pieces. I also reminded them that they were in a business office that represented the base, and they would conduct themselves in a business manner. One of them started to say that Chief Gooden was, and I cut her off at point and reminded her that Chief Gooden was no longer there, and I was now in charge.

With that it got very quiet in the office, and I saw that Mrs. Andersen, who was an older civilian clerk, in charge of the ID card section, slip into the Division Commanders office. I had not met her yet, but I could tell that she had been there for a while and felt very secure in her position. I ignored her and told the clerks to get me the tickets for the pending traffic court.

They could not produce anything and said it would take some time to find and go through the tickets. I told her to show me their system for handling the tickets and they did not have a system. The tickets were scattered everywhere and open to anyone who wanted to find them. I knew that my first priority would be to start a basic system. Get file boxes for them and get them sorted out into two files, pending, and completed.

It was getting late into the day, so I went into the security Commander's office to brief him on what I was finding and my plans to fix it. I would need a purchase voucher for the supplies I would need. He greeted me but with a somewhat confused look on his face. I told him that I had been inspecting the Security Section and had some concerns that I would talk to him about, and he nodded his head and said, "Oh yes, I know, I have started receiving complaints already".

I gave him a brief overview of what I had found and explained what I wanted to do first. I also asked if he could assist me in getting some temporary help to get the tickets all sorted out because we had a lot of them to find and go through. He liked my idea and said he would make some calls for some extra help.

The next morning when I got to work things were different. The office looked more like a business office and was a lot cleaner. I complemented the clerks on how much better the office looked and told them that we were trying to get some help sorting out the tickets. I remember that when I asked one of the clerks where the forms were for open purchase vouchers, she got one for me and was ready to type it up for me. She even knew what the maximum allowable amount was and asked me how much to make it out for, and how I wanted it completed and she typed it out.

The Commander came in, and I went into his office, and he had found us four additional recruits that we could use for a couple of days. They were available that morning, and while I arranged transportation for them and briefed the clerks on what I wanted them to get started on the commander confirmed that we would pick them up. Then the Commander briefed me on another problem that I was going to have.

Each month there was a meeting between all the Chiefs assigned to the base and the Base Commander, who was Captain Smith. My boss called it a barbeque of the security division. All the chiefs got to express all their complaints and the security division had become the designated whipping boy.

Chief Gooden had been representing the Security Division and they had been walking all over him. The meeting was at 10:00 AM and I had to make it. I went through our recent mail and found an item marked for my attention. It was a correspondence from the Bureau of Naval Personnel marked Confidential and all it said was that new regulations concerning Dress Code requirements for Military Dependents on military bases were forthcoming. I looked for any complaints on file and did not find any, so I attended the meeting.

I went into the meeting room and sat down with my cup of coffee and notepad. The captain was going to be late, and the base Master Chief, Chief Stanton, was opening the meeting. I think he was the only one in the room who knew who I was.

The complaints started as soon as the meeting was opened. The first complaint was directed at the Security Division about how sloppy the sailors on the base looked, and the Security Division was not doing anything about it, and Chief Gooden was aware of it. The next one was also directed at security, and he wanted to know where we got the authority to tell them how they could park their car and how we determined how the car was reversely parked. Then another loudmouth jumped in with a complaint about how sloppy the dependent wives were dressing when they came to the base exchange store, and he had seen a directive about the dress code for dependents.

At that time, Chief Stanton said that he would like to introduce Chief Barber to you. He is now the Security Chief. I stood up, and with my loudmouth, I responded to their questions.

I said, first off, the appearance of the sailors on this base is not the responsibility of the Security Department. Every sailor on this base is under the supervision of one of you. And as his supervisor, you are responsible for mustering and inspecting him each day. If you do your job, they will not look sloppy. And as for the question about where we get our authority, it comes from the Eleventh Naval District. As for how we can tell if the car is in reverse and parked, well, I can help you with that.

I said, "Chief, if you park your car in a parking lot with painted lines around the stall, then pull your car into the spot through the open end and put your front bumper, which is the end where you open the hood to check the oil, over the line at the end of the parking stall. However, if the end you put your beer in is over the line, that is the rearend, thus you need to turn the car around."

In answer to the next question I said, "Now about the dependents, they are your responsibility, but if you need help with how they should dress, we will try to help you with that, but I am more concerned about a possible security communications violation. I got that same directive this morning, and it was marked Confidential. I received it on a need-to-know basis, and it did not provide any information about how dependents should dress. I don't know if everyone here is cleared to receive that directive." With that, I sat down.

There were a couple of other questions, but they were good questions and not directed at the Security Division. Captain Smith, the base commander, came in about that time and took over the meeting and Chief Stanton briefed him on what was discussed before he came in.

The captain agreed that the appearance of the enlisted men was not security's responsibility and that he noticed a lot of Commissioned Officers were also looking sloppy and that was his responsibility, and he said he would handle that. Then he said that the supervisors should handle the sailors. The captain had also seen the confidential message and expressed concern about it being discussed in the meeting.

After the meeting broke up, I went back to the office and the clerks were doing a good job of getting the tickets straightened out. The Division Commander asked me to find out how many ID cards he needed to order for the next year and of what type. They are a controlled item and must be ordered as a part of his budget.

I thought that would be a simple job for Mrs. Andersen, who was in charge of them. But nothing involving her was simple. All ID cards are controlled by a serial number, and they are sequentially numbered. I was going over to the administrative building to talk to personnel and the Executive Officer, and I told Mrs. Andersen to get a list of each type of ID card that had been issued and the numbers issued for the past twelve months. Her response was I don't have time for that. I explained that it was her job and asked if her job was getting too big for her, and I am sure that the tone of my voice conveyed the rest of that message.

I asked her if she knew how to get the figures that I needed, and she said no. I explained to her that if she looked up the first card issued one year ago and wrote down the serial number of the card, and then looked at the last card of that type she had issued, she could just subtract the smaller number from the larger one and that would be what I needed for each type of card. Then I told her I needed them today.

She went and complained to the Division Commander, but she did her job and got the numbers. I confirmed through the XO that the base had no plans, any new projects, or anything that would change the number of personnel on the base for the next year. So that meant that we would use the numbers from last year. I came back and collected Mrs. Andersen's number and gave it to the Commander. He was amazed that I had done in an hour what had failed to do in six weeks.

The new system for handling the traffic tickets was now completed, and all the findable tickets were filed and ready for traffic court. I began to notice that the other military personnel in the department were starting to show more interest in their jobs.

I got my first opportunity to work a shift as an armed security guard when the mid-shift guard called in sick. I got a security officer's badge and gun belt and took his shift. We had a system of the guard carrying the time clock and placing a coded security clock key at each of the hot spots that was being watched, like ammo storage facilities. We had a total of nine at that time. We also had parking lots, barracks, and aircraft to check on.

We had been getting some theft reports about things being stolen from parked cars and some reports of prowlers being seen on the base. I reviewed the reports and wanted to know how much time the guards were spending making their rounds of all their checkpoints and how much time they had to watch for suspicious activity. I had heard complaints that the guards were spending a lot of time in the guard shack playing cards. So, my first security trip was to locate all nine of the hot spots. Then the second trip was to time how long it took me. The run took about twenty minutes.

On the next trip, I hit all the hot spots and areas of concern and still had time left over. I knew that the time clocks used a paper disk to record all the key impressions. They were turned in at the end of the shift, and a new blank one was inserted. I checked the turned-in disk and with a quick look at the timed key impressions, I could see a constant pattern.

The guard was working a system of starting his rounds just before the end of the hour and reversing his run at the beginning of the next hour. This would give him an hour of time off between runs. How he used that time was unrecorded. The other shifts had different patterns, but the swing shift also had some questionable patterns. Anyone observing their activities would know how much time they had between the security officer's rounds.

I met with the Commander the next morning as soon as he arrived and showed him what I learned. He showed a lot of interest in it, and I explained that I had worked all night and was going home. It was about nine AM when I got home, and I was still up when the Division Commander called me at home and asked if I had some civilian dress clothes like suits or sports coats; when I said yes, he asked me to wear them and meet him at his office as soon as I could. So, I showered and put on my best Hong Kong suit, and I wondered if I was in trouble as I rushed to the office.

As soon as I entered his office, he said good, let's go and he headed out of the office without explaining anything. It was a short walk over to the Base Commander's office, who was Captain Smith, and we did not even slow down and was waived straight into his office by his secretary.

Captain Smith was sitting at his desk when we entered his office, and the Division Commander said, "I think I have found your Chief Investigator," and he introduced me to Captain Smith. This was a total surprise to me, and I had no idea what a Chief Investigator was.

Captain Smith greeted me and started to explain that he needed someone to work directly under him to handle special investigation needs. I was not to appear in uniform at any time, and I would have a new ID card that would only identify me as the Chief Investigator for NAS Imperial Beach.

He had an investigator for the Security Division, and he was located in a separate office space. I would work out of the same office and be in charge of that office. I would need to brief Captain Smith every morning at 8 AM on things he needed to know before he held his division head meeting. I would work through the security department, but Captain Smith would be the only one sending me any orders. I was issued a concealed weapon, a new ID card, and authorized to use security vehicles when needed. The Security Commander would know who I was, and I was to go through him for any special needs I required.

I left the captain's office and wondered what I had just gotten into. They would not have my ID card ready until the next day, so I went home and tried to get some rest.

The next morning, I went to the Investigators Office and met with Rick, the Division Investigator, and explained what was going on. He had requested some help and was glad to see me.

Rick had a good handle on what was going on, and he had good clerical abilities, which I definitely did not have. This job required a lot of paperwork, and it was all legal paperwork, and you had to make a copy for several people. For most of our transportation needs, we just used our own vehicles, and that helped us with any undercover work we were doing. After getting briefed on what he was doing, he drove me over to the security office to get my new ID and a special security badge.

Some of the security problems Rick had been working on involved drug trafficking on the base. Some of them were coming over the back side station fence. Tijuana, Mexico, was only about 8 miles south of the base, and he had information that someone on the base had been meeting illegal aliens who had the drugs at the fence. We had some small aircraft parts like 8-day clocks and standby compasses missing. These were common parts that people liked to install in their trucks and jeeps. Rick also had information on visitors bringing drugs to the barracks parking lot and selling them. He also knew that the immigrants were using our base lights to navigate by.

I had no more direct contact with the armed security guards, but Rick had one who was always helping him out. This one Rick trusted, and I was introduced to him. He was currently working the swing shift, and that proved to be helpful to us.

We started making plans on how to catch the back fence drug runners. There was a pistol firing range with a high backstop just inside the back fence and it made a good observation point. The problem was that we needed to work at night, and it was too difficult to see.

The US Navy Seal Team training base was on the strand in Imperial Beach, and I contacted them about borrowing a Night Vision Scope. At that time, they were just coming into use and not as efficient, and they became and still are listed as Top Secret. I scheduled a meeting with the officer in charge of the Seal Training Unit and he verified that my Top-Secret Clearance was still valid, and I signed one out to me to use for base security only.

Rick and I could not wait to start playing with our new toy. It would show only black images of the people, but you could see them, and you could tell what they were doing. I checked on the security clearance of Rick's friend in the Armed Security Guard Unit, and his Top Security Clearance was still valid. I started using him as a backup when I was chasing suspected runners.

We could always tell the drug runners from the migrant workers. The drug runners were the only ones carrying anything on them. We watched their routes and got a layout of where their trails were. Rick and I got a couple of horses and spent a day mapping out their trails to and around the base.

Knowing where the trails were, we could spot the ones carrying the bags, but we could not cut them off. They were slick and they would mix in with the workers and make them come out first and that would force us to go after the workers and the runners would escape.

To catch them, we would have to be ahead of them and nab them when they passed us. One side of the base had a large area of brush with deep grass and was open all the way to the beach. I picked out a good spot where I had a large thick brush to hide in while I watched their main routes around the base. I had no idea how funny that was going to be.

I made arrangements for my backup to work with me and I tried to find a good flashlight to use. I found an old six-cell flashlight that needed batteries. It was late, and I did not have any new batteries, so I robbed three two-cell flashlights from the security office and finally got the light to work. It had a good beam. I knew it was going to be what I needed.

It was already after dark when we found a good spot in the brush. It was in the known traffic lane used by illegal workers and drug traffickers. It also provided a good hiding spot with an open pocket inside for us, so we would not be seen and a perfect place to put the scope. The viewing end of the scope had a three-inch lens. That was the only thing you could see from outside the bush. All we had to do now was stay out of sight and wait.

While we waited, I relaxed and snuck inside the building spot for a smoke, being careful not to let any of the light get out. My backup was manning the scope and I was waiting to jump out of the brush and grab our first visitor. My backup spotted a group heading our way. He counted about a dozen and two of them were carrying bags. I told him to watch for the bags and to let me know where they were heading. They were crawling through the grass, and he could see them coming but could not get a full view. All he could say was they were almost here.

With only a single lens to look through, you lose your depth perception, but I could hear them rustling through the grass, so I knew they were close. My backup was getting excited and was saying he was here, and he was looking at us. With that, I grabbed my big flashlight and started out of my hiding spot.

The first thing I saw was a Mexican about six inches from the end of the scope staring into the lens while my guy was three feet away in the bush staring through the other end. It was so funny that I was laughing until I pushed on the switch of the flashlight and nothing. The Mexican just sat there, and I bet he thought he was watching a rerun of the Key Stone Cops. We rounded up five more workers, but no drugs.

My jurisdiction did not cover anything off the base, but I listed it as assisting the Border Patrol. Everyone I detained I turned over to the Border Patrol. I did very little reporting on that activity. But one night, our Armed Security had a car come onto the base by running past the gate guard, and when they caught him, he was an illegal alien driving a stolen car.

I had to handle his case, and he was so high on drugs that he had no idea where he was. I ran a check on the car and confirmed it was stolen. It belonged to an elderly couple living in an apartment complex.

The car was in the parking lot; he had hotwired it. He had gotten lost and thought he was at the Mexico Border crossing. I turned it over to the police for the jurisdiction where the car was stolen. I went to court for his hearing, he was so happy to see me. I think it was because I was the only one, he knew at the hearing. He pled guilty. All he wanted to do was get back to Mexico.

Our paperwork requirements were driving us crazy because of the amount of time we had to spend trying to type all those reports. One of the young females I had taken the radio away from at the office was bugging me to work with us in the investigation's unit. After turning her down a few times, she tried a new way of getting my attention.

After one of our drug raids on a barracks resulting in charges being filed on four people, she came into the office with her steno pad and started reading something to me. I had no idea what she was talking about, and I was very busy. The interruption made me a little upset. So, I stopped her and asked what she was talking about.

She looked at me and asked, "Did you watch the debates last night"? I still had no idea what she was talking about. She explained that there was a presidential debate, and to practice her shorthand, she had written down every word each candidate had said. Well, I suddenly realized that she was not a ding bat I was. She was an excellent typist, and that was exactly what we needed.

She took her steno pad, and while Rick and I explained everything we had during the drug raid and arrest, she took notes. While we tagged and recorded all the evidence, she typed up the report. By the time we finished and were ready to leave, she had both my report and Rick's report typed and ready for signature. I was amazed at how professional her work was. The next day I got her assigned to us for three half-shifts a week. She handled our paperwork from then on.

Rick and I solved the cases involving the theft of aircraft parts and worked with an FBI Agent by the name of Dennis Languas. He was a rookie agent, and we became good friends. Our suspect's home was in the state of Utah. He drove a Dodge Power wagon truck, and when we got ready to charge him, he was at home, and some of our evidence was in his truck.

When Dennis checked to see if a local FBI agent could assist in the recovery of our evidence, he discovered that our suspect's vehicle was of interest to the FBI in an unrelated case, so we set up a double hit. At the same minute we hit his locker in the barracks for a search while the FBI hit his truck and home. They confirmed that the parts were in his truck and placed him under arrest.

Dennis and I also worked on a case involving one of the people stationed at Imperial Beach and the Tijuana Mexico Police. Our guy owned an old sports car that was just a piece of junk, and said he owned more than the car was worth and tried to pull an insurance fraud.

He drove the car to Tijuana and left it, came back and reported it stolen. The Tijuana police spotted the car as a suspicious vehicle and found it listed as stolen. The car was registered at the base address, so I received a call from the police.

The FBI would not allow their agents to work on a case unless the case went through them and they assigned it to an agent. But if they happened to be at the location when the crime was discovered, then they assisted if requested. Dennis and I had a system so when I had something coming up that I wanted his help with, I called his dispatcher and told them I had some more information for him about something he was working on. He would come to the base to pick up information and assist me with my case.

Well, an international incident is always of interest to the FBI, so we worked the case and got a confession from my suspect.

Activity at the base had slowed down so I was able to take some time off. Keiko and I took a trip to Colorado to see if we wanted to consider taking a job with the Sheriff's Department in Arapahoe County. We had a nice trip and were impressed with what we saw. I filled out all my paperwork and was interviewed by Sheriff Roy Volt. He agreed to hire me based on a good polygraph test. Due to the schedule of the polygraph operator, I had to wait for a test.

When I returned to the base, I learned that Rick had finished getting our cases set up for trial by court-martial. We had twenty-one cases scheduled for hearings. While we were waiting for the court martial board to convene, I got my appointment for my polygraph test. My test was scheduled for 8 am on the following Tuesday and I was able to schedule a flight to Denver on Monday afternoon before the test and a return flight on 5 pm the day of the test.

We were busy and worked in the office Monday morning, but Rick took me to the airport in time for my flight. Ray Ross picked me up at Denver airport and I spent the night at his house. He took me for my polygraph test the next morning. After the test was completed, he got me to the Denver airport in time for my return flight.

Rick picked me up from my return flight and he and Keiko were the only people who knew that I left town.

I needed to know when I would be available to start my new job with the Arapahoe County Sheriff's Department, so I requested my earliest retirement date, it was the first week of July 1973.

Rick and I had 21 cases going to Court Martial, and after I retired from the military, I was planning on taking a couple of months off before reporting to the Arapahoe County Sheriff's Department for my new career. I had been in military so long that I had forgotten that in the Civilian world, things are done differently.

I was planning on taking a trip to my hometown in High Springs Florida, for a nice vacation before starting my job. I had to sell my house in California and find one in Colorado and move all my personnel stuff.

Everything was going good; I had confirmed my retirement date and accepted an offer on my house. The Court Marshal Board was selected, and a starting date for the hearing was set. The Navy had assigned a lieutenant to act as the legal officer for trials and act as our advisor.

On the first day of the hearings, the Court Martial Officer laid down the rules for the hearings. The Court Marshal would be conducted by the rules for Court Marshals and not a Court of Law. He stated that the attorneys could advise their clients but not speak for them. He said that this hearing is not going to be made into a Perry Mason-type trial.

After he had the attorneys state their names and qualifications, then each stated the name of his client. Then asked if there were any questions. One of the attorneys said there may be questions about the defendant's rights. With that question, the Court Marshal's office asked who his client was and picked up a case report, which happened to be my report. Then he looked at the attorney and said, "You are an attorney, aren't you?" The attorney responded with yes. The CM officer said, "Then you can read."

With that, he opened and read my statement about advising the defendant's advisement of their rights. Then picked up Rick's report and started reading it. He stopped reading and said, "They both say the same thing." He laid down the reports and said, "If you have any questions, then read the report." Then he went on to say that he was not going to keep these people, referring to Rick and me, standing around there all day, they have work to do, and with that he dismissed us.

Shortly after the hearings got started, I got a call from My friend Ray Ross in Colorado telling me that Sheriff Roy Volt had died of a heart attack. Volt did not have an undersheriff, so the county commission had to appoint someone to fill in as sheriff until the next election.

I had set my retirement date with the Navy and put my house up for sale to get ready for my new career, and now nothing was certain about my future. All I could do was wait and see if I still had a job offer from the sheriff's department.

The Arapahoe County Commission appointed Phil Baker to be the acting sheriff. Ross talked to Baker about my situation, and he agreed to keep me on the hire list. Things were looking good again, and Court Marshals were doing good. Everything on the base had quieted down, and Rick and I were just cleaning up some reports and follow-ups.

I got another call from Ross in Colorado, and Baker wanted me to start in a month. He had an opening and wanted me to fill it. I explained that my retirement date was not coming up that soon and I would need a later starting date. Then I learned that in a small department, you had to have an opening in the department to fill before you could hire someone.

There was no way of knowing when the next opportunity would be. That sure put a kink in my plans. I explained that I had enough leave time to move out there to start the job, but I would have to come back if I had to testify in the middle of a bunch of Court Marshal cases, and if needed, I would have to come back to testify. I would also have to come back for my retirement. I would need six weeks before I could report for work.

Baker thought about it overnight and said that he would pay the overtime for six weeks, but if I was not there on the Monday following my retirement, he would issue a warrant for my arrest.

I now knew that I would not be able to take a vacation between jobs, so I started making different plans. I contacted our Legal Officer and asked him if I could fly home and be on call if needed. If the Court Marshal officer needed me, just tell him that I was out of town but would be back the next day and ask for a continuation. Call me, and I would go straight to the airport and catch the next flight back to San Diego. He agreed to try that, and I took the next flight home.

I had left all my phone numbers at home and the High Springs Police Department with them. I spent over a week at home, and nobody called. My dad was upset that I was going into law enforcement and that I was not coming home. My daughter, Pat, was not happy about it either. I don't think my mother ever understood why I left in the first place. But we had a nice visit anyway. By the time I got back to Imperial Beach, the Court Marshals were over, and we only lost one charge on one defendant.

My house sold and the new owners did not want to move in until after I had to leave. I was to live there and let them store their boat in the garage and we transferred the utilities over to their name. All I had to do was lock the door on my way out and leave the keys in the mailbox.

I shipped all our stuff to Denver to be stored until we got a place to live there. I had a new E300 Ford Econoline van, and I sold my T-Bird. I packed the van with the stuff we were taking with us and put sleeping bags on the floor for our last night in our home.

The night before I left on retirement, I got a call out to investigate a fight so I had to report to the captain the next morning.

On July 6, 1973, at 0730 hours, I reported in and let the XO know I was there." He came out of the Captain's Office snickering to himself and guided me into the office. This was very out of character for the normal procedures, and I had no idea what was going on. The captain was searching through everything on his desk for something. Then turned to the Executive Officer (XO) and said," We have a Chief Petty Officer retiring, and I cannot find anything on his retirement ceremony". He also said that this wasn't right, he served twenty years, and he has earned a ceremonial send-off. With that, the XO said, let me introduce you to the Chief who is retiring, and he pointed to me.

When I told the XO when I was going to be retiring, I told him that I did not want any ceremony, just a quiet exit. The captain knew that I was retiring but had not made the connection that I was also the Chief that was retiring. The XO was having fun watching the captain trying to figure that one out.

We had a nice sendoff conversation, and he tried to get me to consider a new program that was coming out for the Navy called the Naval Criminal Investigation Services (NCIS). Well, I could not resist having a little fun with him also, so I told him that I had to report to the Arapahoe County Jail on Monday morning. I did not include that I was to start work. The captain was thinking that I had gotten in some trouble and was trying to find out if there was some way, he could help me out. The XO explained that I had a job with the Sheriff's Department there and that I had to report to work there on Monday.

All I had to do was to brief the captain and turn in my gun and ID. Pick up our new ID cards and hit the road. Well, I was already getting started later than I had planned.

I went to the Security Office, and Mrs. Andersen got her last lick in. She did not have our ID cards ready as I had requested, so we had to wait for her to drag everything out.

I brought Keiko inside the office, and she used the restrooms. I visited with the crew while Mrs. Andersen tried to delay us as much as possible. The crew was watching her, and they knew what she was doing, and they started letting her know that they were displeased with her behavior. She delayed me about a half hour, but we got our new ID cards and hit the road to Colorado.

# Chapter 43

# LEAVING THE MILITARY

On July 6, 1973, I left California heading for Aurora, Colorado, with my wife Keiko and our dog. I had just officially retired from the US Navy at 9:30 A.M. that morning and I was heading to my new job with the Arapahoe County Sheriff's Department. I was driving my 1971 Ford E300 Cargo van with all of our personal things that we would need until we found a place of our own to live. I had to report to work on Monday 9, 1973 at 8:00 AM and move over the weekend.

I knew that crossing the desert in midsummer was going to be a hot trip. When I bought my van, the dealership told me that it had what they called the desert cooling package. That included a larger radiator to create more air flow over the engine, water cooling system, and cooler running thermostats controlling the flow of the cooling water for the engine. This was to keep the engine running cooler.

It was a hot trip and the van had two bucket seats, and the engine console came back between the seats. We put a pan of water with ice cubes in it and used wet towels to keep us cool. I even had one for our little dog.

It got so hot that the asphalt was getting soft, and the truck tires were slinging asphalt under the van like a good undercoating job. We stopped in Blythe, California at noon. It was 110 degrees in the shade. We got more water and ice, and we headed across Arizona.

We spent one night in a motel on the road and made it to Ray Ross's house in Aurora, Colorado, late Saturday evening. We stayed with him until we found a place to live. I rode to work with him for my first week.

The first week on the job I received my orientation to the department by spending each day with a different division of the department. The Sheriff's department was located in the city of Littleton, and I rode back and forth the first week with Ray. I got the weekend off and started working the Jail Division at midnights starting on Monday.

When new deputies were hired, they got their first uniforms from the uniform grab bag and if you made it for a month, you could order new uniforms. Our uniforms were made out of good material, and they had a nice western style. The shirts were blue. They had pearl snaps both down the front and on the epaulets on the shoulders. For headwear we had a blue western style small brim Stetson hat. The trousers were a grey western dress style with black side stripes. They had been custom designed to capture and blend the traditional western style and the new western styles. They were expensive but they sure looked good.

New employees were on probation for the first four months of employment. If you made it off probation, the department would invest in new uniforms for you. I was scheduled to work the midnight shift in the jail for four months, but on my third month of employment, one of our day shift jailers let a 16-year-old female that was being detained for being a juvenile runaway escape. The sheriff put a jail lieutenant by the name of Joseph, Ray Ross, and me on a team to find and bring back the runaway.

I had gotten to know Lieutenant Joseph and Ray Ross when I had served on the USS Hancock together. We got a lead on where she was supposed to be hiding out and we found the location. It was a small house on the backside of a large lot with the main residence on the front side of the lot. The area around the small house had not been kept up and the weeds were waist high around the house.

We worked our way onto the lot without anyone seeing us and stopped at the edge of the tall grass. We were now out of our jurisdiction and had no backup support. I was able to crawl through the grass to the house where I could see in the windows, and I could see a large man with a big beard sleeping in one of the bedrooms.

I slipped back to where Ross and Lt. Joseph were and told Ross, "At least we have a body to talk to." Ross heard body, and thought I was talking about a dead person. We slipped back to the house and got into position to cover it. I knocked on the door. Ross was covering the window and the guy suddenly sat up in bed and yelled out "Who is out there?" Ross, thinking that the guy was dead, jumped and yelled back at him, Sheriff's department and to get out here right now.

The guy opened the door, we went inside and checked the house, and there was no one else in there. He was cooperative and told us that the suspect had been there, but she had left for another hideout and told us how to get there. As we walked back to our car, Ross stopped and told me that if I ever told him there was a body again, it better not sit up and yell at him or I was going to be in big trouble.

We found the other location and our runaway and brought her back to the jail. It was around midnight when we got there and I was supposed to work the mid shift, but Sheriff Baker had already called in someone else to work the shift. We booked our prisoner back into the jail and completed our reports while Sheriff Baker expressed his dissatisfaction with the officer that let the Juvenile escape. He had violated some jail rules and it turned out that this was not the first time he had gotten into trouble, so Sheriff Baker told the deputy to be in the Sheriff's Office at 8 AM. He suggested to the deputy that he consider resigning before the meeting.

The sheriff transferred me to swing shift effective immediately. I went home, got a little sleep, and reported to my new shift. He assigned me a senior deputy for training. The officer was Gene Martin, and we became friends and worked on several assignments together during the rest of our careers.

Shortly after starting on swing shift, I found myself being the only one working the receiving area after the day shift all left the building. The main security problem that I observed was that everyone entering the building after hours had to enter the building through rear door of the jail. The rear door had a buzzer system and an electric lock that was controlled from inside the booking area. The problem was that you could not see who was at the back door from inside the booking area.

To find out who was at the rear door was to either buzz them in before you saw them or break security by opening a side door and stepping outside the building. I did not find either of them satisfactory. I remembered that I still had my old rearview mirrors that I had taken off my van so the next day I brought one of them with me and secured it to the side of the building where I could see the back door. After mounting and adjusting it, the mirror worked great that I got an attaboy.

Shortly after installing the mirror, I was working alone in booking when someone pressed the buzzer. I looked in the mirror and saw two large Englewood police officers with a very large male Indian. He had blood on his face and his shirt. Not only was he big, but he was one of the meanest looking people I ever saw.

I asked the police officers with him why they had to beat him up to get him under control. They laughed and said, "We did not arrest him, we rescued him." They told me he was a real Indian Chief, and his little 4-foot 10-inch wife was the one who beat him up. He had come home drunk again and she called the police to get him removed from the house, and when they came in, she was beating him over the head with the base of the phone while talking to them on the hand receiver. They knew the Chief and described him as one of kindest people they knew.

Not only was the Chief a very large man, but the only sound he would make was a low-pitched growl. All he wanted to do was get some sleep. I put him in a holding cell with a bench seat and gave him a mattress pad and let him sleep it off. His hands were so large that to fingerprint him you had to use two cards to roll his prints.

Working swing shift in the Receiving Section of the jail will challenge every skill you have. For the most part, you are dealing with people during times of their worst behavior. Most of the time they are trying to run a bluff on you, hoping you will drop the charges or let them out of jail. One night while I was still trying to learn my job, I received two attorneys on drunk related charges. One was charged with DUI. He was a nice guy, but he told me that I did not have the authority to make him give me a set of fingerprints.

He was not resisting being fingerprinted. He was just trying to advise me that there was no legal support for our procedure of requiring that we complete a full set of fingerprints on everyone as a part of our booking procedure. Well in my mind I was sure he was wrong. All our procedures were in writing, and I could not believe that the Arapahoe County Sheriff's Department would make that kind of a mistake.

The next morning, I asked the Jail Captain where I could find our authorization to take fingerprints from everyone we booked in jail. The captain told me that it was in our booking procedures and that was all I needed to know. His response to my question raised a red flag for me. Normally those answers meant they don't know the real answer.

I asked some of the other supervisors my question and they were not sure of the answer and suggested that I ask our District Attorney. His office is supposed to provide assistance to us with questions about the law. I went to our DA's office and asked one of the Deputy District Attorneys and got another run around. He was sure there was a law covering it. I pinned him down by requesting a copy of legal authorization and told him I needed it in three days. He promised he would get it for me.

The first time I went back to get it, he had forgotten to look it up. This time I put it in a written request and filed it with his office. While I was waiting for the DA's response, I kept searching on my own. No one could show me a copy of anything that addressed the issue.

When I did get a response from the DA's office, they could not provide me with anything, and suggested that I contact the Colorado Bureau of Investigation. They had sent us a request to provide them with one card on people charged with a misdemeanor level crime and two cards on felony charges.

I requested that they provide me a written copy of their authorization to require that fingerprints of everyone booked in jail be collected. The only thing they had was budget approval to set up and maintain a fingerprint file and storage system. When I called them about not being able to provide me with any legal authorization, they referred me to the FBI. Then I was convinced that the attorney was correct.

I contacted the FBI and spoke with Agent Ray Hornsby, who was in charge of their Criminal Fingerprint Section. He was able to provide me with a copy of the FBI's authorization to create a fingerprint file system on convicted felons. The only fingerprint card they worked with was supposed to be convicted felons. That did not answer my question because almost all the people we booked into jail were being charged with something but were not convicted of anything.

During the rest of my career in law enforcement, I had a lot of contact with agent Hornsby about fingerprints, but never found the legal authority for taking prints on pretrial detainees just because they were booked in jail.

Working in the inmate receiving section was interesting and I got to do a lot of studying of criminal law statutes. Colorado had just revised its' criminal law statutes the year before I started working at the Sheriff's Department. Some laws were changed, some added, and some were dropped.

Sometimes I would find inmates that were being charged with crimes that were no longer on the books and others had new charges that were hard to look up. All in all, it kept the job interesting.

I got off to a good start with the Sheriff's Department thanks to my friend Ray Ross. Phil Baker was working in the Sheriff's Department as a Captain and was friends with Ross when Sheriff Volt died. Phil Baker had got the appointment to fill out the rest of Sheriff Volt's term as Sheriff. I was pleased that Sheriff Baker and I got along very well.

At the end of my probation period, I was issued new uniforms, and I was assigned as a Court Deputy. This new assignment gave me the opportunity to get to know all the Criminal Court judges and to study the court system. I would escort the prisoners to and from the court for their court hearings and guard them in court during their trials. I was able to see what made a case successful and what caused it to fail. Some of the prisoners were very dangerous and they were always looking for a chance to escape custody.

The prisoners were always studying everything you did to look for a weakness that they could use. It was somewhat like a poker game, bid and bluff or call.

I was new to the prisoner escort service so I also had to learn how to survive. I never had to shoot a person and I thank God for that, but I had to make the prisoners think I would. I had qualified for Sharpshooter so I always wore my sharpshooter badge to answer the prisoners' questions about if I could hit them. The other main question was would I shoot them.

I never had to find out, but I told myself that if I had to, I would. To pass this on to prisoners, I developed a system of studying them by making eye contact with them and while staring at them I would picture in my mind what their head would look like after a bullet had hit them. Then without changing my expression I would move to the next high-risk prisoner and do the same thing. I noticed a change in their expressions and sometimes their behavior would also improve.

Normally you would have to move up to five prisoners a time. They would try to challenge or test you. One of the little tests they would do was to tell you that they were only charged with a misdemeanor and that I could not shoot them. The statute said that prisoners who were charged with felonies posed enough danger to the public that guards could use deadly force to keep them from escaping. The crime, if escaping from custody, was a felony. So, when they tried to play that game, I would just say, "Yes, but to escape custody is a felony'. I would usually add a little flavor by saying don't do that because if I miss you with any bullet, the Sheriff will have me out here all night looking for it. He will not let me close the case until every bullet is accounted for. Thank God they never called my bluff.

The only training, I had was to ride shot gun on a couple of transports. My first solo transport I made to Canyon City, Colorado's main state prison, I had five prisoners in our Plymouth Station Wagon. I did not know how to get there, and it was a long transport.

I had my roadmap on the front seat beside me with the route marked out. One the prisoners I was transporting had spent a long time in the system. He was what we called a lifer. All he wanted was to get back to a cell in the big house. He turned out to be a nice guy and asked me to hurry up and get him back because he was expecting some good stuff, and he wanted to be there when it arrived. The long-term prisoners liked to brag about how good they had it in jail.

My first turn off the route I was on, was at the city of Colorado Springs and I missed my turn. I realized it but a prisoner called out, "Hey, you missed your turn." He added that he did want to ride around the countryside, just take a right at the next light, go two blocks, and take another right and that will bring you back to your route. He was correct, and I knew that he knew the area, and he knew that I did not.

Then he said, "Don't let the big bug you are going past scare you." There is a very large statue of a bug on the right side of the road. He was right again, it was a monument to the boll weevil, and it was about ten feet tall. With his help, we all made it safely home.

I made a lot of transports while assigned to the Court Service section and most of them were uneventful, but I got one that was a surprise. I was transporting a juvenile to the Juvenile Detention facility, located in Jefferson County, for our Juvenile Court when I got a radio call to pick up a prisoner from the Jefferson County Detention facility and bring him back with me to Arapahoe for court appearance the next day. So, on my way back I went to the Jefferson County Jail.

Normally, non-scheduled transports are low risk cases and is a request from a court that is making a last-minute change to their Court Docket that does not in and of itself create a security risk. When I arrived to pick up the prisoner, The Jefferson County shift supervisor met me and looked a little surprised. He asked me if I knew who I was transporting. I told him no, only that his last name was Hernandez. He told me that he was the leader of the worst Hispanic gang in the Denver area.

I did not know anything about him, his past or his charges. These types of transports normally require two people, the driver, and an armed person to ride Shotgun. I decided to go ahead with the transport and the Deputy helped me get him safely secured in my vehicle. He also volunteered to take his vehicle and follow me to the County line that separated our counties. I got him transported without any problem.

I learned a lot more about him during his court appearances. He had strong control over his gang and some of them showed up in court during his hearing. We also had additional people assigned to court security during his hearings. He would direct his people with eye and head gestures, and they would position themselves where they could try to intimidate the witnesses. They were not causing any disturbances so we could not remove them from the court room without the Trial Judge's permission. We would just take a seat next to each of the gang members.

His Court hearing was a motion to get his Jail sentence suspended or reduced. The Judge denied his motion.

I was contacted by a member of the Denver Gang Unit that Hernandez had put a $10,000 dollar reward out to anyone who broke him out of jail or custody before we got him back in the State Prison at Canyon City.

Since he was already sentenced to and serving time in Canyon City and all his court motions to change his sentence were denied, there was no reason that I could not return him to the State Prison without delay. Considering that he was a security risk to be out of jail. I decided to secretly move him right away. I called my contact at the prison and made arrangements for a late special delivery.

When I made a secret prisoner transport, I did not speak to anyone about it until it was underway or completed that was not a required part of my plan. I would call Sheriff Baker and tell him I was working on something and that is all he wanted to know. He always said that if he knew what I was doing, then I had already told too many people.

I picked me a driver that I trusted, Mike Egbert and quietly pulled him aside and told him I wanted to buy him a cup of coffee I took him to a nearby restaurant and while we were drinking our coffee and eating a burger, I told him we were moving a prisoner and had him call his wife and tell her that he was working late and would not be home for supper. He was going to be the driver and I would ride shotgun.

Our best transport vehicle was a Plymouth Station wagon. That car had an engine that could get unbelievable speeds and drove great. While Mike got the car ready, I went into the receiving area and Gene Martin, who was my training officer, was working in the receiving section running the shift. He was the only one on duty in the receiving area. I told him that I was slipping Hernandez back to Canyon City. I told him to make sure no one knew about it.

The housing area for the prisoners was on the third floor and the only way to get up to it was to use a very secure, special remote-controlled elevator. We had an excellent officer on duty on the third floor by the name of Scofield. He was a retired US Army veteran with a lot of experience. Deputy Martin got him on our secured phone line and told him what to do and to be sure no one could know what was going on. Hernandez was being housed in an isolation cell which made it easier.

Scofield walked up to Hernández's cell, unlocked his door, and told him his attorney was downstairs and had to go over something with him. Hernandez was taken by surprise and wanted to take his papers with him, but Deputy Scofield told him "No you don't need anything, and I will lock your door for you, come on now." He put Hernandez on the elevator, and Martin and I met him, and took him straight into a hold cell dressing room.

Martin had all of Hernandez's personal clothing laid out and told him to change. Hernandez started trying to argue that he could not go because he had something he had to do. Deputy Martin told him that he had two choices, in his clothes or naked, it did not matter, but he was not leaving in our jail clothes, but was going now. By the time we got him cuffed and ready, Scofield had all his personal stuff from his cell bagged up and on the elevator.

We quietly left the jail and did not radio dispatch or anyone. While we were driving that long drive to Canyon City, Mike and I discussed that if Hernandez's people did try to stop us, it most likely would be on the long stretch of highway crossing over the mountain. They would most likely try to block us in, and we had to make sure that did not happen. To give Hernandez something to worry about, I told Mike, you just drive and don't let them stop you, I will take care of killing him if he tries to escape.

Everything went good until we got on the long uphill part of the drive and overtook a slower moving vehicle, and almost, like it was on cue, a faster moving vehicle was closing up on us. Mike flipped on our emergency equipment, floored the old Plymouth, and blew past the vehicle in front of us. It was a false alarm and with the exception of scaring an old man half to death, there was no problem. Canyon City was waiting for us and the only thing we lost was some sleep.

The Sheriff's Department serviced the Eighteenth Judicial Court, and we had a lot of Judges. Each one had his own way of running his court and their own personally. One thing you learned right off is that every court demands respect and when the Judge is in his courtroom you best look sharp and be professional.

I had a lot of free time while watching the prisoners, so I studied the body language of everybody. I watched the prisoners, the jury, the judge, attorneys, and the officers. I learned the tricks the attorneys liked to pull on the police officers and what actions by the officers that the judges didn't like. I could tell the moment someone lost the jury.

I also learned a lot about the law and took advantage of being able to ask the judges and attorneys questions about things that I didn't understand. I spent about a year working the court services assignment before being assigned to a special law enforcement unit.

Sheriff Baker created a special crime suppression unit he called The Special Services Unit. He promoted Ray Ross to Sergeant and put him in charge and assigned me and three other deputies to it. We worked directly for the sheriff and did not handle routine calls. He wanted us to be free to work out projects and available to cover any call involving weapons or violence.

We would check the police call records and look for trouble areas and develop a plan to identify and arrest the people causing the problems. One of our officers, Dave Novotney, was already on the idea and had already developed a lot of good information. He had the names of the juveniles that were causing problems and what areas they were in. I went to the land office, retrieved new maps of the newly developed areas and marked the locations of all homes of VIPs in the county in case there was any threats to them.

My first high speed pursuit came shortly after we got the unit working. We were working an area on the North side of our county next to the Denver County line when our dispatch radioed that Denver was in a high-speed chase with two suspects in a chevy Super Sport sedan. While the call was being aired, they blew past us at a high rate of speed. Without knowing why, they were being chased, we joined in the chase.

They came South into our jurisdiction then turned East on one of our main East-West streets, Hamden Ave. Hamden is a six-lane street, but it makes a 90-degree turn and becomes Havana Street back through Denver. It was late at night, and we now had two Denver units and two Arapahoe County units, and I was one of them. We were all running wide open and too busy to notice the Speed.

The merger of the two streets has a large 90-degree corner with two turn lanes in the middle, I came upon the corner much too fast, but I was in the first left side lane when I entered the intersection. My vehicle skidded and walked across all eight lanes, and I was almost on the grassy part of the right shoulder by the time I completed the curve.

Every police officer we passed joined in the chase. By the time I got around the corner there must have been ten units in the chase. I remember that we were sucking so much sand out of the street that it looked like we were driving through a sandstorm.

My unit was wide open, and everyone was passing me. The next thing I saw was a string of red traffic lights completely across our street. It was the intersection of Mississippi Ave. I was coming back to my senses; I took my foot off the gas pedal and as I reached down to turn off my red lights, I was just slowing down to 100 MPH. I left my lights on and began getting my vehicle stopped. When I crossed Mississippi against four red lights, I was still traveling at almost 100 MPH.

I remembered while at the Police Academy they had told us that anyone driving in hot pursuit like that would be disoriented when they stopped and that they should not be allowed to drive until after the adrenalin wears off. As I pulled my vehicle to the curb, dispatch radioed that the chase had ended, and the suspects were in custody. I looked around to see where I was and how to get back to Littleton, I realized that I was totally lost in an area that I was unfamiliar with.

All I had to do was turn around and go back the same way I came, but in my mind, for me to be sure which way I had to go, I had to look up where I was on the map and drive past a couple of streets to make sure I was going in the right direction. When I got back to the intersection of Havana Street and Hamden Avenue and saw all the skid marks in the corner of that intersection, I thanked God for my safety.

One of our officers, Kip White, was a tall, thin, white male with a pale complexion, blonde hair, blue eyes, and spoke perfect Spanish. He was perfect for working situations involving illegal aliens. They never expected him to be able to understand their language. He looked like a young kid, but he had served in the Army Intelligence Corp and had a lot of special training. We worked great as a team and set some new records for arrests and cases cleared.

At the end of Baker's term as Sheriff, he lost the election to a college professor by the name of Arnold Miller with no experience in the Sheriff's Department duties or responsibilities. We had a large Sheriff's posse who were all volunteers. They provided us with special equipment we did not have, like horses and four-wheel units. Sheriff Miller dropped the posse and renamed the unit as Reserve Police Officers. We lost all that service and most of the members and a large portion of them were from the Denver Bronco football team.

Our uniforms were expensive, and the County Commission balked at paying for a complete change in uniforms. and told him he would have to pay for the uniforms out of his own pocket. To change uniforms, you also had to get the new design approved through the County Procedures and go through the Government bid process and approval for a contract to make them.

He did make changes to our uniforms. We went from black ties and side stripes to maroon ties and side stripes. The black background on our shoulder patch also went to a maroon background. Now, instead of getting compliments on our uniforms, we got a lot of laughs. He also tried to change our western hats to campana hats, but that also got stopped and uniform hats became optional.

I was assigned to the Patrol Division and the morale there was low for a while. I had missed the opportunity to get that experience by being transferred to the Special Services Unit, so I made the most out of it. Now I was able to get enrolled in community college and majored in Criminal Investigation with a minor in computer technology.

Being assigned to regular patrol duties after being in the Special Services Unit was quite a change. You still had some time to prowl the area and try to catch people committing criminal acts, but you had to spend most of your time investigating complaints, crime scenes, and writing reports. The fully equipped and marked patrol units made it harder to slip up on anything in progress.

Shortly after I got assigned to the Patrol Division, I was assigned to work the swing shift. It was in November, and we were having some heavy snowstorms. One of the biggest problems with working patrol is you have to drive in all kinds of conditions. Snow and frozen streets are one of the worst conditions. Most of your time was spent helping stranded motorists to get home. Most of your attention was diverted to finding them and getting them the assistance that they needed.

On one of my shifts, we were having a bad snowstorm and I started receiving calls to assist a stranded motorist as soon as I got in my patrol car and reported myself in service. Every unit we had was covering wrecks, traffic problems and stranded motorists. I was the closest unit to Headquarters and I got a call to pick up a couple of cases of the Red Traffic Flares and distribute them to the units that needed them.

By the time I got that job completed, my shift log sheet was two hours behind. It was dark and snow fall was heavy. I made it back into my assigned district and pulled into the first place I found that I could safely stop. I was at one of our convenience stores. I could see the clerk inside the store, and everything appeared ok. He was waiting on someone at the counter and had his back to me. We worked out a system on how to signal us if he had a problem. He would first look at us then turn his back if he needed assistance. I recognized that he had not looked at me, but it was hard for me to see through the store window. I started filling in my log sheet.

The clerk came outside to my unit and said that he had just been robbed and walked back into the store. I was surprised and first I thought he was trying to pull a prank on me. But he had come out to my car in a snowstorm wearing a short sleeve shirt. I jumped out of my car and followed him inside the store. He was already on the phone with his boss telling him that he had been robbed.

I questioned him about what they looked like, and he told me that they were the three that had walked right by my car. Then I remembered seeing them leave the store and the only details that I could remember was that one of them had looked at me as he walked out of the parking lot. I can still see that fat little face with the wire rimmed glasses. He looked like he was just a kid.

I put the robbery call out on the radio and started following their tracks through the snow-covered parking lot. There were three sets of footprints in the snow, and they went directly across the street in front of the store and to a set of tire tracks of a parked car. The tire tracks looked like those left by a Volkswagen. I later was able to establish from the clerk that they all looked like juveniles and the oldest looking one was the one with the wire rimmed glasses. He was the one with a small handgun. We never got any more information on the robbery or the robbers.

Normally in bad weather, the weather causes more risk to you than the people. That was the case with Sergeant Ross. We were working day shift after a couple of snowy days followed by an overnight hard freeze. We were having one of our worst Black Ice Days. It had frozen the night before and it was hard to get patrol cars out of the parking lot. The first car I tried to use had regular summer tires with the tire tread worn down and did not have enough traction to hold the car on any unlevel surface without sliding out of control. I had to return it to the parking area. I was able to find a unit with new studded snow tires and I drove it.

Ross was the Shift Sergeant that morning and he had sent me back to the jail to help transport a prisoner that had sliced his wrist in an attempt to commit suicide, and his guard to the hospital. While I was still on my call at the hospital, I heard dispatch air a stickup alarm call from one of the banks in our area. Sergeant Ross had tried to cover the bank call and skidded off the road at about 30 miles per hour. His car hit a support cable to a power pole and flipped over and slid into a large hole.

No one saw the accident and Ross was pinned in the car hanging upside down. He could not use his vehicle radio but was able to get a weak signal out on his handset. He calmly called Dispatch and reported that he had just had a vehicle accident and was stuck in his vehicle and needed some help getting out.

It was a freak accident. The road curved to the left to go around the ditch and was a bad area between the road and the railroad tracks. The black ice was so bad that his car would not turn to follow the road. It slipped off the road into the ditch and turned over, and then just skidded along the ground until it fell into the hole. One of the city offices, also covering the bank stickup alarm, was familiar with the area and he found where Sergeant was and arranged his rescue.

I was still at the hospital when they brought Ross in. He had broken his collar bone, his side arm had bruised his right hip. The hospital kept him overnight for observation and he recovered just fine.

Charley Brownlow was an ex-Texas State Trooper hired and assigned to the Patrol Division. He was 100 percent Texan. Charley stood 5 foot 10 inches tall and weighed over 200 pounds. His High School Football coach was so sure that Charley was going to be a professional football player and had overdeveloped his shoulders and neck. Charley had no neck; his shoulder muscles went all the way up to his ear lobes. We never could get his tie to fit him.

Charley was assigned to my shift, and we became good friends. We worked well together and I always enjoyed having him for my backup. Charley's hero was Buford Pusser from the Walking Tall story. Charley liked to act like him and had a four-foot stick in the trunk of his patrol unit. Charley also carried a four-cell steal flashlight. With his size and swager, and that big flashlight, he always looked intimidating. Normally on any call involving a disturbance or resistance to arrest, the problem would just clam down as soon as Charley arrived on the scene. Most of the time the people would rather be his friend than tangle with him.

One of our worst problem areas was what we called the Parker Road District. It was a small area that was located between the Cities of Aurora and Denver. The strip of land was still unincorporated. and had three large apartment complexes, three convenience stores and some other small businesses, all of which invited unwanted transient people to cause trouble.

The Parker Road District was always an interesting area to work. If you worked at it aggressively, you would not get many calls and you could spend your time aggressively working all your problem areas. If you missed being assigned to the district for a few days or could not aggressively work the area for a few days, you would be swamped by so many complaints that you would not have time to aggressively patrol the area.

We had been having some stickups at some of our convenience stores and we had one store that was always a prime target. It was located between the three apartment complexes and was surrounded by Aurora and Denver jurisdictions, but Arapahoe County had jurisdiction over the part where the store was. It was also located at a main crossroads intersection with a lot of escape routes.

I cruised by the store just after dark and observed a tall black man just hanging out in the store. There were a couple of people checking out with the clerk and the suspect was staying away from the counter. I thought that they were about to be robbed. I called Charley on the radio to cover the front of the store while I checked the back side of the store. I drove around behind the store and there was a pickup truck parked next to the building in the dark with the engine running. I was sure he was the getaway driver and I got ready to take him as soon as Charley covered the front. Charlie radioed that he had the front of store covered and I told him that I had the getaway driver and for him to watch the suspect until I could disable the getaway vehicle.

I could see someone in the driver's seat, but I could not tell what he was doing. I drew my service revolver and approached the driver's window. I pointed my weapon at the driver and yelled freeze, police. Then I could see his hands. He had a death grip on a cheeseburger and all set to take another bite.

He was a construction worker on his way home from work and had gotten his supper, a cheeseburger, and French fries. He had tried to make it all the way home, but the smell of that food got the best of him. He pulled into the first place where he could get out of traffic to eat his supper.

To make matters worse, Charley called me on the radio and said the suspect was getting ready to leave the store and appeared to be friends with the clerk. I said to let him go Charley, I was wrong everything is ok.

One day when I was not on duty with him, he got a loud noise complaint from one of our apartment complexes that was in one of our bad areas. When he went to the apartment, he found that a large party was going on and everybody there was black. He also observed that the males were all large people. He spoke with the person in charge of the party and explained the noise ordnance for the area and told them to just keep the noise level down. They agreed and he left.

By the time he got in his vehicle, dispatch was giving him another complaint of load noise from the same apartment. He returned to the apartment with some back up and the music was just as loud as the first time. He walked to the center of the room and was met by one of the large black men, who asked what he wanted. Charley responded well boy, "I just told you about the noise complaint. Before he could finish his statement, the large man confronted Charley with "Boy? Did you say boy?"

Charley knew that his bad choice of words was going to get him into trouble, so he looked at the guy and tried to think of what to say. Nothing was coming to Charley to say, so he had to stall for more time. To do so, and not look intimidated, he took his steel flashlight and put it on a table where he was standing. He still could not think of what to say so he stalled for more time by taking off his handheld radio and placed it on the table. Then he looked straight at the guy and said, "Boy, mister, sir or whatever you want to be called, you will have to close this loud party."

It was quiet for only for a second before some of the party guys started laughing. As it turned out, most of them were Denver Broncos Football players and had belonged to the Sheriff's Posse at one time.

They knew that Charley had not meant any harm by his bad choice of words, and as members of the Denver Broncos, they could not afford any bad press.

I always enjoyed working with Charley as my backup. We had a lot of fun and also did a lot of good police work. On one of our day shift assignments, Charley and I were working on a disturbance complaint at one of the apartment complexes in the Parker Road District and had just finished that call, when our dispatch aired an Officer Needs Assistance call.

The officer was Steve Keller from our squad. He was at the Water Reservoir Recreation area, which was on Parker Road about five miles from where we were. When you hear any call that an Officer Needs Assistance, you stop whatever you are doing and start in his direction immediately.

I was closer to the parking lot exit than Charley was, and I just turned on all my emergency equipment and accelerated my vehicle into the traffic as fast as I could. Charley was trying to follow our department procedures and get our dispatch on the radio to tell them we were responding, and I got ahead of him in the traffic.

The first emergency vehicle will normally be in the safest condition because the other traffic will try to get out of your way, but as you pass, they close up behind you and concentrate on watching you. The second unit will have to fight their way through the traffic.

I had a wide-open roadway and was running wide open. I could see Charley in my review mirror. He was being blocked by the traffic I had just passed, and he was fighting from road ditch to road ditch to get through the traffic. Dispatch aired the additional information that the security gate guard at the recreation park could see our officer and he was down on the ground with the suspect close to the gate.

I had to slow my unit down to make the turn into the entrance at the gate and my entrance lane was open and passed through the gate at about 50 MPH. I don't think that made the gate guard in that little booth very happy, but I got to where Steve was, and he was ok.

He had the suspect face down on the ground with his hands cuffed behind his back. I got out of my vehicle to help Steve get the suspect standing up. As soon as we got him on his feet, he kicked the side of Steve's door in an attempt to get away from us. My vehicle was right next to me, and we threw him on the hood of my car. The problem was he did not have a shirt on, and my vehicle had been on a high-speed run and the hood was not the coolest place to be right then.

Charley got there just as we threw the suspect on the hood of my car and Charley was mad about the traffic slowing him down. He asked what the problem was, and I told him that the suspect did not want to get in the back seat of Steve's car and Charley said, "Well, let me help you with that." Then he very delicately opened the back door to Steve's vehicle and brushed off the seat. Then Charley grabbed the suspect and pulled him off my car and threw him in the back seat. Steve and Charley secured him in the back seat and Steve transported the suspect to jail.

The suspect had no identification on him, but he had given Steve a name that could not be confirmed. I went through the suspect's vehicle and found some papers in the glovebox that showed a four-part name, The first name was John the second name was Wayne and the last two were parts of a Hispanic name. When I did a warrants and records check on the name he gave Steve, I got no response on it, but I did get two small warrants on the name with John Wayne in it.

I took the warrant information to the Booking Officer that was processing him and asked the officer what name he was being booked under and he told me the name he had given to Officer Steve Keller. I acted real happy about the name and said, "Great; that is the name I got these two big felonies warrants on."

That comment got the suspect's attention. He admitted that the Four-part name was his real name. He had a civilian security guard position at one of the Federal Facilities and Steve was charging him with reckless driving and resisting arrest, and he knew the charges and warrants would cost him his job.

I had a lot of good memories about things that Charley and I did, but I also had one that was not so good. I was taking a week of vacation time to work on my house. I was putting up drywall in my basement and was just finishing up the main part of the job. I was not used to that much physical work and I was so sore that it hurt me to breathe.

The good news was that I was at the end of a very long and hard day, but the job was ending, and I was so tired and sore that all I could think of was soaking in my hot tub and sleeping for the rest of my vacation, but my wife brought me the phone and said it was an emergency, it was Charley Brownlow.

He was working the midnight shift on Patrol and was scheduled to work that night, but he was on his way to Texas to take care of a personal emergency there and the officer that was supposed to take his shift had suddenly called in sick. The department had some good policies on being able to swap shift assignments, but if you were on the schedule to work, you were the one held responsible if no one showed up to work the shift. Failure to show up for your shift normally meant you would be fired.

Every muscle in my arms, legs and back felt like they were on fire. I did not have the strength to walk. I tried to tell Charley that I could not help him, but I knew he could not afford to lose his job.

It was the midnight shift, and he was assigned to the Parker Road District. Somehow, I got a shower, something to eat, got my uniform on, a bottle of aspirin and made it to the Department before the off-going officer filed a complaint about being late getting off his shift. I explained to the off-going officer what was going on and his pass down information on the district was it was a slow day. He could see how bad I was hurting and helped me service the unit.

I was hoping that it would stay quiet, and I could stay out of trouble. I had not reported into dispatch to advise them that I would be covering the shift, I just called myself in service over the radio. Dispatch acknowledged me by giving me a pending call to one of the convenience stores that was having trouble with a customer. It was not given as an emergency call, so I responded I was enroute. I was not in any physical condition to try to make a hot run with any type of vehicle.

I took my time getting to the store hoping they would have everything worked out before I got there. No luck with that because both the customer and the store manager had dug in their heels and was set on not changing their mind.

The customer had lost his ring of keys while shopping in the store and had searched everywhere in the store except behind the counter. The store manager would not let the customer go behind the counter. The manager had searched the area behind the counter twice and had not found any keys.

The customer had sworn that he would not leave the store until he got his keys. The store manager had suggested that the customer find himself a sleeping bag because it was going to be a long night. The store owner had a rule that none of store employees would ever let a customer behind the counter for any reason and I had no justification for breaking the rule.

I was hurting too bad to try to walk around so I made the customer and the manager come out to my car. I had each one of them explain their side of the story. All they could confirm was that a full set of keys were missing and no evidence that they were ever inside the store.

The duty store manager, that had tried to find the keys, was sure they were not inside the store. He had a rule that he could not break that customers are not allowed to go behind the store counter.

I advised the customer that he should give all his information to the manager and that the manager would call him if the keys were found. I also advised the customer of Colorado's Trespass law and that I would have to take him to jail for trespassing if a complaint was filed. With that information they came to an agreement, and I called myself back into service and left the area.

I found a parking lot at one of the apartment complexes to watch and I took some more aspirin. It was a quiet night and every few minutes, when I could, I would get out of the vehicle and walk around it trying to ease the hurting in my legs. I knew that parking a police car in a private parking area would get some complaints called in on you, so I had to move before that happened.

I remembered that there was a small service road that a couple of the apartment complexes used as a back way to get past some of the morning traffic rushes. It was just a strip of black top about a half mile long that was on private property. I had worked some traffic calls on it and remembered that it was in the area where I was. I decided to check it out while I was killing time. I drove down the roadway at about 10 to 15 MPH toward the other apartments.

Suddenly a large old rotten tree fell across the road right in from of my vehicle. I stopped instantly and it was so close to my front bumper that some of the small debris bounced up and fell on the hood of my vehicle. My front bumper was only inches away from touching the log. I was in an open area with no rhyme nor reason for the tree to fall. I spotlighted the area and there was nothing or anyone in the area.

When I realized how close the tree came to falling on my vehicle, it scared me. Yes, it was old and rotten and eaten up with termites, but why it had fallen that close to me I will never know.

I knew that in a couple of hours there would be a string of cars trying to use that road, but I was hurting too bad to try to move it off the road, so I called dispatch to get our street cleanup crew to clear the road. But this was a private road, and the property owners would have to move it.

It was broken into pieces, so I took my vehicle and used it to push part of it off the road clearing a traffic lane. Then I got back in my vehicle and took a long slow drive back to the department and spent the rest of that shift writing my reports.

Charley made it back to Colorado, but he resigned and moved back to Texas. About 90 days later I took the test for investigation and was promoted to investigator and transferred to the Investigation Division.

# Chapter 44

# INVESTIGATION DIVISION

My first assignment was to work burglaries with Investigator Dean Northup. Dean was also the Arson Investigator for the department, so I worked with him on all suspected arson cases.

Dean was divorced and raising his two teenaged sons. His mother and father kept them during his working hours so he would drop them off on the way to work and pick them up on his way home. He was what you would call a good company man. He would always show up on time, followed all the rules and never complained. He wasn't ready for a loose cannon like me.

In investigations, we worked as a two-man team. Most of the time your partner was your only backup. You needed to know what he was thinking, as well as what he was doing. How he would react to any situation at any time. Well in our case, we were total opposites.

The Sheriff's Department issued a department vehicle to each of the investigative teams. The team was required to have one person on call at all times and he would be the one driving the vehicle. We had a Dodge Dart. To say that the car was useless for what we needed would be a compliment. The only thing good about it was the radio and PA system.

In Investigations, we worked as a two-man team. Most of the time your partner was your only backup. You needed to know what he was thinking as well as what he was doing, how I was going to react to the situation at all times. Well in our case, we were total opposites.

The first day I worked with Dean he was going to show me some of the riskier areas that we had to work cases in. I was driving and I had just come from the midnight shift in the Patrol Division. On the midnight shift, stop lights with no traffic had become slow and go as normal operation. To stop and just sit there by yourself for minutes just waiting for the light to change was not going to happen very often.

I was driving on one of our rural roads and came to a "T" intersection where it merged with a main route into the Denver city area. There was no traffic, so I slowed down and made a left turn onto the street without stopping. Dean was talking about his wife leaving him and the boys and still could not understand why she had left. Suddenly he went into shock and yelled," you ran a redlight. I said, "Well Dean, don't tell anyone or I might get a ticket". My actions completely blew his mind. He just kept staying, but the light was red.

After Dean settled down and we switched positions, he did the driving for a while. I got bored just riding in the shotgun position. I took the PA system microphone and as we passed one of our popular golf courses there were some players that were teeing off, I keyed the microphone yelled, "Four!" Dean wasn't sure what he heard or where it came from.

The next area we drove through was one of the bad areas of Denver. Dean was telling me not to come to this part of Denver by myself because these peopled hated cops and it was dangerous. As we were driving through the neighborhood, the only people I saw was two Mexican adult males that were dressed nice and was standing on the sidewalk talking to each other. While Dean was still telling me how dangerous everyone was, I keyed the PA microphone and yelled, "Hey, my name is Dean Northrop and I'll whip all you SOB's."

Dean called me a crazy something or other and just about stomped the floorboards out of that little Dart trying to get out of the area. The two guys on the street just went on with their conversation and looked confused about what the noise was.

I was trying to get Dean to loosen up and have some fun. He was taking everything too serious and not really paying attention to what was going on. After he settled down, I got him to laugh about what we had just done. Dean was a good officer but at that time he was carrying too many personal problems to keep his mind on the job.

When I was first assigned to the Burglary team, which was a two-person team. We investigated both residential and business burglary cases. Dean was also the arsons investigator, and we investigated those cases also. We would also be assigned as extra help on larger special investigations.

Investigating criminal activity was aways interesting. Most of the criminals look at committing criminal acts as just another job. They will develop the necessary skills to commit the acts and stick to the ones that provide the best payoffs. As they perfect their skills to commit the acts, and when they learn what works best for them, that will become their Modis Operandi.

The act of burglary requires that the person unlawfully enter a secured place like a residence or business and commits a second crime while inside. Some states will require the additional wording of, "With specific intent to commit a crime therein." Most burglaries are committed to steal something of value.

During my assignment to working burglaries, I met some interesting people. The youngest of them was a pair of 12-year-old identical twins by the names of Michael and Patrick. I will not use their last names to protect their families. These kids had two brothers and one sister older than them, and a father, but no mother at home. They all had criminal records or were being investigated for criminal activity.

The twins were constantly being accused of being illegally in someone's home or business and stealing things. But even at 12 years old, they knew not to be together at the same place or at the same time so the witness could not identify them. They also knew to lie about everything and never to admit to anything. They were identical and when they dressed alike, you could not tell which one was Michael or which one was Patrick.

I filed so many cases involving them that Judge Foote, our Juvenile Judge, ordered them to be split up by sending Patrick to live with his grandmother in the state of Oregon. That only lasted about six months before she shipped him back.

The Father of the twins filed a theft and forgery case against his son John Jr, who was 16 years old at the time for stealing his Social Security check and cashing it. John Jr.'s defense was that his dad had not paid him for the Marijuana that he had sold his dad. John Jr. got convicted of forgery of the check.

I had additional cases against John Jr., and he wound up in a Juvenile Detention facility. There were other cases against different members of the family, but they were not my cases.

One other juvenile related burglary case that I worked involved a 16-year-old male and a very antique silver water pitcher. This case was in the incorporated city, Greenwood village. Normally, the Sheriff's Department would not be working on their law enforcement cases, but they had their incorporation procedures challenged and were going through a court challenge. During this time the arrest authority of their police officers suspended, and the Sheriff's Department was handling their Law Enforcement duties while their case was in court. I was assigned to the case.

The case indicated that the person committing the burglary was not an experienced burglar. He took mostly junk items and passed up a lot of very expensive items. Only the water pitcher that I was pursuing was an item of great interest if it was once owned by King Louie III. The owner could not tell me what he had paid for the item because of his bid agreement. He did tell me that it cost him $10,000 just to be able to bid on it.

The water pitcher was about 12 inches tall and held about a quart of liquid. It was pure silver and double lined with an attached lid and the handle still had part of the bamboo that originally covered the handle. It was completely handmade and had beautiful hand carved patterns on the complete body of the pitcher. My fear was that the thief would sell it to someone who would melt it down. All the real value was in its' antique value.

I got a lead on the Juvenile who was suspected by the neighbors and contacted his mother. The boy was not at home and the mother wanted me to talk to his stepfather first. He was an ex-priest and said they would cooperate with me. Later that day I met with his stepfather and explained the situation to him, and he promised to find the kid and have him and the water pitcher information the next morning.

The next morning the stepfather and the boy met with me, and they had the water pitcher, and it was not damaged. I got all the items back that the owner wanted, and the Judge gave the juvenile a suspended sentence. His file will also be removed when he turns 18 if he stays out of trouble.

The next case I got from Greenwood Village involved a career criminal by the name of Anthony Leo Gonzales Jr. He went by the name of Tony Gonzales and over the next 10 years I got to know him well. Tony was burglarizing a home in Greenwood Village when a spunky 17-year-old girl came home and surprised him. She heard him making a noise upstairs and she grabbed an umbrella and started upstairs after him. Tony started down the stairs at the same time and when she threatened him with the umbrella, he told her that he had a gun and she let him pass.

She gave a good description of him to our artist, and I was able to get him recognized in a line- up. My witness picked him out of the line up. I charged him with the burglary and got him convicted.

One of the things about Tony's case was that the family who lived at the house he burglarized was on vacation at the time. The lady that lived there had hid all her jewelry in the bottom of one of her dresser drawers, under a drawer full of clothing. Tony was going through that dresser drawer when the girl came in. He heard her enter, stopped, and ran out. He was within four inches of her $40,000 worth of jewelry when he stopped and ran.

I used that information to aggravate Tony while I investigated him for other burglaries in the area. By the time I got his case to trial, I had been able to add five additional counts of burglaries to his conviction.

For an intruder to gain entrance into a secured building, he needs a quick method that will not attract attention. The most common method is to walk straight up to the door and force it open. To accomplish this, a lot of them use a large pair of either vice grips or adjustable pliers.

They call the burglars using this method "vice griper's". The good ones can walk from the curb to the door and open it about the same time as it takes the owner to get in with the key. They take pride in their skills and earn titles like King of the Vice Grips. Tony was one of the vice gripers, but not very good at it.

Probably the second-best method of entry was through a window. This method normally would require a very small person, sometimes a child. They would force the window open enough for the small person to squeeze through, and the child would open the door from the inside and let the rest of the intruders inside.

To gain entry to the inside of a business, sometimes the rooftop is the preferred method. It can provide better hiding and is often easier to cut through. Most businesses have alarm systems that protect doors and windows, and coming in through the roof will bypass them. Motion detector systems provide more protection for a business or residence.

Motion detection systems can also cause a lot of false alarm calls. I remember one case where I worked in Littleton, Colorado involving a pizza restaurant. The Patrol Division was getting regular calls to the restaurant for early morning false alarms. All the alarms would be at about the same time and almost every day would always be false calls.

The Patrol Division requested my help to try to find out what was setting off the alarms. They would always be within a few minutes of each other between seven and eight AM, and almost every day. I went to the area where I could watch the restaurant and on the first day, while I was watching it, we had an alarm. There was no one in or around the building at the time of the alarm. I was satisfied that it was not a person causing the alarm.

I went back to look for a common denominator that could cause the alarm to trigger. The first thing I noticed was that the time of each alarm was always close to the same time, but never the exact same time. There would be one to two minutes between the times. Also, sometimes it would skip a day.

First, I checked the time of the sunrise on the days of the alarms and found that it was consistently just a few minutes before the time of the alarm. That raised the question of what about the days when there were no alarms. When I checked the weather for those days, there were early morning clouds. The next day I watched the building and shortly after the sun hit the windows, the alarm went off. The change in temperature inside the building was triggering the alarm. The alarm company adjusted the sensitivity of the system with stopped the alarms.

There were so many burglaries being committed that no one could clear them all and sometimes you don't have anything to work with. I always worked hard and got lucky on a lot of my cases, but I had two cases involving the same victim that I would like to tell you about. The victim was an elderly widow by the last name of Deem. Her husband was a medical doctor and an extraordinary businessman.

Dr. Deem had left Mrs. Deem in excellent financial position. They had no children. She had a small, but beautiful home. The home was built on top of a hill overlooking the countryside in the incorporated part of Arapahoe County just East of Denver. It was an excellent location for her with quick access to the city of Denver. The bad part was that it was a prime target for transit burglars.

When I got the first burglary report involving Mrs. Deem, I had no information about her. The report looked like a typical forced entry burglary. The crime scene investigation had not found any workable leads, but the items taken made it look like the work of an experienced burglar. A closer study of the items taken raised some interesting questions.

The items included two long white goat skin rugs, but no value for them was listed. The jewelry was mostly silver and turquoise, which was very popular at that time. There was also some diamond jewelry listed. The total value of the jewelry was 40,000 dollars. The last thing listed was a full-length fur coat with a value of 50 dollars.

The crime scene investigator had remarked that there were no neighbors close enough to have witnessed anything, so none were contacted. I phoned the number listed for the victim, Mrs. Deem, and scheduled an appointment to interview her about the items taken.

Interviewing Mrs. Deem was a challenge. She was very opinionated and only wanted to discuss her point of view. When I entered her house, I observed a nice upright piano in the living room and on the top, I saw a stack of business type checks. The stack was about a half inch tall and covered with dust. I could tell that they were real but I had no idea how much they were worth. I asked her if they were there when the burglary occurred and her response was, "Oh, they been there a long time, someday I've got to get them in the bank."

She talked about where and how she had gotten the jewelry and who gave her different items, but never about the cost. When I asked about the white goat skin rugs, she just said that they were trophies from one of her husband's hunting safaris. She only referred to the coat as "Her coat" and never said anything about the cost or how she got it, but she kept telling me that she knew who took it.

She had a lady friend who lived in the area that had a problem teen aged son who was always in trouble. I don't recall her name. but I do remember that her initials were K R. I checked on her friend and she was just a friend trying to help Mrs. Deem when she could and both her and her son were not in Denver when the burglary occurred.

There is a communications network that the police were using to notify other police agencies of crimes committed and to request assistance in solving them. I posted a notice about the Deem case and the items stolen after interviewing Mrs. Deem.

The next day, after the interview, I got a notice from Mrs. Deem's insurance company that the value of the Fur coat had been raised from 50 dollars to 2,000 dollars. In view of that information, I thought that I was looking at insurance fraud. I met with the agent and questioned him about the increase in the price of the coat. Her agent was the one who had made the change.

He explained that he had been the Deems insurance agent for about twenty years and she had never wanted to be bothered with filing any claims even though she was entitled to the money. This time he was able to get her to let him file the claim. He knew that what she had listed as a fur coat was a very expensive top of the line full length Mink coat. He had talked Mrs. Deem into increasing the listed value of the coat.

He had the information about the coat and where it was purchased from but not the value of the coat, so I went to interview the store manager. I don't remember the name of the store, but it was a very exclusive store. I sure remember the lady who was the manager. She walked as though she was floating to keep her feet from touching the floor. As she approached me, she looked me over as if to say, don't let your cheap suit touch anything.

I told her who I was and that I was investigating the theft of a mink coat that Mrs. Deem had purchased from her store. She responded that the store does not give out any information about any of their customers or their purchases. I explained that I needed to confirm that the value she had listed was valid because she initially listed it at 50 Dollars and then raised it to 2,000 dollars.

That information caused a shocked expression on the store managers' face, and she said that she would not tell me the cost of the coat but that amount of money would not even start to cover its cost. She went on to explain that the coat was a special order, and the store was only authorized to sell two of them in the Denver area. Then she said that she would not discuss anything else about the coat. I thanked her and was glad to depart the store.

There was no new information about the Deem case for a couple of months then I got a call from a detective in Salt Lake City, and he had recovered the coat and goat skin rugs. He also had the suspect in custody on other charges. He had one of his female officers put the coat on and model it for a picture so I could get conformation on being the right coat. He also sent pictures of the goat skin rugs.

I took the pictures to Mrs. Deem to confirm that it was her coat and she was very mad about somebody wearing her coat but made no comment about getting it back. I explained that the person who stole her things was a transient on his way through Denver and needed money and that he had confessed to it. Mrs. Deem was acting irrational and still insisted that her friend had something to do with it.

To make matters worse, when we got the two rugs back, we noticed that the letters K and R, small in size, had been stamped-cut in both of the rugs. We had no way of knowing who, where or what time that had happened.

The D A and I both was afraid to let Mrs. Deem testify during the trial, but she was the victim and did testify. She also blurted out that she thought someone else had stolen her things. Thank God no one in the court believed her and got a conviction.

The Salt Lake City detective testified that the suspect's girlfriend had turned him in. She stated that he had promised her the coat and then changed his mind, and when she found out, she got mad and reported him to the police.

We had multiple burglaries every day, but none to match the last one that Mrs. Deem suffered. She had started investing in top quality jewelry and she invested very heavily in it. About one year later her house was burglarized again.

This time the only physical evidence that was found at the crime scene was one size six shoe impression. The footprint was in the dust on top of a stereo speaker directly under a vertical crank out window. The burglary was accomplished by very professional people and the only items taken was her collection of high value jewelry. The estimated value was approximately one-half million dollars.

Every possible suspect was thoroughly investigated and cleared. There was never a single trace of what happened to the jewelry.

In addition to working burglaries, I also got to assist in other cases, where additional help was needed like homicides and unusual cases. One of the unusual cases was about strange noises in a residence where one of the owners thought it was paranormal activity.

It was a nice little tri-level three-bedroom residence in a nice small community. The community was located between two main routes with small business districts on each side. The owners were from Israel, and they had two teenaged girls ages ten and twelve. The male owner was a well-known gynecologist who worked shifts at three different hospitals in the Denver, Colorado area and was on call for two other hospitals. He received a large total salary, but his time at home was limited.

The noise complaint was that loud banging noises would be heard at different times and sometimes at night the kids would hear the sound of footsteps outside their room. The owner had purchased a sound recording system and had microphones hidden on the steps and did get a good recording of the sound of footsteps walking up to the door and the girls screaming. The girls stated that they had heard the sound and thought they saw someone at the door.

The only damage that was discovered was a hole knocked out the drywall paneling in the hallway. Based on the size and shape of the hole, it appeared to be for a baseball bat. There was a bat in the house that belonged to one of the girls, but the crime lab could not match the bat to the hole.

The banging noise was loud and random, but it was occurring two to three times a week. It always sounded like someone beating very hard on the walls. Our investigator tried to duplicate the sound but could not. When all our physical searches for some type of electronics that could have caused the sounds were exhausted, we had the state crime lab do a search on the types of signals from any type of remote equipment. They also failed to find anything.

We investigated the possibility of someone in the community doing something to try to drive them out of the community. We interviewed the neighbors and found no evidence of that. One of the next-door neighbors had a window in their attic that provided an excellent overview of the roof of the house. We got permission to put someone in the attic to watch the house and we set up a surveillance team.

We had one officer in the attic, two members to cover the yard and the team leader was set up inside the victim's house. I was one of two covering the yard. From my location I had a full view of the front of the house and one side yard. The other member cover the back and other side.

With the house completely covered we waited for something to happen. The member of the team who was inside the house was in the living room with all four of the family members. He had a sound recorder setup and we all had radios.

After about two hours of waiting, the ten-year-old girl went into the bathroom that was close to the living room. Within about 10 minutes there was a very loud banging noise in the house. The girl in the bathroom screamed and we were all alerted by a radio call that something was happening.

All the sounds were recorded and there were three sets of three bangs in rapid order, which sounded like someone banging a wall. Both the parents went to the girl in the bathroom and checked her. She was scared and still sitting on the commode. She had not caused the noise.

No one on the outside of the house saw or heard anything. We tried every way we could to duplicate the sound inside the house, but we failed to find a way to create the same sound.

After reviewing the case, the captain in charge of Investigation Division closed the case. There did not appear to be any danger of anyone getting injured and we did not have the funds to continue the investigation.

We were visited by four different paranormal investigators, and we were all interviewed by each of them, and we gave them a copy of our case file. After that, we did not hear any more about the situation.

Our patrol division had a traffic accident involving a death that I assisted with. I named it our "Accidental vehicle Homi-suicide case". The case involved a semitruck driver that was hauling a truck load of Coors Beer that was found dead in the driver's seat of the truck.

The Coors Beer company is in Colorado and just released their product to be sold outside of the state of Colorado. The driver was from the state of Florida and was driving a Budget Rental Tractor and trailer with a full load of Coors Beer. He was heading East on Interstate 80, had just cleared Aurora, and was passing through a large road construction area when the truck hit some of the construction barricades and stalled out.

The speed limit through the construction zone was posted at 30 MPH. His traffic lane was restricted to one lane with the large concrete barricades on both sides of the lane. It appeared that his truck was almost stopped before it hit a barricade. The driver was still sitting in the driver's seat and was slumped over the steering wheel. He was dead.

The impact of the accident was so minor that it should not have caused any physical injuries to driver. The driver was the only person in the truck cab and when the first responders reached the truck both doors and all the windows were closed. When the door was opened to check the driver, they discovered that he had been shot in the chest and there was a nine-millimeter simi automatic pistol on floor by the driver's feet.

When I arrived at the scene, the body and the firearm had been removed from that cab and truck door closed. My primary concerns were whether anyone else could have been in the cab with the driver or if he had been shot from the outside of the truck. All glass in the windows and the windshield was in perfect condition confirming that nothing had entered the cab from outside of the vehicle.

I checked the inside of the cab and there was a good layer of dust on everything inside the cab except where the driver was. The passenger's door was locked from the inside. I failed to find any evidence that anyone else had been in the cab of the truck.

When I arrived at the scene the Crime Lab team had not arrived and the driver's seat had not been tampered with, the bullet was still in the back of the seat. It appeared that the bullet had passed through the driver's body in an upwards angle and entered the back cushion of the seat. This indicated that the driver had shot himself.

The truck cab had a sleeper compartment behind the driver. I had to wait for the Crime Scene investigators before I could check it. Some of the drivers that carry a firearm with them on trips kept it in the sleeper. It is normally loaded and ready to shoot and stored in the sleeper within their reach.

My theory was that he had taken the gun out while slowly driving through the construction area and was setting it up by loading a round in the chamber and it went off accidently. To load a round in the chamber he would have had to use both hands. That could have caused the gun to be directly in front of him when it went off. The Crime Scene Investigators agreed with my conclusion. That is why I jokingly called it an "Accidental vehicle homo suicide case".

While I am talking about cases other than burglary, I would like to tell you about the time I completely lost my mind and challenged one of our Eighteen Judicial Judges. Judge Naugle was an older one of our judges and was fighting some health problems. I had a lot of dealings with him, we both liked fly fishing and we had become friends.

I handled a case involving the theft of a Citizen Band Radio from one of our Radio Shack stores. It involved two young black males and a sharp store clerk. One of the suspects was short and the other one was tall. They were driving a Silver colored 1957 Chevy car. This was a classic example of what not to do if you are going to commit a crime.

First off, this made identifying who did what was narrowed down to two statements, the short guy, or the tall guy. Next you can spot and recognize a Silver 1957 Chevy for miles.

The store clerk watched the two customers enter the store together, split up and go to different parts of the store. He recognized this as a well-known action used by shoplifters to distract a store clerk. The tall guy went to the back of the store and started handling items and boxes while the short guy went to where the clerk was and asked him to show him a CB radio from the display. While the store clerk was showing the short guy the radio, the tall guy dropped something in the back of the store.

While the clerk was checking on the tall guy in the back of the store, the short guy left the store. The clerk had been hit with this action before, so he immediately checked the display rack, and the radio was missing. Now the tall guy was exiting the store. The clerk watched them get in the Silver Chevy and leave.

The clerk immediately called in the complaint, and our dispatcher immediately broadcast it to our patrol officers. The officers in the area of the Radio Shack store covered the main exit routes to the Denver area. In less than 10 minutes they spotted the silver Chevy and stopped it. The tall guy was driving. The short guy was in the front passenger's seat and appeared to be hiding something under the seat.

When one of the officers asked if he could search the vehicle, the response was yes. When the officer asked them to step out of the car they refused and withdrew their agreement. The officer, realizing that this was a case where the exigent circumstances should apply to search the vehicle anyway and found a new CB radio under the front seat.

The officers got the suspects to drive back to the Radio Shack. The clerk identified the radio, the suspects, and their car. The box the radio came in was still in the store and it contained the paperwork and accessories that belonged to the CB radio. The suspects were arrested, and I filed the case in court.

The short guy was well-known in the area for being involved in theft cases. I had met his dad, who was a very nice person and was retired military. The tall guy did not have a prior record.

The case wound up in Judge Naugle's court for a felony theft trial. The two defendants were split up and being tried on different dates. The short defendant was the one on trial and he was in jail at that time. Since he required a deputy to escort him for his hearing and I had to be in court, I escorted him through the hearing.

Normally, in these types of cases there is a suppression hearing on all questionable evidence before a preliminary hearing. The preliminary hearing was to be determined if there was enough evidence to support a trial. When we got to the court, they were getting ready to panel a jury.

After some discussion between the District Attorney, Eaton Feldman, the Public Defender, and the Judge, the discussion was not going well, and the judge moved the hearing to his chambers. The defendant could not go in the Judge's chambers, and I had to provide guard duty for the defendant. Therefore, I could not go in the chambers either.

After a half hour or more, they came back into the courtroom. Eaton looked at me, shrugged his shoulders and said "We ain't got a case." I was very upset and yelled back at him "What the hell do you mean I ain't got a case, I came in here with a good case and I am not going to accept this. I want an open court hearing on what happened to my case behind closed doors.

I had never had an outburst in court like that and I was sure that I had just ended my law enforcement career. I had just lost all my respect for the system and some people that I had high respect for. Then I heard myself saying that if there is something wrong with my evidence, I want to know what it is and why it is wrong. Then I repeated that I wanted an open court hearing the decision to suppress my evidence.

Just as I was winding down, the Judge came back on the bench and called the court back into session. The first question the judge asked was if we were ready to move on. The District Attorney told the Judge that there was an issue that needed to be addressed. He said, "Detective Barber was the investigating officer in this case, and he has requested an open court hearing on why the evidence was suppressed." He added that I needed to know what was wrong about how we got the information and why it was wrong so I could train my officers.

I expected to have the roof cave in on me, but instead the Judge just asked for a hearing date. A new date was set and the judge reversed his decision on suppressing the evidence and it was all reinstated. We went to trial and won the case. There was never any repercussions for challenging the court and the judge and I stayed friends.

Things under Sheriff Miller were not running as smoothly as they should have been. I saw employment ads for experienced officers offering starting salaries that were higher than my pay was at that time. I could not remember having ever questioned the salary that I was paid for any job. I always trusted my employer to treat me fairly. But now I was getting inexperienced officers to train and their salaries were higher than mine. I checked on the salaries of other officers with basically the same level of experience and found that my salary was well below theirs.

For the first time in my career, I asked for a meeting with the sheriff about my salary. I brought a copy of the employment ad, and asked if I resigned and was rehired, would my experience with the department qualify me the same starting salary. Both the Under Sheriff and the Sheriff were unaware of their new policy on hiring was causing any conflicts with existing salaries. What concerned me more was that they did not appear to know how to correct the problem. They promised to look into the matter and that was all the answer I got.

Even if they adjusted my salary to the starting salary of experienced officers, I would still be six per cent below where I should be. All longevity and merit raises were based on two per cent. All promotion salaries were based on a preset starting amount. If I was promoted to Sergeant, I would get 10 per cent increase in salary. I requested to be put on the next list for the next Sergeant's test. I took the test and was promoted to Sergeant.

# Chapter 45

# BACK TO THE PATROL DIVISION

Being promoted to sergeant required that I be reassigned, and I was transferred to the patrol division. Each patrol squad had two sergeants assigned to it. The sergeants had a dual responsibility, to supervise the squad seven days a week and to cover the duties of Watch Commander for your assigned shift.

Gene Martin, who was my first training officer and still good friend, was made sergeant the same time I did and was assigned to the same squad. I was happy because Gene and I worked well together. This assignment required that we split the Watch Commander's duties and share the squad supervisor's duties.

When we worked out the scheduling assignments for the squad, we had to cover every day with a balanced crew. The duty assignments were based on eight-hour shifts, and everyone had two days off a week plus any holidays that had to be covered. Gene and I had to cover the Watch Commander duties for eight hours every day. When either one of us had a day off, the other one had to be on duty at the department. We had to cover the patrol duties for the entire county which covered an area that was 13 by 68 miles.

All our patrol units were single manned units, so you had no backup with you. Should you have a bad situation you had to call for backup and sometimes there was not anyone within thirty miles of you.

Sheriff Miller had been voted out of office at the end of his term and Ed Nelson was elected Sheriff. He reestablished the all-volunteer posse program. Our posse unit provided excellent assistance to the Sheriff's Department. The four-wheel drive division provided a much-needed assistance during the heavy snowfall times in reaching isolated locations for rescue or assistance in our rural areas. The mounted unit were great for crowd control and searching for lost or missing persons.

The Department had a special training program for the posse and some of them became certified as special deputies. They also provided extra manpower to the Detention Division for controlling unruly inmates.

Each member of the posse came from different backgrounds, and they brought their own special skills and personalities with them. Most of the time that was good, but sometimes it could be an obstacle.

I remember one of the posse members that I really enjoyed working with. His first name was Bill. He was very serious about everything but sometimes he would get overly excited. He was riding with me when I received a call to cover an alarm at the residence of one our very wealthy citizens. I was about four miles from the residence and had to use South Havana Street to Hamden Avenue to get there.

As soon as we started, Bill started getting excited and saying let's go let's go. I remember the route from the first high speed chase I was on. There was a hard 90 degree turn where Havana joins Hamden. The only thing on the south side of the curve is a golf course. Havana and Hamden are both heavily traveled streets with three traffic lanes in each direction with two turn lanes in the middle of the street.

The South bound traffic lanes were a little more congested than the North bound lanes. I was headed South on Havana when I got a radio call from the deputy assigned to the call. He was telling me that he had one of two exits to the residence blocked off. He needed me to close off the other exit. Bill was really getting excited now.

I turned on my emergency equipment and took the middle lane to pass the Southbound traffic. Things went well until I reached that 90-degree turn. To make a 90 degree turn to the right at a normal speed is difficult enough, but I thought all I had to do was stay in the middle lane and go with the traffic.

I approached the curve at about maximum speed that I felt that I could safely negotiate the curve. As I started to round the corner, I saw a car in the turn lane directly in front of me, right in the middle of the curve. He was trying to exit the road by crossing the Northbound traffic lanes to make the entrance to the golf course. I saw him lock up the brakes on his car right in front of me. To avoid hitting him or the Southbound traffic I had to pass him by entering Northbound traffic lane.

I first had to turn left into the Northbound traffic lane and then do a hard right turn to accomplish a 90 plus degree turn through the traffic. While I was trying to keep my police car from turning over or skidding out of control. Bill was yelling obscenities at the driver of the car ahead of us. I am not sure how I managed to get safely through that curve, but just as we passed the car, Bill started laughing and yelling did you see the eyes on that guy?" They were big as saucers."

Somehow with the help of God, we made it safely through the curve. Bill just kept on laughing at how scared the guy driving the other car was. I am glad he did not see how scared I was. We got safely to the residence only to find out it was a false alarm.

I had one more frightening encounter with that corner at Hamden and Havana. It was in the Wintertime. We had just gotten all the new Pontiacs for patrol cars. All of the patrol units had new studded snow tires on them. I was at the station when I got a call about a fight involving weapons at a truck stop just East of the City of Aurora, Colorado. It was in our jurisdiction, and it involved multiple people and injuries. I dispatched all my available units to the call, and I followed in my brand-new unit.

From the department to the scene was about 15 miles. Everyone, including the paramedics, was running full emergency. I had to go out East Hamden to Havana and make that 90 degree turn again. This time I slowed down and took the full inside lane into the curve like I did in that first high-speed chase.

Those steel studded tires are not designed for high-speed driving. They are designed for the studs to protrude out of the tire when it spins so they can grab the ice on the surface and give you some traction. When you are driving at high speed the studs are the only part of the tire touching the road. You lose most of the traction from your rear wheels. When I entered the curve that car just walked right across the road. By the time I got the car stopped, I had walked across all six lanes and was going onto the shoulder of the Northbound Lane.

We got to the fight, and it was between the truckers and the local cowboys. There was twelve people total in the fight, and it was a bloody mess. They had grabbed anything they could use to fight with including a three-foot piece of two by four.

They were drunk and to prove how bad they were, they were refusing medical treatment. We got four of worst injured in an ambulance and sent them to the hospital. We told the rest of them to either go with the paramedics or get in the police cars. Three of them got in the police cars and we took them to jail.

Our medics at the jail treated two of them, but one had a gash in his head about three inches long and we got him to go to the hospital for some stitches. He was confused as to why his side had lost the fight. He explained to me that he had started the fight. He had been trying to date one of the waitresses at the truck stop and the truck drivers were trying to move in on the waitresses and they did not live there. The cowboys were local and they did not like that.

He decided that he would teach the truck drivers a lesson and he hit one of them. To his surprise the trucker attacked him and whipped him. He then went and got the two by four to even up the fight and came back and hit the truck driver with it, but the truck driver took it away from him and hit him with it.

He really thought that was wrong and just could not believe that they had lost the fight. I think he had been watching too many movies.

Working as the shift supervisor was a lot different than being a patrolman. Most of the time you were working on a complaint or processing paperwork. The amount of time you could spend working in the field with the patrolman was limited.

When you did get out of the office, you were going to all the districts to meet with officers assigned to the district. You would get a briefing from them and check their paperwork.

One thing about working patrol was you never knew what the next radio call would turn into, what you would see around the next corner or behind the next building. On some nights you would be running from one thing to the next during the shift. Other times it would be so slow you had trouble staying awake.

I recall on one of my swing shifts, we got a call for a rape and kidnapping. The kidnapping consisted of the victim's boyfriend being forced into the trunk of the suspect's car. After a lot of driving around the back roads in the area, the victim escaped from the car. The car drove away with the boyfriend still in the truck of the vehicle.

After the victim found some help, she called in for help. Her description of the car was vague. We had a dark colored four door sedan and that was all. Every law enforcement agency in the area checked every back road and street in their assigned areas for the rest of the night and we never found the car or boyfriend.

Missing people was another problem. It seemed like with them we got better descriptions. A lot of them simply went for a quiet walk and most of them returned before we found them. Some were adults just trying to find some privacy.

The biggest problem was juveniles. We always considered them to be in danger. Stolen vehicles were also a big problem. Welfare checks on elderly and sick people were always a major concern. Looking for reported DUI drivers and hit-and-run drivers also required a lot of our time.

Most of the calls turned out to be just routine events, but I remember one that was unusual. I was working the midnight shift and at about 3 am I was returning to the office. As I was passing through the main intersection in a shopping center, I stopped for a traffic red light. While waiting for the light to change, I noticed that the lighting was dimmer through the intersection than they should be. We had two banks located at the intersection and normally the lighting was very bright in that area and that concerned me. I started checking for the reason for the lights being so dim.

At first everything seemed normal, but then I noticed a power pole in the middle of the sidewalk did not look right. The only thing holding up the power pole was the electrical power cables. The bottom of pole no longer touched the sidewalk. Someone had driven off the street and right through the power pole.

About six feet from the base of the pole I found a fresh stream of water. I tracked the stream of water about four blocks and right up to the garage door of a residence. All the lights in the residence were out and no one would answer the door. I called for the District State Patrolman to back me up. They handle the vehicle accidents in the unincorporated parts of the county.

We put the spotlights from our units on the front of the house and pounded on the door until someone answered the door. I could hear a woman's voice tell someone that they had to go to the door. A middle-aged male came to the door pretending that he had been asleep for hours. The water was still dripping out of the heavily damaged front end of his car.

He admitted to owning the vehicle, but he denied driving it. When I asked him how many keys he had for the vehicle, he said two. I told him that it must have been his wife that was driving the vehicle and would not say any more. He went to jail charged with a DUI and leaving the scene of an accident.

After a six-month tour in the patrol division, I transferred to the Detention Division. Although I missed working the streets, I was getting tired of those bad weather shifts.

# Chapter 46

# DETENTION DIVISION

Jail had become a bad choice of names for a place where you locked people up for violating the law. Jail houses were now called Detention Facilities. The term incarceration facilities were also used. This was mostly used by the courts when they sentenced someone convicted of violating a law to be locked up for a period of time.

There is a long history of the use of lockup facilities to hold unwanted people. I think it started before we had established communities. If people were camped together, they had rules that you were expected to follow if you shared the camp. Failure to follow the rules would get you expelled from the camp.

When communities were formed, rules for bad behavior expectations were established and you would be thrown out of the community if they were violated. This would solve your problem temporarily, but you were only transferring the problem to another community. When the violator was thrown out of that community, he would return to your community. To keep the peace between communities, you had to learn how to deal with your own problems. This led to building a place to lock them up. This became known as a Jail.

One of the rules that got established was called vagrancy. If a person could not prove they had the means to support themselves, they would be declared a vagrant and would be locked up. This created a new set of problems and expenses for the community. Someone had to be hired to catch and lock up the problem person. The person being locked up had to have food and other forms of care or he would die. The community leaders now had to raise money to support someone they did not want in their community. To solve this problem, they would make the person work for their care. This opened a new source of problems and fraud.

The prisoners now became a source of cheap labor for projects. Property owners and contractors could also save money on labor costs by using prison labor. As the communities grew, things changed. The number of people locked up grew and the jail keeper soon became the Sheriff. The Sheriff was now the one locking up the prisoners, but he was also supplying the cheap labor to cover his expenses. Today we would call that a conflict of interest.

Prisoner labor in its most basic form started with what was called simply a work list. When people were locked up, their meals were delivered from what was called the work list. If you failed to get your name on the work list, no meal was ordered for you, and you did not eat. When you were arrested, you were held until the Judge heard your case. In some cases that could be up to 30 days if the Judge only held court once a month. Prisoners were now taken out of the jail and worked all day for meals until a Judge would hear their case.

The judges would normally hear the case, find them guilty and sentence them to the number of days that had been confined and give them credit for time served and release them. This caused a new Constitutional problem. People who were arrested and charged with a crime were pretrial detainees until they were tried and found guilty. The Judge could sentence them to serve time at hard labor in the jail. The procedure of making pretrial detainees work for food before being sentenced was without any legal standing. This law was abused by so many places that it was declared unconstitutional by the supreme court.

As the judicial system developed throughout the country, refinements in the laws provided better constitutional guidelines for enforcing the law and protection for the defendants. Judges now sentenced convicted defendants to serve their time in confinement based on the severity of the crime they were convicted of. Less serious crimes were called misdemeanors, which carried a maximum of two years to be served in the county jail. More serious crimes were called felonies the defendants would be sentenced to serve their time in the State Prison.

When I was first assigned to the Detention Division, the facility was not adequate to safely house and process the amounts of detainees we were required to service. The number of inmates we were receiving was steadily increasing. The court system was also being overrun by the number of cases they were assigned to handle. I remember reading some statistical data that the current percent of the population that had to be incarcerated was 1 percent. The population of the country was growing and so was the percentage factor. There was some concern that new drug laws in Colorado would increase the percentage factor.

My first supervision position assignment in the detention division was midnight supervisor. Our new Sheriff, Ed Nelson, had hired a staff of new captains to run the different departments. He had hired a retired Denver Police Captain named Glenn Reichert as supervisor of the Detention Division. For my first two days on the job, I had avoided meeting him. On my third shift, one of our young inmates committed suicide by hanging himself during shift change.

At shift change, both the incoming and the outgoing shifts did a complete prisoner count, called a head count, together and the information was passed down. Just after we passed his section, he tied a home-made rope, made from his bedding, around his neck and somehow jumped or fell from the top bunk. After we completed our head count and passed it down to the oncoming floor officer then did his check of everything and found the inmate hanging there.

We cut him down from the rope, and attempted to revive him, but were unable to save him. I phoned Captain Reichert's residence and introduced myself to him at that time. I advised him we had a death in the jail. This is not the way you want to meet your boss.

The County Corner came and removed the body. I chose to process the crime scene myself. Just as I was photographing the crime scene, Captain Reichert walked right through the scene. Yelling to get out of the crime scene is also not the recommended way to introduce yourself to your new boss. I did not get off to a good start with my new boss, but after he had completely checked me out, we became good friends. I worked for Captain Reichert until his death from lung cancer about three years later, and I was one of his best friends.

I had finished my associate degree in criminal Investigations at the Arapahoe Community College and started working on a bachelor's degree program. Some of the universities and colleges in the area ran some of their outreach programs in our facilities. I had been attending classes through both the Metropolitan State University and Columbia College. I felt like I was not getting the basic education material that I needed from them and switched back to the Community College. The Arapahoe Community College offered some excellent general educational and computer science courses on an early morning schedule. I could now take the early morning classes I needed.

The job requirements for being the midnight shift supervisor were less demanding than being watch commander for the patrol division. My main job was booking in new arrestees and keeping peace and security. During the first part of my six-month tour on midnight shift, I had a lot time to study but by the end of tour, the overcrowding and the old, outdated equipment was requiring all of my attention.

Upon rotation to dayshift supervisor, I became aware of a lot of new problems. I did not have enough manpower to meet the demands of work requirements. The court was issuing orders for special things for some of the inmates, like additional phone calls, additional visitation times and authorized counselling sessions. We had to monitor all telephone calls made by the inmates to ensure that they were not calling a witness or victim of their charges.

Our system for inmate phone calls required that the inmate fill out a request form for the call showing the name and number of the person to be called and listing the best time to call them. An inmate request was called a Kite. Then an officer would have to set up a special phone line in a private area for the inmate to use. The officer would have to dial the number, confirm who was receiving the call and that they were willing to talk to the prisoner. Then the officer would have to remove an extension phone off the hook so the inmate could not hang up the phone and redial a different number.

Inmates are called Cons and that has nothing to do convicts, it stands for con artist. They will run every possible con or trick on you they can. Lying is a normal part of the communication process with a large part of the inmate population. I have had several of them lie to their judge and say that the officers would not let him call his attorney. The only phone number they provided was for their girlfriend. Even when the judge knew the inmate was lying, he would order another call.

The Detention Division was not the only part of the Judicial system that needed additional support. The entire State of Colorado's Judicial system needed updating and new facilities. Canon City, the state prison, needed to be rebuilt and expanded. All the courthouses needed additional space and support. The financial support just was not there. Years of neglect of the system had resulted in a situation that had to be dealt with at both the state and local levels.

Arapahoe County needed a new jail, new court facilities and a larger County Commissioners building. The problem was put on the ballot and sent to the voters. The only item that passed was the jail. The jail was the most expensive item on the list and the County could not afford the cost of a new jail. The County Commissioners authorized a new building for them and gave their old building to the County Court. They also approved the jail to be remodeled.

## Chapter 47

# REMODELING THE JAIL

The jail was on the third floor of the Sheriff's Department. When the remodeling started with the oldest part of the jail, which was the two-man lockdown cell block section, we had one dorm type room we called the drunk tank or the bull pen. Everyone booked in at night or on weekends went to that cell until he bonded out or went before a judge. If you didn't bond out or get released by the judge, then you were assigned a cell. If we received a female or juvenile, then we had to find or create a special place for them.

The cell block area was remodeled into a dorm with bunks, tables, and a bathroom for the inmates. This made providing the service required for the inmates a little easier to accomplish. They lost the security of the lock down cell, but it gave them more freedom of movement. They could also play cards and board games on the tables.

The area inside the dorm had to be open so the guards could see everything always going on. The world had now been introduced to the number one babysitter of the times. The television set. We got one for the dorm and the TV could only receive three channels at best. If the inmates could not decide which channel to watch, we would remove the TV; however, for the most part this worked ok.

I put together a plan to get the telephone company to put a pay type phone in the dorm. This required some special arrangements and I met with local phone company representatives and worked out the details.

The telephone unit would only allow operator-assisted calls. All calls would be made collect only. The telephone company would have complete control of the unit and assume all responsibility for any fraudulent use of the system by the inmates. The phone company would receive all monetary proceeds collected for the use of the system. Each operator assisted call cost fifty cents per call.

The phone company would take the call from the inmate, obtain the number, and confirm that the person receiving the call agreed to talk to the inmate and have their account billed for the cost of the call. No third-party billing.

When I discussed this with the telephone company representatives, they assured me that if there was no one present at the phone number being billed, the call would not be completed. I knew that was not correct because I had placed a call from a floating boat dock on Table Lake in Missouri and charged it to my house phone in Littleton, Colorado.

It only took one billing cycle to start getting complaints from citizens about getting billed for third-party calls. I referred them back to the phone company.

Criminals are criminals because they want to be criminals. Being in jail will not stop them from doing criminal acts. The next problem I had to deal with was hogging the phone. The largest inmate in the cell would make a call to his girlfriend and have her leave her phone off the hook. When another inmate needed to use the phone, he would have to pay the big guy to hang up the phone so he could use it. There was no time limit on the calls.

To get a time limit per call put on the phone I had to meet with the Public Utilities Commission. They could not understand why a phone in a jail cell could not operate the same as a pay phone in public shopping centers. It took a lot of explaining to them that the reason a person is in jail is because he refuses to obey the rules. A cross section reference of the crowd in a shopping center would represent the general population, however, the inmate is 100 percent of that and .01 percent of the general population that has to be incarcerated.

After the meeting I got the time restriction on the phone; but I had to function as an advisor to the local unit of the Public Utilities Commission on all inmate phone questions.

The challenge of the jail modification grew more complicated when the City of Littleton and the Railroad company decided to recess the railroad tracks that ran by the Courthouse and the Sheriff's Department. The main route for the coal trains coming from Wyoming runs right through the middle of Littleton, and a lot of these trains pull over 100 boxcars full of coal and blocked traffic at each crossing for long periods of time. This had become a major problem for all first responders.

To solve this problem, the railroad would recess their tracks below all the main routes and put bridges over the Railroad Tracks. This required shutting down the street that ran in front of the jail and the courthouse. There were a lot of closed in parking spaces on the street for people doing business with either the Sheriff's Department or the District Court. All other public parking was shopping centers that were located three to four blocks away.

Our parking lot for employees was one block away and we opened it up to the public while the construction was going on. The District Attorney's office building was next to the court, and they had a nice small parking area in-between the courthouse and their building. It was a perfect location for people trying to find the Courthouse or Sheriff's department for the first time. The District Attorney was Bob Gallager. He had every parking space between his office and the Courthouse reserved for his employees.

I met with Gallager, and the Littleton Police Chief. We explained the traffic and parking problems that the construction was going to create for the citizens trying to do their business in the area. I explained we had temporarily moved our employee parking and asked Gallager if he would help out by allowing his parking area to be open to the public until the street could be reopened. Not only did he refuse to cooperate with us but he ordered the Littleton Police Chief to ticket any vehicle parked in front of any of his signs.

The next morning was when the Littleton Police Department had to close the street. The police department was responsible for the area around the Courthouse, but the Sheriff's department was responsible for the security of the Courthouse. That night I went to the parking lot and removed every Reserved Parking sign and stored them in the evidence locker for safe keeping. Three weeks later, when the street reopened, I took a night off and replaced all the Reserved parking signs. No parking tickets were issued.

# Chapter 48

# JAIL OVERCROWDING

While I was on dayshift, I was asked to work with the courts on the overcrowding problems. I knew all our judges and got to have meetings with them to discuss problems of overcrowding and try to find solutions. The obvious problem was too many prisoners and not enough room.

The main cause of the problem was failure to modernize to keep up with the changing situation and expectations. No one wanted to spend any money on the prisoners' needs.

In view of the rising number of lawsuits being filed by the prisoners for their living conditions, Governor Richard Lamm had requested funds to make some of the improvements that the Penitentiary at Canon City needed, and his request was turned down. The prisoners won their lawsuit and were awarded several million dollars, but the conditions that led to a suit still existed.

The third floor of the Sheriff's Department was being completely remodeled to house prisoners more efficiently. On the first floor of the building was our prisoner receiving and processing area, our kitchen for preparing their food, the laundry processing and inmate property storage. It was also the main entrance to the building, the security control for the first floor. It also was the office space for the jail administration, and prisoners' records storages.

The increase in the number of people being arrested was putting stress on the courts and the detention facilities. The court dockets were overfilled with cases and to try to make time for the cases to be heard, every case possible was being plea bargained.

The courts were trying to help with the increasing number of pretrial detainees that could be released on bond. They created a special unit to check the jail logbook each morning and collect the background information. The judge would need to consider flight risk on everyone scheduled for their first court appearance. The courts also created guidelines for authorizing Personal Recognizance Bonds, and authorized the Sheriff's Department to give PR Bonds to those who qualified for them.

The State Prison was filled to its maximum capacity, and they were all sentenced prisoners. They were being sued for overcrowding and could not move their new prisoners from the County jails. This created a backlog of prisoners and increased our overcrowding, and those prisoners could not be released. The only relief that the County got was the cost per day per prisoner reimbursement.

Governor Richard Lamm was in office during our struggle with overcrowding. He was pro law enforcement and we had meetings with him about the overcrowding problem. His view of the problem was from a statewide point of view. A lot of Colorado's Counties were rural and impoverished. They could not support a proper jail or staff.

While I was working with our judges, I learned that one of the main problems regarding the lawsuits facing the courts was that there were no written guidelines about what a constitutional jail should be. The agencies like ACLU that were bringing the lawsuits were telling the courts what they would like the guidelines to be, but nothing from the state to help them reach a fair and balanced decision.

During this mad rush of new problems, the County Commission authorized some new employee positions in the Sheriff's Department.

One of them was for an additional lieutenant to be in charge of the jail operations. I applied for and got a promotion and filled that position.

About the only thing that changed for me was that now I got to work 24 hours a day and 7 days a week. I had to have a phone, radio, or pager with me at all times.

I had six sergeants, each with a squad of deputies. They had to cover all jail operations for our 24-hour, 7-day operation. One squad worked Sunday through Wednesday and other squad would work Wednesday through Saturday.

I had to reduce the number of college classes I was taking, but the County increased our training budget. I was willing to go to any training that was available. There were several outstanding two- and three-day management seminars available to us and I tried to attend all of them. Most of supervisors did not want to go to them so I would attend them and teach the relative information to our people during their scheduled department training.

Suddenly, one morning I got a call to meet with Captain Reichert. He explained that the State of Colorado had received a Show Cause Order from a Federal Court that wanted to shut down all the prisons and jails in the state from housing prisoners. As a defense against this order, the State was setting up a team of instructors to create and teach a 40-hour jail training course to all the jails in Colorado. He had assigned me and Sergeant Ira Karr to represent Arapahoe county.

Our training was scheduled for two weeks at CSU in Boulder, Colorado. There was a screening process and some of the applicants were dropped before reporting into Boulder. The training started with 40 students, but only 24 of us graduated.

The first part of week one was to teach us how to teach adult training classes. It was basic common sense and did not require much extra time. The second part of the first week was to select the subjects for the jail training program, and who would write and teach them.

We would turn in our written procedures and at the end of the first week, we would be video filmed teaching one of our lessons. We were graded on our ability to write lesson plans and teach at the end of the first week. We lost about half of the class at the end of the second week.

The second week was all about setting up the overall training course. We went over all the lesson plans written during the first week and selected the ones to be part of the training program. We were matched up into teams of four members to travel and teach the program. Each member had 10 hours of lessons to learn and teach.

Even during the two weeks in Boulder, I still had to be available for calls and decisions relating to the jail operations. Teaching on the road was normally a three- or four-day program. Most of the small departments could not afford to let people off for a week at a time.

I remember that in one of our classes I had a county sheriff, an 86-year-old retired rancher that was the jail administrator, a one-armed deputy and a 20-year-old that could not carry a gun. I also had both of the deputies from one County.

I was teaching the class on food service and the requirements that the meals have the proper amounts of calories and one of the deputies asked the others how many calories are in a cheeseburger with fries. The reply was "I don't know, but I get them all the way." They were the only two deputies in the county and one of them worked days and the other one worked the night shift. When they had someone locked up in jail, they stop at a truck stop on their way to the office and got them a cheeseburger for their meal, give it to them and go on patrol. The other would do the same thing every day.

Colorado Springs had opened a new jail and we taught the new deputies hired to work in it and the average experience of the group was one day. While I was teaching a class on Documentation to protect yourself against lawsuits, I used a lawsuit that I had just received from one of our inmates, and when I stated his name, half the administration came charging down to see the paperwork. He had been in their jail, and they had got about 5 lawsuits from him. I can't use his real name, but he always signed everything as Dr., his complete name and PHD on the end of signature.

We had a lot of interesting groups and when some of them learned what they were responsible for some of them quit their jobs. Some of small county sheriffs stopped housing prisoners and entered in contracts with larger jails to house their prisoners.

While we were teaching the correction courses, we still had to maintain our regular assigned duties. I would have to go to the office and clear up all pending situations before going home after a trip. Sometimes I would have to go to office early before I departed and pickup material so I could study it while at training assignment before deciding on how to manage it. The work went on day and night.

Captain Reichert's cancer problem required a large part of his time and when he was receiving treatment, Al Powers, the administrative lieutenant, and I would have to carry his workload. Most of the court's requests were about inmates and I had to manage them. The department was expanding, and new jail employees were being hired for the expansion and Lt. Powers and I processed all employment applications for our division.

After we had conducted several correction training sessions, we were asked to write a model manual for the State of Colorado for a constitutional detention facility. This was something the courts had been requesting.

We were given two weeks and some top-rated Constitutional attorneys to help us. We would be using a court facility in the city of Aurora, and I could not turn down this opportunity to advance my knowledge of Constitutional law. This was my chance to ask if we had the legal authority to take fingerprints from pretrial detainees. I still had not received a valid answer to that question.

On the first day of our new project, we were introduced to our support team. One of the attorneys, who was specializing in constitutional law, was a female. During our one-on-one interview, I told her of my quest to find the legal authority for taking the fingerprints of everyone booked into detention facilities, explaining that most of them were pretrial detainees. She did recall having researched that question, but she would research it again and have me an answer the next day.

She contacted me the next morning and told me that she did not find any legal reference to if, but she knew a judge in California who was hearing lawsuit cases pertaining to fingerprints being taken by detention facilities. She had made arrangements for a conference call to him for that afternoon.

We made the call, and the judge told us that there was no written authority for it. He stated that it was a procedure that got started and it worked so well that everyone had adopted it. He also said that personally he did not see why people were objecting to it. That was the last update that I got on the matter.

To accomplish our task, we divided the workload into areas of concern and we each selected the ones that we wanted until they were all covered. I took the medical services because of all the isolated areas in Colorado. Medical services are also a problem for the citizens who live there.

I called all my contacts in ACLU, American Medical Association, AKA AMA, and rescue units that was servicing the less populated areas. Each of the outlying areas have their own unique problems. The standard I wrote that everyone agreed on was, "Each facility shall provide the same level of medical services that is available to the local community. And that all facilities must establish an agreement with a hospital to have a phone connection with a hospital that will have a medical doctor on duty to handle the call in an emergency." We finished the manual on time, and it turned out good.

For the procedures to be enforced throughout the state, a large amount of money would be needed. Governor Lamm attempted to raise the money by getting a Sales Tax increase, but it failed to pass. That was the last I heard about our Constitutional Standards Manual.

My situation was getting worse. The overcrowding situation in the jail had reached a point where I had 1.5 inmates for every bed space. Maintaining discipline in the prisoner population was near impossible. To make matters worse, we were getting a bigger backlog of State prisoners.

There was no such thing as a full night's sleep for me anymore. I was getting phone calls during the night about problems, and I would give instructions on how to handle it and would not remember it until I read the officer's report the next day.

Our number of female inmates were increasing, and I had been able to get the sheriff to hire more female deputies for the Detention division. I was now able to assign two to each squad and this had worked out good overall, but it resulted in a new problem coming up.

We had some married couples working for the department and they had children. This created a babysitting problem. When they worked on different shifts they could care for the children, but when they got on the same shift they had to find and hire a babysitter. When they were assigned to the midnight shift, there were no babysitters available.

At that time, we were not rotating our work shifts and the employees that had the shift they liked would not trade shifts. I was able to attend a management seminar on managing multiple shifts and they pointed out that to be fair to all employees you had to rotate the shifts.

I made the decision to put the operations part of the division back on rotating shifts. I took my idea to Captain Reiker, and he was from the old system where you started at the bottom and earned your way to the better positions. He took the idea home to study it over. He called other department heads he knew, and all had already changed to rotating shifts.

The next morning, he gave me the ok to start rotating the shifts. He also advised me that he had already been getting calls from what we called the prima donnas saying that everyone was going to quit if we tried to rotate the shifts.

I had a very efficient clerk working as my secretary, Diane McHenry, and we put a lot time in working out the shift rotation schedule and new shift assignments. We also worked out the procedures for swapping shifts. We had the same small group of employees spreading the word that everyone was going to resign if they had to change shifts.

Diane worked late the night before the official notification of the new assignments getting all the copies ready. The next morning when I came into my office, she had placed two paperwork baskets on my desk. She put a sign on the one that held the new schedules that read "NEW SHIFT ASSIGNMENTS HERE" and on the other basket she put a sign that read "RESIGNATIONS HERE." The shift change went smoother and there were no resignations.

When we finished remodeling the jail a lot of the ceiling that had been our side of the secured area was now part of the secured area. The old ceiling had some sky light areas that had steel bars over them. Those areas were now supplying natural light for parts of the housing area. They looked good and strong, but in the past, the roof structure had some sever rot damage and had been repaired.

They were not properly tested, and we did not know that one of them was a weak point. The sky light was in a housing unit that we had housed a prisoner charged with murder and armed robbery. He had escaped from a prison in Oklahoma, and he found the weak skylight and forced it open from inside the housing unit. With blankets and bed covers he made a rope and escaped with three other prisoners.

Two of the prisoners were apprehended within 24 hours of the escape and the other two the next day. They were wearing men's boxer shorts and had convinced someone that they were jogging and someone had stolen their clothing. No one was victimized by any of the escapees.

After the bad publicity of the escape by the press, the County Commissioners released the information that the county would be building a new detention facility and a new justice complex. The county had purchased a large portion of land in the unincorporated part of the county near the Centennial Airport and that would be the home of the justice center. Suddenly everyone became an expert on jails.

# Chapter 49
# OVERLOAD BURNOUT

Reichert had passed away from lung cancer and Captain Taylor, someone I had known and admired from my first day with the department, was assigned to the jail. At first, I was happy to have him and was looking forward to having his help. Soon after Captain Taylor started, I noticed that things I was trying to do were getting blocked. I also noticed that the undersheriff was now writing procedures for the jail just to make himself look good. Also, they did not fix anything and we could not cover them.

They were being automatically approved and not being questioned as to where we would get the additional resources to comply with them. This was setting up the employees to fall guys if something happened. I had seen this scheme run before.

I did not realize that I was getting such a bad case of burnout. I knew that I was getting very bitter, and I was not happy with the way I was acting. I knew that I needed some time off, a long rest, but right now I had to take care of the jail. I felt like I was the only one who understood how bad things were.

Looking back at the situation, I was acting like an alcoholic who knew he had to get his drinking under control but first he needed one more drink. I would clear up this last problem then I would take some time off.

Well, those were the things that brought it all to a head. I challenged his decision in an unprofessional way and was put on suspension from duty with pay until it could be investigated. I had over 90 days of vacation time accumulated and took a total of six weeks off.

After a couple of days off and some good sleep. Keiko and I decided to take a trip to see my brother in High Springs, Florida. I was giving some consideration to trying for a job with the Alachua County Detention Center.

I had a lot time to kill before having to be back to Colorado. At that time, I was not sure if I wanted to continue working for the Sheriff's Department. I knew that I did not want to keep the same position there, so we loaded up our Motor home and took off.

I had been so conditioned to feel like if I was not there that everything would just fall apart, that it took a few days to realize that it was just a job. I was concerned about the hearing I would face when I got back, but I was not expecting to be terminated.

After a few days off, I began to realize how good it was not to have to jump up and go to the office. I had not been there for a few days and it had not fallen apart and no one had called me for anything.

We had a nice trip and enjoyed a couple of extra nights on the road. We stopped at the Will Roders Museum in Tulsa Ok and in Cairo, Georgia to see my daughter Pat. By the time I arrived at my brother's house, I was getting a much clearer look at everything. I was beginning to understand why they gave you vacation time.

I called the Alachua County Detention Center and made an appointment to meet with their operations lieutenant. I was there on time, but he was running late.

When I walked into his office, I got a reality shock that changed my outlook on everything. It was like seeing myself. He had a tired look and was drinking a large cup of vending machine coffee, talking on the phone, and signing papers. He had an inmate who would die if he did not get his Dialysis Treatment and he was refusing to go because he had to wear jail clothes. He was also trying to move a couple of inmates to a more secure area because of a valid threat to blow a hole in their part of the jail to get them out.

I could see that the pace he was going was stressing him out to the point it was like a heart attack looking for a place to happen.

After our meeting, I had no interest in getting a job there. We spent some time comparing our jails and most of the problems were the same. We exchanged ideas about how to deal with them, things that failed and what had worked. I remember leaving his jail and relieved that I did not have to deal those problems anymore.

I enjoyed the rest of my vacation and returned to Colorado early, checked in to stop my vacation time, and went back to just being on suspension. It took them another two weeks to have my hearing and I went back to doing anything I wanted to.

By the time of the hearing, I had decided that I did not want to lose or quit my job and I did not want to leave the Detention Division. I enjoyed the challenge of the work and I liked working inside and out of the weather. I expected to be reduced in rank and reassigned and that is how it went. I was reduced to Sergeant and assigned to the court services supervisor.

The primary duty of court services is to get inmates to their assigned courts on time. It sounds simple but it becomes very complicated when you have several courts and each judge thinks you work directly for him and his court is all you have to worry about. Each of the court bailiffs has to maintain the Judge's Docket. To maintain their workloads the Judges and trail attorneys are constantly changing the cases on their dockets.

I knew that we were getting complaints from some of the courts about not getting their defendants there on time. I had observed that there was total confusion in court services almost every day. To find the problem I went into the office early and laid everything out. As soon as the crew came in the office the court list started to get rearranged. There were two phone lines in the office and both were ringing. Each transport officer was getting changes to the dockets. We had 5 county courts, 3 were within walking distance, 2 in a different city, and 4 district courts.

The second morning I came in early and laid out all the court dockets and took the second phone and unplugged it. I took control of the main phone and would not let anyone use the other phone. This forced all the bailiffs to deal with me. All of our officers were able to get their original dockets and get their prisoners on the move to their courts.

I took every request for changes to their dockets and put them on a list for the next available transport officer. That made every bailiff mad as all get out. I would remind them that they were very important, but they were one of nine courts that we had to service.

The biggest complaint I got was that no one answered the phone when they called. I sent the rest of that week getting chewed out by judges and bailiffs, but the work went smoother and more defendants got to court on time. Once I was ordered to bring the prisoner myself. I explained that I would love to do that, but he would have to explain to all the other judges why there was no one to assist them.

The next big problem I had to deal with was court security. Captain Reichert had always used me to deal with unusual court security request. Now that was someone else's problem and when one of the judges called me personally, I would explain why I could not help them and get them in contact with the correct person. I was enjoying working regular hours.

Well, all good things have to come to an end. The court services supervisor's position was on 6 months rotation schedule. Sheriff Nelson had died, and we had a new sheriff by the name of Patrick Sullivan. Captain

Taylor had been replaced in the Detention Division by a new Captain by the name of Jeffery Spoon. I had hired Spoon when he first started and I had worked with him during his career. When I was lieutenant, he worked for me and now I worked for him.

He called me to his office to give me a new assignment. Sergeant Susie Mock was one of our senior sergeants and she was requesting to be assigned to court services. He had a special assignment he wanted me to handle.

# Chapter 50

# SPECIAL ASSIGNMENT

He needed someone to work with Jim Heartly, our computer programmer, to convert the division from paper to computers. The department had purchased an IBM Systems Ten computer system and Heartly had written the jail a program for the jail's inmate booking and records control. Hartley had a test program ready to run but it was receiving a lot of resistance from some of the employees. Sheriff Sulivan, our new sheriff, wanted to see more progress being made.

Captain Spoon also received approval for a new position in the Detention Division which was for an Administrative Sergeant. He had gotten me approved for that position. With this position my area of responsibility would be assigned by the Division Captain. My first assignment was to convert the detention division from paper files to computer files. I accepted the assignment.

The county had approved the funding of building the new Justice Complex which included the first phase of our new jail and a new building for the district court. The funding for my project was from the new jail transition funds and the project was to be completed before we opened the new jail. I had to hire, train, and supervise all the new data clerks until the system was operational, test, checkout and approve the computer programs written for the Detention Division.

I also had to convince the judges that the computer recorders were reliable and could meet the legal standards for court records. I also had to merge the old paper jail records with the new computer records.

The division had started getting the system installed. Hartly had installed the IBM computer terminals that we would be using for the test program. Some additional clerks had been hired for Booking Clerks. They were to assist the deputies in the receiving area with the paperwork and they would be converted to Data Entry Clerks.

Hartly needed the clerks to use the test system to help him find and debug his program. This is when everything stopped. None of the line supervisors knew how to use computers and some of them did not want to have to deal with them and they would not let the clerks spend any time playing with the terminals.

First, I had to develop the qualifications for the position of Data Clerk. I had to put all the booking clerks under my supervision. They would still be assigned to shifts and would function as booking clerks to assist the squads, but in their spare time they would start learning their new jobs as Data Entry Clerks on the computer. Our objective was to have the old jail fully on the computer system before the new jail was completed.

I needed a lot more education about computers and was cramming in all the computer classes I could through the community college. Hartley was an excellent programmer for the IBM Systems 10 computer. There are many functions in the Detention Division that we needed programs for. He had covered most of them in his test program.

All the clerks were now learning the program and constantly crashing it. Everyday Heartly got a new list of program bugs to work on and we were starting to make progress.

I was meeting with judges and slowly getting them to start thinking about the possibility of using computer files. Our new presiding judge was Judge Stewart and he had started as Public Defender the same time I started with the Sheriff's Department, so we had worked together for a long time. He agreed to get the other judges to meet with me so I could explain the new system to them and get their approval for the changeover.

Getting the Judges to accept the computer system was easier than getting our line supervisors to work with it. I had hired and trained all the Data Entry clerks and conducted training classes for the Officers. While the younger officers were excited about working with the new system, the older ones were avoiding the training.

None of our Sergeants showed up at any of the classes. I recognized that they were afraid of being embarrassed in front of subordinates by not understanding how the computer worked. To help them with this problem I tried to set up a special training class for just the supervisors. None of the sergeants agreed to attend the class, they all had different excuses.

I knew that I had to exercise more authority over them to get them on board. I scheduled a time for each one of them to be trained. I officially notified each one of them that I would be conducting required training for the supervisor of their shift at the scheduled time, and I hoped it would be them. If they could not attend the training, then submit their resignation so I could train the new supervisor of that shift. Some of the hardcore cases complained to Captain Spoon but he supported my decision. Everyone got trained and no one resigned.

We created a new numbering system for identifying prisoners. It was a sequential system starting with the two-digit number of the year. The computer would assign the first inmate booked in the year of 1987 the booking number of 8700001, each number after that would increase by 1. This is the same system that is now used by hospitals today. Everything about that person would be controlled by that number. Hartly also wrote a search program that connected all inmates prior files together.

The Inmate Commissary was another big problem for the deputies. Inmates would fill out an order form for the items they wanted to purchase. Someone would have to bag up the items and charge the inmates money to account for the items. If the inmate was at court when he was called to pick up his commissary order, some other inmate would show up and steal it by claiming to be the other inmate. When we found out about it, we would have to refund his money and we would lose the amount of the sale.

A lot of our vendors were using the Universal Product Code which was the new barcode system used to track and control information about each product. This gave me an idea that led to the barcoded arm band system of identifying and tracking inmates.

I would convert their Booking Numbers to a barcode, print out labels with the barcode and the inmate's name, and put it on an armband that the prisoner would have to wear. I would control all the inmate's files and activities to his booking number.

Hartley started writing the programs to convert the booking number to a Barcode and to print out the labels. I contacted a company in California by the name of Precision Dynamics to produce the arm bands and do the medical research on them.

We got the armband system developed, but we ran into problems. The first problem was with the quality of the current Dot Matrix printers. The print was not sharp enough for the barcode. The second was with the paper labels, they were inserted under the clear plastic cover on the arm band and condensation caused the fibers in the paper to separate.

To prevent this, we needed paper with higher plastic content. We had to switch to laser printers and they generated more heat. The plastic and glue on the labels did not work well with the heat. The next model of Dot Matrix printers produced a higher quality print and eliminated the need for the Laser Printer.

By the time Precision Dynamics got the condensation problem fixed the unit cost of the armband exceeded the price we had planned on. We switched the armband for a lapel ID card, which also had a picture of the inmate on it. With the ID card we lost the security of having the item physically attached but we had all inmate's activities connected to a barcode. Without the ID, the inmate got no service and was restricted to his cell and was given feed bag lunches until the ID was recovered.

The first County that I know of to implement the inmate armband system was Decatur County, Georgia and it spread through the system.

When we moved into the new jail, we subcontracted the inmate commissary to a private vendor. A computerized form would be printed out for each inmate for their Commissary Day showing a list of all available items and the cost per item. The inmate would fill out and sign the order form. The commissary clerk would check the list, total up the cost and allocate the funds from the inmate's account. The vendor would pick up the commissary order forms, fill the order, and deliver it to the inmate. The vendor would then send us a voucher and we would send them a check.

## Chapter 51

# THE NEW JAIL

When we made the move to the new jail, I got some additional assignments. We installed our own phone system for the Detention Division. The system was made by the Sieman's Company. The phone distribution was controlled by a computer that controlled all the phones for the Administration. My position was moved to the new facility, and I was put in charge of the new phone system. All the initial wiring was installed by the local phone company, including the punch down room, AKA Wiring Distribution Room. We only had limited instructions that came with the system, but I was able to attend a four-day factory training school on the system. The school was located in Boca Raton, Florida.

The school was scheduled in April and while it was still cold in Colorado, it was already hot in Florida. I was scheduled fly from Denver, Colorado to Fort Pierce, Florida, rent a car and drive to Boca Raton. Everything had been arranged by the Department.

The first problem I encountered was at the beginning of the flight. I got on the plane ok, but we sat in the plane at the terminal for over three hours. We were scheduled to stop in Houston Texas, but due to the overloading of the plane, we would have to make a fuel stop before Houston.

Bad weather over our refueling stop caused us to be four hours late getting started. The delay caused us to miss our connecting flight to Fort

Pierce, but the airlines had rebooked us on a flight to Miami and then to Fort Pierce. Our first flight was not scheduled for an in-flight meal so all we got to eat was a bag of salted peanuts.

When we got to Houston, we learned that they were holding our flight for us on the first leg of an overseas flight, and it did not have an in-flight meal scheduled. One more bag of salted peanuts. When we reached Miami, we were supposed to be met by someone to take us to our Shuttle flight to Fort Pierce.

The flight to Miami was crowed and uncomfortable. I had the seat by the aisle and had a twelve-year-old seat banger between me and the older guy in the seat by the window. The old guy acted like a grouchy old man and for a long time he would not acknowledge anyone. Finally, he got bored and decided to talk to me.

He asked if I was going on vacation, and I said no I am going to a school on telephone systems. Then he said in a commanding sounding voice, "When are they going to get phones that we just tell them what we want?"

There was no way I could let that pass, so I said, "We had those when I was a kid. You just turned the crank on the side of phone and say Operator give me the feed store."

He got so mad at me that I think he would have thrown me off the plane if he could. I thought that was one of my best spontaneous come backs to a question. He did not speak another word to me on the rest of the flight.

There was no one to meet us at Miami and the airlines had no information on us. After another delay, the best they could offer was a bus to take us on to Fort Pierce without our luggage. There was a delay at Fort Pierce while they tried to find information on the location of our luggage, and we filled out the claim forms for it.

I got a shuttle to the car rental agency, where my car was reserved. I had to get in the end of a long line of people from Europe that had cars rented, but the wrong type of driver licenses. After another long delay, I found out that they did not have my car. They had the reservation for it ok, but the car they scheduled for me had not been returned. The only car on the lot was a dirty little compact that had a transmission fluid leak and stunk really bad. I had to take it to get to my hotel in Boca Raton.

The Hilton Hotel had a contact with the school for reduced rates on rooms for students. They had a room for me and when I checked in and gave them the Department Credit card it was not valid. They had not reset it from the last time it was used. I had to put the room on my own credit card. Our Logistics Officer had never been very reliable.

I checked in without my luggage okay and if the airlines found it, they had agreed to rush it to the hotel. The hotel restaurant was already closed for the day, so I had to find somewhere to eat my first meal for the day and I was hungry. I was able to find a nice little steak house restaurant in the area.

I got back to the hotel and the room was nice and it had a study area. I got a shower, but I had to wrap up in a towel to get some sleep. At about 5 AM I was woken up and told my luggage was at the check-in desk. I got up and retrieved my luggage. I got ready for a school that I only had a map to find. I made it to school on time, and it was an excellent school.

The school was a full four days, and I had a return flight booked two hours after the last class. I made it to get the car returned and to the airport just before boarding time. I was hungry and I remembered the last flight and I was going to eat before I got on the flight back. I paid a Red Cap to make sure my luggage got on the plane, and I got me a food meal.

The flight was a night flight routed back through Houston, then onto Denver with no changes. We got off on time and soon as we leveled off, we were served a nice in-flight meal with steak and potatoes. Just what I needed after I had just eaten.

We had a short stop in Houston. Just enough time to stretch your legs and make a bathroom trip. I had just got back in my seat when I saw my neighbor walking to her seat. She and her husband and another couple had been windsurfing in Texas, and the husbands were driving the equipment back. The ladies were flying back early to make it to work on Monday morning. I have no idea what the odds were on that connection, but it sure made the rest of trip go fast.

When I returned to work, I had a lot of inmate phones that were not working. The inmate phones were the ones installed by the local telephone company when we moved into the jail. The people who were making the decisions for the jail at that time had made arrangements with the same people that had put the first phones in the jail. They had wired and installed a phone in each inmate housing day room. I quit taking care of the inmate phones when I quit being a lieutenant. Now I had all the phones in the new jail complex dumped in my lap.

The phone company had put the same type of phones they were using for payphones in the jail and programed them to only do outgoing operator assisted calls. The problem was the phone was programmed from inside the phone with small switches called dip switches. The inmates had learned how to pop the phone off the wall and reprogram the dip switches. They could hang the phone back on the wall and you would not notice it if you did not check it.

Once the inmate had popped the phone loose from the wall, he could hang it back on the mounting plate, but could not secure it. If you bumped the phone it would fall. The officers were finding the phones that were not secured and removed them from the cell.

Three of the four dayroom phones had been removed. I found out what the problem was and contacted the phone company. They put me on a waiting list to get someone to come out and repair them. Inmates without phone service is a problem to deal with. At first, I would reprogram the phone and resecure it to the wall, but the inmates would have it down and reprogrammed before I could get back to my office. I had to find a new company to deal with.

Several things were going on with the telephone business at that time. The break-up of the Bell Company had created opportunities for smaller companies to start up. The payphone business was dropping off due to the development of portable phones like bag phones and car phones. The inmate phones were a good money maker for the company.

A company, by the name of Tripple Crown out of California, was offering rebates on the revenue collected from the inmate system to the County. I contacted the company, and we discussed switching over to them. I don't remember how they worked it out, but the phone company had to be reimbursed for the cost of their phone wire that was installed during the building process. The local phone company was failing to provide the maintenance necessary to keep the inmate phone service running. So, we switched over to Triple Crown.

Tripple Crown came out and installed a large computer to run their system and put new phones in each Dayroom. Their system would automatically connect all the calls to their operators in California. I advised them against allowing any phone contact between inmates and live operators. They insisted that their trained employees could handle everything. For an inmate to call across the street, the call had to go to California then be placed back to the local number. After one year of operations, they went bankrupt and owed us $10,000 they could not pay. I had to take their equipment for payment on their bill.

I wanted a local company I could meet face to face with when I had a problem. We had a company called Silverado Communications that was just down the street and trying to change from Payphones to Inmate phones. The owner of the company was George Livingston, and he was seeking advice on how to get started in the inmate phone business. I invited him to come to my office and let me give him an overview of problems we were having with inmates and phones. After meeting with me, he requested that I train his staff.

I met with his staff several times and we designed a system, including the phone unit itself. The case would be a heavy metal case and mounting bolts would be secured from inside the case. The wiring inside the unit would be only the hook switch and the handset and dial pad. All calls would be processed only by the computer.

The system worked well but after a few phone bills the inmates figured out which number was for each of the units. They also figured out that even though there was no way of knowing when a call was being made to the unit, if you picked up the receiver at the right time you would be connected. Then there was the simple matter of knowing precisely when someone was calling and you could receive free calls. There is no limit to how far some people will go to cheat the system.

As soon as we got the computer system running, Sheriff Sullivan started asking me to compile information about different types of inmate data. He was being given false information about what the computer could do. I would have to explain that if the data was not in the computer, we could not retrieve it.

He would talk to me about projects he was working on, and I would look for data that would support his project. I would try to compile the information and try to put it in a report that I gave him when he needed it. I created a small management of information section, called MIS. I would create grafts and bar charts for him that he could take to meetings when he needed them. I also maintained the form letter to presiding Judge about the overcrowding and number of state inmates we were housing. That letter went out every Monday morning.

I changed my working hours to 7 am until 3 pm Sunday through Thursday. The earlier hours gave me a jump on the rush traffic and

Sunday was a quiet day to do research. I would complete the request for things I needed approval on and present them to the captain for his signature as soon as he came in and before he got fully awake. I would send the form letter and other reports for the sheriff to his printer so they would be available as soon as he came in.

# Chapter 52

# VIDEO COURT SYSTEM

When we built the new jail, it was built with a court room inside the jail for high-risk prisoner cases. Sheriff Sullivan asked me to check on putting a Video Court system in the court room. I did not want that assignment because Lieutenant Reynolds was a communications expert and was in charge of the communications division and thought he was better qualified to handle it than I was, but the sheriff directed me to handle it.

I did the legal research and found no legal requirements that we could not meet, I contacted my ACLU contact about any concerns they may have, and they had none. I talked with judges and got some concerns over to the inmates' advisement of rights, but nothing that we could not cover. The main need for the video court was to reduce the amount of transports of Municipal Prisoners to and from city courts. I got a Municipal Court Judge to work with me through the project.

Building the video transmission system required special knowledge and equipment and I made contact with a small company that specialized in video transmission systems. We needed a system to connect our Municipal Courts, District Court, and Detention Center Courtroom together. These places were spread out over a 12-mile area. The system would use a Microwave transmission system. Each location would require equipment to record, monitor, transmit and receive. Due to the distance between, we needed a relay point in a central location.

The best location for our central relay was easy to find. Right in the middle of our coverage, Chevron Oil company had a beautiful high-rise building. I was able to contact the manager of the building and he gave me, and the project engineers a tour of the roof of the building. It was perfect for what we needed, including electrical power for our equipment.

The building manager arranged a conference call to their headquarters so I could officially request the use of their building for a relay point. They were glad to cooperate with us and we could operate our equipment on their electrical system without charge. However, there was one thing that he would not allow, microwave's four-foot-wide disk. He thought that would make his building look like Micky Mouse. The two-foot disk was ok, so we got the use of the building.

To ensure the legal requirements were met, the system was designed to carry four signals at the same time. One would be the Judge, one the Prosecutor, one for the Defendant and one for his Attorney.

The monitor at each location would be able to display any combination of the video feeds. Normally it would show all four. The Judge, prosecutor, defendant, and his attorney. If witnesses were videoed, they would use any available camera. All Court hearings were recorded and saved in view only mode. If copies of the hearing were requested, they would be recorded on a VCR tape.

I videotaped a judge giving a full advisement of rights and it would be viewed by all defendants before each hearing. Each judge would start his hearing by confirming that the defendant had viewed the advisement and asked if he had any questions. The system worked well, and I don't know of any challenges to it.

My career in the Arapahoe County Sheriff's Department afforded me so many great opportunities that I can't count them. I got to meet, work with, and learn from some of the smartest and most wonderful people in the country. I was able to work on and be a part of some of the most interesting and challenging projects. I have been blessed with so many wonderful memories, but my most enjoyable memories are of the people that I was able to help along the way.

I got to help some of the older employees learn how to use the computer. I realized that it was how older people learn that was causing them to have problems. When we are young our minds are like a sponge, they absorb everything. As we grow older our mind changes. Almost everything new that we are exposed to is similar to something we already know, and we look for the differences between the items. This is what I call learning by comparison.

The older we get the more we rely on that way of learning. When something comes along that we have nothing to compare it to, like the computer system, we are lost. I developed a new introduction to computers course for seniors and taught it to our older employees. I was able to teach other computer-related courses like Word Perfect and Lotus 123 to our employees.

I also was assigned to be a part of what we called the five-year certain and ten-year proposed plan. I went to all the expositions of newly developed products related to law enforcement to see if we needed them.

## Chapter 53

# POPE JOHN PAUL II

The largest event that we covered was in 1993 when Pope John Paul II visited Colorado with the Youth of the World Day. We were estimating up to a million people to attend. It was held in Arapahoe County, and we had to coordinate the security for the event. It was held in a large open field that was being used as an open outdoor park area.

Since the Pope is not head of a government, the military could not get involved. Our local National Guard unit scheduled a training exercise for assisting the local authorities with a local disaster. All local law enforcement agencies assigned people to assist. It was scheduled for Easter Sunday.

The Pope was scheduled to do a Sunrise Service and the visitors would do a pilgrimage to the location the day before and campout overnight. They had a large number of busloads of special guests being bused to the event during the night before the service.

The National Guard unit set up a portable triage center at the location and all the local rescue units sent teams to assist if needed. The weather started out nice, but we had a rain shower, and then a hard drop in temperature. I was stationed at rear entrance of the area where the Pope would enter and even wearing our raincoats over our uniforms, we were cold.

All night long the radios were requesting assistance for people with hypothermia. The National Guard reported treating 32,000 cases during the night. Everything else was minor except for two heart attacks, one was fatal.

We had no way of doing a count of the attendants, but the estimates ranged from over 100k to 300k. I do know that the large field was overflowing and when we hauled off the trash left by the visitors it took 32 trash truck loads to clear the area. The extra cost to the County's budget for the event was $90,000.

The most enjoyable memories I have was talking with the young people. Every one of the young people was a pleasure to meet. This is such a far cry from what we normally had to deal with that all the officers were delighted.

## Chapter 54

# MY SECOND RETIREMENT

I retired November 1st, 1994, and moved back to High Springs, Florida. My brother was still alive, and I got to spend some quality time with him. I also got to spend some time fishing our local river. I spent some time working with my brother and going back to college. I completed a two-year course in automotive technology.

In 1997 I ran for City Commissioner in Alachua County and get elected. In November of 1999 I lost my brother to cancer and in 2000 I had the honor of serving as Mayor of my hometown of High Springs. I lost my wife Keiko in November of 2001, also to cancer.

In March of 2003 I married my current wife Audrey and began playing country music again. We put together a small band of old guys that use to play and still enjoyed it but did not want to play commercially. We started a one-night show in the local civic center for seniors that included a potluck dinner. We wanted it to be a family night they could share with their grandkids, so there was no drinking, drugs or smoking allowed. The seniors liked the music and the dancing, and we liked the good food and friendship.

We created some great friendships, memories and music. We kept it going until Covid shut us down. I also enjoyed being a disk jockey on a local radio station for three years with a show I called "Old Country's Trip Down Memory Lane.

I retired from everything on January 1$^{st}$, 2023, to write this book about Caressing Old Memories.

www.ingramcontent.com/pod-product-compliance
Lightning Source LLC
Chambersburg PA
CBHW030539080526
44585CB00012B/199